A Birder's Guide to Louisiana

Richard Gibbons
Roger Breedlove
Charles Lyon

American Birding®
ASSOCIATION

Copyright © 2013 by American Birding Association, Inc.

All rights reserved. No part of this publication may be reproduced, stored in a retrieval system, transmitted in any form or by any means, electronic, photocopying, or otherwise, without prior written permission of the publisher. Personal reproduction for recreational and educational purposes permitted.

Library of Congress Catalog Number: 2013933425

ISBN Number: 978-1-878788-43-6

First Edition

    1 2 3 4 5 6 7 8

Printed in the United States of America

Publisher:
    American Birding Association, Inc.

Editor:
    Paul E. Lehman

Associate Editors:
    Cindy Lippincott and Bob Berman

Maps:
    Cindy Lippincott

Cover Photography:

    front cover: *Great Egret*
    © Joseph Turner

    back cover: *Tricolored (Louisiana) Heron*
    © Amy Shutt

Distributed by:

    American Birding Association
    1618 West Colorado Avenue
    Colorado Springs, CO 80904 USA

    phone: (800) 850-2473 or (719) 578-9703
    fax: (719) 578-1480

    http://www.aba.org

DEDICATION

This book is dedicated to Louisiana's past and present birders and ornithologists who worked tirelessly for a better understanding of our shared natural heritage. They were, and continue to be, driven by the sense of discovery that awaits every birder as they head out the door.

Acknowledgments

A *Birder's Guide to Louisiana* would not have been possible without the tremendous generosity of scores of friends and colleagues, the Atchafalaya National Heritage Area, and the Louisiana Department of Culture, Recreation and Tourism. A special mention is warranted for Paul Dickson for his support of the Louisiana Bird Resource Office, which provided the final push to completion.

There is no substitute for local expertise. Much of the completeness and accuracy of the information contained in this book is owed to the local experts who reviewed various sections of the manuscript. We would like to acknowledge the excellent contributions by Paul Conover (Southwest and Lafayette), Terry Davis (Northwest), Jay Huner (Central), Mac Myers (Southwest and Lafayette), and Dan Purrington (Southeast). Also of great assistance were the thoughtful comments of Roselie Overby, Steve Pagans, J. V. Remsen, Rosemary Seidler (Northwest), and Steve Shively (Kistachie National Forest). Additionally, we are very grateful for the additional reviews, edits, comments, and suggestions from the following birders: Scott Barnes, Erik Johnson, Nancy Menasco, David Muth, Brian O'Shea, Jane Patterson, and Peter Yaukey.

We are thankful to Kimberly Vetter and Barbara Breedlove for their editing contributions. We are also indebted to J. V. Remsen for providing time and energy in numerous aspects of the manuscript.

Finally, we thank the following friends and colleagues from the LSU Museum of Science and elsewhere for their expertise: Verity Mathis, Prosanta Chakrabarty, and Jeff Boundy.

The book is filled with outstanding photography and art and we are truly grateful to the following photographers and artists for their contributions: Jessie Barry, Darlene Boucher, Jennifer Brumfield, David Cagnolatti, Fred D. Canter, John Elias, Christina Evans, Carol Foil, Jake Fontenot, Michael Harvey, Mark Herse, Erik I. Johnson, Jim E. Johnson, Jessica Kirste, Dan Lane, John Longhenry, Ronnie Maum, Dave Patton, Michael L. P. Retter, Michael Seymour, Amy Shutt, Jason Stuck, Joseph Turner, and USFWS.

We realize this is a far cry from the perfect birdfinding guide to Louisiana, but it is a start. Our goal is to provide accurate and useful information for both resident and visiting birders. It is likely that we got some things wrong; we take full responsibility for these errors and encourage you to send us your suggestions and corrections.

Richard Gibbons, Roger Breedlove, and Charles Lyon

Atchafalaya
NATIONAL HERITAGE AREA — AMERICA'S FOREIGN COUNTRY

The authors and the American Birding Association want to thank the Atchafalaya National Heritage Area for its financial support.

The Atchafalaya National Heritage Area is a federally designated National Heritage Area encompassing fourteen parishes along the Atchafalaya River in Louisiana.

The Atchafalaya Basin is the nation's largest river swamp, containing almost one million acres of America's most significant bottomland hardwoods, swamps, bayous, and backwater lakes.

The basin begins near Simmesport, Louisiana and stretches some 140 miles southward to the Gulf of Mexico. Currently, the Atchafalaya Basin is bound by natural ridges formed by levee building along active and abandoned courses of the Mississippi River.

The purpose of the Atchafalaya National Heritage Area is to establish and maintain interpretive sites; increase public awareness of and appreciation for the natural, scenic, cultural, historic, and recreational resources of the area; and implement programs that recognize the important resource values of the national heritage area.

For more information go to *http://www.Atchafalaya.org* or call 800-404-8626 or 337-228-1094.

LouisianaTravel.com

FOREWORD

If you like seeing large numbers of birds, you'll love Louisiana. Although Louisiana may not have the life-listers appeal of some of the border states, probably no state in the USA can compete with Louisiana in terms of bird spectacles. Bird density in general is higher here than almost anywhere in the country, and some of the concentrations are stunning. This birdfinding guide will help more people appreciate our state for the special birding area that it is.

With a relatively low human population density, Louisiana still supports large areas of contiguous forest and wetlands. Coupling that with productive soils, a warm and wet climate, and large areas set aside for wildlife management makes the number of birds one can see in a day exceptionally high. Even the areas of intensive agriculture, especially those including the working wetlands (rice/crawfish) of southwestern Louisiana, support high densities of birds. For example, a winter trip there would likely yield at least 20,000 Snow Geese, many thousands of White-faced Ibises, thousands of shorebirds, more than 100 individual raptors, hundreds of herons, thousands of Boat-tailed or Great-tailed Grackles, and millions of Red-winged Blackbirds. Several million ducks typically winter in Louisiana, with the majority in the southwestern coastal marshes and adjacent agricultural areas. Catahoula Lake can host thousands of Canvasbacks and 10,000 or more Ring-necked Ducks. Grassy areas can host swarms of Savannah Sparrows, and areas of mixed weeds and grass can support spectacular densities of Swamp Sparrows. Wooded and brushy areas in winter typically have high densities of landbirds, especially Yellow-bellied Sapsuckers, Eastern Phoebes, Ruby-crowned Kinglets, Hermit Thrushes, American Robins, Yellow-rumped and Orange-crowned Warblers, and White-throated Sparrows; eBird high counts for these species in Louisiana are among the highest for North America. November and December sugarcane roosts of Tree Swallows are estimated in the millions, and a visit to one of those congregations impresses even the most complacent non-birder.

It's not just winter when Louisiana can boast about its high numbers of birds. Even summer has its rewards. If you work at it, you can see more than 100 White-eyed Vireos or Prothonotary Warblers in a single morning along Whiskey Bay Road in the Atchafalaya Basin, along with high numbers of other bottomland hardwood species, including Swallow-tailed Kite and Swainson's Warbler. A drive around the suburbs of Baton Rouge can yield counts of 50 or more Mississippi Kites. Breeding colonies of hundreds of herons, egrets, ibises, and Roseate Spoonbills are accessible in a few places, and one can find post-breeding aggregations of thousands of these birds, joined locally by hundreds of Wood Storks in July and August. In fall, the right weather conditions at the right places along the coast can produce hundreds of Broad-winged Hawks, Eastern Kingbirds, Northern Rough-winged Swallows, Gray Catbirds, Yellow

Warblers, Blue Grosbeaks, or Indigo Buntings. Some feeders host hundreds of Ruby-throated Hummingbirds. In November, a rice-harvester can flush over 100 rails, including numbers of Yellow Rails, from a single field. And of course there's spring migration, when the right weather conditions can produce some of the most spectacular birding in North America. Hundreds, sometimes thousands, of migrating landbirds can be seen in a day during fallout weather conditions along the coast between late March and mid-May. Weather radar that detects birds shows that the volume of birds crossing the Gulf of Mexico is as high or higher off western Louisiana as anywhere over the entire Gulf. Shorebirds also concentrate in spectacular numbers in southwestern Louisiana, where many thousands can be found in a day during spring, often involving 20 or more species.

Louisiana also has a long history of producing records of vagrant species, especially western and southwestern species farther east than their normal ranges, e.g., Least Grebe, Harris's, White-tailed, and Zone-tailed Hawks, Mountain Plover, Western Gull, Ancient Murrelet, Flammulated Owl, Vaux's Swift, Magnificent and Blue-throated Hummingbirds, Ringed Kingfisher, Williamson's and Red-naped Sapsuckers, Ladder-backed Woodpecker, Prairie Falcon, Hammond's, Gray, Pacific-slope, Cordilleran, and Brown-crested Flycatchers, Great Kiskadee, Sulphur-bellied Flycatcher, Cassin's, Couch's, and Tropical Kingbirds, Plumbeous, Cassin's, and Yellow-green Vireos, Chihuahuan Raven, Clark's Nutcracker, Rock Wren, Townsend's Solitaire, Curve-billed and Sage Thrashers, McCown's Longspur, Lucy's, Virginia's, and MacGillivray's Warblers, Tropical Parula, Hermit and Red-faced Warblers, Painted Redstart, Cassin's, Brewer's, and Baird's Sparrows, Hepatic Tanager, Varied Bunting, and Hooded and Scott's Orioles, to name some of the most noteworthy. Louisiana also has records of a number of species that would be good finds anywhere in the Lower 48 States, such as Masked Duck, American Flamingo, Yellow-nosed Albatross, Red-footed Booby, Lesser Sand-Plover, Black-tailed Godwit, Kelp Gull, Antillean Nighthawk, Green Violetear, Green-breasted Mango, Crowned Slaty Flycatcher (only record for USA), Fork-tailed Flycatcher, Brown-chested Martin, Northern Wheatear, White Wagtail, and Blue Bunting (first record for USA). So, for those looking for rarities, Louisiana is productive.

For all of this avian wealth, Louisiana is definitely under-appreciated and drastically under-visited by out-of-state birders. This new guide is a critical first step toward changing that.

J. V. Remsen, Jr., Ph.D.
Curator of Birds, Louisiana State University Museum of Natural Science,
McIlhenny Distinguished Professor of Natural Science, and
Professor of Biological Sciences

Table of Contents

Introduction 1
    Food and Fun 2
    Geography 3
    Birding Seasons 5
    Winter Hummingbirds 6
    Pelagic Birding 7
    Birding Organizations and Bird Clubs 8
    Federal and State Agencies 10
    Internet Resources 11
    Citizen Science Opportunities 12
    Precautions 13
    How to Use This Guide 15
    Tree Swallow Roosts, *by Michael A. Seymour* 16

Chapter 1 - Southwest Louisiana 23
    Turf Grass Road and Jefferson Davis Landfill 25
    Sam Houston Jones State Park 27
    LA-108 Loop 28
    Sabine National Wildlife Refuge 30
    Holly Beach 31
    Peveto Woods Migratory Bird Sanctuary 32
    Sabine Bridge 35
    Town of Cameron 37
    Fruge Road 40
    Cameron Prairie National Wildlife Refuge 41
    Little Chenier Road 41
    Oak Grove Sanctuary 42
    Rutherford and Broussard Beaches 43
    Hollister Chenier Preserve 45
    Rockefeller Wildlife Refuge 45
    Lacassine National Wildlife Refuge 46
    Thornwell 47

Chapter 2 - Lafayette Area 51
    Rice Country 53
    White Lake Wetlands Conservation Area Birding and Nature Trail 57
    Palmetto Island State Park 58
    Acadiana Park Nature Station 61
    Lake Martin–Cypress Island Preserve 62
    University of Louisiana–Lafayette Experimental Farm 64
    Spanish Lake 66
    Avery Island–Jungle Gardens 67
    Jefferson Island–Rip Van Winkle Gardens 68
    Sherburne Wildlife Management Area 69

Chapter 3 - Baton Rouge Area **73**
    Louisiana State University Campus and Lakes. 74
    Capitol Lakes and Arsenal Park 79
    Blackwater Conservation Area. 80
    Frenchtown Road Conservation Area 83
    Bluebonnet Swamp Nature Center. 85
    Port Hudson State Historic Site 86
    Audubon State Historic Site 87
    Mary Ann Brown Nature Preserve 88
    Tunica Hills Wildlife Management Area 90
    Morganza Spillway. 91
    Sherburne Wildlife Management Area–South Farm 94

Chapter 4 - Southeast Louisiana **97**
    Houma and South 97
    The Route to Grand Isle 99
    Port Fourchon 100
    Elmer's Island Wildlife Refuge 103
    Grand Isle 105
    New Orleans City Park 109
    Audubon Park 110
    Joe W. Brown Memorial Park 112
    White Kitchen Area 112
    Bayou Sauvage National Wildlife Refuge 113
    Honey Island Swamp and Pearl River Wildlife Management Area 114
    Fontainebleau State Park and Lake Pontchartrain's Northshore 117
    Jean Lafitte National Historic Park 119
    Bonnet Carré Spillway 120
    Venice: Empire to Fort Jackson 123
    Fort Jackson 124
    Venice: Boothville-Venice 127

Chapter 5 - Central Louisiana **129**
    Cheneyville. 129
    Overton Lock and Dam 132
    Elbow Slough Wildlife Management Area 133
    Catahoula National Wildlife Refuge–Dewey W. Mills Wildlife Management Area . . . 135
    Sicily Island Hills Wildlife Management Area 136
    Fort Randolph-Buhlow State Historic Site. 138
    Kisatchie National Forest 139
    Stuart Lake 141
    Little Cypress Pond 142
    Longleaf Trail 145
    Kincaid Reservoir and Castor Plunge Road and Bottoms 146
    Camp Claiborne Loop 148
    Boyce Loop 151

    Indian Creek Recreation Area 155
    Chicot State Park and the Louisiana State Arboretum 157

Chapter 6 - Northwest Louisiana **161**
    Black Bayou Lake 162
    Scissortail Loop 164
    Bayou Bodcau Wildlife Management Area 165
    Cross Lake Area 167
    C. Bickham Dickson Park 170
    Stoner Avenue Recreation Area 172
    Red River National Wildlife Refuge 173
    Yearwood Road Loop 177
    Red River Locks and Dams 179

Chapter 7 - Northeast Louisiana **183**
    Black Bayou Lake National Wildlife Refuge 185
    Handy Brake National Wildlife Refuge 186
    Upper Ouachita National Wildlife Refuge 187
    Poverty Point State Historic Site 189
    Tensas River National Wildlife Refuge 191
    Russell Sage and Ouachita Wildlife Management Areas 192
    D'Arbonne National Wildlife Refuge 195
    Bayou D'Arbonne Lake Spillway 197

Appendix A - Abundance and Status of Louisiana Birds (bar graphs) **198**

Appendix B - Specialties of Louisiana **221**

Appendix C - Checklist of Louisiana Birds **226**

Appendix D - Mammals of Louisiana **243**

Appendix E - Reptiles and Amphibians of Louisiana **246**

Appendix F - Butterflies of Louisiana **251**

Louisiana Birding Routes **256**

Selected Reading **259**

ABA Code of Birding Ethics **260**

Index **263**

INTRODUCTION

Louisiana proudly stands apart from the rest of the country with its unique history of rural French-speaking Cajuns and the jazzy mix of cultures in New Orleans. American literature, music, and art have been inspired by this melting pot of many cultures since the 1700s.

Ornithology in Louisiana shares an equally rich and textured history. Alexander Wilson, the father of American ornithology, worked through the swamps and hills of Louisiana for America's first ornithological account, *American Ornithology*. Soon thereafter, John James Audubon was overwhelmed with the birdlife of Louisiana and gained inspiration there for the majority of the prints in his *Birds of America*. The tradition continued, with ornithological giants such as Harry C. Oberholser, George H. Lowery, Jr., John P. O'Neill, J. V. Remsen, Jr., and Ted Parker honing their craft in Louisiana. Today, a growing group of state ornithologists and committed birders continue to make ornithological contributions.

Louisiana has more than its fair share of outstanding birding opportunities. Spring migration in the coastal woodlots and rice fields is unforgettable. Summer birding provides some of the best opportunities anywhere to see such breeders as Swallow-tailed Kite, Swainson's Warbler, and Bachman's Sparrow, to name just a few. Autumn birding is a long, protracted procession of migratory birds finding their way south. Wintering birds arrive with each passing weather front.

What may be the most exciting aspect of Louisiana birding is the opportunity for discovery. Louisiana is still largely wildlife habitat with cities sprinkled throughout, and that's just the way Louisiana likes it. Although you may run into more people with a rod and reel or Catahoula hound than a binocular and field guide, the outdoor camaraderie is there. The great outdoor tradition is reflected in the large number of state parks and wildlife management areas, not to mention the vast Kisatchie National Forest.

Louisiana is touted as *America's Wetland*. With more than forty percent of the country's coastal marshes, it's easy to understand why. These highly productive marshes provide habitat for millions of birds and act as the natural nursery for coastal fisheries. To the distress of many, these marshes have been eroding at a rate of 25–30 square miles per year due to land subsidence and the impediment of marsh-nourishing sediments. Hurricanes *Katrina* and *Rita* accelerated the problem when they roared ashore at opposite ends of the state in 2005.

These storms were devastating to coastal communities such as New Orleans and Cameron and equally so for the marshes that protected many cities from the brunt of major tropical storms. More than 200 square miles of coastal marsh was converted to open water. The issue is finally receiving the attention and funding to find solutions, but it will be decades before the corner is turned and a new equilibrium found. In the meantime, your visits to the coastal marshes will not only be rewarded with abundant birdlife, but your visit will also help keep the issue of coastal marshes at the forefront and provide witness to our changing landscape.

Despite habitat loss, birding continues to grow in popularity in Louisiana, and state and local governments are responding with new opportunities. Three additional birding trails offer insights to new areas in the northern half of the state, while new citizen-science projects provide that little extra motivation to get observers out there to explore.

FOOD AND FUN

Everyone has heard of the fabled New Orleans Mardi Gras—the party of parties held on "Fat Tuesday" prior to the beginning of the Lenten season. Actually, the parades and balls go on for a couple of weeks leading up to Lent. Although Mardi Gras is celebrated in several smaller cities and towns of the strongly Catholic southern portion of the state, the New Orleans carnival is a spectacle to be witnessed at least once. Nor do the people of southwest Louisiana ("Acadiana") satisfy their need for socialization with Mardi Gras only. The list of local festivals is quite staggering. There is the Couchon (Cochon) de Lait (held annually in Avoyelles Parish), the Corn Festival, the Crawfish Festival (a huge street party in the village of Breaux Bridge), the Rice Festival, and a host of other lesser excuses to engage in merriment.

The cooking of Louisiana is much storied, and for just cause. The two most famous of the cuisines are Creole and Cajun. The Creole variety is centered in New Orleans. Lots of sauces—wonderful seasonings—world-class chefs—great eating. The Cajun style is the work of descendants of the Acadians in southwest Louisiana. The chefs in and around Lafayette don't skimp on the spices. Sausages (such as boudin), crawfish, and other seafood are a delight to the palate. In and around Natchitoches, the tamales from Zwolle and the meat pies are not to be missed. The Chinese may have developed barbecue, but north Louisiana is now as noted as Texas for its smoked meats.

Geography

Generally thought of as no more than a venue for swamps, marshes, and bayous, the truth is that only a small percentage of Louisiana may be so designated. Fields and forests abound. Hundreds of thousands of acres of National Forest lands cover much of the sandy hills of the north-central region. There is even a knob in the north that is almost defiantly referred to as Driscoll Mountain, towering at 535 feet above sea level.

Oak/hickory is considered to be the climax forest type for much of the state. Nevertheless, settlers found considerable prairie in the southwest and a band of pines near the coast, especially in the southeast. The prairie was turned into rice fields and the "Attwater's" Prairie-Chicken and Whooping Crane were soon extirpated. The old-growth bottomland hardwoods were virtually all harvested and sent to local mills. As a result, Ivory-billed Woodpecker was last documented here prior to the early 1950s. Nor were the oaks and hickories safe. They, too, were cut and pines planted in their place by the large lumber companies, who were also the large landowners. The pines, of course, could be cut for market every twenty years or so, while the hardwoods would require a human lifetime to mature.

Coastal marsh Richard E. Gibbons

Longleaf Pine savanna Erik I. Johnson

The four main habitat types found today are pine uplands, coastal marshes, coastal prairies of the southwest, and bottomland hardwoods of the Mississippi/Atchafalaya/Red River floodplains. A sub-classification of the pine uplands is the Shortleaf Pine area in the extreme north, west and east of the Red River. The pine uplands comprise three distinct regions. They are in

4 INTRODUCTION

Upland hardwood forest — Richard E. Gibbons

Beach near East Jetty, Cameron — Richard E. Gibbons

Cypress/tupelo swamp — Richard E. Gibbons

the west-central portion, the northcentral district, and the parishes north of Lake Pontchartrain. The coastal marshes extend from the Gulf inland for some 20 to 25 miles. Generally treeless, the marshes do support low oaken ridges, called cheniers, that serve as resting and foraging points for trans-Gulf neotropical migrants. The bottomlands are dotted with cypress/tupelo swamps that exist in areas where runoff is poor or nonexistent. It should be remembered that during the eons the Mississippi River has flowed through a great deal of Louisiana. An abandoned river bed, therefore, stands an excellent chance of becoming a swamp at some point. A number of reforestation projects center around the bottoms in northeast Louisiana.

BIRDING SEASONS

Louisiana's birding year begins with the arrival of the first Purple Martins, usually in mid-to-late January. In late February and early March, the Sandhill Cranes move north, a few shorebirds come through, and waterfowl meander away from the coast. In mid-March, Blue-gray Gnatcatchers begin to turn up in most of the state. Ruby-throated Hummingbird, Yellow-throated Vireo, Louisiana Waterthrush, Northern Parula, Yellow-throated Warbler, and Summer Tanager put in appearances at the cheniers. The first kites and Broad-winged Hawks sail past Cameron Parish.

Without question, the best time to visit Louisiana is during the latter part of April. Nesting has begun and the influx of neotropical migrants is at its peak. Grand Isle and Cameron Parish offer birding opportunities that equal those just across the Sabine River at High Island and elsewhere on the Upper Texas Coast. The concentration of trans-Gulf migrants may be staggering—depending on the weather conditions—particularly at Peveto Woods in western Cameron Parish. In April, the neotropical migrants turn what had been a trickle into a huge stream that reaches flood stage during the last week or so of the month. The swell then subsides until it is no more than a trickle again by mid-May. By this time, the myriad sparrows are no longer found. The Yellow-rumped Warbler has abandoned its winter haunt, along with Orange-crowned Warbler and American Goldfinch. But *Empidonax* flycatchers peak in early May, along with Mourning and Canada Warblers and several other late-migrating passerines. Shorebirds continue to slip through for another month or so. In late April and early May, Red-cockaded Woodpecker is feeding young and Bachman's Sparrow is singing. Late May to early June is the season to find breeders on the nesting grounds. Hooded Warbler is heard from the brushy understory and Prothonotary Warbler flits about in the swamps. Also present are Yellow-throated Warbler and Northern Parula (in mossy forest).

In June, hummingbirds have completed nesting and begin to show up in numbers at feeders. By month's end, a few shorebirds have already begun their return journey to the south and returned to the state, and Wood Storks are present—the product of a post-breeding dispersal from Mexico. In July, a few more shorebirds are congregating along the coast and the Purple Martins begin to stage. Flocks of this latter species numbering in the hundreds of thousands use the south end of the Lake Pontchartrain Causeway as a roosting site; somewhat lower numbers may be seen under the span across the Red River in Shreveport.

By Labor Day, southbound Mourning, Yellow, and Canada Warblers and several species of migrant flycatchers have reached the cheniers. Wintering hummers show up at Lafayette feeders. Teal numbers increase, as well. As the heart of fall approaches, more and more neotropical migrants filter through until they peak in early to mid-October. By month's end, many ducks are again present, along with overwintering Sandhill Cranes and Vermilion Flycatchers. The autumnal exodus lacks the crescendo associated with the vernal pageantry, but not the excitement. The crest of the tide is lower, but the stream lasts longer. Despite many species having donned their more cryptic basic plumage, there is no lack of color. Neotropical migrants continue to pass through the cheniers well into November.

By mid-December, it is generally thought that "all are ashore that are going ashore" and the Christmas Bird Counts begin. Winter birding in Louisiana tempts because of the several vagrants that are always about. Brant, Ferruginous Hawk, Golden Eagle, *Myiarchus* flycatchers, Ringed Kingfisher, Northern Wheatear, Mountain Bluebird, MacGillivray's and Black-throated Gray Warblers, and Black-headed Grosbeak—to name just a few—have been found in winter.

WINTER HUMMINGBIRDS

Feeding, tracking, and gardening for the myriad hummingbirds that spend the colder months of the year in Louisiana enjoy no less than cult status here. Some dozen species have been recorded, although some of these only once or twice. All have been observed at feeders. While most of these birds are found south of Interstate-10, a very few have been seen as far north as Shreveport. Ruby-throated, the only hummingbird to breed east of the Mississippi River, winters here in small numbers. Usually, a Broad-billed puts in an appearance each winter. Broad-tailed is seen regularly in the state, as is Allen's and Calliope. Anna's is almost annual in occurrence. Black-chinned is always present, as are Rufous (the most numerous) and Buff-bellied. Also recorded no more than a couple

Rufous Hummingbird   Joseph Turner

times each are Green-breasted Mango and Magnificent and Blue-throated. The state's few Green Violetear records are of individuals in summer.

Upwards of 800–900 individual hummingbirds may be documented in a single winter in the state. It appears that the epicenter of winter hummingbird activity in Louisiana is Baton Rouge. For locating wintering hummers, visit the Louisiana Ornithological Society website *http://www.losbird.org*. Two additional list-servs provide information about wintering hummingbirds, as well: check the Humnet Birding list-serv *http://www.museum.lsu.edu/~Remsen/HUMNETintro.html* or the Louisiana Birding list-serv *http://www.museum.lsu.edu/~Remsen/LABIRDintro.html* for recent posts. Many messages from the HUMNET list are archived by subject. Topics include gardening, feeder cleaning, hummingbird ID, pests, and supplies.

Magnificent Frigatebird and Audubon's Shearwaters Dan Lane

PELAGIC BIRDING

Louisiana has had a spotty history of pelagic birding, due largely to the low number of species and individuals of pelagic birds generally encountered. With that in mind, the species that are most likely to be encountered between late spring and early autumn are Wilson's Storm-Petrel, Band-rumped Storm-Petrel, and Bridled Tern. Cory's Shearwater, Audubon's Shearwater, Leach's Storm-Petrel, Masked Booby, and Sooty Tern are recorded less frequently, but are regular offshore. Pelagic trips generally departed out of the Venice area due to its proximity to the Mississippi Canyon. This deep trench, scoured by the river over uncounted millennia, brings deep blue water much closer to the shore off Louisiana than is found at other sites along the continental shelf. Birding expeditions are not currently offered commercially. Still, a good number of fishing boat captains are familiar with at least some of the more common pelagic species. Be prepared, however, to spend some serious money for a private charter. With the coastal fishing fleet recovering from Hurricanes *Katrina* and *Rita*, it may be time for a state birding group to resume organizing these outings. An inquiry to the LABIRD list-serv would be the best way to know if a trip is in the works.

BIRDING ORGANIZATIONS

Louisiana Ornithological Society
Website: http://www.losbird.org
Address: Louisiana Ornithological Society,
  504 Whitebark Drive, Lafayette, LA 70508

This is the statewide birding and ornithology organization. LOS organizes gatherings three times per year (fall, winter, spring) in different parts of the state, publishes a journal on Louisiana ornithology, publishes a quarterly newsletter for its members, and has loads of information regarding Louisiana birds at their website. The LOS website is also the online site of the Louisiana Bird Records Committee (LBRC), where birders can find the state's Review List of rare bird species. Visiting birders are invited to check this list and report any sightings of rarities to the LBRC.

Louisiana Bird Resource Office
Website: http://birdoffice.lsu.edu
Email: birdoffice@tigers.lsu.edu
Address: LSU Museum of Natural Science,
  119 Foster Hall, Baton Rouge, LA 70803

This office is a component of the Louisiana State University Museum of Natural Science charged with facilitating a better understanding of Louisiana birdlife through the gathering and dissemination of information on the distribution and ecology of Louisiana birds. Check the website to see how your birding can help contribute to these goals.

BIRD CLUBS

The Loose Alliance of Casual and/or Keen Bird Watchers of Central Louisiana
Contact: Roger Breedlove; rjbandbab@suddenlink.net
Address: 320 Park Place, Alexandria, LA 71301

Baton Rouge Audubon Society
Website: http://www.braudubon.org
Email: president@braudubon.org
Address: PO Box 67016, Baton Rouge, LA 70896

Terrebonne Bird Club (Houma/Thibodeaux)
Address: 1806 Bull Run Road, Shiever, LA 70395
Contact: Pat Allen, co-president;
  piggypoet@sw.rr.com; (985) 851-0422
Contact: Karen Kelly, co-president;
  Kelly2ag@redfishnetwork.com; (985) 594-4215

LABA (Louisiana Birders Anonymous)
Contact: Judith O'Neale; jloneale@aol.com
Address: 504 Whitebark Drive, Lafayette, LA 70508
tel: (337) 981-1011

Gulf Coast Bird Club
Website: http://sites.google.com/site/gulfcoastbirdclub/
Contact: Pete Lund; epltastyl@aol.com
Address: 4159 Longpine Lane, Lake Charles, LA 70611
tel: (337) 855-2023

Northshore Bird Club (Covington/Northshore of Lake Pontchartrain)
Website: http://www.minilogic.com/nsbirders
Contact: Bill Wayman; (985) 727-9759

Crescent Bird Club
Address: 6656 Argonne Boulevard, New Orleans, LA 70124
Contact: Joelle Finley; jfinle@lsuhsc.edu; (504) 488-3996
Contact: Ed Wallace; mottledduck@hotmail.com; (504) 343-1433

Orleans Audubon Society
Website: *http://www.jjaudubon.net*
Email: jj@jjaudubon.net
Address: 801 Rue Dauphine, Suite 304, Metairie, LA 70005-4608
tel: (504) 831-9913

Bird Study Group (Shreveport Society for Nature Study)
Website: *http://www.birdstudygroup.org*
Address: LSU Shreveport, One University Place,
Shreveport, LA 71105-2399
tel: (318) 797-5338

Louisiana Bayou Bluebird Society
Website: *http://www.labayoubluebirdsociety.org*
Contact: Evelyn Cooper; (318) 878-3210
Address: PO Box 983, Delhi, LA 71232

FEDERAL AND STATE AGENCIES

U.S. Forest Service—Kisatchie National Forest
Website: *http://www.fs.fed.us/r8/kisatchie/index.html*
Address: 2500 Shreveport Highway, Pineville, LA 71360
tel: (318) 473-7160

U.S. Fish and Wildlife Service
National Wildlife Refuges
Website: *http://www.fws.gov/refuges/profiles/ByState.cfm?state=LA*
Address: 1875 Century Boulevard, Suite 240, Atlanta, GA 30345
tel: (404) 679-7152

Louisiana Department of Wildlife and Fisheries
Business Hours: 8:00 AM–4:30 PM, Monday–Friday
Website: *http://www.wlf.louisiana.gov/*
Address: 2000 Quail Drive, Baton Rouge, LA 70808
tel: (225) 765-2800

Birders between the ages of 16 and 60 need to obtain a hunting or fishing license or another, less expensive, non-consumptive permit (e.g., "Wild Louisiana") to enter state wildlife management areas. They can be obtained through the LDW&F website, as well as at some retail outlets where hunting/fishing licenses are sold.

Louisiana State Parks

Website: http://www.crt.state.la.us/parks/
Address: PO Box 44426, Baton Rouge, LA 70804
tel: (888) 677-1400

Louisiana State Parks camping reservations

tel: (877) CAMP-N-LA (877-226-7652)
Louisiana State Office of Culture, Recreation, and Tourism
Website: http://www.louisianatravel.com/birding
Address: PO Box 94291, Baton Rouge, LA 70804
tel: (800) 677-4082

Atchafalaya National Heritage Area

Website: http://www.atchafalaya.org
Louisiana State Office of Culture, Recreation, and Tourism
Address: PO Box 44243, Baton Rouge, LA 70804
tel: (800) 404-8626

INTERNET RESOURCES

LABIRD

Website: http://www.museum.lsu.edu/~Remsen/LABIRDintro.html

The LABIRD list-serv is the principal forum for Louisiana's birding community. Instructions for joining the list-serv are found at the Louisiana Bird Resource Center.

eBird

Website: http://www.ebird.org/

The Cornell Laboratory of Ornithology's free web-based listing program receives millions of observations per month and is a massive searchable database. Many Louisiana birders submit their checklists here, thereby putting their birding efforts into a database and toward a better understanding of birdlife.

All About Birds

Website: http://www.allaboutbirds.org/

This is the Cornell Laboratory of Ornithology's free web-based bird information site. It includes profiles of all North American birds including information on their distribution, identification, and vocalizations.

Louisiana Breeding Bird Atlas

Website: *http://www.manybirds.com/atlas/atlas.htm*

Mark Swan, co-author of the published version of the Louisiana Breeding Bird Atlas, hosts a digital version of the document. There is a wealth of knowledge distilled on these pages, thanks to the many volunteers and technicians who gathered the data from 1994–1996.

Bird Louisiana

Website: *http://www.birdlouisiana.com/*

A current list of birding festivals and current organization contacts can be found at the Bird Louisiana website.

CITIZEN SCIENCE OPPORTUNITIES

Christmas Bird Counts (CBCs)

This program was started in 1900 by Frank Chapman and 27 enthusiastic birders as a way to supplant the holiday side hunt and gather information on North American birds. Led by the National Audubon Society, it runs between 14 December and 5 January every year. A single date is chosen for each count. There are about 25 CBCs in Louisiana, well distributed throughout the state. To read more about the CBCs, visit National Audubon's website *http://www.audubon.org/bird/cbc/index.html*. For local information such as contacts and dates, the Louisiana Ornithological Society *http://www.losbird.org/* maintains a list of local CBC dates on their website.

Breeding Bird Surveys (BBS)

This late spring and early summer survey regime is a large-scale, long-term international program coordinated by the U.S. Geological Survey and the Canadian Wildlife Service. The impetus for the program was the rapid avian population declines noted in the 1950s and 1960s. Volunteers across North America conduct roadside bird surveys to develop long-term population trends. The Louisiana Department of Wildlife and Fisheries coordinates Louisiana's survey routes. Contact information is found above.

Reporting Unusual Sightings

If you locate a bird that you believe is noteworthy due to its overall rarity in the region, or because of its seasonal rarity, or you find it in particularly unusual numbers, take careful notes and/or photos and recordings and report your observation promptly to the regional editor(s) of the Arkansas and Louisiana Region of *North American Birds* http://www.aba.org/nab. Also, you should send your report to the LABIRD website http://www.museum.lsu.edu/~Remsen/LABIRDintro.html. Birders in Louisiana have a list of reporting recommendations and these are summarized by the Louisiana Bird Records Committee at the Louisiana Ornithological Society's website http://losbird.org/lbrc/instruct_lbrc.html.

PRECAUTIONS

It has often been said that Louisiana has only two seasons, summer and gray. The summers are long, hot, still, and humid, while the gray is rainy, windy, and muddy—the only real respite coming during the precious few days between cold fronts. Although this is somewhat of an exaggeration, the comfort level in summer ranges from unbearable to unbearable. Going out-of-doors is much like walking into a damp electric blanket. The ambience in winter vacillates between very mild and cold. Late January through February is the coldest time, when freezing temperatures are most probable. Visitors are urged to dress appropriately and have raingear handy, even in summer, as convection showers are always possible. Sun block is recommended, particularly in summer.

Long-billed Curlew   Erik I. Johnson

The **trespass** law in Louisiana is extremely strict. It is "no fault" and requires no intent. Simply stated, it is a violation to merely enter upon the property of another without specific permission. Ergo, it is advisable—if that permission has not been obtained—to observe only from the roadside. Ah, the roadsides. Road shoulders are very narrow to nonexistent, and often of poor quality. It seems we lack the hard, rocky subsurface found in many other parts of the country and the roadbeds must be built up. This construction is generally done without any regard for legitimate needs to park off the roadway (emergencies, flats, etc.), much less for a casual driver to muck about. Always use extreme caution when pulling over to the side.

Be careful when birding in wildlife management areas and wildlife refuge lands during **hunting seasons**. *Be aware that anyone between the ages of 16 and 60 needs a hunting or fishing license or another, less expensive, non-hunting permit (e.g., "Wild Louisiana") to enter state wildlife management areas.* These can be obtained through the LDW&F website *http://www.wlf.louisiana.gov/*, as well as at *some* retail outlets where hunting/fishing licenses are sold. In 2013, the cost was no more than $5. Violators are subject to stiff fines.

Birders should always be aware of their surroundings and this is especially true if you are alone. Louisiana is not without opportunistic **theft**, and making it tempting by leaving valuables in plain sight will increase the chance of a broken window and stolen gear. Cover your valuables, keep your phone handy, and let someone know where you are going. Urban areas can concentrate the downtrodden, and if birding a new area in a city, ask locals if it's safe, and go with someone. You'll probably see more birds, too.

Snakes are not a particular problem in Louisiana, but the visitor would be well advised to be at least "passing familiar" with a few of the species. Most snakes are absolutely harmless, but there are five that should be avoided. The least likely to be encountered is the Texas Coral Snake. This small colorful reptile uses a neurotoxin, unlike the more common pit vipers. Short and slender, its coloration resembles that of a species of kingsnakes, but its yellow bands are juxtaposed with the red ones. The rhyme, which we are taught as youngsters, refers to the color separation and goes, "red next to yellow, kill a fellow — red next to black, friend of Jack". The Eastern Diamondback Rattlesnake is also not likely to be found, but exercise care in the "Florida Parishes," which lie directly north of Lake Pontchartrain. The Canebrake Rattlesnake occurs, sporadically, in other regions. Copperheads are found in woodlands throughout the state, but sightings are relatively rare and the species is generally somewhat docile. In spring through fall, encounters with the Cottonmouth (Water Moccasin) are possible, even likely in the proper habitat. It prefers swamp edges, riverbottoms, and the backwater of lakes and ponds. It is best to leave it be and look for other avenues when one bars the way.

Insects are a bane, especially in summer and fall. Deer flies and mosquitoes can be a problem in spring, summer, and early fall. The former can be a serious and painful distraction to birding, especially in late spring and summer; these insects seem to ignore repellent and can be blocked effectively only with netting. Mosquitoes appear to be worst in late summer and early fall. Ticks are abundant in grasses and weeds, along with chiggers. Chiggers can leave a lasting memory. These "redbugs" are tiny mites that will find their way to a good stopping point such as sock lines and undergarments. Here they gnaw away at your flesh. Their saliva creates a strong persistent response resulting in a two-week welt. To bypass these lovelies, avoid walking through tall grass in the warmer months. Putting your pants in your socks, wearing rubber boots, and using insect repellent or sulfur powder helps when you choose to traipse through the grassy gauntlet.

Spiders are harmless for the most part, but the Black Widow and Brown Recluse (or Violin Spider) are present and should be avoided.

Poison Ivy, particularly near the coast, is abundant and should be avoided. If a birder has a question about whether an individual plant is harmful, there is yet another rhyme which might be helpful. It is, "leaves five, let it thrive — leaves three, let it be."

Despite this ominous foreboding, Louisiana birding is extremely rewarding if the prudent birder takes but a few precautions.

How to Use This Guide

A Birder's Guide to Louisiana was written from the perspective of birders with automobile transportation. Roads are given standardized abbreviations, e.g., Interstate 49 is I-49 and Louisiana Highway 14 becomes LA-14.

Bird names and order follow the *American Ornithologists' Union Check-list of North American Birds,* 7th Edition (1998), with 42nd through 53rd (2012) supplements, http://www.aou.org/checklist/north/print.php.

The American Birding Association's *ABA Checklist: Birds of the Continental United States and Canada* (7th Edition, 2008, and supplements through 2012), Version 7.0 http://www.aba.org/checklist/, is the appropriate checklist for the ABA Area. And the Louisiana Ornithological Society's *Official Louisiana Check-list* is provided as an appendix to this guide.

Tree Swallow — Jessica Kirste

TREE SWALLOW ROOSTS

The Great Swallow Tornado of Vacherie

by Michael A. Seymour

Reprinted with permission from *Louisiana Conservationist*

"I'll tell you what you should do. Hang up the phone and get down here right now!" And so began a friendship between two avid outdoorsmen and me, the Louisiana Natural Heritage nongame bird biologist. It sounded like so many similar tales from fellow birders, our own big fish story. "Millions of birds are descending into sugarcane fields near Vacherie, Louisiana," said the caller. Indeed, I had heard the story before, but had never witnessed the spectacle myself. It was time to change that.

The Tree Swallow is a small, bicolored, iridescent blue and white, aerial predator that feeds primarily on flying arthropods such as flies, beetles, ants, ballooning spiders, and emerging adult aquatic insects. Like other birds with similar diets, during colder months, this species migrates southward to ensure ample food resources during the non-breeding season. Decreasing temperatures and the conclusion of the nesting season send Tree Swallows from their nesting grounds in Canada and the northern half of the US to their wintering grounds in Florida and the margins of the Gulf of Mexico as well as places farther south into Central America and the Caribbean. Louisiana's wintering population of Tree Swallows may be greatly affected by cold snaps, sending birds farther south of our state should insect numbers be adversely affected. In times of extreme weather, they may even augment their diet with seeds and Wax Myrtle fruits; Tree Swallow is one of only a few bird species that can digest bayberries.

It was several days before I could join Lawrence "Squint" Laiche, the caller, and his nephew Bret Acosta in Gramercy, Louisiana, about forty minutes southeast of Baton Rouge. They had promised quite an unbelievable show just days before, but on this November evening, I was met instead with long faces as Squint and Bret informed me that the roosting field in Vacherie, La. had been harvested that very day! Instead of millions of swallows returning to roost, or sleep, in the cane as they had for several consecutive days, I would be lucky to see a fraction of that number. And I was lucky; by sunset that evening, I had watched hundreds of thousands of birds drop into an adjacent, uncut cane field to spend the night. Swallows that had been cruising the Mississippi River all day where air temperatures were conducive to flying insects, now perched and chattered inside thick stands of cane. The sheer number of birds alone was enough to leave a lifelong birder mesmerized, but the process itself was, perhaps, the most fascinating.

Imagine, if you can, standing on a dirt, farm road leading into one of Louisiana's most famous crops under a near empty, blue sky darkening as the sun falls into the western horizon. At first, a few Tree Swallows zip about low to the road picking off the

Tree Swallows milling above the sugar cane field Michael Seymour

last few insects of the day. But within minutes the sky is peppered from horizon to horizon with the birds seemingly milling about in no particular direction. The swallows may be inches above the cane stalks or a few hundred feet above softly chirping. As the sky turns from dark blue to orange and red, a binocular scan of the sky reveals swallows for miles in all directions. One binocular field may be a cube of birds composed of 30x30x30 individual swallows—a block of 9000 birds! Suddenly, the flock begins to form a cohesive unit, and the once seemingly random motion is replaced by a large swirling mass similar to a funnel cloud. Soon thereafter, the birds begin vocalizing together, their cadence quickens, and without further warning dive at a near ninety-degree angle into the cane. Just below the tops of the stalks, the birds spread horizontally through the plants. The funnel cloud has touched down in the crop as a tornado with a column several birds thick. On that first visit in late November 2007, I witnessed a flock of several hundreds of thousands of Tree Swallows. It was a number of birds that I was simply not comfortable estimating; the trip was a nice taste of what was to come, but in no way had I expected to witness such an incredible phenomenon a few weeks later.

Tree Swallow roosts are frequently found in cane fields and natural stands of cane throughout Louisiana during migration and during winter. Historically, the species likely utilized cane growing along the Mississippi and Red Rivers for such purposes and probably still does where the plants are still extant. In fact, natural canebrakes are considered one of the nation's most critically endangered ecosystems, with only remnant, patchily distributed stands remaining. President Teddy Roosevelt described this rare ecosystem and its rare inhabitants, including the Louisiana Black Bear and the Ivory-billed Woodpecker, in an article entitled "In the Louisiana Canebrakes" (1908); the height and density of the cane made travel and hunting tremendous challenges. In the present-day, stands of native Roseau Cane or Phragmites in our coastal zone may provide substantial roosting habitat for millions of migrant swallows. For generations, Rockefeller Wildlife Refuge in Cameron and Vermilion Parishes with its vast marsh and expanses of cane has hosted immense flocks of swallows during migration, especially fall, or in winter.

Depending upon the season, up to seven species of swallows may occur in Louisiana—Tree, Bank, Northern Rough-winged, Barn, Cliff, and Cave Swallows and Purple Martin. Only four of these are common nesters—Northern Rough-winged, Barn, and Cliff Swallows, and Purple Martin. Cave Swallows and, even the abundant Tree Swallow, are very rare nesters in Louisiana, and Bank Swallows simply migrate through. Most swallows are cavity-nesting species that rely on woodpeckers and other cavity excavators or even manmade nest boxes and or other structures for nesting. To be sure, martin houses can be found in almost every neighborhood that recognizes the value of these insect predators. Like their smaller Tree Swallow relatives, martins also form very large and very prominent roosts in our state. Undoubtedly more famous to birders and non-birders than the "Vacherie swallow tornado" is the roost of Purple Martins at the southern end of the Lake Pontchartrain Causeway. Some sources estimate that 100,000 to 200,000 martins may roost on the understructure of the bridge during the peak activity in July. If total population estimates are correct—roughly 10,000,000 martins in North America according to Partners in Flight (PIF), a bird conservation organization—then one of every fifty martins on the continent may be roosting in Metairie on any given night in mid-July. Other Louisiana swallows likely form large roosts during migration, but none have built roosts of seemingly mythical proportions, as have Tree Swallows and Purple Martins.

Tree Swallows swoop into the sugar cane field — Michael Seymour

In early December 2007, I received another phone call from Mr. Laiche. The flock that had been fractured in November had reformed to its previous splendor. On this occasion, I brought reinforcements, two biologist colleagues, to assist in estimating the number of birds. The event occurred similar to that I had witnessed in November—swallows seemingly magically appearing until the entire sky is filled. On this evening, however, there was one very obvious difference (other than an increase in mosquitoes). Whereas, there were hundreds of thousands of Tree Swallows before, there were now millions! By the Department's estimates, we viewed some two to five million swallows that evening! Comparing this estimate to PIF's calculation of the North American Tree Swallow population (20,000,000 Tree Swallows), at least ten percent of the world's population of Tree Swallows was spending the night in Vacherie, La. It became clear after this event that the Vacherie swallow tornado is likely the most underappreciated natural phenomenon in Louisiana! I strongly advise anyone who might be interested to visit this stretch of the Mississippi River during peak flights from mid-October to early December. I thank Bret, Squint, and Ken Prestenbach, who have tracked the flights for years, for introducing me to this awesome sight!

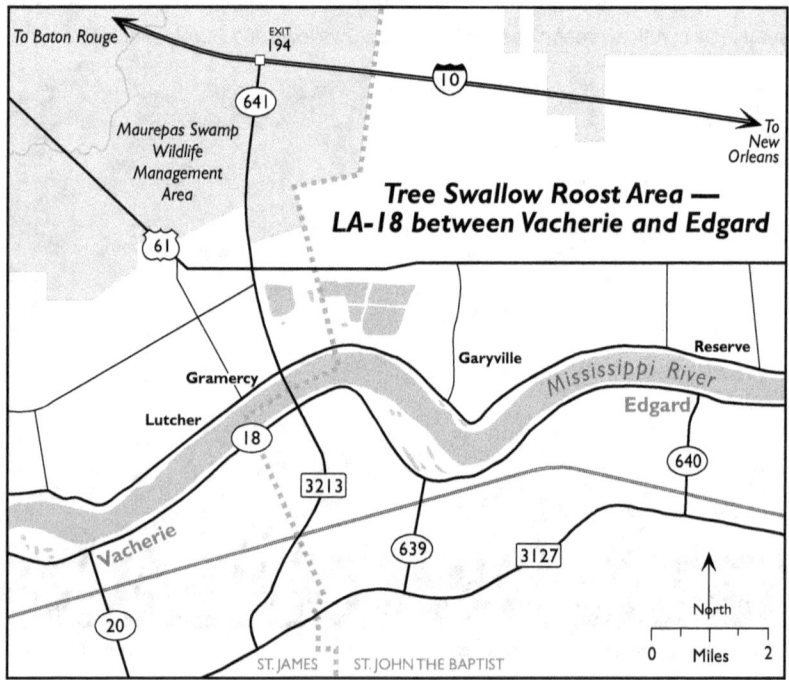

Getting There:

This underappreciated, but overwhelming event is exceptionally easy to view, because a public highway takes one immediately adjacent to prime roosting habitat. Louisiana Highway 18 on the south side of the Mississippi River—particularly the stretch between Vacherie and Edgard—can be especially rewarding for swallow tornado watchers.

The event is weather dependent on two scales. Cold weather in the northern half of the continent will push many more swallows into Louisiana than a milder fall and winter might, when birds do not have to travel as far for adequate foraging. As such, it is difficult to estimate when a peak day for viewing might occur, but mid-October through, at least, early December are best. Also, depending on the harvest schedule of the cane, roosting sites may be removed at any time. Locally, periods of thunderstorms may preclude the formation of a large roosting flock altogether. Overcast skies bring about an artificially early sunset, which might make the flock enter the sugarcane earlier than expected.

The best time of day for viewing is just prior to sunset; the morning exodus of the flock from the cane is not as spectacular as the evening entry. Plan on arriving by 4:00–4:30 PM so that you may situate yourself to best view the flock; you may have to drive the highway back and forth to figure out where the flock will most likely alight. Backlighting (having the sun in your eyes) is actually best for viewing and can make for spectacular pictures and video if the sky is slightly cloudy. If you would like to photograph the action, bring a tripod to steady the camera, as shutter speeds will suffer from the dimming light. Once the sun starts to drop into the horizon, the lighting becomes ideal for viewing. The sky may be filled with birds by 5:00 PM or so, and emptied of birds by 5:30 PM. The actual swirling funnel cloud only lasts a few minutes. The entire flock of millions of birds may pour out of the sky in five minutes. This means that if there are two million birds aloft, more than 6500 individuals will land in the cane per second!

As you ready yourself for the viewing, there are, at least, a few considerations: (1) Bring bug spray as mosquitoes will be present even in colder temperatures; (2) Park legally and safely; and (3) Do not trespass! Do not enter fields without the permission of the landowner! Although, I have seen the amazed reaction of sugarcane landowners firsthand during these events, many more may not have witnessed this event for themselves and may not readily appreciate your enthusiasm. Remember that there is a flipside to every coin; in this case, the huge congregation of birds means that farmers and their workers are subjected to intense levels of ammonia from buildup and degradation of bird droppings. Be respectful and thankful to the landowners, and they will, certainly, respect you. Enjoy the spectacle, and be careful!

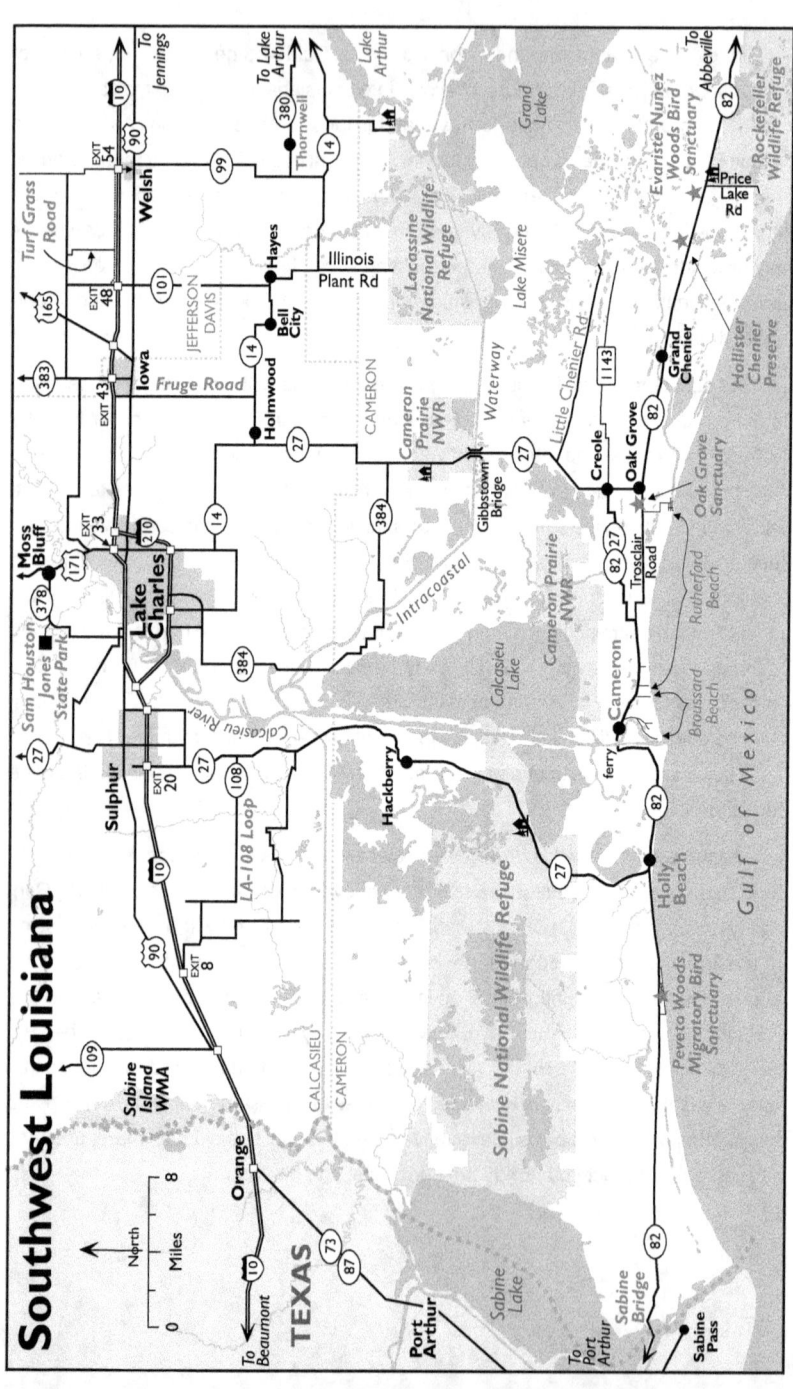

SOUTHWEST LOUISIANA

Southwest Louisiana in general, and Cameron Parish in particular, are relatively unknown to North America's birding community. There are areas along the Louisiana coast that rival the venerated (and rightfully so) Texas sanctuaries at High Island and Sabine Pass and Alabama's Dauphin Island. Regardless of where they might start out, all Louisiana Big Days of note have ended in Cameron Parish. In recent years, several of these Big Days, performed by LSU Museum of Natural Science ornithology students, have surpassed the 200-species barrier. In all, over 420 species have been documented in Cameron Parish. All spring and fall meetings of the Louisiana Ornithological Society are held here. Most of the parish is marshland and is virtually inaccessible. The areas that are accessible, however—such as the freshwater marshes, beaches, and oaken ridges (cheniers)—provide marvelous bird habitat.

Waterfowl hunting is big business in south Louisiana. Much of the marshland and even many of the rice fields are leased during the season, which runs roughly from September to late January. Even so, the winter birder may see a staggering number of ducks and geese. Greater White-fronted, Snow, Ross's, and Cackling Geese may be found. Gadwall, American Wigeon, Mallard, Blue-winged Teal, Northern Shoveler, Northern Pintail, and Green-winged Teal are common. Mottled Duck is a permanent resident. Cinnamon Teal is rare but observed in some years, mostly during spring migration. Offshore waterfowl rafts often contain thousands of Lesser Scaup, and any of these flocks occasionally may harbor any of the three scoter species or a rare Long-tailed Duck. Bufflehead is sometimes present in these Gulf waters, and Common Goldeneye is a possibility. Red-breasted Merganser and Ruddy Duck are also present off the beaches. Both Canvasback and Redhead may be seen. Greater Scaup will occasionally put in an appearance in a large marsh pool.

All twelve members of the heron family normally found in the U.S. may be seen here in a single day, particularly in late summer and early autumn. Roseate Spoonbill is a common permanent resident along the coast. Sandhill Crane is a regular winter visitor to the area around the town of Holmwood in Calcasieu Parish.

Shorebirds are also numerous. Snowy, Wilson's, Semipalmated, and Piping Plovers all may be observed along the coast in the proper seasons—the former two species are permanent residents, though only a few pairs of Snowies are known to nest. American Oystercatcher nests at a few Cameron Parish locations and is most readily observed on a sandbar just south and east of the LA-82 Sabine River bridge from Texas. American Avocet is a permanent resident, although in much reduced numbers in summer.

Draining rice fields in spring and fall may temporarily hold thousands of shorebirds, including Semipalmated, Western, Least, and White-rumped (spring) Sandpipers. Western and Least remain through the winter. Baird's Sandpiper uses the sands and dried mud behind the beaches, also during migration. Willet and Sanderling may be found close to the Gulf. Long-billed Curlew is local in fall and winter. Marbled Godwit may be observed in all but the breeding season, and its smaller kin, Hudsonian Godwit, is a visitor to the rice fields in spring. Short-billed Dowitcher is seen on the salt flats of Gulf beaches (oversummering birds are uncommon). Long-billed Dowitcher is more prevalent away from the coast, joined in migration by Stilt Sandpiper.

Lesser Black-backed Gulls can be found in small numbers among the more common gull species during fall and winter. Caspian Tern is a permanent resident, along with Gull-billed and Royal, and Sandwich Terns are present except in winter. Least Terns breed.

Birding the precious few wooded sections of the coast that are accessible to the public can be a terrible disappointment during the middle of summer. However, in winter, an uncommon Black-and-white Warbler, Northern Parula, Black-throated Green Warbler, American Redstart, or rare Black-throated Gray Warbler or Yellow-breasted Chat are possible, along with the more common Ruby-crowned Kinglet or Hermit Thrush. But, during the migration periods each spring and fall, these copses and woodlots are spectacular places. Almost every regularly occurring wood-warbler in the U.S.—Kirtland's and Olive (which is not a true wood-warbler) excepted—has been documented here. It is not at all unusual to see 20 or more warbler species in a single day. In addition, the trees and undergrowth are alive with flycatchers, thrushes, tanagers, grosbeaks, buntings, and orioles. The daily counts of the Louisiana Ornithological Society at its spring and fall meetings generally push the 200-species mark and always contain a few rarities.

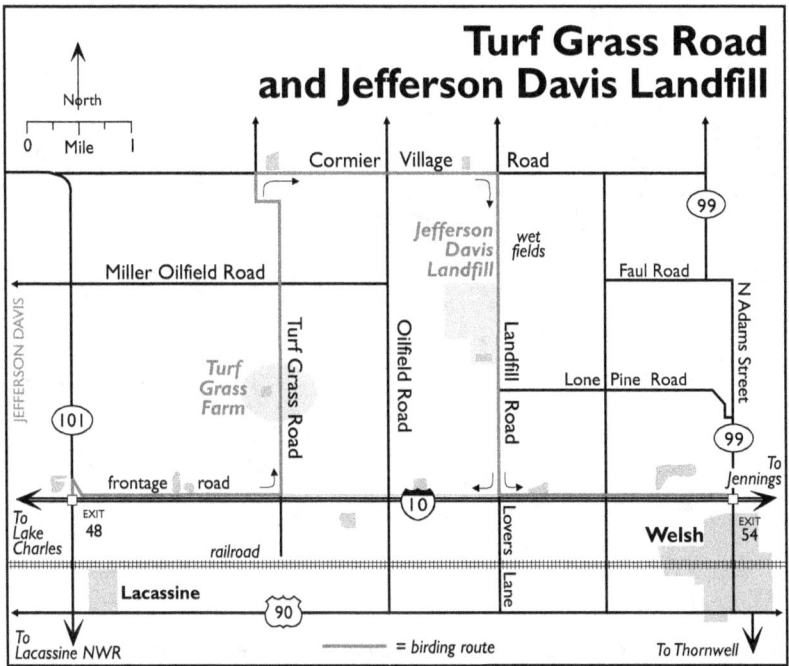

TURF GRASS ROAD AND JEFFERSON DAVIS LANDFILL

For a short trip from Lake Charles, head east on I-10 from the I-10/US-171 junction (Exit 33) for about 14 miles to LA-101 (Exit 48). Turn left under the freeway, drive north about 0.5 mile to the eastbound frontage road, and turn right onto it. Go east 2 miles to Turf Grass Road and turn left (north). The brushy hedgerows and fallow fields leading to the grassy fields can be excellent for sparrows and buntings, including Painted Bunting and Dickcissel. Swainson's Hawk and Crested Caracara have been seen here, as well. Continue north on Turf Grass Road for 0.75 mile to the turf grass farm. Sod farms are apparently irresistible to "grasspipers" in spring, making this the best site in the state to find Upland and Buff-breasted Sandpipers in April and early May. A scope is helpful for scanning the vast turf fields for distant buffy blobs. American Golden-Plover is also expected in spring. Check the power lines at this season for Scissor-tailed Flycatcher.

After working the fields, continue north on Turf Grass Road about 2 miles, with a dogleg to the left, to Cormier Village Road. These agricultural fields are good for sparrows and buntings. A flock of Bobolinks in late April or early May isn't out of the

Buff-breasted Sandpipers work the turf John Longhenry

question. At Cormier Village Road turn right and continue 2.3 miles, checking the ponds on the right for King Rail and other waterbirds. Turn right (south) at Landfill Road and head back toward the interstate. This road has excellent wet fields on the left that can be loaded with waterbirds. The large landfill on the right—a.k.a. Mt.Trashta—attracts a loyal following of Laughing Gulls from the coast along with other offal-philes. Hedgerows and fallow fields are good for sparrows and buntings. In spring, listen for the seemingly incessant and jumbled song of Painted Bunting.

Turn left (east) at the frontage road to return to I-10 (Exit 54) at the town of Welsh (2.3 miles) or right (west) to return to LA-101 / I-10 Exit 48 (4 miles).

SAM HOUSTON JONES STATE PARK

Located about 12 miles northwest of Lake Charles, this 1,068-acre park offers an array of amenities as well as a glimpse at natural Louisiana. You'll find about a dozen cabins equipped with heat and air conditioning, six dozen campsites with water and electricity, a playground, restrooms, showers, and boats for rent. Two trails meander through the park, and the Calcasieu River offers boating, fishing, and a good place to find Belted Kingfisher. (See map on page 22.)

The stands of pines in the forested regions of the park once harbored Red-cockaded Woodpecker, now absent. Even so, the habitat holds many other pineywoods species. Permanent residents include Eastern Screech-Owl, Barred Owl, Hairy and Pileated Woodpeckers, Carolina Chickadee, Tufted Titmouse, Brown-headed Nuthatch, Pine Warbler, and Eastern Towhee. Winter residents include Yellow-bellied Sapsucker, Eastern Phoebe, Blue-headed Vireo, Brown Creeper, House and Winter Wrens, Golden-crowned Kinglet, Cedar Waxwing, Orange-crowned and Yellow-rumped Warblers, White-throated Sparrow, and the occasional White-eyed Vireo or Gray Catbird.

Migratory breeders include Chimney Swift, Ruby-throated Hummingbird, Acadian and Great Crested Flycatchers, Yellow-throated and Red-eyed Vireos, Wood Thrush, Kentucky and Hooded Warblers, Northern Parula, Summer Tanager, and Indigo Bunting. During migration, thrushes, a host of warblers, Scarlet Tanager, Rose-breasted Grosbeak, and Baltimore Oriole can be found.

To reach Sam Houston Jones State Park from Lake Charles, head north on US-171 from I-10 (Exit 33). Travel 3.9 miles to LA-378 (Sam Houston Jones Parkway) in the town of Moss Bluff. Turn left (west) and drive 3 miles to a right turn onto LA-378 Spur, which leads to the park's entrance in 1 mile.

White-tailed Kite   Erik I. Johnson

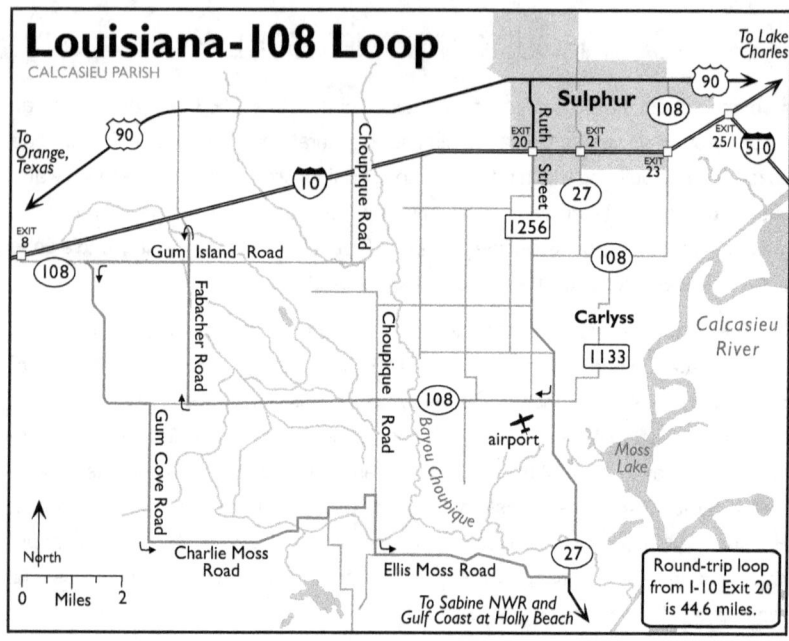

LA-108 LOOP

Good birds for Louisiana, such as White-tailed Kite, Short-eared Owl, and Grasshopper and Harris's Sparrows, might be spotted on this 45-mile loop, but the real jewel is a population of Crested Caracaras that occurs in the patches of vegetation that dot the area. The loop always provides good birding, but it's a "must see" in winter.

Head west on I-10 from Lake Charles to Exit 20 (Ruth Street in the town of Sulphur). Zero your odometer at the stop sign, then turn left onto LA-1256. In 2.2 miles, LA-1256 becomes LA-108/27. At 5.4 miles, turn right (west) with LA-108, zeroing your odometer at the turn. Explore the fields and hedges along the road. The airport fields on the left at 0.6 mile should be scoped during migration for grass-loving shorebirds such as Upland and Buff-breasted Sandpipers.

At 8.1 miles, turn right onto Fabacher Road. The 42,000 acres along here are maintained primarily for duck and deer hunting and may be birded only from the road. The security guard who patrols the roads is used to encountering birders and may be able to point you in the direction of Crested Caracaras, which may nest on the property.

Pay attention to the treetops, snags, and power poles for perched raptors. White-tailed Kite is somewhat reliable. Check hedgerows in fall and winter for Lincoln's and Harris's Sparrows.

At 11.2 miles, you will reach Gum Island Road. The field on the northeast corner harbors Grasshopper Sparrow during winter. If Crested Caracara hasn't been seen yet, drive north through the intersection to examine the pastures on both sides of the road. Then return to Gum Island Road and turn right (west). Watch the power poles for raptors and the hedges for sparrows. During summer, look for Blue Grosbeak, buntings, and Dickcissel.

Crested Caracara John Elias

In 2.4 miles, Gum Island Road intersects with LA-108. Zero your odometer and turn left (south). After 4.2 miles on LA-108, turn right (south) onto Gum Cove Road. Explore the brush and fields, especially during winter, for the next three miles. Turn left onto Charlie Moss Road (7.2 miles) and follow its zigzags to Choupique Road. At the bayou crossings, check trees for wintering finches. Turn right onto Choupique Road and follow it and Ellis Moss Road for 6 miles to reach to LA-27. Turn left (north) to return to I-10 in Sulphur or turn right (south) to head toward Sabine National Wildlife Refuge and the coast.

Sabine National Wildlife Refuge

The main bill of fare here is the waterfowl. Sabine National Wildlife Refuge is primarily an open, freshwater marsh with a small amount of scrub and a stand of oaks at refuge headquarters. It is in these oaks—and in the scrub just across the road—where Louisiana's first Townsend's Solitaire was found, but that area is currently off-limits (since Hurricane *Rita*). Neotropic Cormorant is usually present along the waterways on either side of the road. During winter, Belted Kingfishers perch on the power lines waiting for a minnow to swim into range. Ospreys patrol overhead.

The flats north of headquarters often fill with feeding sandpipers, but stopping to see them is usually difficult because the road is very narrow with only a few small turnouts. The colder months are excellent some years for Short-eared Owl, which can be seen from the refuge's main parking area as they begin their crepuscular search.

To reach the refuge from Lake Charles (see map on page 22), take I-10 west to the LA-27 exit in Sulphur (Exit 20) and head south to the small town of Hackberry. From here it is about 8 miles to refuge headquarters on the left. If refuge personnel are around, it is best to let them know you will be birding the grounds as many areas of the refuge are off-limits. The main parking area for the refuge is on the right, just 3.6 miles farther. Amenities include restrooms and 1¼ miles of boardwalks with several observation decks.

During migration, thrushes, warblers, tanagers, grosbeaks, buntings, and orioles can often be found in the trees and scrub along the waterway to the south and the treeline on the east. Mottled Duck, Least Bittern, Green Heron, Black-crowned Night-Heron, Roseate Spoonbill, Purple and Common Gallinules, and Black-necked Stilt all nest in the vicinity.

During winter, the duck population swells as Blue-winged Teal—around since late summer—is joined by Gadwall, American Wigeon, Mallard, Northern Shoveler, Northern Pintail, Green-winged Teal, and every now and then a rare Cinnamon Teal. The shallow lakes and ponds on the property hold Canvasback, Redhead, Greater Scaup, and, although rare, Common Goldeneye. Other winter denizens are Yellow Rail, the even more elusive Black Rail, Virginia Rail, and Sora. (The Yellow and Black Rails are very, very rarely seen here; your only real chances for seeing Yellows are in the rice fields during harvesting—see pages 49 and 52.) Gull-billed Tern is found working along the borrow pits on either side of the highway and Neotropic Cormorant is always present.

Neotropic Cormorant   Dan Lane

HOLLY BEACH

From Sabine National Wildlife Refuge, continue south on LA-27; at about 6.6 miles from the entrance to the parking area, check the water tower on the left during winter for a Peregrine Falcon that uses the tower to keep track of activity in the surrounding marsh.

Shortly (0.4 mile), LA-27 makes a 90-degree turn to the left as it joins LA-82 coming in from the west. Zero your odometer at this intersection and head east into the hamlet of Holly Beach. From this point on—until the highway wanders away from the beach—mine the shore for shorebirds and mixed gull flocks, particularly during winter and migration.

Snowy, Wilson's, Semipalmated, and Piping Plovers can be seen along with several species of peep. Black-bellied Plover, Willet, and Ruddy Turnstone are generally present, as are American Avocet and Black Skimmer. Late summer and early fall is an excellent time for Reddish Egret.

Laughing, Ring-billed, and Herring Gulls and Caspian and Royal Terns often are found here, with Bonaparte's Gull also around during the winter. Sandwich Tern is uncommon. Many gull rarities have been recorded here, so check the gull flocks if you have the patience for it.

On the north side of the highway, watch the wires and fence posts for raptors, especially during winter. Northern Harrier, Red-tailed Hawk, and American Kestrel are common. The patient birder might tease out a Merlin.

During colder months, the nearshore waters usually harbor rafts of Lesser Scaup. All three scoters—Surf, White-winged, and Black—can sometimes be seen, whereas Red-breasted Merganser and Ruddy Duck are easier to spot. Rare, but sometimes present, is Long-tailed Duck.

When LA-82 veers away from the beach, the fields on both sides of the road should be scanned for migrants in April, when Bobolink and Yellow-headed Blackbird are possible.

Piping Plover   David Cagnolatti

PEVETO WOODS MIGRATORY BIRD SANCTUARY

If you are new to Louisiana, you may not be familiar with the term *chenier*. It is a French word meaning "place of oaks." These are oak mottes to our Texas neighbors, but you ain't in Texas, *mes amis*. The slight elevation permits oaks and other trees to persist and serve as a forested habitat island in a sea of marsh. This habitat is a welcome respite to migratory songbirds heading north, south, or along the coast. For this reason, they can be excellent birding spots and have the potential to be

SOUTHWEST LOUISIANA 33

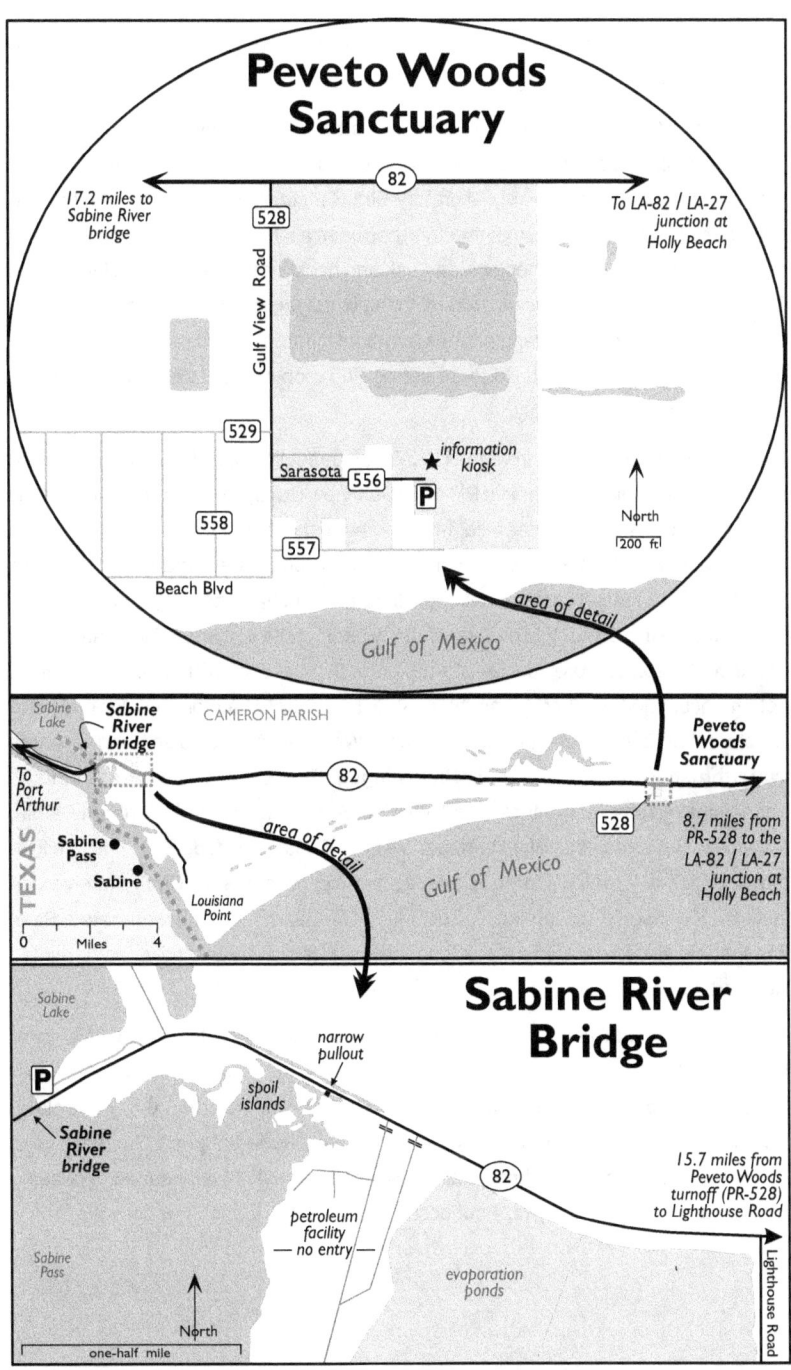

mind-blowing in April and early May if the winds are out of the north or there is substantial rain.

Peveto Woods Migratory Bird Sanctuary is owned and maintained by the Baton Rouge Audubon Society. (In the past it was known by a variety of other names, including the Holleyman-Sheely Migratory Bird Sanctuary.) Considering the last few hurricanes to strike the area, maintenance has been a tall order. Trails leading to views of windblown scrub, fields, hedges, and oak and hackberry woods dot the landscape. The woods here are best visited during spring when migrants can be seen coming in off the Gulf, although this island of trees may hold interesting birds at any season. The deer flies and mosquitoes build to an unforgiving mob by late spring or summer, so dress and slather accordingly.

To reach the sanctuary from the LA-27/82 intersection at Holly Beach, drive west on LA-82 for 8.7 miles. Turn left at PR-528 (Gulf View Road), heading south toward the Gulf of Mexico. After a quarter mile, take another left onto the first gravel road, which leads to a parking area. Pause at the metal donation box at the entrance to the woods to contribute to the sanctuary's upkeep. Bring a lawn chair and use insect repellent. One of the best areas in this chenier is the watering hole just east of the sanctuary's entrance. Fifteen or more species of warblers within the span of three or four hours is not an uncommon number during the peak of migration. The more regular-occurring warblers that can be seen include Ovenbird, Worm-eating, Louisiana and Northern Waterthrushes, Golden-winged, Blue-winged, Black-and-white, Prothonotary, Tennessee, Nashville, Kentucky, and Hooded, American Redstart, Northern Parula, Magnolia, Bay-breasted, Blackburnian, Yellow, Chestnut-sided, Blackpoll, Yellow-throated, Black-throated Green, Canada, and Yellow-breasted Chat. Rarely seen include Swainson's, Mourning, Cape May, Cerulean, and Black-throated Blue. Exceptional finds are Virginia's, Connecticut, Hermit, Townsend's, and Painted Redstart.

Eastern Wood-Pewee, *Empidonax* flycatchers, and Great Crested Flycatcher forage in the sanctuary. Yellow-billed and Black-billed (uncommon) Cuckoos, Yellow-throated, Warbling, and Philadelphia Vireos, Veery, Gray-cheeked, Swainson's, and Wood Thrushes, Scarlet Tanager, Rose-breasted Grosbeak, and Baltimore Oriole are found almost daily. Lesser Nighthawk, Black-headed Grosbeak, and Lazuli Bunting are very rare but possible.

American Oystercatcher   Christina Evans

SABINE BRIDGE

To get to Sabine Bridge at the Texas state line from Peveto Woods Sanctuary, return to LA-82, zero your odometer, and turn left (west). At 16.8 miles, stop at a small pullout on the left. The island to the southwest is one of the most reliable places in the state for American Oystercatcher. In fact, they breed here.

In spring, check the fields to the north of the road for Whimbrel and also listen for Sedge Wren and Seaside Sparrow. A half mile to the west turn right into a parking area at the beginning of a new swing-bridge over the Sabine River into Texas. During spring and summer, Cliff Swallows dart about, foraging and nest building. Look carefully among them for the pale face and throat of a Cave Swallow; a few individuals have nested here several years.

The backside of the island that was visible from the small pullout is visible across the highway. Set up your scope on the south side of the roadway to examine it.

36 SOUTHWEST LOUISIANA

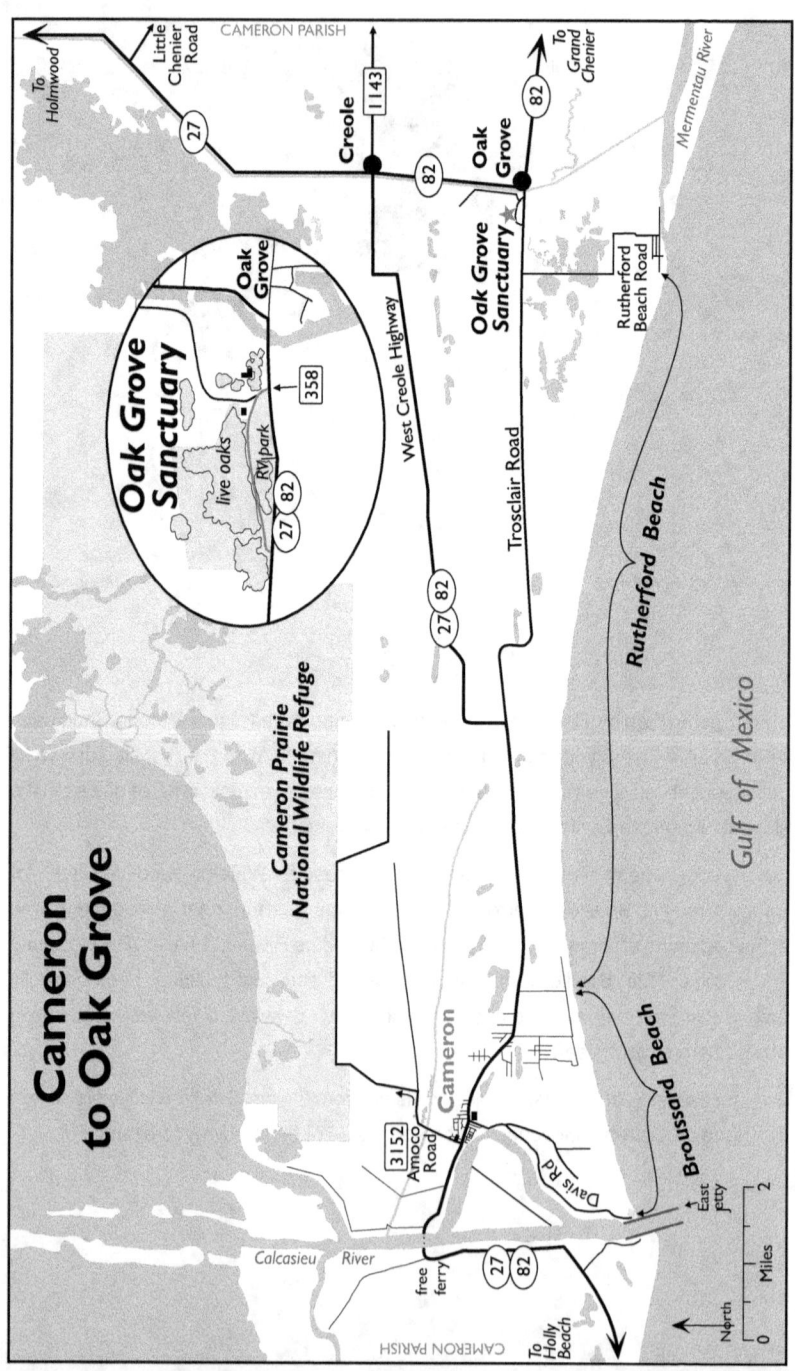

TOWN OF CAMERON

Return to Holly Beach on LA-82 and continue eastward on LA-27/82 for about 8 miles to the Calcasieu River ferry, a short crossing necessary to reach the town of Cameron. You might have as much as a 20-minute wait for the next ferry, an opportunity to check out a small woodlot on the right that usually contains a few migrants, the odd vagrant, and mosquitoes seemingly the size of dragonflies.

Cameron Parish is one of the most rural areas in Louisiana with only one stop light and one caution light, both in the village of Cameron. The village is void of a police department and depends on the Cameron Parish Sheriff's Office to handle any criminal activity. The town's few residents are not suspicious of tourists. They are accustomed to seeing binoculars, especially during the fall and spring. But, they might ask you about your visit.

The village of Cameron formerly supported trees that were very attractive to migrants during spring and fall. But extensive hurricane damage has resulted in few such opportunities at present. However, White-winged and Inca Doves and Bronzed Cowbird are fairly common year round. A cowbird flock tends to persist in Cameron and should be sifted through for Yellow-headed Blackbird. If the flock is in town, it's hard to miss.

Behind the courthouse, which lies about half a mile west of the elementary school, Amoco Road leads north to a marshy expanse of Sabine National Wildlife Refuge. This road dead ends, but provides a nice elevated entry into the brackish coastal marshes where geese, ducks, rails, gulls, and terns are the general fare.

Blue Grosbeak, Indigo and Painted Buntings, Dickcissel, and Orchard Oriole visit the areas of grass and low shrubs. To find them, drive south on Davis Road—located just west of the elementary school.

Painted Bunting   Joseph Turner

Nelson's Sparrow — David Cagnolatti

Continue south on Davis Road. The road traverses marsh and ultimately leads to the beach and the east jetty of the Calcasieu River. Gravel parking lots along the way usually host resting gulls and occasionally small sandpipers. Mind the fences, pools, and poles as well. Clapper Rails may be seen and heard in the mud adjacent to the grasses.

Cormorants, herons, ibises, Roseate Spoonbill, gulls, and terns use the area as a roost at all seasons. Whimbrel and Long-billed Curlew often visit the drier grass to the east, near the beach entrance. The shrubs on the left side of the road are used by a variety of spring and fall migrants. The marsh is a winter home to Nelson's Sparrow and a permanent home to Seaside Sparrow. Vireos, wood-warblers, Blue Grosbeak, Indigo and Painted Buntings, and Orchard Oriole also can be seen.

The road ends at a site maintained by the Cameron Parish Police Jury. There is a small fee for parking. Toilets, camp sites, a jetty walk, and an observation deck are among the site's amenities. The observation deck provides a grand view of salt marsh, nearshore waters, and the western tip of Broussard Beach. Check the sand near the rocks for American Oystercatcher. Black Skimmers often patrol near the shore in squadrons. American Avocets, especially in winter, spring, and fall, wade in the shallows as they feed with their delicately recurved bills.

Brown Pelican (the once-extirpated state bird) is now common along the sands. American White Pelican is almost always spotted, although it might be missed in mid-summer. Laughing Gull is a fixture, along with Forster's Tern. Common and Sandwich Terns are uncommon. More likely are Ring-billed and Herring Gulls and Caspian and Royal Terns. Franklin's Gull and Black Tern are always present in spring and fall, whereas Bonaparte's Gull is relatively easy to find in winter.

Many a rare gull has been scoped on these sands—California, Lesser Black-backed, Glaucous, and Great Black-backed Gulls, and Black-legged Kittiwake have been reported. If you're a gull guy or gal, this is your spot.

Check the river for wintering Horned Grebe. In late winter, this is an excellent place to scope for scoters and Northern Gannet. Snowy, Wilson's, and Piping Plovers, although not common, can be found in winter by the patient observer willing to walk. Black-bellied Plovers are almost always somewhere along the beach. Sanderlings are always running on the beach.

An alternate route to the Gulf Coast and Cameron from Lake Charles takes you down the eastern part of the LA-27 loop, visiting Fruge Road and Cameron Prairie National Wildlife Refuge on the way to the intersection with LA-82 at the town of Creole. See map on page 22.

Fruge Road

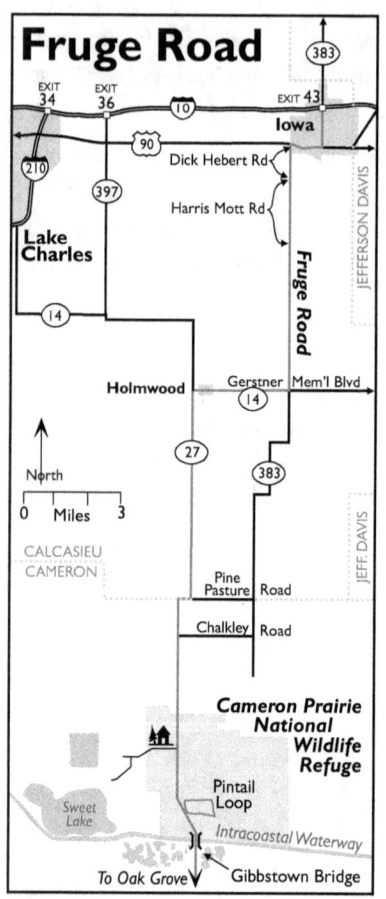

East of Lake Charles, get off I-10 at the town of Iowa, Exit 43, and turn south onto LA-383. At 1.2 miles this road intersects US-90 at a caution light. Turn right, drive one mile to Dick Hebert Road, and turn left. Follow this road for 7.4 miles—after a mile, the road changes to Harris Mott Road, and after 3 miles it becomes Fruge Road.

During winter, check the fields for Crested Caracara, shorebirds, vagrant flycatchers, and sparrows. In summer, Eastern Kingbird and Scissor-tailed Flycatcher are evident. Look for transient flycatchers in migration.

At 7.4 miles, turn right (west) onto LA-14 (Gerstner Memorial Boulevard) and drive 3 miles to the community of Holmwood, where LA-14 turns north toward Lake Charles. To reach Cameron and the Gulf Coast, turn left onto LA-27. Just south of this junction is an area where a flock of Sandhill Cranes has wintered. Geese and ducks are usually present here during winter, too. The shoulders along LA-27 are very poor, so park with extreme caution. (An alternate route from the Fruge Road/LA-14 junction to Cameron Prairie National Wildlife Refuge is shown on the above map.)

CAMERON PRAIRIE NATIONAL WILDLIFE REFUGE

Eleven miles south of Holmwood you will see Cameron Prairie National Wildlife Refuge headquarters on the right. Check the trees and ponds here during migration and the fields behind the main building during winter for geese and ducks.

A short wildlife drive called Pintail Loop starts 2 miles south of the headquarters or, for birders approaching from the coast, 1.4 miles north of the south foot of the Gibbstown Bridge over the Intracoastal Waterway.

During spring and fall, there are numerous possibilities for migrants and vagrants. If water levels are appropriate, shorebird numbers here can be very impressive. During summer, Least Bittern, Green Heron, Purple Gallinule, and Orchard Oriole can be seen. During winter, Tricolored Heron, Virginia Rail, Sora, and Marsh Wren are present, as are loads of puddle ducks.

LITTLE CHENIER ROAD

After you cross the Gibbstown Bridge, zero your odometer. (See map on page 22.) At 4.8 miles, turn left onto Little Chenier Road, which continues east for 14 miles.

Gull-billed Tern   David Cagnolatti

Along this path, Wilson's Phalarope is possible during migration. American Bittern can be seen in the marsh during winter. Least Bittern and Purple Gallinule are fairly common during spring and summer. Virginia Rail and Sora are often spotted during winter.

Wooded patches might contain a few migrants during fall and spring, and Western Kingbird could stray during these seasons, as well. Roseate Spoonbills are common, along with Little Blue and Tricolored Herons, Snowy Egret, and White and White-faced

Ibises. Gull-billed Tern is often seen during winter in the large bays of the Mermentau River at road's end.

Return to LA-27 and turn left (south) toward the town of Oak Grove. At the junction in Creole, the road you are on joins LA-82 coming up from the south. The combined route becomes West Creole Highway and leads west some 15 miles to Cameron. As you continue driving south (now on LA-82), the canal bordering the road between Creole and Oak Grove can be good for Neotropic Cormorants. A left turn with LA-82 in Oak Grove will take you eastward to Abbeville by way of Rockefeller Wildlife Refuge.

OAK GROVE SANCTUARY

Many birders who bolt for the coast during spring weather fronts will stop at Oak Grove Sanctuary to see if their meteorological mindfulness was on the money. (See map on page 36.) If there are going to be birds on the coast, this small group of hackberry and oaks with its healthy understory is often the first woodlot where they can be sampled. A side road can be used for parking and you can work the trees for any trans-Gulf migrants that have stopped in for a break. In non-breeding months there is often a cowbird flock in the area that you should be sure to check for Bronzed Cowbird and for a rare, spring Shiny Cowbird.

To reach the sanctuary, turn right (west) at Oak Grove onto Trosclair Road. Just across the canal, at 0.1 mile, Parish Road 358 leads to the right. This poorly maintained blacktop passes through Oak Grove Sanctuary, a marvelous old stand of live oaks that should always be examined during migration and winter. *Empidonax* flycatchers, Warbling and Philadelphia Vireos, Cape May and Black-throated Blue Warblers (both rare, spring only), and a host of other passerines can be seen during migration; Black-throated Gray Warbler has wintered here. A pair of Great Kiskadees has been fairly reliable in this area in recent years and birders should keep their ears alert for their *kis-ka-DEE!* call. Birding from the road is the *modus operandi* unless you have permission from the owners, who can sometimes be found in the area.

Seaside Sparrow   Jennifer Brumfield

Rutherford and Broussard Beaches

To reach Rutherford Beach from Oak Grove Sanctuary (see map on page 36), continue west on PR-358 until it rejoins Trosclair Road in a few hundred yards. In another 0.8 mile, Rutherford Beach Road, which is adequately signed, intersects from the left. Turn south and travel 1.2 miles to where the road turns left. This *Spartina* marsh is an excellent place to see and hear Seaside Sparrows. In another 1.2 miles the road ends at the beach. Drive all of the streets in the area. Groove-billed Ani might be seen in the nearby brush in fall and winter. During winter, look for flycatchers and Palm Warbler. It is at this season that hawks and falcons are numerous.

Broussard Beach is the stretch of sand and mud running east from the Calcasieu River jetty to a cut between Cameron and Oak Grove. Rutherford Beach runs from the bayou's mouth south of Oak Grove west to the cut (see map). At one time, it was possible to traverse this entire sea-washed stretch in a two-wheel-drive vehicle, but erosion has made this almost impossible. A more prudent tactic would be to make tentative forays from either end.

Snowy and Piping Plovers are relatively common during winter; Wilson's and Semi-palmated Plovers are also present. Rare gulls, including Thayer's and Glaucous, have been reported on these shores.

These beaches are two of the best places in Louisiana to find Reddish Egret during fall. Short-eared Owl is a regular visitor to the grasses behind Rutherford Beach during winter. Burrowing Owl and a

Wilson's Plover — David Cagnolatti

vagrant Chestnut-collared Longspur have also been recorded here. Saltcedar stands during winter can hold Palm Warblers. The quiet ponds between the camps at Rutherford Beach and Oak Grove occasionally hold Greater Scaup during winter. Also during winter, tens of thousands of Lesser Scaup undulate among the waves of Cameron Parish's surf. Look for Red-breasted Mergansers—Surf, White-winged, and Black Scoters, and Long-tailed Duck are sometimes found among them. In winter, Northern Gannet may be seen offshore plunge-diving into the Gulf waters.

44 Southwest Louisiana

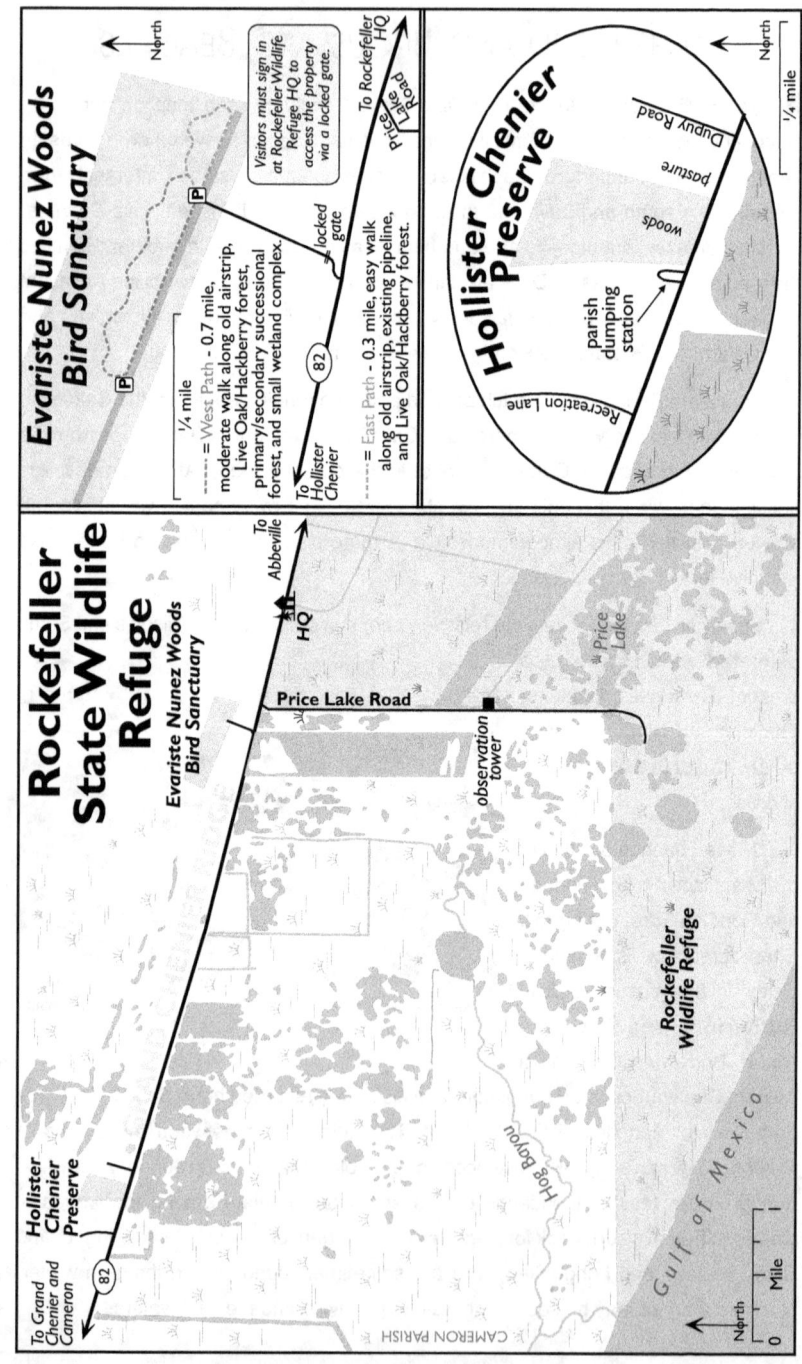

HOLLISTER CHENIER PRESERVE

Owned and operated by The Nature Conservancy, this 54-acre coastal woodlot (chenier) stands on an ancient elevated ridge. The property is currently open to the public during daylight hours 15 March–15 May and 1–31 October. For other times of the year, telephone The Nature Conservancy at (225) 338-1040 for permission.

To get to Hollister Chenier from the town of Grand Chenier, travel east on LA-82 for approximately 5 miles and look for the parish dumping station on the left. The property begins just east of the dumping station north of the highway and ends at a pasture.

ROCKEFELLER WILDLIFE REFUGE

Rockefeller Wildlife Refuge is a massive (722,367 acres) state-owned wildlife preserve located between LA-82 and the Gulf of Mexico. Refuge habitats range from coastal chenier—Nunez Woods—to open beach, although the beaches are not accessible by road. The closest you can drive to the ocean is along 3.3-mile-long Price Lake Road, which skirts the western boundary of the preserve past fresh and brackish marshes, providing several open-water views, but stopping well short of the Gulf. An observation tower about two miles out gives visitors a little better view of the surrounding area and is a good place to set up a scope to examine shorebirds and waterfowl. Wintering ducks are about the same as those found at Sabine Refuge and elsewhere, with Gadwall and Green-winged Teal being especially common.

Evariste Nunez Woods Bird Sanctuary, a coastal woodlot located just north of where Price Lake Road meets LA-82, offers a mile of trails arranged in a figure-8 pattern. Once an airstrip, this site offers the observer a long wooded edge to bird on the West Path. The potential for migratory birds in spring is similar to that at other coastal woodlots, i.e., very good. A recent addition to the list of birds you might encounter here is Great Kiskadee. This large and raucous flycatcher is fond of water and has been fairly reliable at Nunez Woods for the last few years. It is usually heard giving its *kis-ka DEE* call before it is seen, and vocalizations tend to be more frequent in the morning. Access to Nunez Woods is limited to Monday through Friday, 7 AM to 5 PM, between 1 March and 31 August. Visitors must sign in at Rockefeller Wildlife Refuge headquarters 1.8 miles to the east on LA-82. Here, you can ask about recent sightings and also get a key to the locked gate at the beginning of the long driveway.

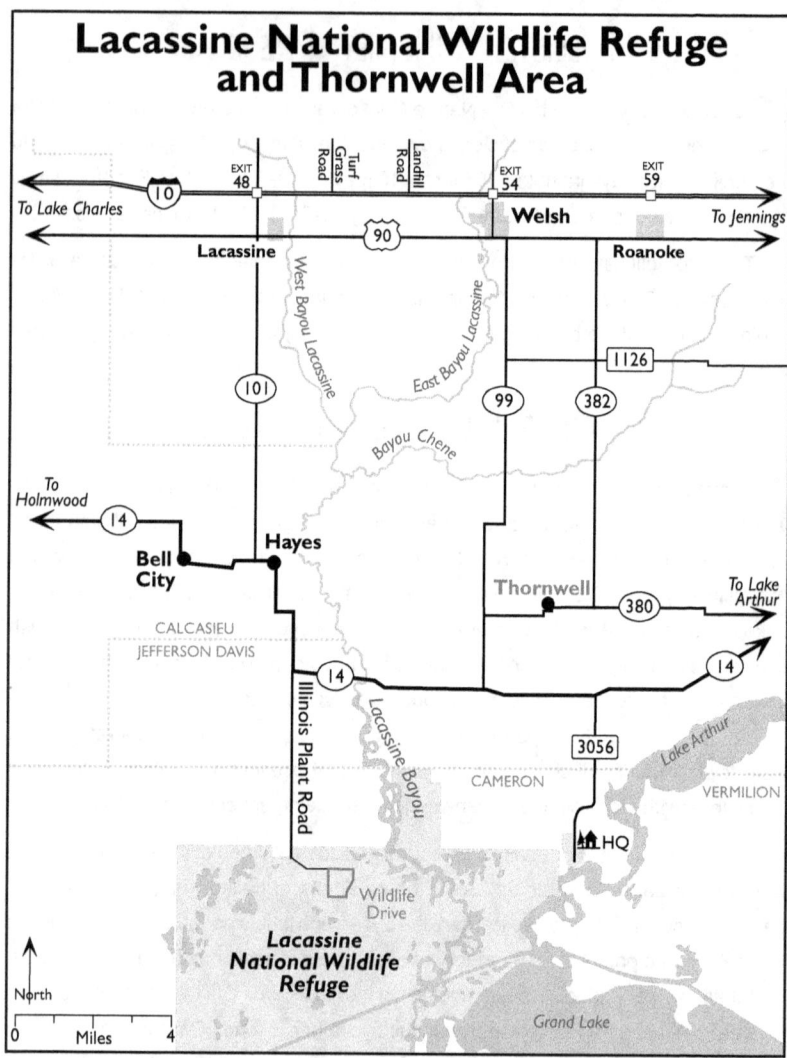

LACASSINE NATIONAL WILDLIFE REFUGE

Located in northeastern Cameron Parish, Lacassine encompasses a wonderful freshwater marsh with a permanent population of Black-bellied Whistling-Ducks. During spring and summer, Fulvous Whistling-Ducks are also present. Least Bitterns may be seen flying above the marsh or doing the splits between stalks of marsh grass along the wildlife loop drive. Green Herons can be ridiculously common during spring migration. This is perhaps the easiest place in the state to see Purple Gallinules as they work the canal edges during spring migration.

Neotropic Cormorant claims a home here year round. Almost every winter, most dabbling ducks, American Bittern, and Vermilion Flycatcher (scarce) are seen. Merlin is no stranger here during winter, and Peregrine Falcon is not unexpected. Occasionally, a Crested Caracara will cruise by.

The access to Lacassine departs LA-14 some 13.7 miles east of the town of Holmwood. Pass through Bell City and Hayes, then turn right at the sign for the Illinois Plant Road. This road will empty into the refuge in 4.5 miles. The gravel portion of Illinois Plant Road used to access Lacassine Pool is private property. The U.S. Fish and Wildlife Service has an easement agreement in place to ensure that the public has a right of access to the refuge. A condition of the easement is that visitors accessing the Pool may use the road only for vehicle travel (i.e., no stopping) and may do so only during refuge operation hours (currently one hour before sunrise to one hour after sunset).

Purple Gallinule   Carol Foil

Yellow Rails and Rice Festival participants   Dave Patton

THORNWELL

When you leave Lacassine National Wildlife Refuge, you are close to an interesting birding area near the community of Thornwell, where plenty of roads and byways warrant inspection. A tractor working in a dry field during summer will often kick up Swainson's Hawk, a species known to nest in the area but rare throughout most of the remainder of the state.

Turn right (east) onto LA-14 from Illinois Plant Road and drive 5.2 miles to LA-99. Turn left (north) to LA-380 in 2 miles.

To reach Thornwell from I-10, get onto southbound LA-99 at Welsh (Exit 54) and follow it for about 11 miles. Thornwell is not shown on all published maps.

Anhinga, Snowy Egret, Little Blue, Tricolored, and Green (rare in winter) Herons, White-faced Ibis, Black-necked Stilt, and Eastern Screech-, Great Horned, and Barred Owls are seen year round. Migrant breeders include Great Crested Flycatcher, White-eyed Vireo, Blue Grosbeak, Indigo and Painted Buntings, Dickcissel, and Orchard Oriole.

The many fields and rice plots provide habitat in winter for Short-eared Owl, along with geese and ducks.

Shorebirds are plentiful during migration as well. American Golden-Plover, Semipalmated Plover, Solitary and Upland Sandpipers, Hudsonian Godwit (spring only), and Semipalmated, White-rumped (spring only), Baird's, and Buff-breasted Sandpipers pass through annually. In winter, Western and Least Sandpipers and Long-billed Dowitcher are regular.

Ferruginous and Rough-legged Hawks and Golden Eagle are very rare visitors. Say's Phoebe has been found and Ash-throated Flycatcher is rare but not unexpected during this season. Winter Wren is seen along the wooded waterways. Yellow Rail is fairly common, but generally is seen only in fall (shortly after its arrival) during the rice harvest.

The mere mention of Yellow Rail raises eyebrows among birders due to the difficulty of seeing one. It wasn't until the autumn of 1943 that George H. Lowery, Jr. discovered a Yellow Rail wing in a cut hayfield and began searching for a live rail by accompanying the field machinery. Since that time, if you wanted to see a Yellow Rail, you found a rice combine, set up a scope on the highway shoulder, and waited patiently for the telltale white secondaries when the bird flushed. Eventually, birders made it onto a rice combine and sent out tantalizing reports of multiple rail species observed from the combine cab or deck. Yellow, King, Virginia, and Sora Rails were seen in good numbers. In 2009, what was the privilege of a few became available to the public through the Yellow Rails and Rice Festival organized by Steve Cardiff and Donna Dittmann of the LSU Museum of Natural Science in concert with the local rice growers' association and LSU Agriculture Extension Service office. As this festival flourishes, it provides a pioneering example of how agriculture and nature tourism can work together. Check the Bird Louisiana website *http://www.birdlouisiana.com/* for details.

Yellow Rail   Jennifer Brumfield

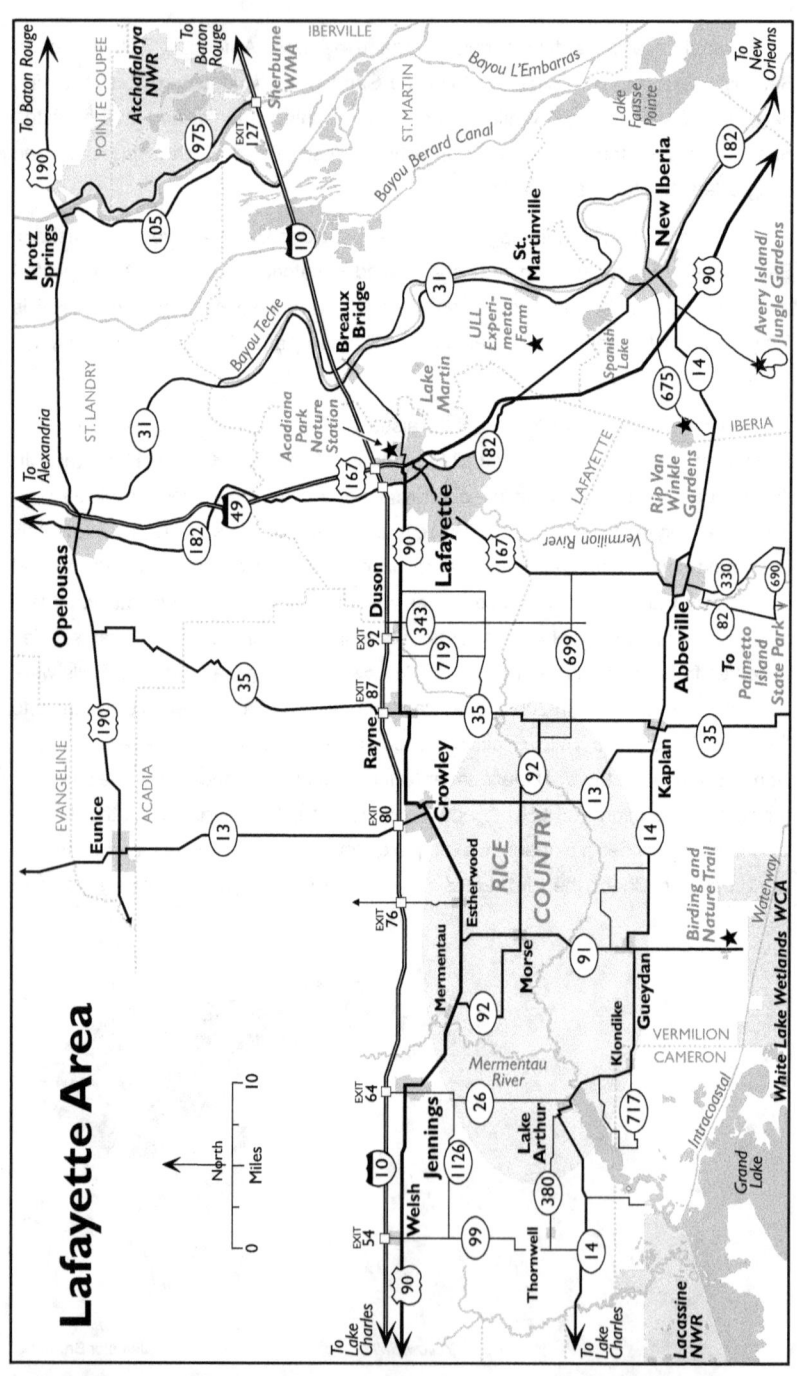

LAFAYETTE AREA

This is Cajun Country, home of the descendants of 18th century French-Canadian refugees. The prairies and swamps were sparsely populated when these French speakers immigrated and their influence is strongest in the small towns of the region. The prairies are mostly gone now, converted to rice and crawfish production, but there are still remnants of the avifauna in the hedgerows and vestigial pastures. Lafayette, the major city in the region, sits on an ancient prairie escarpment carved by glacial runoff thousands of years ago. Today, birders can enjoy the rice country's spectacular shorebirding, the Atchafalaya Basin's rich songbird soundscape, and leisurely walk the summit of a 42,000-foot salt dome.

Fulvous Whistling-Duck   Jessie Barry

52 LAFAYETTE AREA

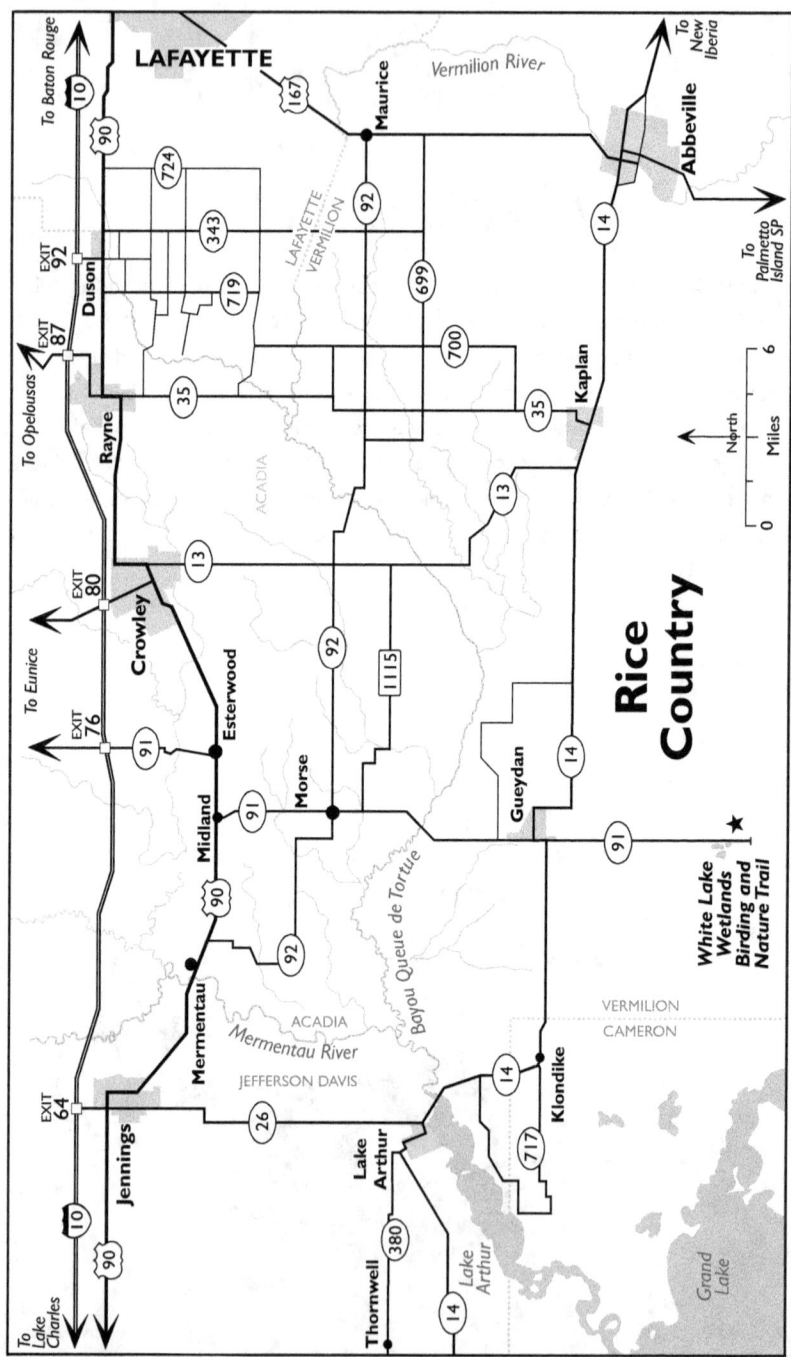

Rice Country

The Louisiana rice country, for purposes of this chapter, is the land west and south of the city of Lafayette—loosely bounded on the west by the Mermentau River, on the south by LA-14, and on the north by US-90. LA-91, LA-13, and LA-35 are the important north-south arteries, whereas LA-92 aids in traversing the rice field habitats east to west. Well known to Louisiana residents is the intimate connection between rice and crawfish cultivation in what the industry calls "working wetlands." Crawfish is cultivated in the cool months in the same fields in which rice is cultivated in the warm months. This assures a shallow water/moist soil food-rich environment for all manner of waterbirds as water is added and removed from the landscape to accommodate both crops. This has accounted for a geometric increase in wading bird populations in the region over the past several decades. The value of this landscape has resulted in the National Audubon Society's designation of the area as an Important Bird Area. This is not to say, of course, that rice isn't grown in other regions, or that shorebirds aren't found elsewhere. Indeed, there are rice fields far to the north in the state and great shorebirding may be had in those areas, as well as along the coast. Nevertheless, this is the very heart of Louisiana shorebirding. This is where our only Black-tailed Godwit was found in 1994 and where, some years, a Curlew Sandpiper or a Ruff is located. The state's first Fork-tailed Flycatcher was also a product of the rice country. Vagrant Say's Phoebe, Northern Wheatear, and Mountain Bluebird have been documented in this rectangle. Winter visitors also include scarce-but-regular Vermilion and Ash-throated Flycatchers.

There are many approaches to a day of shorebirding that include such an extravagant number of venues. An advisable route would be to drive west on US-90 from Lafayette to Duson and explore to the south between LA-343 and LA-719, checking the fields that can be accessed by public roads. Return to Duson and continue west on US-90 to the town of Rayne, a village that advertises itself as the *Frog Capital of the World*. Turn left (south) onto LA-35 and continue 15 miles or so to the town of Kaplan. Along the way, check all of the intersections, particularly the one with LA-699. Explore the side roads for fields containing shorebirds. In Kaplan, turn right (west) onto LA-14 and proceed for 1.5 miles to its intersection with LA-13. Turn right (north) and drive about 15 miles to Crowley, checking side roads for suitable habitat. At Crowley, turn left onto westbound US-90. Two miles west of Estherwood (a junction marked Midland on some maps), turn left (south) onto LA-91 and drive (remember to check the side roads) about 12 miles to Gueydan, a town which self-bills as the *Duck Capital of the World*. At Gueydan, turn right onto LA-14 and go west for 7.7 miles to LA-717; turn left (south). This road is a loop that eventually winds back around to LA-14 and passes through some of the best goose and duck habitat to be found anywhere in the state in winter. When LA-717 again intersects LA-14, turn right to explore the section of LA-14 between Gueydan and Kaplan not yet traveled; then turn left at Kaplan onto LA-35. LA-92 intersects LA-35 about 8 miles north of Kaplan. Turn left here and check the fields for shorebirds along this road for about 13 miles to the village of Morse. At Morse, take a right onto LA-91 to return to US-90 at Estherwood.

Because of the ephemeral nature of rice (and crawfish) farms, it is impossible to know from day to day, much less from week to week, which intersections are hot or which road will be the most productive. One simply drives the area watching for flocks of shorebirds. Dry, bare ground generally requires only the briefest of glances, but may harbor an American Golden-Plover or two in spring. Dry fields that are just beginning to be flooded are the best places to look for Buff-breasted Sandpiper. Very wet rice fields with the green shoots reaching high above the water, though they may contain herons, ibises, Black-necked Stilts, and yellowlegs, are not usually shorebird hotspots. Shorebirds seem to particularly prefer mudflats. The trick is to find a field in which the farmer is changing the water level. As the water moves from one field to another, it exposes vast, soaked flats, often teeming with life near the surface upon which the shorebirds thrive. After a few days of frantic feeding, the birds drift away to find rich new fields. It is not unusual to find 10–15 species sharing the same half-acre in mixed flocks numbering in the hundreds. Occasionally, they will be found by the thousands.

Clapper Rail Jason Stuck

Not exactly electrifying, summer birding in the rice fields nevertheless may be interesting. Fulvous Whistling-Duck, Neotropic Cormorant, Green Heron, both night-herons, Roseate Spoonbill, Eastern Kingbird, Scissor-tailed Flycatcher, Indigo and Painted Buntings, and Dickcissel nest here, in addition to Mottled Duck and King Rail. Wood Storks put in an annual appearance as post-breeding dispersers from Mexico.

Following the summer birding, business picks up in fall with the arrival of rails and migrating shorebirds. These fields collectively represent the most reliable place in the state to see Yellow Rail in late autumn. The rice farms in south Louisiana often are cut for a second crop in late October and early November. Knowledgeable birders will look for a combine (a harvesting machine) working a field near a road and then focus their gaze on the rice stalks just in front of the reaper. Virginia Rail and Sora will often flush as the machine bears down upon them. With a little luck and a modicum of patience, one will be rewarded with the sight of a Yellow Rail as it begrudgingly flies away from the combine to a less hazardous locale.

Winter birding here is outstanding. Least and Western Sandpipers and Long-billed Dowitchers are common, interspersed with a few Stilt Sandpipers. Geese (including Ross's) and dabbling ducks abound. Every so often, a Golden Eagle or a Ferruginous Hawk will be spotted. These fields are the winter haunt of Short-eared Owls, best observed in early evening as they begin their dusk patrols in search of rodents. In late winter both yellowlegs species are around in fair numbers, as are Black-necked Stilts. And, there is always the chance for a rarity. The Crowley CBC has turned up several over the years and boasts exceedingly high numbers for an inland count. Look for Horned Lark in the drier fields, along with Lapland Longspur. The dry, grassy areas between the fields may contain a Grasshopper or Le Conte's Sparrow. Lincoln's Sparrow is present in the hedgerows and Harris's Sparrow has been found here. Look for Sprague's Pipits, always present in small numbers, in shortgrass areas such as roadside shoulders and grazed pastures.

Springtime, however, is the pride of the rice country. Great flocks of Greater and Lesser Yellowlegs, Semipalmated, Western, Least, and Stilt Sandpipers, Dunlin, and Long-billed Dowitcher are commonplace. In lesser numbers, but present, are Semipalmated Plover, Whimbrel, Hudsonian Godwit, Ruddy Turnstone, White-rumped, Baird's, and Buff-breasted Sandpipers, Wilson's Snipe, and Wilson's Phalarope.

Before birding the rice country, insure that you have ample gas, a Louisiana roadmap, and your spotting scope. As in many other parts of the state, road shoulders are at a premium. Park as far off the highway as possible and set up your scope, where practical, in front of your vehicle.

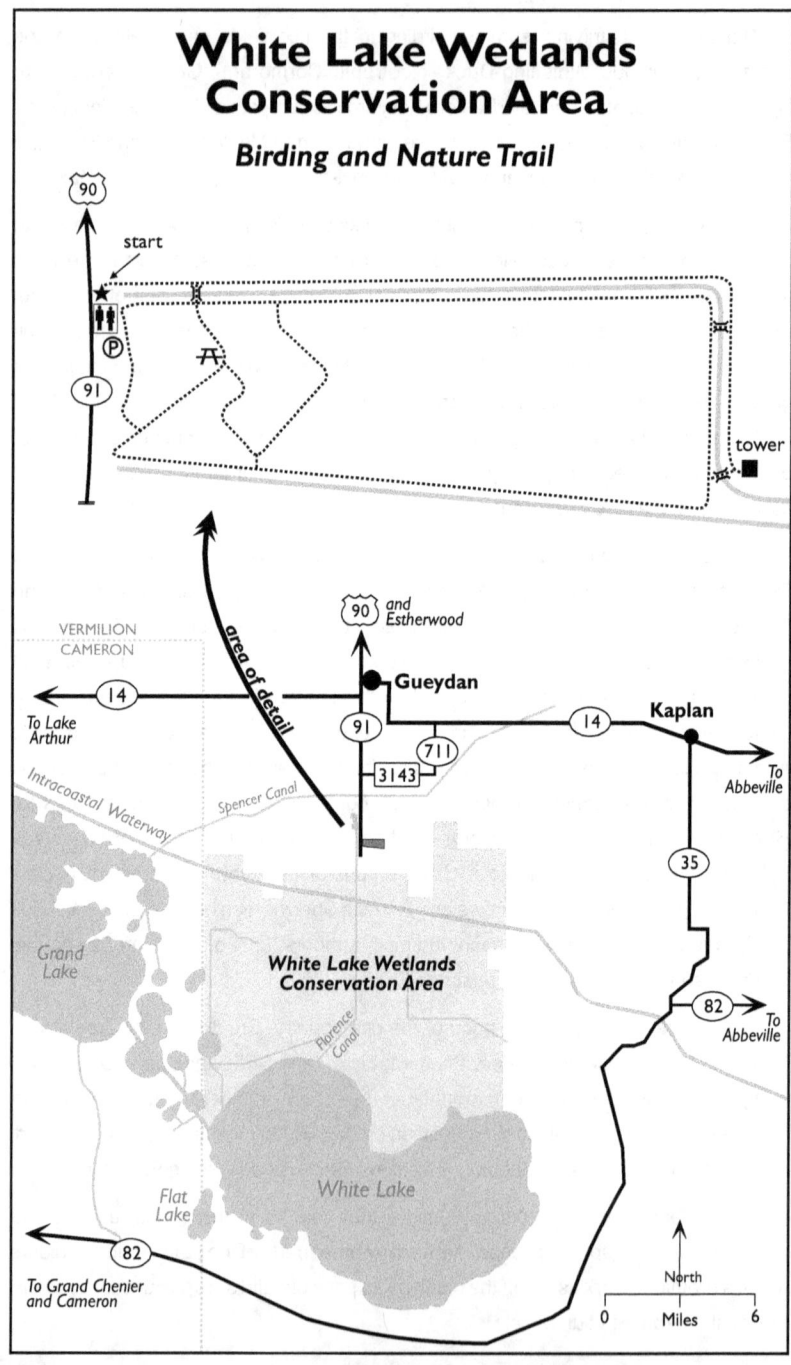

WHITE LAKE WETLANDS CONSERVATION AREA BIRDING AND NATURE TRAIL

This freshly minted birding destination went from idea to done in just three years. The main attraction of White Lake Wetlands Conservation Area is probably the recently introduced experimental flock of Whooping Cranes. After being extirpated from the state in 1950, Whooping Cranes are once again flying the coastal wetlands. The experimental flock was raised in captivity and released at White Lake WCA in hope of returning a lost native species to the rich Louisiana wetlands. Unlike the wild flock of migratory whoopers in Texas, these reintroduced birds are expected to be resident like the crane flock that was here before. White Lake WCA is massive and the chance of seeing these reintroduced birds is unknown, but probably currently very low at this location. Still, the chance is there and as the program continues and more birds are reintroduced, that chance may increase substantially. If the Whooping Cranes are what you want to see, check the Louisiana Birding list-serv http://www.losbird.org and also check out the White Lake Wetlands Conservation Area website http://www.wlf.louisiana.gov/refuge/white-lake-wetlands-conservations-area.

Otherwise, the two-mile-long birding trail is worth a visit. It accesses freshwater marsh and clumps of trees that undoubtedly attract migrants in spring. An observation tower is located in the southeast corner of the 32-acre property, providing a panoramic view of coastal wetlands. No fees or permits are required for this site.

The trail and birding area are located at the south end of LA-91 approximately 7.4 miles south of Gueydan. A parking area and information kiosk interpreting the birds and nature is located near the trailhead.

PALMETTO ISLAND STATE PARK

One of Louisiana's newest state parks, 1,299-acre Palmetto Island State Park is located along the Vermilion River about 6 miles south of Abbeville in Vermilion Parish. The park features 6 cabins, 96 improved campsites, a primitive campground, a water playground, boat launch, and a 0.7-mile nature trail. The park preserves a section of *L'Isle de Grand Bois*, also known as the Big Woods. This remnant of the Big Woods presumably survived conversion to farmland due to the wildness and density of its bottomland forests. Even today, surrounded by farmland and with industry situated nearby on the banks of the Vermilion, a walk through Palmetto Island State Park can give the visitor a strong sense of the what life must have been like when panthers and Red Wolves roamed these dark woods. The occasional presence of Black Bears in the park is a reminder that such a past is maybe not so distant, after all.

In the summer, the park hosts many of the characteristic species of bottomland forests. Eye-catching Barred Owl and Pileated Woodpecker can be easy to see and

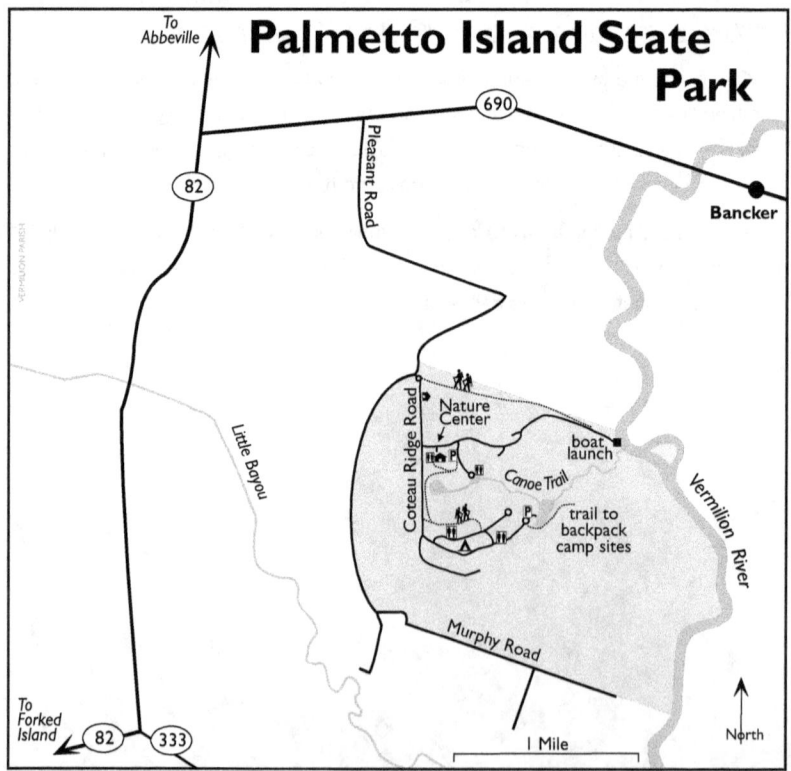

hear in Palmetto Island, while the summer chorus is dominated by the songs of Acadian Flycatcher, White-eyed Vireo, the abundant Prothonotary, Hooded, and Northern Parula warblers, and the ubiquitous Carolina Chickadee, Carolina Wren, and Northern Cardinal. Swainson's Warbler is a summer resident in the park as well, although in smaller numbers. Openings in the woods should reveal Mississippi Kites coasting in the sky above the treetops, perhaps joined by Swallow-tailed Kites, which are believed to recently have begun nesting in the Big Woods. Winter birding is typical of the area, with the resident woodland birds such as Ruby-crowned Kinglet and White-throated Sparrow.

Boating through the park can provide a scene worthy of a visitor's greatest fantasy of a wild Louisiana bayou. The forest pushes to the bayou's edge, and many of the park's nesters can best be seen and heard from the open space that the wide bayou provides. Pileated Woodpeckers flash across the bayou while Red-shouldered Hawks and kites circle above, and nesting Ruby-throated Hummingbirds patrol the trumpet creeper vines that grow thickly in the canopy along the forest's edge.

The agricultural areas surrounding the park are rich in birdlife as well, including local specialties such as Black-bellied Whistling-Duck and Mottled Duck throughout the year, and Fulvous Whistling-Ducks mainly during the breeding season. Local ricefields and crawfish ponds can attract Neotropic Cormorant, White and *Plegadis* ibises (mostly White-faced), and Tricolored Heron throughout the year, Wood Stork in summer, and swarms of shorebirds at all times except early summer.

To reach Palmetto Island State Park from Abbeville, take Highway 82 south for 6 miles. Turn east (left) onto Highway 690, then travel about 0.9 mile to Pleasant Road. Make a right onto Pleasant Road, and continue 0.6 mile to the well-marked park entrance.

Palmetto Island State Park: 19501 Pleasant Road, Abbeville, LA 70510; (337) 893-3930 or (888) 677-0094. For reservations, call 877-CAMP-N-LA [(877) 226-7652]. Email: palmettoisland@crt.la.gov.

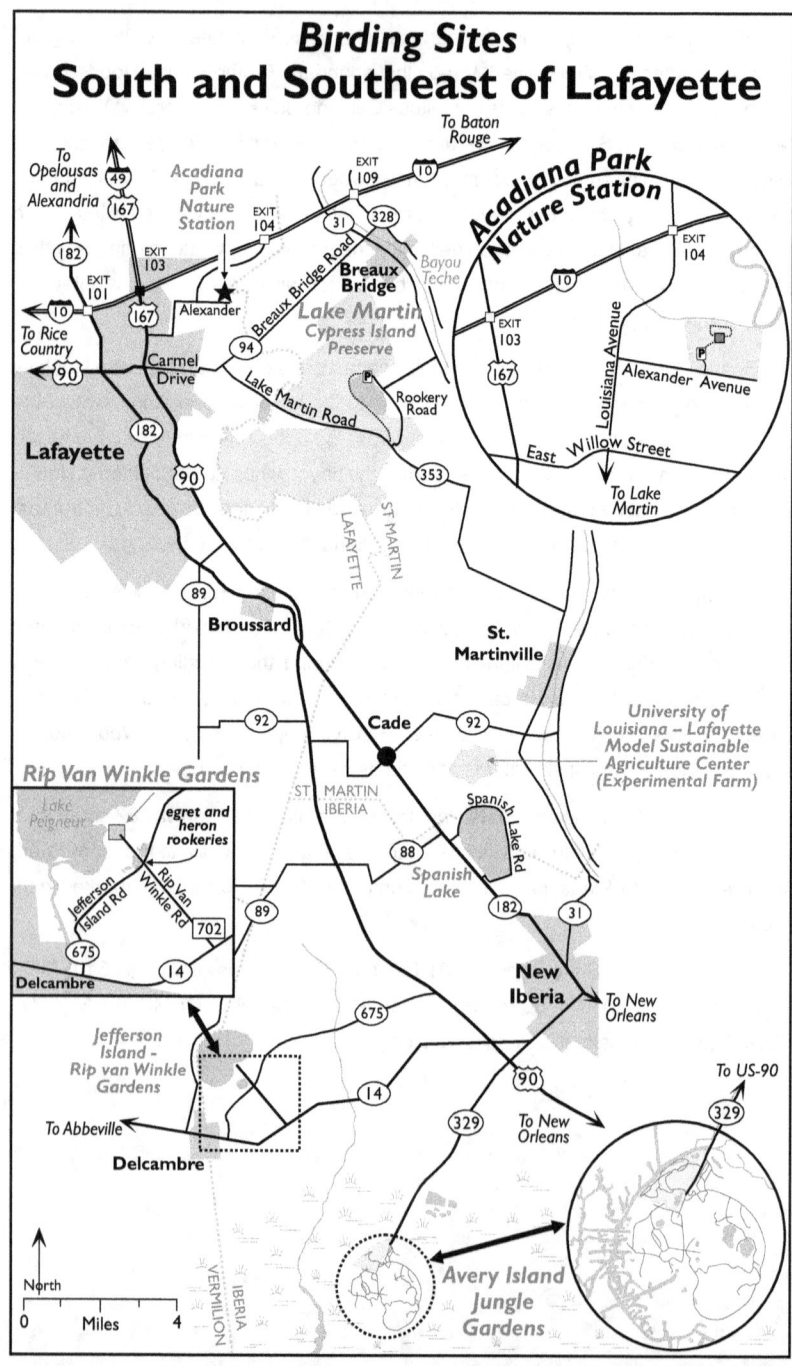

ACADIANA PARK NATURE STATION

To get to this hardwood haven from I-10 in Lafayette, take Exit 104 (Louisiana Avenue) and drive south for 1.0 mile to East Alexander Street. Turn left (east) for 0.7 mile to the entrance to Acadiana Park on the left. Stay left at the fork to reach the Nature Station, located in the center of over 40 acres of hardwood forest dominated by stately old live oaks. Camping and picnic sites are available, and you'll find several miles of trails to explore. The station is an urban wonder, offering not only the opportunity to observe, but also to learn. Nature center staff offers birdwatching and wildflower tours on the first Saturday of the month and a night tour on the last Saturday of each month. The staff will entertain requests for group tours at other times by advance reservation.

A few of the park's more common species are Barred Owl, Red-bellied and Downy Woodpeckers, Carolina Chickadee, Tufted Titmouse, and Brown Thrasher. Some of the birds that migrate here to breed include Broad-winged Hawk, White-eyed and Red-eyed Vireos, Prothonotary and Kentucky Warblers, and Northern Parula.

Spring and fall migrations can be colorful experiences indeed. Acadian and Great Crested Flycatchers, Yellow-throated Vireo, Swainson's and Wood Thrushes, Black-and-white and Hooded Warblers, American Redstart, and Bay-breasted, Chestnut-sided, Yellow-throated, and Black-throated Green Warblers are often participants in the pageantry as countless migrants returning from the Neotropics wend their way along in answer to some ancient, unheard and unseen signal to migrate.

Nature Station Richard E. Gibbons

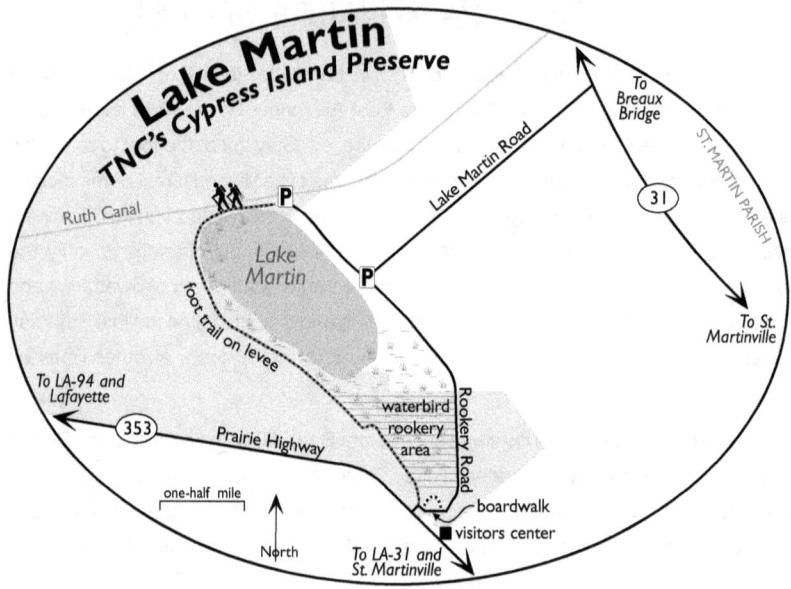

LAKE MARTIN – CYPRESS ISLAND PRESERVE

To continue on to Lake Martin from the Nature Station, return to Louisiana Avenue and turn left (south) at the traffic light. Drive 1.4 miles to Carmel Drive (also signed LA-94) and turn left (east). From this intersection, drive 1.5 miles to well-signed Lake Martin Road (LA-353) and turn right (south). From here, it is 5.2 miles to Rookery Road. (To find the visitors center, restrooms, and a picnic area, turn left into a driveway 150 yards south of Rookery Road.)

Turn left at the *Lake Martin Bird Sanctuary* sign and follow the gravel road as it winds around the south side of the lake. The Nature Conservancy has undertaken the management of a portion of these varied habitats. While the lake has its points of interest at any season, the rookeries in spring are nothing short of incredible! It is one of those rare phenomena that really must be seen to be fully appreciated. Even the non-birding local folk, as well as casual tourists, line the roadsides in April. The cypress limbs bend with the weight of birds. The sight of thousands of herons and egrets of every description attending upon their nests is staggering. Hundreds of Anhingas, ibises, and Roseate Spoonbills add to the drama. The occasional Neotropic Cormorant will be spotted.

Lake Martin is of interest beyond the rookeries. Wood Thrush, Prothonotary and Hooded Warblers, Northern Parula, and Yellow-throated Warbler can be heard singing during the breeding season, while a plethora of songbirds use the area as a stopover in migration. House and Winter Wrens, Golden-crowned and Ruby-crowned Kinglets, Orange-crowned Warbler, and a host of other species overwinter.

Tricolored Heron — Jennifer Brumfield

White-faced Ibis   Carol Foil

UNIVERSITY OF LOUISIANA – LAFAYETTE MODEL SUSTAINABLE AGRICULTURE CENTER (EXPERIMENTAL FARM)

To reach this interesting mixed bag of habitats, travel south from Lafayette on US-90 for about 5 miles to the town of Broussard. Exit at LA-182 (East Main Street), head southeast for 4.1 miles to LA-92 (Smede Highway), and turn left (east). From here, drive 2.5 miles and turn right onto PR-183 (W. J. Bernard Road) which leads to the ULL Experimental Farm. After entering the property, bear left at the Y to get to the Crawfish Research Center. Although the farm willingly suffers the presence of birders—and even encourages it—visitors must check in.

    The farm encompasses some 600 acres, about half in the Lower Mississippi Alluvial Valley and the other portion on coastal prairie. The crawfish ponds cover roughly 50 acres in the former habitat. Just east of the ponds is a small woodlot and adjacent to the west are a wooded wetland and a field. Other wooded areas nearby may also be explored. Research personnel suggest that at least half a day be set aside to do justice to the birding opportunities at the farm.

The crawfish ponds are visited by waders such as Great and Snowy Egrets, Little Blue and Tricolored Herons, ibises (White-faced is the more-common dark ibis west of the Atchafalaya Basin), Roseate Spoonbill, and Black-necked Stilt.

In winter, expect to see several species of dabbling ducks, especially Northern Shoveler. The field to the west may contain sparrows, while the woodlands should have Blue-headed Vireo, House Wren, kinglets, Hermit Thrush, and Orange-crowned and Yellow-rumped (Myrtle) Warblers aplenty.

Migration-season birding at the farm produces a vast array of migrants such as *Empidonax* flycatchers, Kentucky and Hooded Warblers, American Redstart, Magnolia and Blackburnian Warblers, Summer and Scarlet Tanagers, Rose-breasted Grosbeak, and Baltimore Oriole. The numbers of Blue Grosbeaks and buntings, especially during the fall, can be staggering. Quite a few breeders occur on the farm, among them Downy Woodpecker, White-eyed Vireo, Yellow-throated Warbler, Blue Grosbeak, Indigo Bunting, and Dickcissel.

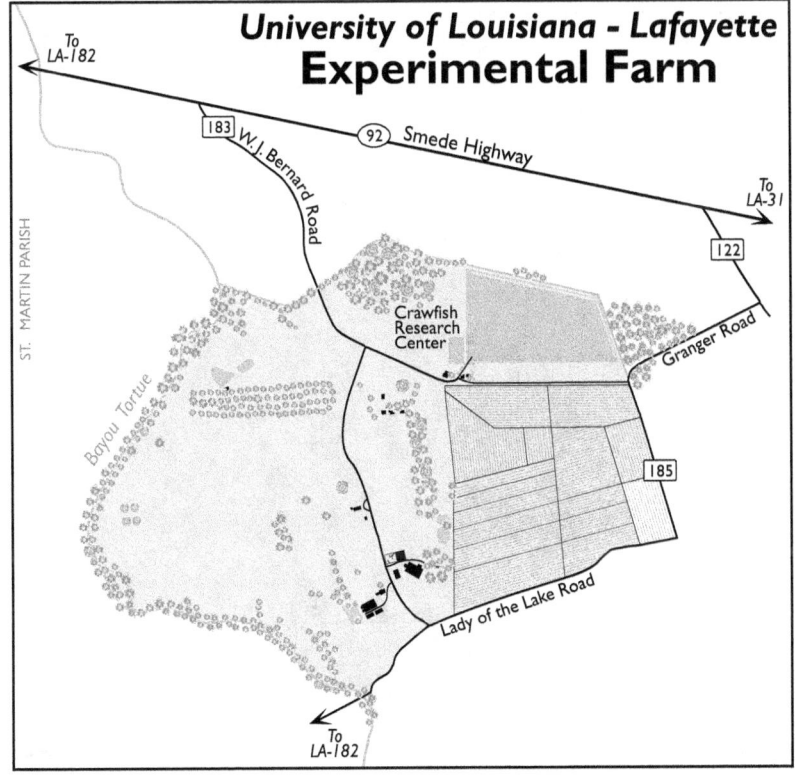

Spanish Lake

Although somewhat ignored by many of south Louisiana's birders, nearby Spanish Lake boasts at least one devotee. Mike Musumeche has been keeping records here for a number of years and his checklist, at last count, exceeded 220 species. To reach the lake from the ULL farm, retrace your route for several miles to the intersection of LA-92 and LA-182, turn left (south), and drive 4.0 miles to the *Spanish Lake* sign on the left. There is a small fee for day use. Diving ducks such as Lesser Scaup and Ruddy Duck are often present in winter, along with Double-crested Cormorant and American Coot. Year round, look for Pied-billed Grebe. Bald Eagle is an infrequent visitor, as is Peregrine Falcon. Cooper's Hawk is often observed, particularly during the colder months. Red-shouldered Hawk is a nesting raptor. The woods that ring the lake contain many of the same species of breeding and wintering birds as you might find at ULL farm and Lake Martin. Even so, you will be impressed by the huge wintering flocks of Yellow-rumped (Myrtle) Warblers. Lots of Orange-crowned Warblers are also present at this time of year, and Blue-gray Gnatcatcher and Wilson's Warbler aren't unexpected.

Mottled Duck   Michael L. P. Retter

Avery Island – Jungle Gardens

Avery Island isn't an island in the typical sense of the word. Instead, it's the very tip of a massive salt dome that spreads underground for more than 40,000 feet. The island comprises the 150 feet of the salt dome that rises above the surrounding marsh. Avery Island is best known for the world famous McIlhenny Company Tabasco hot sauces. In addition to their hot sauces, the McIlhennys developed the elaborate Jungle Gardens and were pioneers in bird conservation. In a time when herons and egrets were still struggling to recover from the millinery trade plunder, E. A. McIlhenny constructed Bird City, a large artificial nesting area. The birds took to it and it is still occupied today. Hundreds of Great, Snowy, and Cattle Egrets continue to use the nesting platforms maintained at Bird City. This colony is the showpiece of Jungle Gardens, a 250-acre exotic garden with ancient live oaks, exotic bamboos, and scads of azaleas. Admission to Jungle Gardens is $8.00 for adults and $4.50 for children under 12.

Avery Island is best birded in spring when this large island of trees provides a welcome break for trans-Gulf migrants. This isn't to say it wouldn't be worth the trip at other times. Jungle Gardens has a driving loop and a few trails that wind through the massive live oaks and gardens. Canals and ponds provide habitat for a few waterbirds, and the number of alligators is impressive.

To get there from Lafayette, take US-90 east for 20 miles to the LA-14 exit west of New Iberia. Head east for less than a mile and then turn sharp right onto LA-329 (Avery Island Road) and travel 7 miles to Avery Island.

Great Egrets nesting at Bird City Richard E. Gibbons

Jefferson Island / Rip Van Winkle Gardens

Kentucky Warbler Dan Lane

A smaller, less elaborate version of Avery Island and its exotic gardens exists at Rip Van Winkle Gardens near Jefferson Island. This 25-acre estate is located on another of the massive salt domes in this region and boasts an historic home as well as paths that meander through a lovely series of interlocking gardens. It also comes with a story—legend has it that the pirate Jean Lafitte buried treasure under the spreading live oaks that reign over the house and gardens. From a birder's perspective, however, a wonderful feature of this location is found just outside its wrought-iron gates. The small lakes near the oak alley support an impressive egret and heron rookery from spring through summer. Hundreds of Great, Snowy, and Cattle Egrets, Tricolored Herons, White Ibises, and Roseate Spoonbills all compete for nesting spots among the cypress trees. Perhaps the best feature of this special place is your proximity to the birds. While standing on the small levee that surrounds the lake, you are only a few yards from the nests and are treated to the cacophony of grunts, whistles, and groans as well as some outstanding photo opportunities. Don't, however, get so caught up that you forget to watch for the large alligators that cruise the area! The gators patrolling the moat keep terrestrial predators away from the nests and that is a big part of what sustains this rookery.

This spot would be a great addition to a rookery tour of Lake Martin and Avery Island. To reach it from Lafayette, travel south on US-90 East for 22 miles. Turn right (west) onto LA-14 toward Delcambre. After 6.5 miles turn right onto Rip Van Winkle Road (PR-702) toward Jefferson Island/Rip Van Winkle Gardens.

SHERBURNE WILDLIFE MANAGEMENT AREA

Located on the eastern edge of the Atchafalaya Basin, this extensive hardwood habitat has historically been one of the best and easiest places in the state to encounter Swallow-tailed Kites between late March and the end of June. To get to this area from either Baton Rouge or Lafayette, take I-10 (west from Baton Rouge or east from Lafayette) to Exit 127 (just east of the Whiskey Bay bridge over the Atchafalaya River) and turn north onto LA-975. This mostly gravel road, while not exceptionally well maintained, is generally passable. Caution should be exercised as all-terrain vehicles and other auto traffic are often present and there are many blind curves where your view is blocked by the river levee. LA-975 winds about for 17.4 miles until it intersects US-190 to the north, just across the Atchafalaya River from the little village of Krotz Springs. Obey the speed limit in this town, where the law is quite diligent about monitoring the passing motorists.

The birding along LA-975 can be interesting in winter, but it is excellent during migration and in early summer. There are a couple of side roads leading away from the river (toward the east) that allow auto traffic and may be explored. Watch for Wild Turkey, or at least listen for the gobble of the males in early spring. Keep an eye to the sky during the breeding season for the many soaring species. In addition to Swallow-tailed Kite, you are likely to see Anhinga, several species of herons and

Prothonotary Warbler Amy Shutt

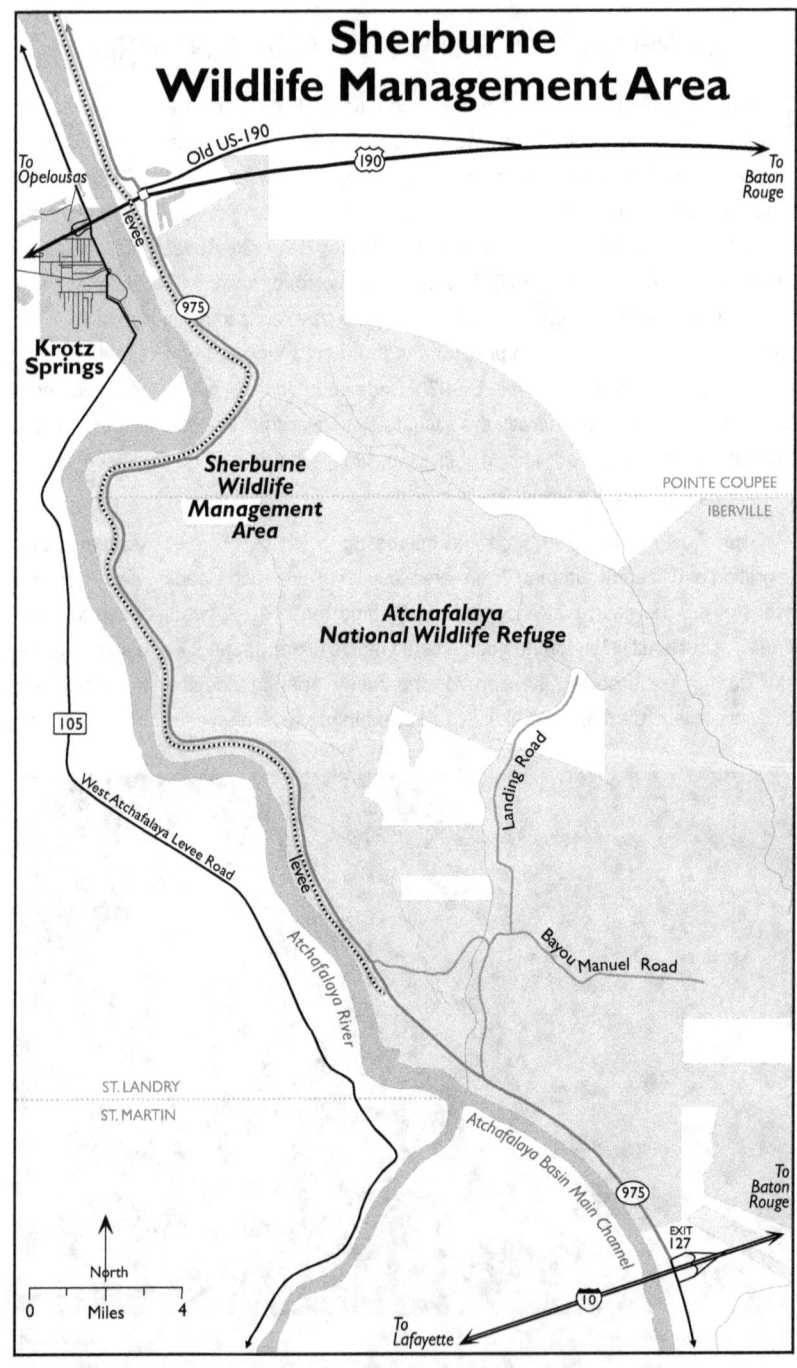

egrets, Mississippi Kites by the dozen, and Red-shouldered Hawk. In late summer, Wood Storks may be seen taking advantage of the free transportation that the thermals provide. Other nesters of the basin include Downy, Hairy, and Pileated Woodpeckers, Acadian and Great Crested Flycatchers, Red-eyed Vireo, Blue-gray Gnatcatcher, Black-and-white, Kentucky, and Hooded Warblers, American Redstart, Northern Parula, Yellow-throated Warbler, and Summer Tanager. Around stream crossings and side-road canals, listen for the soft whistle of Prothonotary Warbler and the sharply insistent call of Swainson's Warbler.

Birding the west (levee) side of the road can be equally productive at times. The levee is posted, so driving or walking on it is prohibited. Nevertheless, Indigo and Painted Buntings and Orchard Oriole are extremely conspicuous from the roadway in summer. In fact, Breeding Bird Surveys conducted in this area for a great many years by Van Remsen have shown this overall area to contain the state's highest concentration of breeders that migrate from the Neotropics. In winter, the entire area is great for wintering wrens and sparrows.

It is possible to drive on for many miles on the continuation of LA-975 (which might be signed by some other name) north of the US-190 junction. Return to US-190 and head east to reach Baton Rouge. You can get to Lafayette by heading west to Opelousas on US-190, then turning left (south) onto I-49 to its end at I-10.

There are many birding sites to explore in this region, the heart of the Atchafalaya National Heritage Area. Worth mentioning in addition to those covered in this chapter are:
- Thistlewaite Wildlife Management Area
- Bayou Teche
- Henderson Lake
- Atchafalaya River
- Lake Fausse Pointe State Park
- Lake Dautrieve
- Indian Bayou

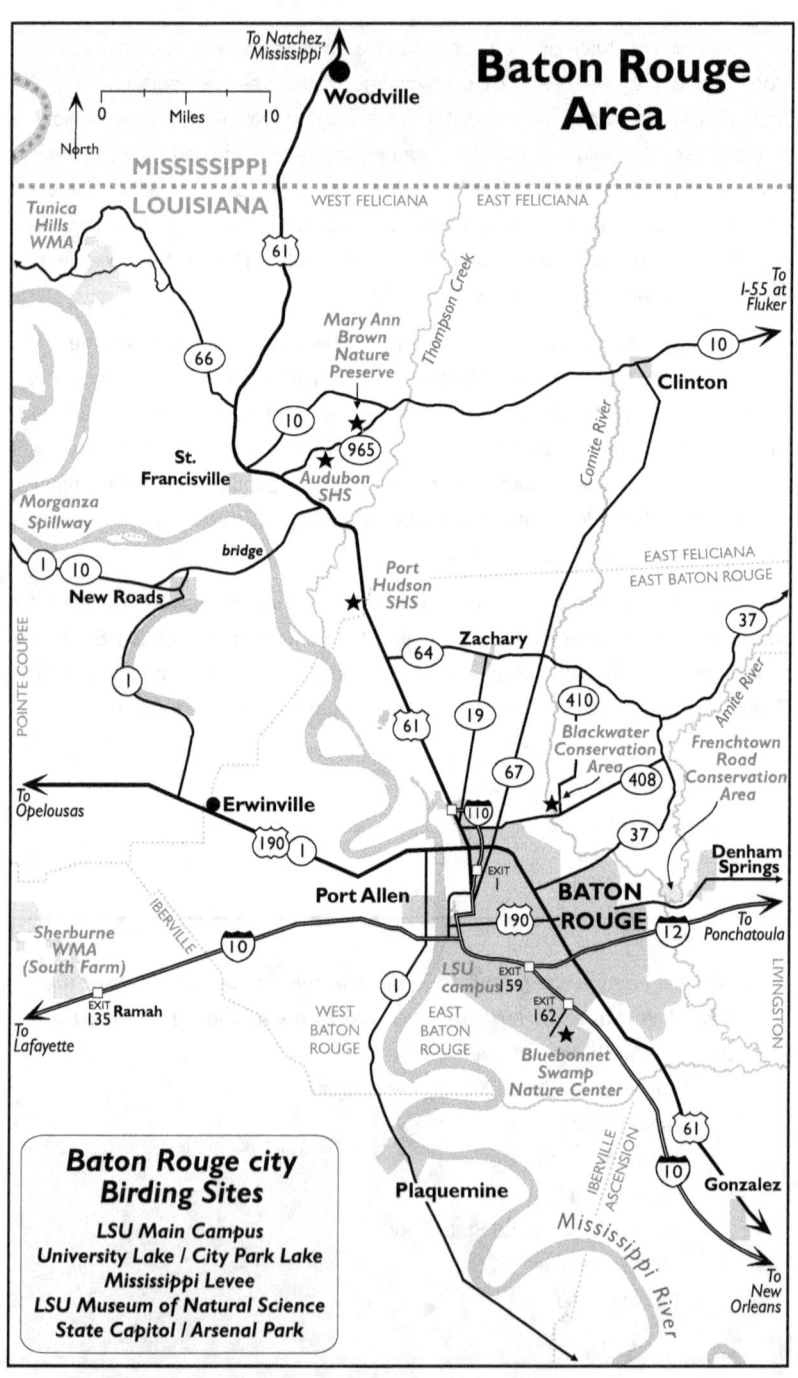

BATON ROUGE AREA

Although not a birding destination comparable to Grand Isle or Cameron Parish, the state capital and vicinity offer several areas where birders can make good use of a few hours. During spring migration, some of these locales would even qualify as hot spots.

In winter, the local population of hummingbirds reaches considerable size—so great that the Baton Rouge Christmas Bird Count boasts the largest number of individuals of any count in the state, now surpassing even New Orleans and Lafayette. Fall migration is more spectacular here than spring, due in large measure to the effect referred to as the *coastal hiatus*. In spring, migrants from the Neotropics that are taking advantage of the strong southerly winds will not descend to feed and rest until far inland. They tend, therefore, to simply sail on by the coast and southern interior lands, including Baton Rouge, on days with favorable winds. On the other hand, in fall the birds tend to filter through the woodlots and ponds on their way south and stack up along the coast. Baton Rouge is close enough to the coast that it benefits from the stack-up.

American White Pelicans Richard E. Gibbons

Louisiana State University Campus and Lakes

Thanks to an active group of birders at LSU, the campus and lakes have nearly 200 species in their combined eBird checklists. This section is treated in four parts: main campus, the lakes, Mississippi River overlook (the levee), and the LSU Museum of Natural Science.

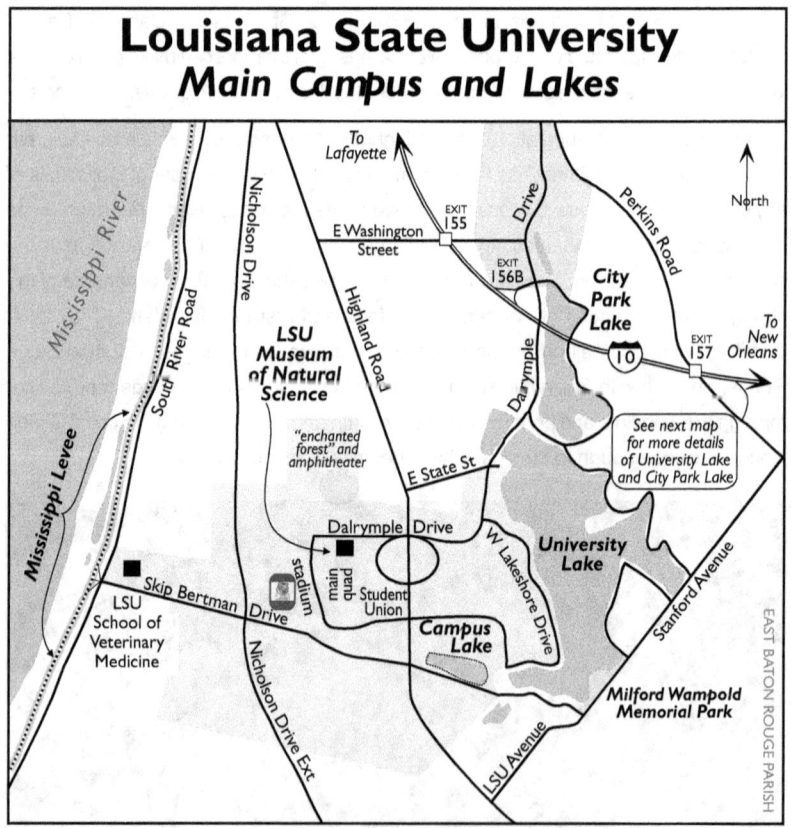

Main Campus

LSU's campus has rows of impressive live oaks, cypress groves, pine patches, a small lake, and open fields. Bordered roughly by the lakes to the northeast, River Road to the west, Nicholson Drive Extension to the south, and Stanford Avenue/LSU Avenue to the southeast, this pedestrian-friendly location can be good for an hour or two of birding—one never knows what might show up in the mix. Year-round residents are the expected Eastern urban species, e.g., Downy Woodpecker, Blue Jay, Carolina Chickadee, American Robin, Northern Mockingbird, Northern Cardinal, and House Finch. The winter months provide an influx of northern migrants that take advantage of the well-tended trees and include Blue-gray Gnatcatcher, Golden-crowned and Ruby-crowned Kinglets, Orange-crowned, Pine, and Yellow-rumped Warblers, Dark-eyed Junco, and American Goldfinch. Spring and fall are unpredictable for migratory birds, but migrants are always possible, so be on the lookout.

The summer months are characterized by the two-note call of Mississippi Kites, the constant chatter of Chimney Swifts plying the aerial plankton above, and the sporadic *weep* from Great Crested Flycatchers. When birding campus, consider walking the "enchanted forest" and Greek amphitheater just north of Dalrymple Drive and west of Infirmary Drive; the main quad south of Dalrymple Drive and Infirmary Drive; the Parade grounds south of Dalrymple Drive and west of Highland Road; and the oaks surrounding the Student Union between Highland Road and Tower Drive. Next, make your way to Campus Lake, which is about two city blocks southeast of the Student Union east of Highland Road.

Campus Lake is more like a pond with patches of willows and Bald Cypress near the water's edge. This water body and patch of woods can be good for Wood Ducks (year round), Pied-billed Grebe (winter), Anhinga (year round), Great and Snowy Egrets, Green Heron (summer), both night-herons, American Coot (winter), Forster's Tern (winter), Belted Kingfisher (winter), and Orchard Oriole (summer). A paved sidewalk provides a vantage to most of the lake and a path skirts the northern edge.

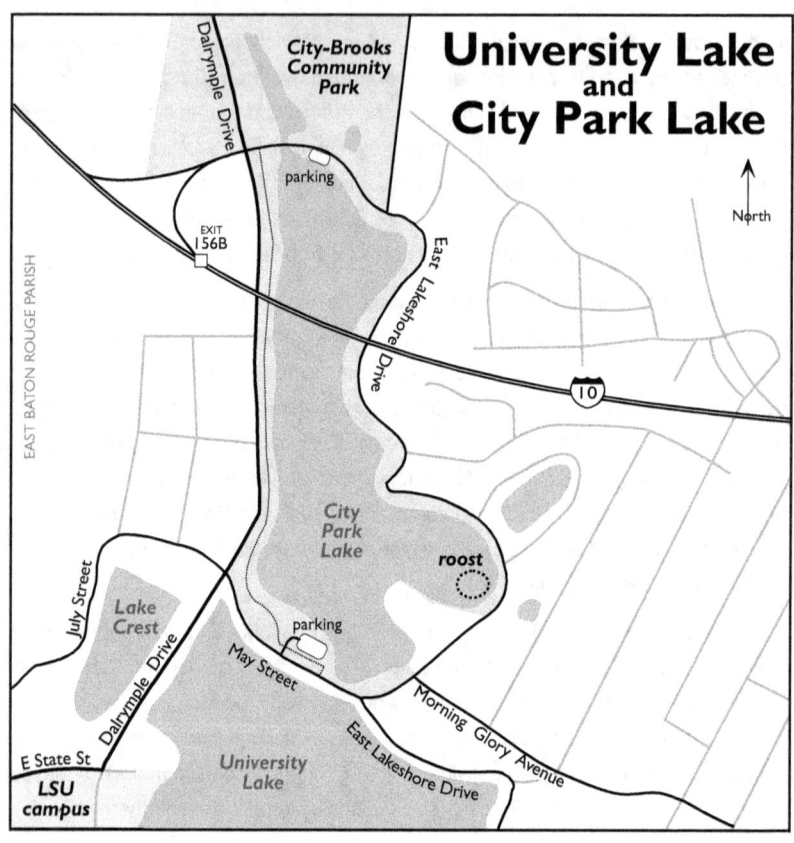

University and City Park Lakes

Perhaps the most impressive birding attraction of the lakes is the roost at East Lakeshore Drive just north of Morning Glory Avenue. From late fall through early spring, the clump of cypress trees is filled with Double-crested Cormorants, the occasional Neotropic Cormorant or two, and a mix of herons, egrets, and ibises. In spring, the cormorants migrate north and most herons relocate to heronries for breeding, leaving the few Wood Ducks to rule the roost for several weeks. Post-breeding birds begin showing up by late June and their numbers build to an impressive congregation of herons until the cormorants return in the fall. Parking is a challenge here and it may be best to walk from the parking lot at May Street between Dalrymple Drive and East Lakeshore Drive. The walk itself is a good way to see some of the regular species found at the lakes. A spotting scope can be useful for identifying birds far out in the lakes such as Bonaparte's Gull (late fall through spring) and

Forster's Tern (late summer through spring). The lakes are visited more often in the cooler months for a few good reasons. The milder weather is reason enough to explain the disparity, but the big draw is the certainty that each passing weather front will bring new birds, e.g., wintering waterfowl, American White Pelicans, or wintering flocks of songbirds. Even more interesting than this are the small number of records of Vaux's Swifts. For more than a decade a handful of Vaux's Swifts has wintered in Baton Rouge and the best way to find them is to go to the lakes during cold, wet, and foggy weather. It is thought that most of their prey is inactive at these times so the swifts will hunt the warmer air just above the water where some prey items remain active.

Late summer and fall is hurricane season, and when such a tropical system makes landfall anywhere nearby, any major inland body of water can become a concentration point for normally pelagic or coastal waterbirds such as Magnificent Frigatebird and several tern species.

The lakes and campus are easily reached from I-10. Take Exit 156B south, Dalrymple Drive, which skirts the western edge of the lakes. Other lake access points include the Milford Wampold Memorial Park on Stanford Avenue and the parking area on East Lakeshore Drive just east of Dalrymple Drive and north of I-10 (see map on page 76).

Mississippi Levee

Old Man River is the defining geographical feature of the Baton Rouge area. It seems only natural then, that one would like to see the mighty Mississippi. A good access point is the overlook near the LSU School of Veterinary Medicine at the western end of Skip Bertman Drive. A paved walkway continues north to the downtown area from here providing a levee-top view of *batture*, the alluvial land between the river and levee when the river is low. This site has stairs and ramps for easy access to the levee trail. There is also an open area of batture below the levee that often has shallow pools visited by migrant shorebirds. The batture can be good for wintering birds such as Hermit Thrush, White-throated Sparrow, and Purple Finch. The mowed levee is apparently good wintering habitat for American Pipits, which invariably work the levee slopes in patchy flocks. The shallow ponds may host Wood Ducks and Anhingas year round. In spring and fall, songbirds may be found using the strips of woods along the river and ducks, herons, and shorebirds use the ephemeral ponds. Some of the more interesting breeding birds include Yellow-billed Cuckoo, Great Crested Flycatcher, and Eastern Kingbird.

Mississippi Kite   Dan Lane

LSU Museum of Natural Science

Another attraction worth a visit is the LSU Museum of Natural Science. Visitors can check in and park at the Visitor Center located on the northwest corner of the Highland Road and Dalrymple Drive intersection. The museum is located two blocks west in Foster Hall, LSU's original dining hall, and is open Monday through Friday, 9 AM to 4 PM. Inside you will be treated to dioramas of many different habitats and the George H. Lowery, Jr. Hall of Louisiana Birds. Here you can see all the birds of Louisiana in one place— granted, they are taxidermy mounts, but to have them all in one place gives you a very nice sense of the rich diversity of Louisiana's birdlife.

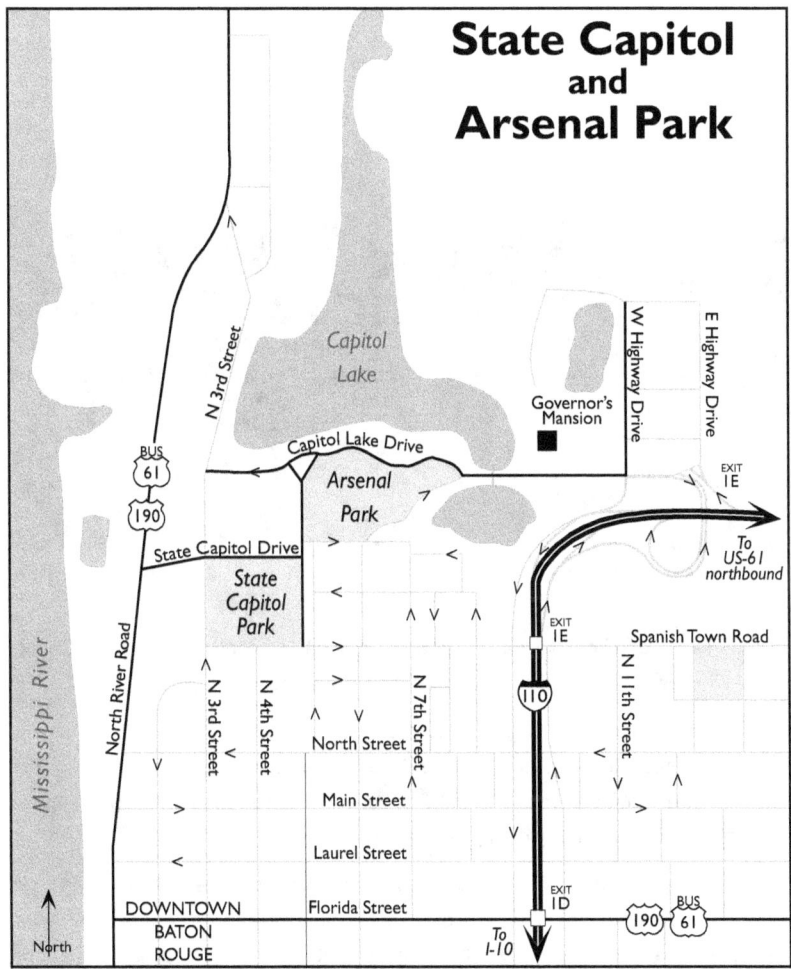

CAPITOL LAKES AND ARSENAL PARK

The Louisiana state capitol is the tallest capitol building in the United States. Completed in 1932, this 34-floor landmark can be seen from throughout the area. The observation deck on the 27th floor provides an impressive view of downtown Baton Rouge and the Mississippi River.

To reach the capitol from east or west, get onto Loop I-110 north from its juncture with I-10 just east of the Mississippi River. Take Exit 1E (also signed *Capitol Access Road/Capitol Park*) and turn left (west) toward the capitol grounds, following the

Capitol Lake and Arsenal Park Richard E. Gibbons

well-marked street. The road passes through Arsenal Park and to the south of Capitol Lake. The best place to park is along the road in Arsenal Park.

The lake should be surveyed, particularly in winter, for waterfowl. Canvasback, Redhead (rare), Ring-necked Duck, and Lesser Scaup are present in the colder months. The park contains a number of mature hardwoods that can become something of a migrant trap during spring and fall.

Peregrine Falcon has been a regular around the capitol in recent years. You can walk around the gardens to the south of the main entrance—and in Arsenal Park. In fall and spring, search the old oaks there for migrants. During the colder months, be especially watchful overhead—downtown Baton Rouge is one of the best places in the state to see rare, wintering Vaux's Swift.

Be sure to check the small lake near the Governor's Mansion and Department of Transportation (to the east of the Capitol—turn left on West Highway Drive). It often hosts birds that prefer more solitude and shallow water, such as Yellow-crowned Night-Heron and White Ibis in summer and Gadwall and Hooded Merganser in winter.

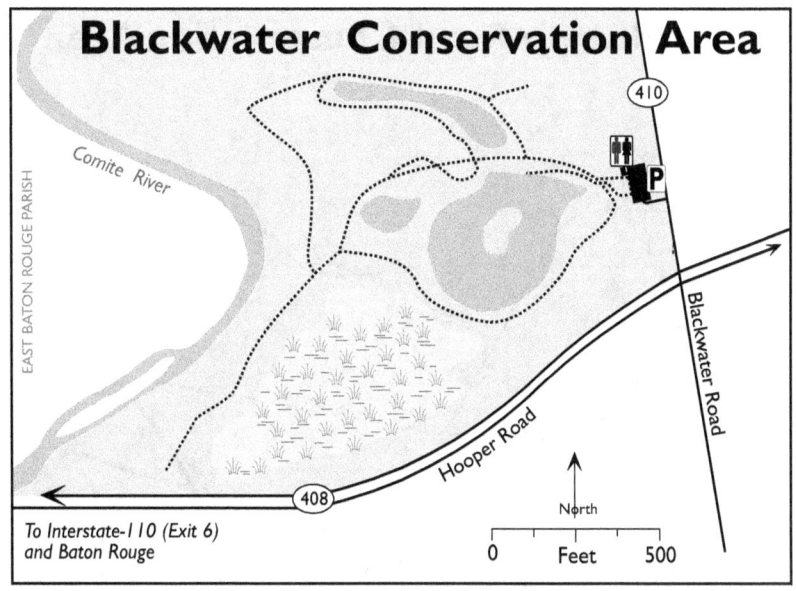

BLACKWATER CONSERVATION AREA

Just north of Baton Rouge, this site is far enough from the urban center to attract a few nesters and less-urban-tolerant wintering birds. It is a mix of upland and bottomland forest near the Comite River with just over a mile of trails. To find the park, take I-110 north to LA-408 (Exit 6, Harding Boulevard, also the exit for the Baton Rouge Regional Airport). Turn right and head east on Harding Boulevard, which becomes Hooper Road, for 4.6 miles. Turn left onto Blackwater Road (LA-410) and the conservation area parking lot is 200 feet ahead on the left. The habitats include young trees, open meadow, some open water, and a small riparian section along the Comite River. This relatively new wetland restoration project is designed to provide birding and nature experiences. To that end, a parking lot, gravel paths, bathrooms, and a water fountain are provided to make your exploration more comfortable. This park is a little remote, so it is best to keep your valuables out of sight.

In summer you might find Wood Duck, Anhinga, Green Heron, Red-shouldered Hawk, Prothonotary Warbler, Northern Parula, Yellow-breasted Chat, Indigo and Painted Buntings, and Orchard Oriole. The cooler months offer Forster's Tern, Belted Kingfisher, Yellow-bellied Sapsucker, Common Yellowthroat, and Orange-crowned, Pine, and Yellow-rumped (Myrtle) Warblers. Wintering sparrows include Field, Savannah, Song, Swamp, and White-throated. Eastern Towhee is resident.

82 Baton Rouge Area

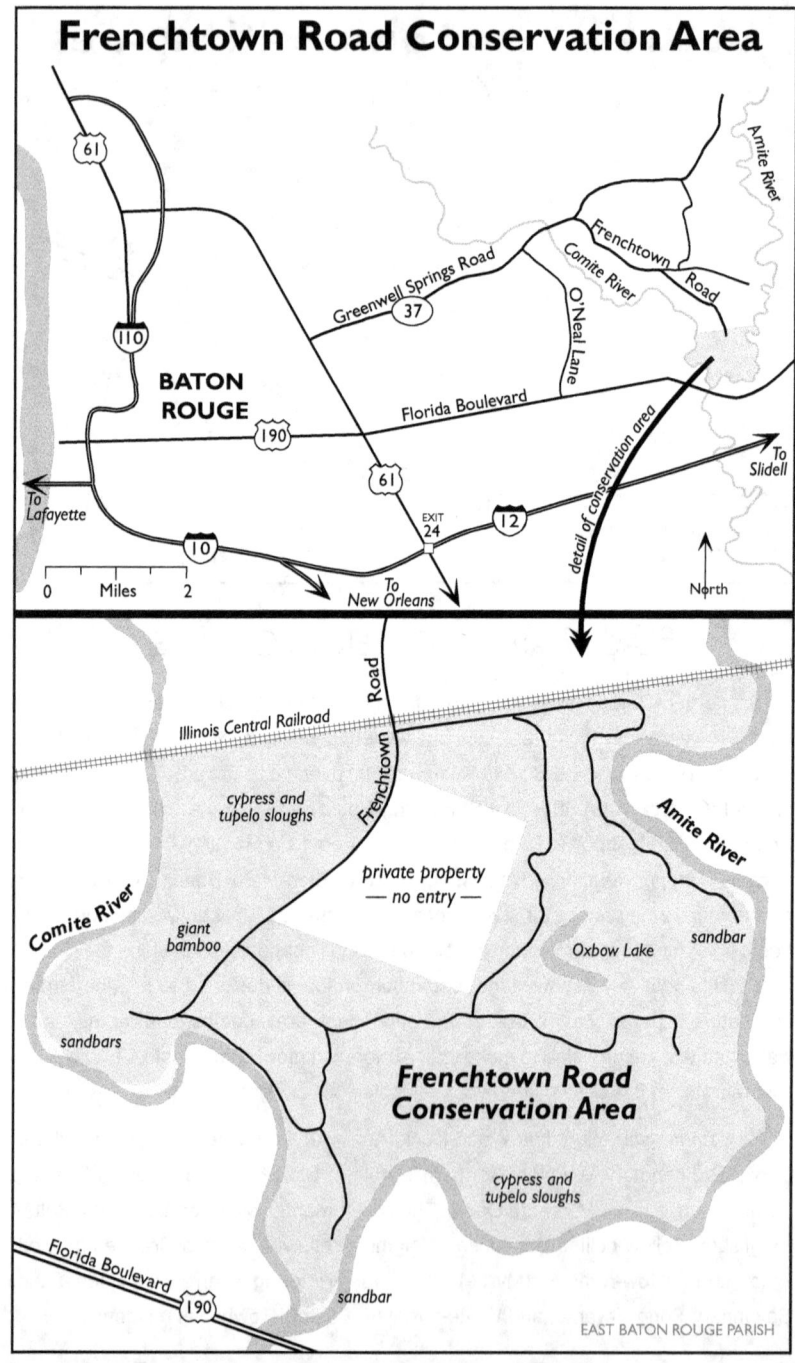

Barred Owl   Ronnie Maum

FRENCHTOWN ROAD CONSERVATION AREA

This is the East Baton Rouge Recreation Commission's newest conservation area and also the largest, with nearly 500 acres of bottomland hardwood sloughs and upland ridges. There are more than five miles of trails and great access to the Comite and Amite Rivers, which merge at the southern edge of the property. The park was designed with birders in mind, and park signage provides links to the eBird checklist and species accounts for some of the species of conservation concern such as Prothonotary and Swainson's Warblers. This is Swainson's Warblers' closest breeding site to Baton Rouge. More common Prothonotary, Kentucky, and Hooded Warblers are also here from April to July. Wood Thrush, increasingly scarce throughout its range, still holds on here. Given the remoteness of the site, take the proper precautions.

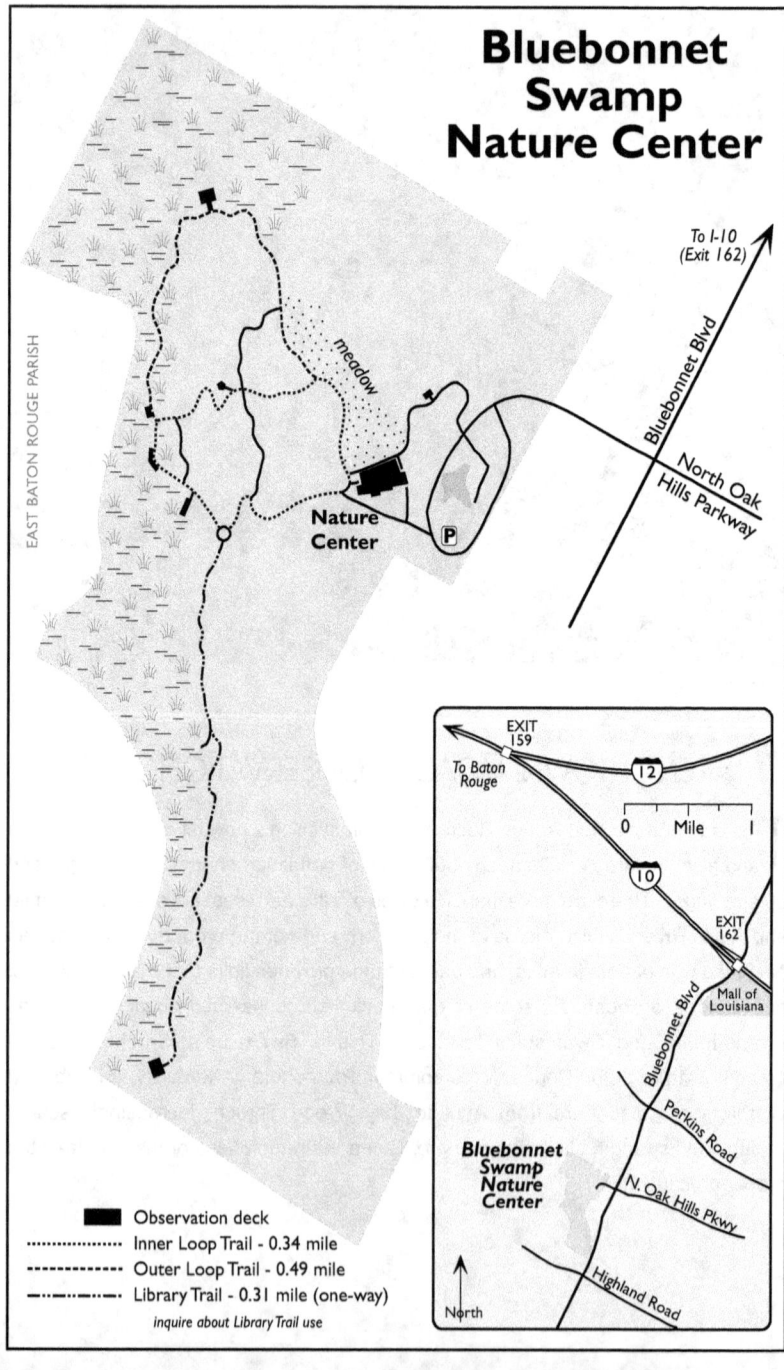

BLUEBONNET SWAMP NATURE CENTER

Another unique habitat located in the midst of suburban sprawl is the Bluebonnet Swamp Nature Center. Comprising some 101 acres, the tupelo swamp boasts several hiking trails. At least a half day should be set aside in order to do justice to this wooded lowland. A $2 fee is charged for adults; the center's hours are 9 AM–5 PM Tuesday– Saturday and 1 PM–5 PM on Sunday; closed Monday.

To reach Bluebonnet Swamp from Baton Rouge, take I-10 east to Exit 162 (Mall of Louisiana/Bluebonnet) and turn right (south), following Bluebonnet Boulevard for 2.0 miles to North Oak Hills Parkway; turn right. This short lane empties into the parking area for the nature center. A bird list is maintained at the nature center. Breeders include Barred Owl, Red-bellied Woodpecker, Acadian Flycatcher, Yellow-throated Vireo, Black-and-white and Prothonotary Warblers, American Redstart, Northern Parula, and Yellow-throated Warbler. This patch of woods attracts migratory species in spring and fall.

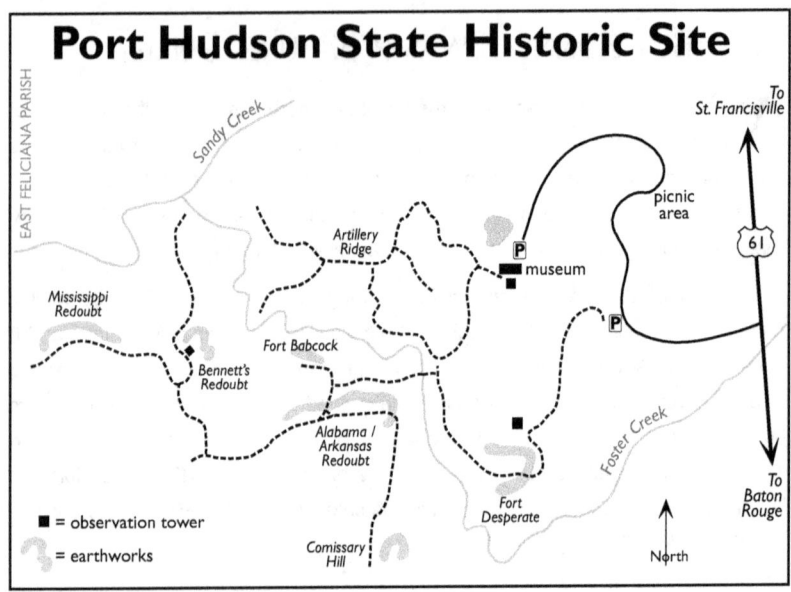

PORT HUDSON STATE HISTORIC SITE

Quite the historic venue, Port Hudson was the setting for the longest true siege in American military annals. In fact, the fort did not negotiate surrender terms until after the fall of Vicksburg. And, contrary to many notions, it was also the scene of the first action involving African Americans. During the siege these untried troops, comprising the 1st and 3rd Louisiana Native Guards, acquitted themselves admirably well against a determined Confederate resistance. The ultimate capture of the fort gave the Union forces unfettered control of the Mississippi River. In the pre-Civil War era, this area was an active shipping port/railhead. Today, it is only a small unincorporated community.

To reach this site from Baton Rouge, take Loop I-110 north to the US-61 exit and turn right (north). Follow US-61 for 11.6 miles and just past the East Feliciana Parish line, turn left into the park. The site contains 909 acres, most of which is accessible to the public. There are a number of picnic areas available for a daily fee of $2. Three observation towers offer grand vistas, and the riverbottom hardwoods boast 6 miles of hiking trails.

Habitats found here are hardwood forest, woodlots, and a smattering of open grass. Acadian and Great Crested Flycatchers, Eastern Kingbird, Red-eyed Vireo, Hooded Warbler, Northern Parula, Summer Tanager, and Orchard Oriole are representative of the nesters, while Red-shouldered Hawk, Red-bellied, Downy, and Hairy Woodpeckers, and Fish Crow are year-round residents. During the summer months, Mississippi Kites sometimes seem to fill the sky as they float above the canopy, feeding on the wing. Wintering birds include Yellow-bellied Sapsucker, Eastern Phoebe, Blue-headed Vireo, House and Winter Wrens, Pine and Yellow-rumped (Myrtle) Warblers, and the occasional Palm Warbler. Migration can be impressive in this good habitat adjacent to a major river corridor.

Oakley House   Richard E. Gibbons

AUDUBON STATE HISTORIC SITE

From the entrance to the Port Hudson site, drive north again on US-61 for a distance of 8.8 miles to LA-965; turn right (east) and follow this state byway for 2.8 miles to the entrance to this preservation site (see map on page 72). The grassy fields and hedgerows along the way can be checked for sparrows. A $2-per-person fee is collected at the gate. Although this 100-acre park may lack the historical significance of a major Civil War battlefield, it is nevertheless steeped in history. John James

Audubon arrived here in 1821, staying at the Oakley House Plantation. Audubon had been hired to tutor the landowner's daughter, and he was afforded half of each day to survey the grounds and pursue his painting interests. The estate (now fully restored) provides the visitor with a brief glimpse into this era in our history. A few common species such as Red-bellied Woodpecker, Blue Jay, Carolina Wren, Brown Thrasher, and Northern Cardinal can be expected. The best bet for birding is the half-mile-long Cardinal Nature Trail that winds through a hardwood/pine upland. Great Crested Flycatcher, Brown-headed Nuthatch, Kentucky and Pine Warblers, Summer Tanager, and Orchard Oriole are found during the breeding season.

Wintering birds include Yellow-bellied Sapsucker, White-eyed Vireo, Brown Creeper, Ruby-crowned and Golden-crowned Kinglets, Hermit Thrush, Yellow-rumped, Orange-crowned, and Pine Warblers, White-throated Sparrow, and Common Grackle. This is also a good place to search for Red-headed Woodpecker. The fence line and pastures just outside the entrance is a good place to find Field, Savannah, and Song Sparrows.

MARY ANN BROWN NATURE PRESERVE

From the entrance to the Audubon State Historic Site, head east (right) onto LA-965 for a distance of 2.9 miles. The Mary Ann Brown Preserve, owned and managed by The Nature Conservancy, is located on the north side of the highway.

This 109-acre plot of mixed pine/hardwood uplands is similar in composition to that of the Audubon State Historic Site. Camping facilities, kitchen, and picnic area are all available for a small fee with prior arrangement. Contact can be made through The Nature Conservancy's website. Visitors can explore the hiking trails without charge.

In winter, Sharp-shinned Hawk, Yellow-bellied Sapsucker, Eastern Phoebe, Blue-headed Vireo, House and Winter Wrens, Hermit Thrush, Cedar Waxwing, Orange-crowned and Yellow-rumped (Myrtle) Warblers, Chipping Sparrow, and American Goldfinch mix with the permanent residents.

Yellow-billed Cuckoo, Yellow-throated Vireo, Kentucky and Hooded Warblers, and Summer Tanager breed here, while Pileated Woodpecker, Carolina Chickadee, Tufted Titmouse, Carolina Wren, Eastern Bluebird, Brown Thrasher, and Pine Warbler are resident. This is the southernmost breeding area in the state for Louisiana Waterthrush. To find one, listen in spring for its descending song along the streams in the eastern half of the preserve.

BATON ROUGE AREA 89

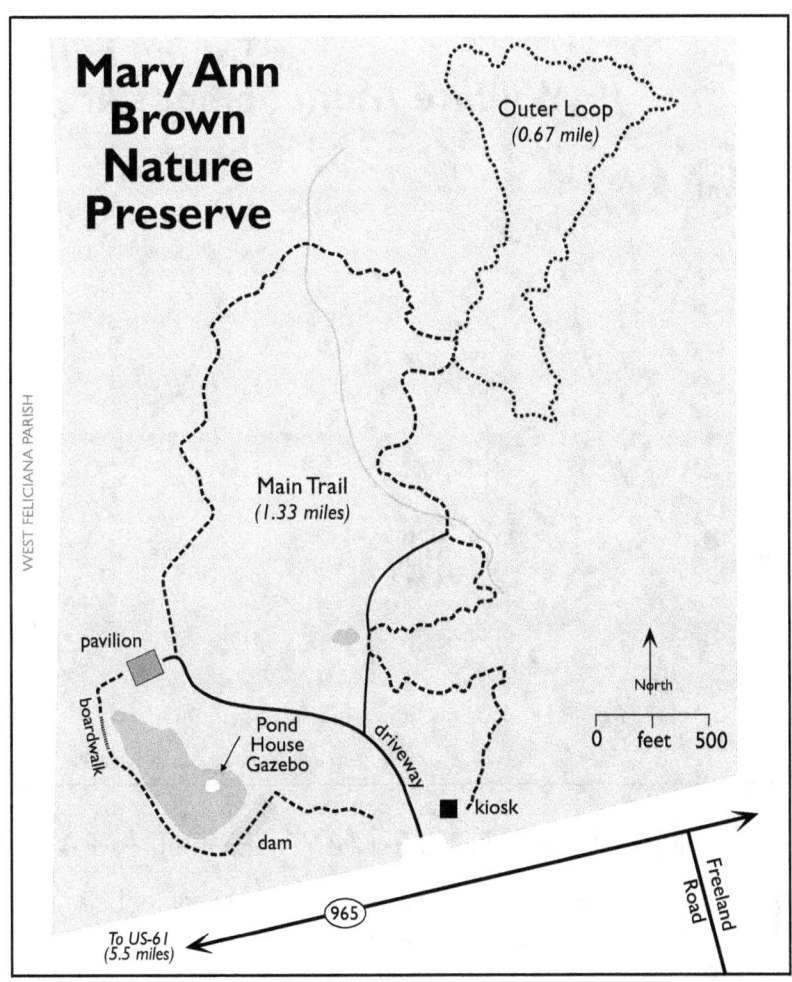

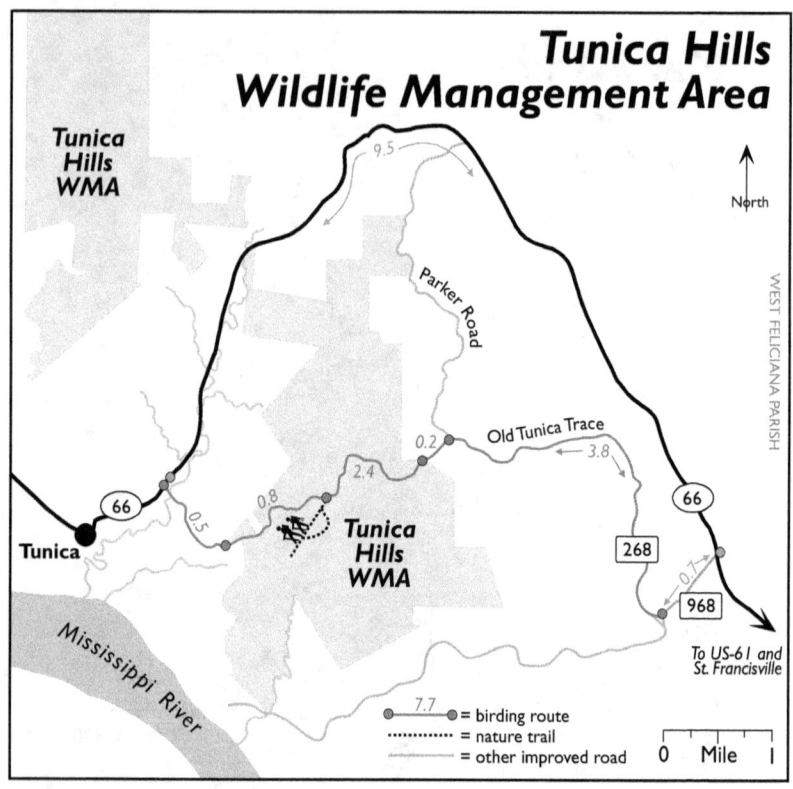

TUNICA HILLS WILDLIFE MANAGEMENT AREA

To find this much-storied region, return to the intersection of LA-965 and US-61. Turn right (north) on US-61 and drive 5.3 miles (through the town of St. Francisville) to an intersection with LA-66 (Tunica Trace). Turn left (west) and continue on this road as it winds about for 7.8 miles. At LA-968, turn left (west), zero your odometer, and drive 0.7 mile to Old Tunica Trace. Turn right and continue 3.8 miles to where the pavement ends and the passage becomes primarily a one-lane gravel road. The rainy months of winter often make the road into little more than a mud trough. Parking and shoulder space is at a premium along this stretch. If you must pull over, be very careful. At 4.0 miles, the Tunica Hills WMA begins. At 6.4 miles, there is a nature trail on the left side of the road with limited parking. At 7.2 miles, you leave the WMA, and at 7.7 miles the Old Tunica Trace intersects LA-66. Turn right to return to St. Francisville, about 21 miles via LA-66 and US-61.

Tunica Hills is a hardwood-forested wonder. Steep slopes, bluffs, and creek bottoms predominate. Not unlike Sicily Island Hills WMA in central Louisiana, the beauty of these timeless hills is in their understated elegance. Like many a wild place in Louisiana, the WMA owes its existence not to some collective aesthetic sense or penchant to preserve, but to a love of hunting. For that reason, it is suggested that visitors plan their trips to coincide with spring migration or the early breeding season. Virtually any species found here in fall or winter may be seen as easily at other locales. Although the woods reverberate with the sound of gunfire from early autumn through early spring, they are almost entirely devoid of human activity during summer when Wood Storks and herons ply the shallows.

Among the permanent residents are Red-bellied, Downy, Hairy, and Pileated Woodpeckers, Carolina Chickadee, Tufted Titmouse, and Eastern Towhee. Migration can be alive with vireos, thrushes, and warblers. Breeders include White-eyed, Yellow-throated, and Red-eyed Vireos, and Black-and-white, Swainson's, Kentucky, Hooded, Pine, and Yellow-throated Warblers, to name a few.

MORGANZA SPILLWAY

Hydrologists tell us that the Mississippi River is wont to switch the direction of its flow in Louisiana every 1,500 years or so. For a time, the bulk of the river will sweep past New Orleans, as it does now. Then it will alter its course and the main body (using the Atchafalaya bed) empties into the Gulf south of Morgan City. It appears that the river currently is trying to effect this change. The economic impact of such a situation would be devastating—far greater than might be wrought by the worst hurricane imaginable. The resultant trickle that would ease by Baton Rouge and New Orleans could not support the commercial river traffic that these ports now enjoy. The effects on Morgan City are less certain, but it is likely that they would not be positive. The only barricade that presently impedes the Mississippi's selected future path is Three Rivers Dam. It was constructed at a point where the Red River joins the Mississippi and where the Atchafalaya River departs from it. This huge undertaking is a project of the Army Corps of Engineers. The idea is to divert most of the flow of the Red River just before it enters the Mississippi and empty it behind the dam into the Atchafalaya. Then, the Mississippi's waters, or most of them, are refused entry into the Atchafalaya and instead are funneled toward Baton Rouge. The engineers working on this great structure admit that the river will eventually win and churn past the dam. Nevertheless, crews labor to keep the Mississippi at bay, repairing and reworking the facility, 24 hours a day, 7 days a week.

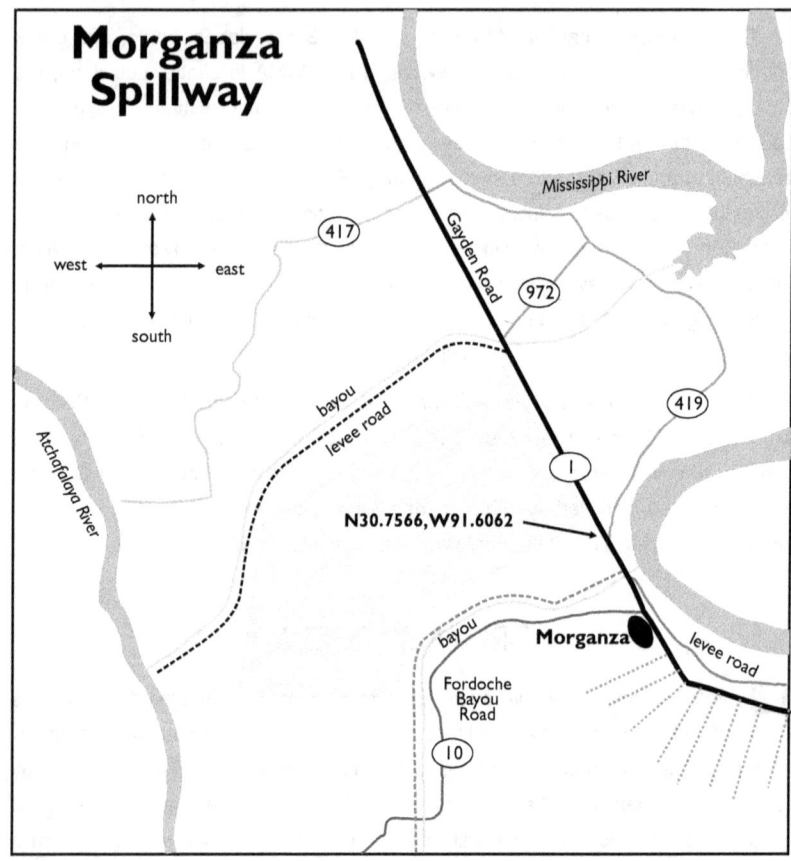

Until a finger in the dike no longer stems the flood, it will be necessary to protect Baton Rouge and New Orleans (particularly the latter) from potentially extremely high waters during spring. To this end, two massive works have been constructed; both are several decades old. The Bonnet Carré Spillway is located about 20 miles upriver from New Orleans, a birding site covered in the Southeast region (see page 120). The Morganza Spillway was established about 30 miles northwest of Baton Rouge. If opening the gates of this latter facility in order to save the cities downriver became a requirement, a huge gush of water from the Mississippi (which would be well above flood stage) could be diverted past the levee and into the Atchafalaya drainage.

This landscape of ponds, mudflats, drowned timber, and weeds teems with bird life virtually the entire year. A rookery for Anhingas, herons, egrets, ibises, and Roseate Spoonbills, it provides adequate sanctuary for hundreds of these birds. In winter, shorebirds visit the flats, but during migration, they descend upon them in large numbers. American White Pelican is also in evidence during the colder months. Dozens of Wood Storks earn a living here during their post-breeding dispersal from Mexico. In point of fact, this is one of the most reliable spots in the state to find this bird.

Morganza Spillway Richard E. Gibbons

Red-headed Woodpecker inhabits the timber at all seasons. Geese and ducks show up in fall, along with an occasional Osprey, Bald Eagle, or Peregrine Falcon. Blue Grosbeak, Painted Bunting, and Dickcissel nest in the area, as does Orchard Oriole. During spring and autumn, a very long list of possible migrants exists.

To reach the Morganza Spillway, drive west from Baton Rouge on US-190 through the small community of Erwinville. At 1.9 miles past the town's only traffic light, turn right (north) onto LA-1. Follow this scenic lane as it winds about in a lazy-C configuration, marking the western levee of False River, a long-abandoned oxbow of the Mississippi. The town of New Roads is reached at about the 15-mile mark. Continue north on LA-1 to the village of Morganza, about 9 miles. The road leads onto the levee and the floodgates just north of this sleepy hamlet. Some of the byways that border the spillway are off limits, while some may be traversed. As of this writing, the road leading to the right (east), just as the spillway is encountered, has always been open to automobile traffic. There are trails leading away to the south that empty into wooded backwaters. Just watch for signs and travel only where there is no prohibition.

Birding sites worth mentioning in addition to those covered in this chapter are:
  False River in New Roads
  Raccourci Old River
  Bayou Manchac

Wood Storks   Jessie Barry

Sherburne Wildlife Management Area – South Farm

Better known to birders simply as South Farm, this parcel of mixed-use land is part of the massive wooded Atchafalaya Basin and has the expected woodland birds. The main attraction at this location is the network of shallow impoundments that are managed for crawfish and waterfowl. These impoundments are drawn down in the summer to promote vegetation growth for wintering waterfowl, stopover habitat for shorebirds, and foraging areas for wading birds. The WMA hosts a "Wood Stork and Wading Bird Event" each summer with the main draw being hundreds of Wood Storks taking advantage of the shallow-water foraging. From the parking area, an old two-track service road serves as the trail out to the ponds. This long walk can be brutal in the summer sun, so plan to do it in the early morning or evening. A Bald Eagle pair nested on the east side of the levee near the parking lot in 2010 and 2011. Although it is impossible to know if these birds will continue to nest here, the chance of seeing them here is better than at many other state locations. The pair has used a large tree on private property but which is visible from the levee road or from the top of the levee as you approach the parking lot. Take care not to disturb the eagles and the private landowners.

BATON ROUGE AREA 95

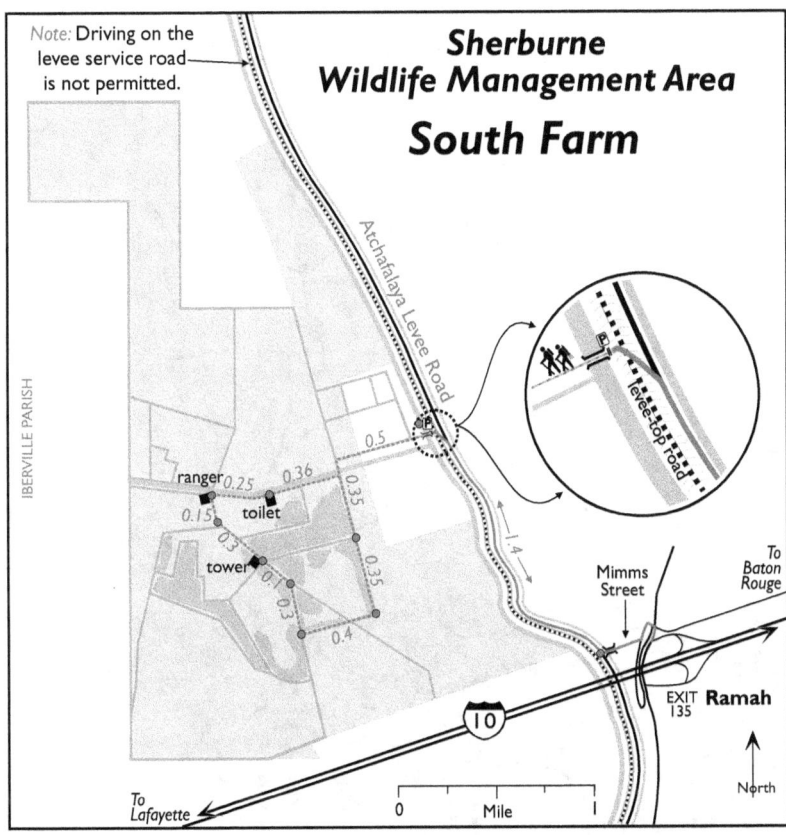

South Farm is a half-hour drive from Baton Rouge. Take I-10 to the Ramah exit (Exit 135). Drive north to the first road on the left and then turn right on Mimms Street. Cross the short bridge and turn right onto the gravel road, Atchafalaya Levee Road. Drive 1.3 miles or until you see the *South Farm* sign and then cross over the levee and enter the parking lot.

Like all state wildlife management areas, anyone between the ages of 16 and 60 is required to have either a valid Louisiana hunting or fishing license, or a Wild Louisiana stamp, to visit an LDWF Wildlife Management Area. These are available for purchase at any license vendor selling LDWF hunting or fishing licenses, on-line at http://www.wlf.louisiana.gov, or by phone at (888) 765-2602.

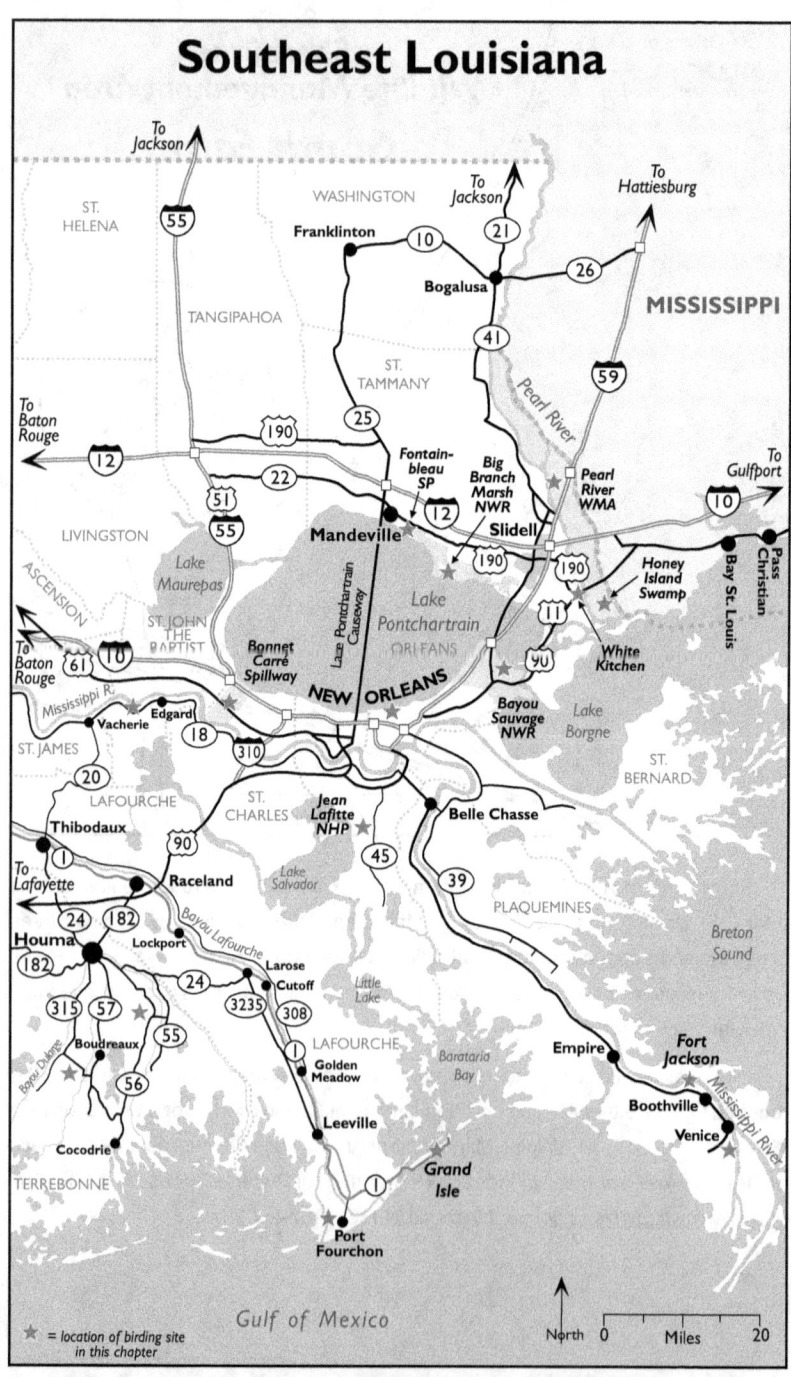

SOUTHEAST LOUISIANA

HOUMA AND SOUTH

This region is a tapestry of woodlands and swamps that transition into marsh and barrier island as one travels southward. The marshes and woodlands between Houma and Grand Isle are given short shrift as most birders head to the coast. The town of Grand Isle, which sits on the barrier island of the same name, is accessed by one of the few Louisiana highways that penetrates the marshes and reaches the beach. Birding can be outstanding during spring migration, and the beaches and woodlots have hosted many rarities through the years. Gray Kingbird, Black-whiskered Vireo, and Shiny Cowbird (at least formerly) turn up regularly on the island in spring, and fall migration has its own rewards and is more likely to yield vagrants.

Houma is referred to as the *Venice of the Americas* and is the heart of the swamp and bayou country. No fewer than 55 bridges traverse the seven bayous that meander through this small city. Houma's Jim Bowie Park with its stately live oaks can be good for migrants during spring and fall migrations. Waterbirds are abundant in this rich environment. Various duck and heron species, Double-crested Cormorants, Anhingas, and Ospreys are among the expected finds.

To fully experience the beauty of Louisiana's wetlands, travel south from Houma on LA-315, also known as Bayou du Large Road. This 23-mile drive traverses cypress swamps, deciduous woodlands, and marsh. Red-shouldered Hawk, Barred Owl, Hairy and Pileated Woodpeckers, Brown Thrasher, Common Yellowthroat, and Red-winged Blackbird are permanent residents. During winter, these habitats also support Anhinga, Belted Kingfisher, Yellow-bellied Sapsucker, White-eyed Vireo, Tree Swallow, House, Winter, Sedge, and Marsh Wrens, Orange-crowned, Yellow-rumped (Myrtle), and Pine Warblers, Song and Swamp Sparrows, and Dark-eyed Junco. During late summer, Wood Storks often patrol the swamps' edges. Bald Eagles, which nest from November to March, are increasingly common.

Similar habitats can be seen along LA-57, which runs south of Houma for 25 miles. At about 16 miles, just north of the town of Dulac, take a left turn toward Lake Boudreaux. Here, several species of ducks (including Mottled as well as Blue-winged

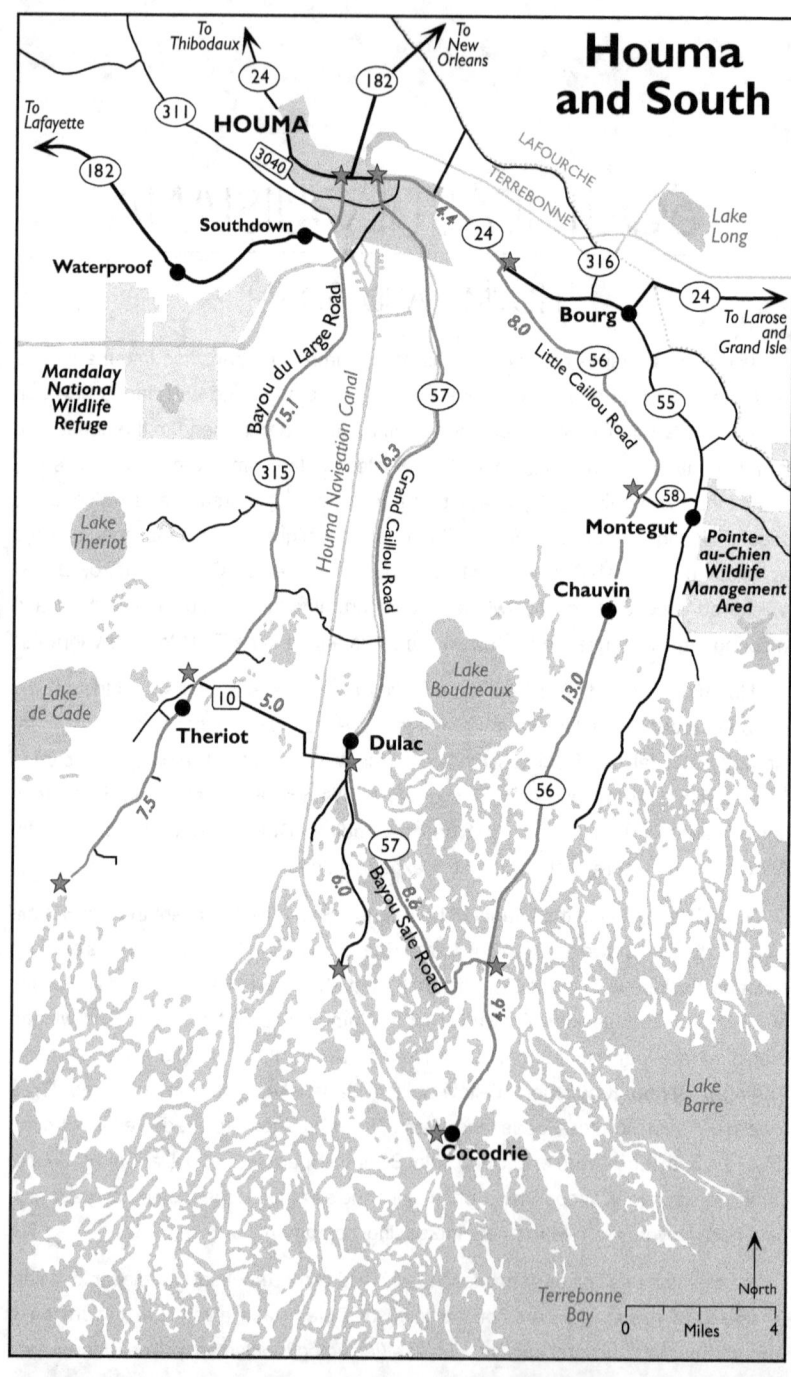

and Green-winged Teal), pelicans, herons, Glossy and White-faced Ibises, shorebirds, gulls, terns, and Peregrine Falcon can be seen. Some 9 miles south of Dulac, LA-57 intersects with LA-56, where you can turn right to explore to the south for an additional 4 miles. Northbound LA-56 will take you back to Houma.

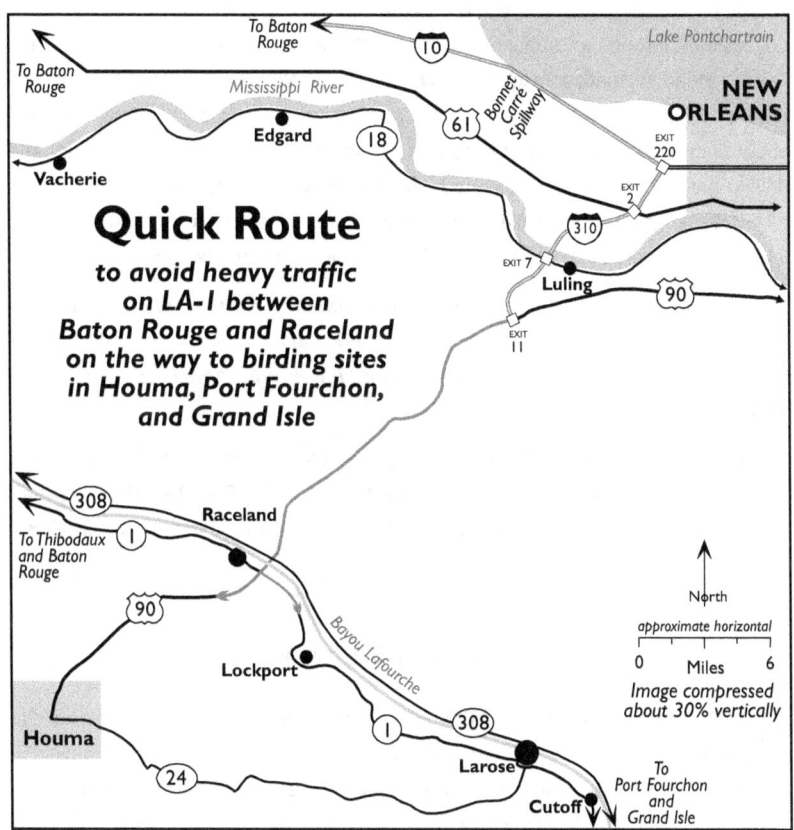

THE ROUTE TO GRANDE ISLE

Coming from New Orleans, take I-10 west to I-310 south. At the end of I-310, exit right onto westbound US-90 toward Raceland. Follow US-90 to Raceland where it intersects with LA-1. Coming from Baton Rouge, because of heavy traffic along LA-1 between Baton Rouge and Raceland, it is typically best to take I-10 east from Baton Rouge to I-310 (Exit 220), just before entering the western suburbs of New Orleans. Turn right (south) onto I-310.

Rather than taking LA-1 all the way to Grand Isle, you can exit US-90 just before it crosses Bayou Lafourche and turn left (south) onto LA-308, which parallels LA-1's path on the east side of Bayou Lafourche. LA-308 ends in 32 miles at Golden Meadow, where you can cross the bayou on a drawbridge to reach LA-1 and continue farther south.

The 65-mile stretch from Raceland to Grand Isle travels along the bayou past shrimp and oyster boats, eventually terminating on the island. As it tracks southerly, LA-1 passes through a number of small towns (Lockport, Larose, Cutoff, Galliano, and Golden Meadow) that seem to spill into each other, making it difficult to tell where one ends and the next one begins. In Larose, 17 miles from Raceland, you have the opportunity to speed up your trip by turning right at LA-657 (West 15th Street) and driving half a mile to LA-3235, a four-lane highway that is much faster than LA-1. LA-3235 rejoins LA-1 in Leeville in 15.5 miles. Mind the speed limits in the area, as they fluctuate considerably, especially the 50-mph limit in Golden Meadow.

Another option at Larose—perhaps for your northbound return from Grand Isle—is to take LA-24 west toward Houma through bottomland hardwoods and cypress that harbor typical breeding birds such as Northern Parula and Prothonotary and Yellow-throated Warblers.

Just south of Golden Meadow, the highway crosses a flood-control levee and traverses the mostly salt marshes alongside Bayou La Fourche. The dominant vegetation is *Spartina alternaflora,* home to resident Seaside Sparrows, and, in winter, Nelson's Sparrows.

Port Fourchon

At the town of Leeville, the new (2009) LA-1 Expressway toll bridge must be used to access points farther south. A one-way toll ($3) is required for southbound travelers, and this can be paid with cash, debit or credit card, or geauxpass (online via geauxpass.com). The elevated highway crosses the bayou and continues south 7 miles to Port Fourchon, where you go directly onto LA-3090 (also signed as A. O. Rappellet Road). At 0.4 mile, the road becomes the eastern boundary of a large impoundment bordered by saltmarsh. Nelson's Sparrow is present October through April and Seaside Sparrow is a permanent resident in the smooth *Spartina* and Black Needlerush *(Juncus roemerianus)* marsh. Listen also for Clapper Rail (year round) and Sedge and Marsh Wrens in winter and early spring. As usual, be mindful of where you park your vehicle.

Depending on the season and the lake's water levels, this shallow body of water can host an impressive assemblage of ducks, pelicans, herons, ibises, spoonbills,

SOUTHEAST LOUISIANA 101

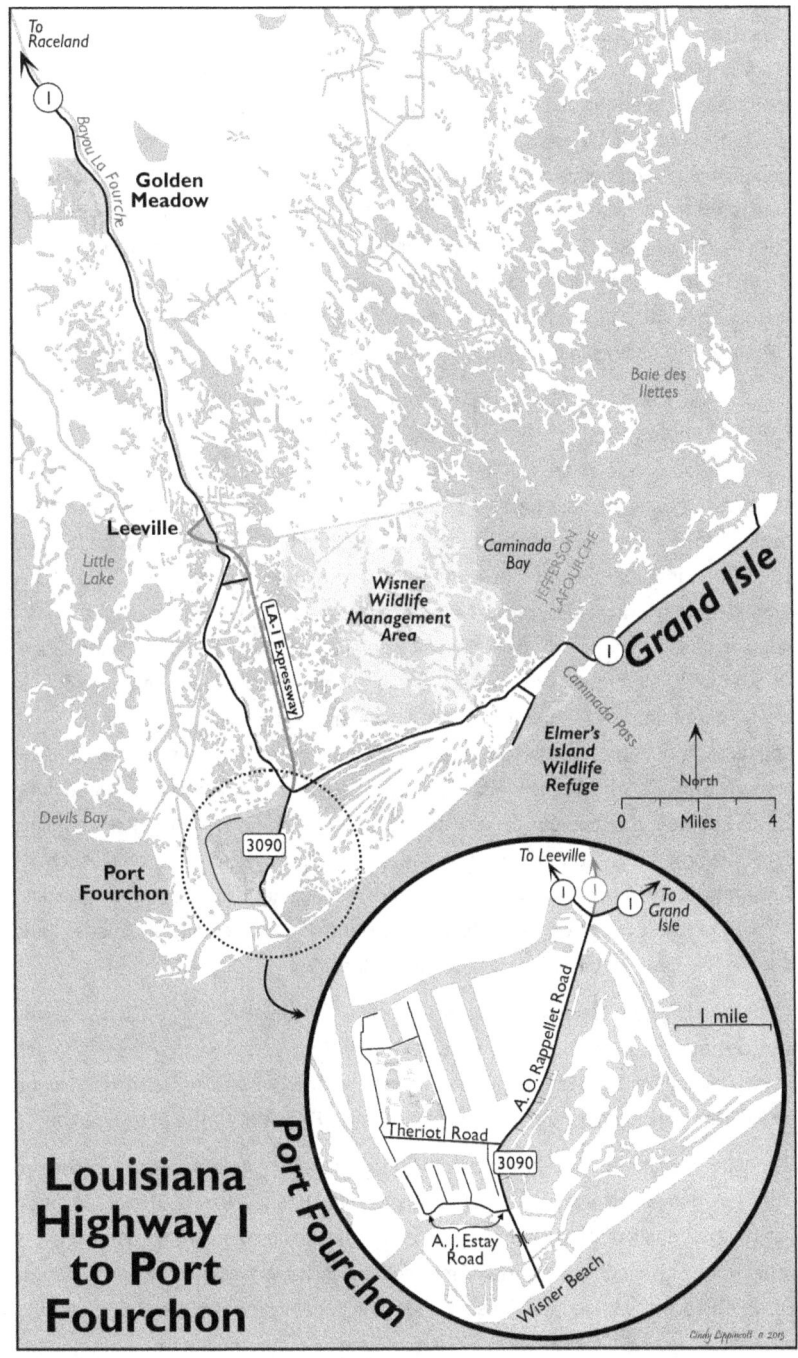

shorebirds, gulls, and terns. Black-bellied and Semipalmated Plovers, Marbled Godwit, Red Knot (mostly on the beach), Stilt Sandpiper, Wilson's Phalarope, and many more shorebirds can be seen during migration months. Reddish Egret is usually present. In winter a Peregrine is often perched on the water tower. A scope will greatly enhance your experience here. If you stop along the road, pull well off onto the grass. Two roads leading to the right can be explored. In fall, Yellow-headed Blackbirds may flock with Red-winged Blackbirds and Brown-headed Cowbirds, especially along Estay Road. Be careful not to block traffic, which usually consists of large oil-field trucks. An occasional Merlin or Peregrine will show up to size up the fare. Passerines will make use of available cover during migration if conditions are favorable.

To head toward the Gulf of Mexico, return to LA-3090 and take a right. The road crosses a narrow bridge leading toward the Gulf to Fourchon (or Wisner) Beach. Beach access was restricted because of the 2010 oil spill and ongoing beach restoration projects; check locally for up-to-date information. The beaches, mudflats, back-beaches, and marshes should be explored during all seasons. A scope focused offshore during late winter (mid-January through early April) may reveal the "double-ended" shape of Northern Gannets as they feed in the offshore waters. Winter rafts of Lesser Scaup will occasionally contain a scoter or a Long-tailed Duck. Red-breasted Merganser, Ruddy Duck, and a few other duck species may also dot the waves during the colder months. A rare Pomarine or Parasitic Jaeger will put in an appearance offshore, mainly in migration but sometimes during midwinter. A good strategy to find a jaeger is to watch gull flocks behind active shrimp boats. Laughing Gull is the most common gull on the coast, but non-breeding months see the addition of Bonaparte's, Ring-billed, Herring, and a smattering of other species such as California (very rare), Lesser Black-backed (occasional), or Great Black-backed (rare). The sandy beach continues for seven miles to the east, ending at Elmer's Island Wildlife Refuge (see below), and two miles to the west.

Sanderlings are common along the shore from fall to spring, along with a variety of less common shorebirds including Black-bellied, Snowy, and Piping Plovers, Willet, Ruddy Turnstone, Western and Least Sandpipers, and Short-billed Dowitcher. During spring migration, this can be an excellent place to find Red Knot and Baird's Sandpiper.

When leaving the beach, especially during migration, note the small patches of woods on both sides of the road, before crossing the bridge. Neotropic migrants often use the cover as a rest stop after a long trans-Gulf journey. Also, when the wind is out of the north or it is raining, trans-Gulf migrants will fly low over the water and put down on any scrap of vegetation. These woods are private property, so stay along the roadside.

Reddish Egret Darlene Boucher

ELMER'S ISLAND WILDLIFE REFUGE

Return to the intersection of LA-3090 and LA-1 and zero your odometer before making a right turn onto LA-1. Look for Ospreys along the road, and perhaps Seaside Sparrows flying across the road. The entrance road to Elmer's Island Wildlife Refuge is on the right, 6.8 miles to the east. This 230-acre peninsula, established as a state wildlife refuge in 2008, provides excellent access to marsh and beaches. The refuge is open from sunrise to sunset, and visitors should try to obtain one of the following before entry: a valid Wild Louisiana stamp, Louisiana fishing license, or a Louisiana hunting license, even though there is little enforcement. The 1.5-mile drive to the beach cuts through rich saltmarsh habitat. The birds found on the beach and mudflats here are much the same as at Port Fourchon: all the small plovers in winter and migration, Red Knots on the beach, all the regular terns in season (including Sandwich in summer, Least breeding), Northern Gannets offshore, and ducks (including Hooded and Red-breasted Mergansers). Perhaps the biggest attraction is the wintering shorebird mix. It can be impressive, with Snowy and Piping Plovers topping the bill.

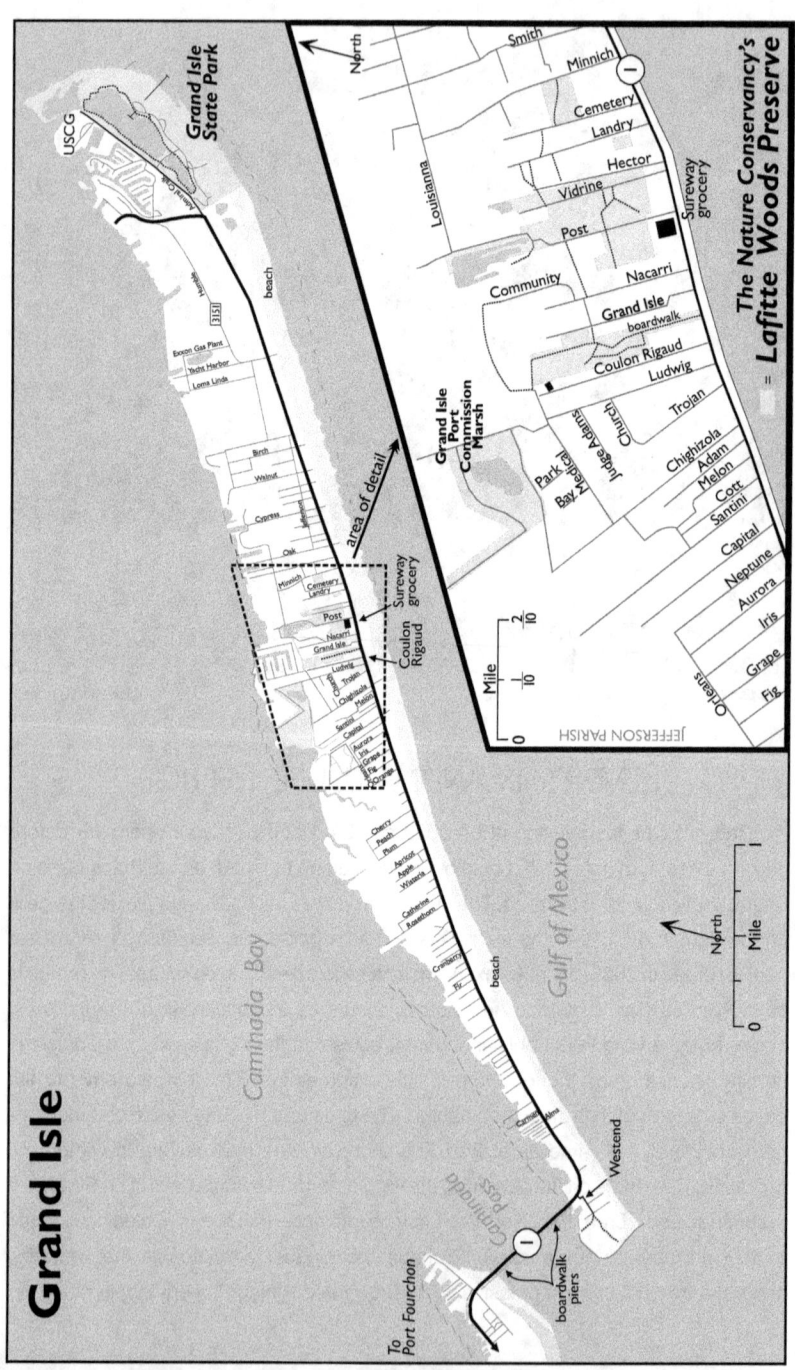

GRANDE ISLE

Returning to LA-1, turn right. Just across the short Caminada Pass bridge is one of Louisiana's premier birding destinations, Grand Isle. This is the only Louisiana barrier island that is accessible by highway. From New Orleans, an approximately 2.5-hour drive provides access to a wide range of habitats that provide forage and cover for an incredible number of birds. There are several woodlots and miles of beach and mudflats to explore. In spring, when Louisiana birding is at its peak, the island may swarm with birders—and birds (though this is highly weather-dependent). One of the reasons for the enduring draw of the island is the open and inviting hospitality of Grand Isle residents.

Immediately after crossing the bridge, take a right toward the beach levee. The west end of Grand Isle can be explored by walking the approximately one mile of beach and back-beach vegetation. The jetty has hosted Purple Sandpiper (very rare). This area offers a good view of the Gulf of Mexico and Caminada Pass, both of which can be great for coastally restricted species. Gray Kingbird, though not to be expected, has been found at least a dozen times in spring on the island, and one place was in the back-beach shrubbery here. Along LA-1, there are several short streets to the left that end at Caminada Bay, and a number to the right that have walkways onto the beaches. These can be surveyed at any season.

White-winged Dove　　　　　　　　　　　　　　　　　　　　　　　　David Cagnolatti

Gray Kingbird   Fred D. Canter

Driving east toward the center of the island, there are two Nature Conservancy sanctuaries. The first, just past Coulon Rigaud Lane is the Grilletta Tract. About three blocks farther, immediately past the Sureway Supermarket (on Post Lane), is Laffite Woods. Both woods are worth spending several hours in, especially if there is a fallout in spring. Fallout conditions are usually caused by thunderstorms offshore or the penetration of a cold front with northerly winds. The Grilletta Tract can also be accessed from the rear on Coulon Rigaud Lane, though parking is limited. The easiest way to access this site is by parking at the entrance on LA-1 (signed). This wooded patch should be checked at any time of year, but it can be loaded with migrants in spring.

A quarter mile past the Grilletta Tract, park at the Sureway Supermarket on the left (where you can pick up a snack) and walk north toward the back bay along Post Lane. The woods here can boast an impressive array of neotropical migrants; all fairly common during migration include: White-eyed, Yellow-throated, Warbling, Philadelphia, and Red-eyed Vireos, Veery, Gray-cheeked, Swainson's, and Wood Thrushes, Ovenbird, Worm-eating Warbler, both waterthrushes, Blue-winged, Black-and-white, Prothonotary, Tennessee, and Kentucky Warblers, Common Yellowthroat, Hooded Warbler, American Redstart, Northern Parula, Magnolia, Bay-breasted, Blackburnian, Yellow, Chestnut-sided, Yellow-throated, and

Black-throated Green Warblers, Summer and Scarlet Tanagers, Rose-breasted Grosbeak, and Baltimore Oriole. Blackpoll Warbler is also fairly common, but only during spring. Prairie and Canada Warblers will be found typically only in fall migration. It is not unusual to see more than 20 species of wood-warblers during an April day. Remember that trans-Gulf migrants in spring may arrive in late morning to mid-afternoon.

White-winged Doves may be found here or in the Grilletta Tract, and you may hear an Inca Dove calling. Sureway Woods is one of the best spots in Louisiana for rarer migrants such as Black-whiskered Vireo and Golden-winged, Cape May, and Black-throated Blue Warblers. Extreme rarities seen in these woods include Sulphur-bellied Flycatcher and Varied Thrush.

After birding the woods, continue east on LA-1 for 1.5 miles beyond Post Lane to Humble Road (PR-3151), which provides access to the "Exxon Fields" (now owned by Energy 21). If you drive the network of roads, stay in your car and be polite if challenged. American Golden-Plover, Upland Sandpiper, and Buff-breasted Sandpiper are often present during spring migration. Ephemeral ponds attract ducks and shorebirds. A scope is helpful for combing through shorebird flocks. Unfortunately, the fields drain well and will often be devoid of birds. A Long-billed Curlew is seen occasionally, and American Oystercatchers are sometimes seen on rocks in the vicinity. This is a good place to see territorial "Eastern" Willets in spring and summer.

In summer, Magnificent Frigatebird is a relatively common sight gliding above the island or offshore.

You can take either LA-1 or the road parallel to it toward the east end of the island, birding opportunistically. From LA-1 there are numerous places to park, cross the Gulf levee by foot, and gain access to or a view of the beach and ocean. Farther on, LA-1 reaches Grand Isle State Park, a fee area where you can scan the beach and Gulf. You also may camp here for an additional fee. Often large numbers of gulls, terns, and shorebirds rest on the beach from here west. A three-story tower (currently being repaired) provides a commanding view of Grand Isle and the next barrier island to the east, Isle Grand Terre. The birds found on the beach here are the same species encountered elsewhere along the island's south shore.

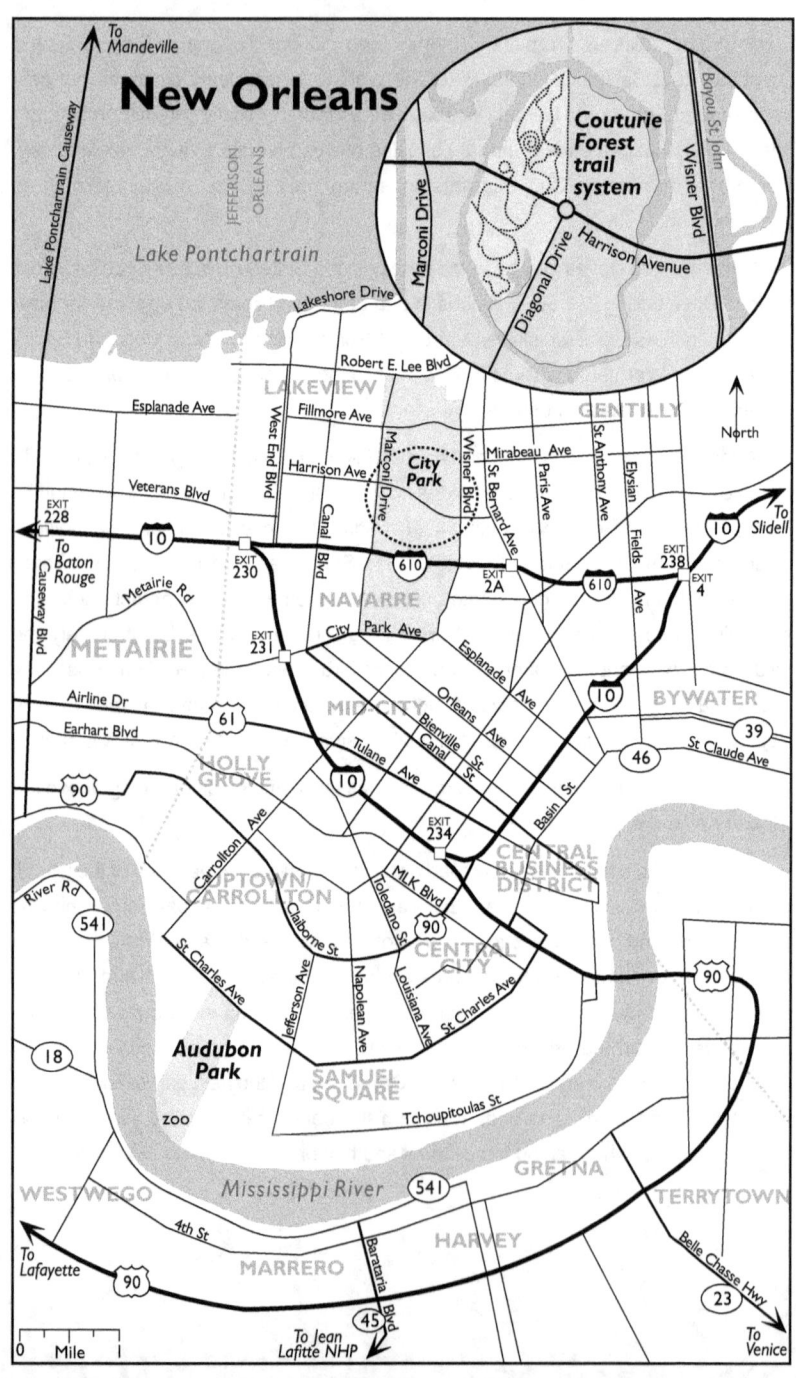

NEW ORLEANS CITY PARK

Most of the "Big Easy" has fully recovered from 2005's Hurricane *Katrina*. Always one of the most intriguing cities in the U.S., New Orleans remains the main draw for visitors to Louisiana. In addition to the various tourist attractions (e.g., food, music), there are a number of good birding opportunities within and near the city. Consult the Orleans Audubon Society's website *http://www.jjaudubon.net* for additional birdfinding information.

New Orleans City Park, the sixth largest urban park in the nation, is located on the north side of the city. Its 1,500 acres has hedges, fields, and majestic live oaks. The oaks collectively form one of the finest migrant traps away from the coast. During fall and spring, migrant flycatchers, vireos, thrushes, wood-warblers, tanagers, grosbeaks, buntings, and orioles can be found when conditions are right. During rare grounding events, or fallouts, the trees may appear to drip with color. In spring, this will usually happen if the timing of a frontal passage or a rain event is right, usually during the early afternoon. In fall, overnight rains usually are the key. Of course, there are also strings of seemingly birdless spring (and autumn) days related to "unfavorable" weather and the coastal hiatus phenomenon (see pages 73, 170).

A good way to bird the park is to visit the Couturie Forest (also referred to as the Couturie Woodlot). Use the parking area just west of the traffic circle on Harrison Avenue, which runs east/west through the park. A trail system can be accessed from this parking lot, providing access to dense understory habitat and a bayou, which is good for Wood Duck, Anhinga (except for breeding time), both night-herons (Yellow-crowned is absent in winter), and usually an alligator. Breeding birds are limited to familiar, widespread species.

Bayou St. John, which borders the park on its eastern edge, is home to winter residents such as Redhead, Ring-necked Duck, scaup, and Common Goldeneye. And, the park's four public golf courses sometimes provide a temporary haven for migrating upland shorebird species, or grasspipers.

City Park has easy access from the central business and hotel districts. You can take the new Canal Street streetcar to the entrance of the park, though that will not leave you near Couturie Forest. Or simply drive up Canal Street north toward Lake Pontchartrain. Turn right at City Park Avenue (you are surrounded by cemeteries at this intersection) for about a mile to Wisner Boulevard, which marks the eastern boundary of the park and provides the easiest entry into the park. Turn left onto Wisner and then left onto Harrison Avenue in about one mile. The Couturie Woods and nature trails are just beyond the traffic circle. Marconi Drive marks the western boundary of City Park and is good for diving ducks north of Harrison Avenue.

Robert E. Lee Boulevard borders the park to the north and City Park Avenue to the south. Coming in from I-10, take Exit 231 and turn onto City Park Avenue.

Audubon Park

Audubon Park, which is about 5 miles up St. Charles Avenue from the Central Business District via the St. Charles streetcar (and across from Loyola and Tulane Universities), is much easier to access than is City Park for the visitor without a car; but at the same time, it doesn't offer as rich birding opportunities. On the other hand, its lagoons are good for Wood Ducks year round, and in winter (September–March) it harbors a huge population of Black-bellied Whistling-Ducks, often numbering in the thousands. Occasionally there will be a Fulvous Whistling-Duck among them. Frequently an Anhinga will be present, as well as a smattering of herons. The heronry, which was the jewel of the park during the breeding season, is no longer active. Check the golf course during late spring and summer for Gull-billed Terns.

During migration there may be birds in the moss-covered live oaks, which are worth the trip in any case, and there are some woods without undergrowth near the golf clubhouse. The zoo, at the river end of the park, is definitely worth a visit and one might turn up an interesting bird there. Behind the zoo, the levee provides a wonderful view of the river, which may host huge rafts of scaup (and possibly other diving ducks) in winter. During tropical-storm weather, a Sooty Tern or other storm-blown waif might be seen along the river. A trip to the park on the streetcar provides a good introduction to New Orleans' architecture.

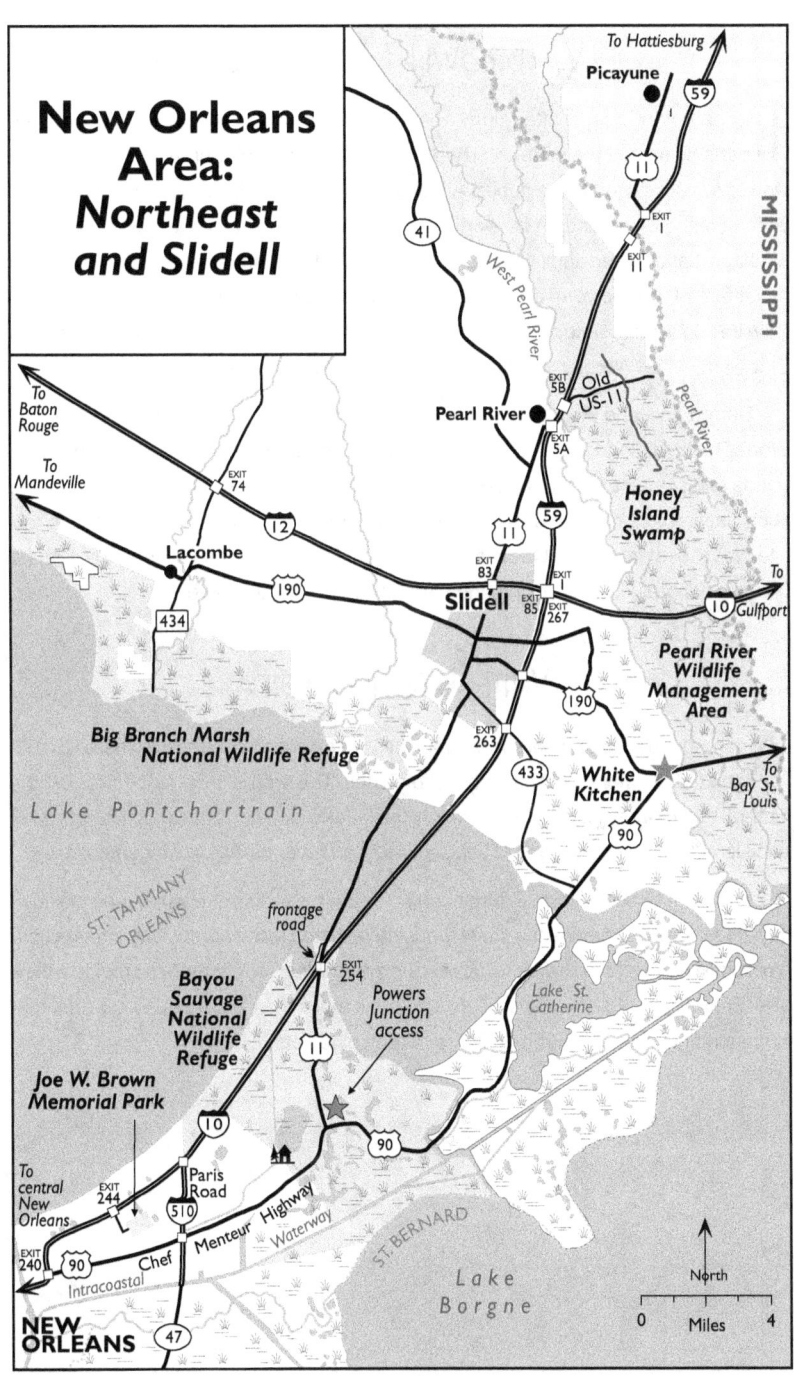

Joe W. Brown Memorial Park

This park was closed after Hurricane *Katrina*, but it has reopened with updated sports fields and paved trails. The Audubon Nature Center here and the adjacent woods remain closed to the public. Although relatively small, this neat patch of woods with a couple of ponds can be worth a visit. Mississippi Kites have nested here and buntings have raised their broods in edge habitats. Wintering species include the usual fare of Ruby-crowned Kinglet, and Orange-crowned, Pine, and Yellow-rumped (Myrtle) Warblers. Additionally, there is always the chance of a wintering Black-and-white Warbler, Northern Parula, or Yellow-throated Warbler.

Barred Owl and Red-shouldered Hawk are permanent woodland residents and Wood Duck, Anhinga, herons, and Belted Kingfisher (fall to spring) can be found in the ponds and along nearby drainage canals. Migration may deposit a bevy of passerines such as vireos, thrushes, warblers, tanagers, grosbeaks, and orioles. To reach this site, travel east from New Orleans on I-10. Take Exit 244 (Read Boulevard) south for 0.4 mile, where you turn left into the park on Nature Center Drive.

White Kitchen Area

A long-gone restaurant of some fame, the White Kitchen once stood where US-190 and US-90 intersect just southeast of Slidell. The area is great for birding and the lack of heavy traffic is a plus. Through the efforts of The Nature Conservancy of Louisiana, the area is now part of Louisiana's Pearl River Wildlife Management Area.

Yellow-throated Vireo, Prothonotary Warbler, Northern Parula, and Yellow-throated Warbler breed near a small roadside rest stop to the north of the intersection. A recently restored boardwalk at the rest stop protrudes into a marsh to provide a view of a Bald Eagle nest that has been active for more than 80 years. Brown-headed Nuthatch and Pine Warbler nest in the nearby pine flats.

Bayou Sauvage NWR — Jake Fontenot

BAYOU SAUVAGE NATIONAL WILDLIFE REFUGE

Bayou Sauvage National Wildlife Refuge occupies a large portion of the extreme eastern part of the city and Orleans Parish. It is one of the largest urban wildlife refuges in the nation and comprises nearly 24,000 acres between New Orleans and Slidell. The refuge and its 26 miles of levees is primarily open marsh and wet woods and provides important stopover habitat, as well as nesting habitat for Black-bellied Whistling-Ducks, Pied-billed Grebes, and King Rails. The usual species of waders are present, and during winter, ducks such as Gadwall, American Wigeon, Mallard, Blue-winged Teal, Northern Shoveler, and Green-winged Teal can be common. American Coots are abundant. During spring and especially early fall, Yellow Warblers can be seen flitting among the drooping willow branches. Here and in the woods, migrants forage before resuming their journey.

The easiest way to access the refuge is from the intersection of Paris Road (I-510) and Chef Menteur Highway (US-90) northeast of New Orleans. From this junction, drive east on US-90 for 4 miles. Just after crossing a canal, you'll see the signed entrance to the refuge on the north side of the highway. There are toilets at the parking lot and a trailhead for the "Ridge," a lengthy boardwalk that leads through woods and marsh. The refuge road beyond the parking area follows a levee for 7 miles through the marsh.

Back on US-90, in 2 miles at Powers Junction (US-11), turn left. Traverse the breadth of the refuge along US-11 for another 5 miles until reaching I-10 at Exit 254. As an alternative to taking I-10 east or west, cross over the interstate and take a poorly marked frontage road to the left (west) just before the highway joins the US-11 bridge that leads to the north shore of Lake Pontchartrain (Pointe aux Herbes). This gravel lane leads to an overlook of a lagoon which is good for both diving and puddle ducks in winter, including scaup, Bufflehead, possibly Common Goldeneye, and perhaps Horned Grebe.

HONEY ISLAND SWAMP AND PEARL RIVER WILDLIFE MANAGEMENT AREA

Pearl River WMA, also known as Honey Island Swamp, is a great bottomland hardwood swamp. Although it is not much of a migrant trap because of the extent of its 35,000 acres of forest and marsh, this area does offer superb birding during spring and early summer. To reach the Honey Island exit from the major freeway junction northeast of Slidell, travel north on I-59 from its junction with I-10/I-12. Ignore the signs for the town of Pearl River, and at 5.7 miles, after crossing the bridge over the West Pearl River, take Exit 5B (Honey Island Swamp). Bear left as the exit empties onto the service road and within a quarter mile you will be at the entrance to the swamp. (You should possess a Louisiana hunting or fishing license or a Wild Louisiana stamp, which can be purchased online at the Louisiana Wildlife and Fisheries website. Otherwise you may be ticketed.) You can bird along the road, stopping at each small bridge, or walk into the swamp wherever water conditions permit.

At 8.0 miles you reach a gravel road that crosses the blacktop. If you turn left onto it, you will end up at a firearms practice range, but the road leading to that facility can be productive. The gravel road leading to the right ends at a parking lot for a nature trail that can be explored in an hour or so. Another gravel road also wanders away to the south at 8.7 miles; you can explore it, too.

All of the breeding birds of southern hardwood swamps are common here, including Barred Owl, Yellow-billed Cuckoo, Acadian and Great Crested Flycatchers, Red-eyed, Yellow-throated, and White-eyed Vireos, Wood Thrush, Northern Parula, Yellow-throated (mostly piney edges), Hooded, Prothonotary, and Kentucky Warblers, as well as American Redstart. This is an excellent site for the reclusive

Swainson's Warbler, a dead-leaf specialist that inhabits the forest understory. To locate it, you will have to know its song and then attempt to track it down. Its song seems ventriloquial. Summer Tanagers are also common, and you might find Blue Grosbeaks in open, brushy edges. One of the most-sought-after species during the spring and summer is the beautiful Swallow-tailed Kite. It can be seen soaring almost daily beginning in late March, although by mid-April it is outnumbered by its more common cousin, the Mississippi Kite. Kites will begin to search for thermals in late morning, so stake out places along the road with an adequate view of the sky.

Swallow-tailed Kite

Jennifer Brumfield

Return to I-59 and head north/right. At 5.1 miles, take Exit 11 (Pearl River). The fields and scrub here provide edge habitats favored by such species as Yellow-breasted Chat, Indigo Bunting, Painted Bunting, Dickcissel, and Orchard Oriole. The vast expanse of open sky here should be scoped for Swallow-tailed and Mississippi Kites. It's not unheard of to see three or four dozen kites aloft during migration, feeding on the wing and making subtle adjustments with their tail feathers to compensate for the inconsistencies of thermal heating and breezes.

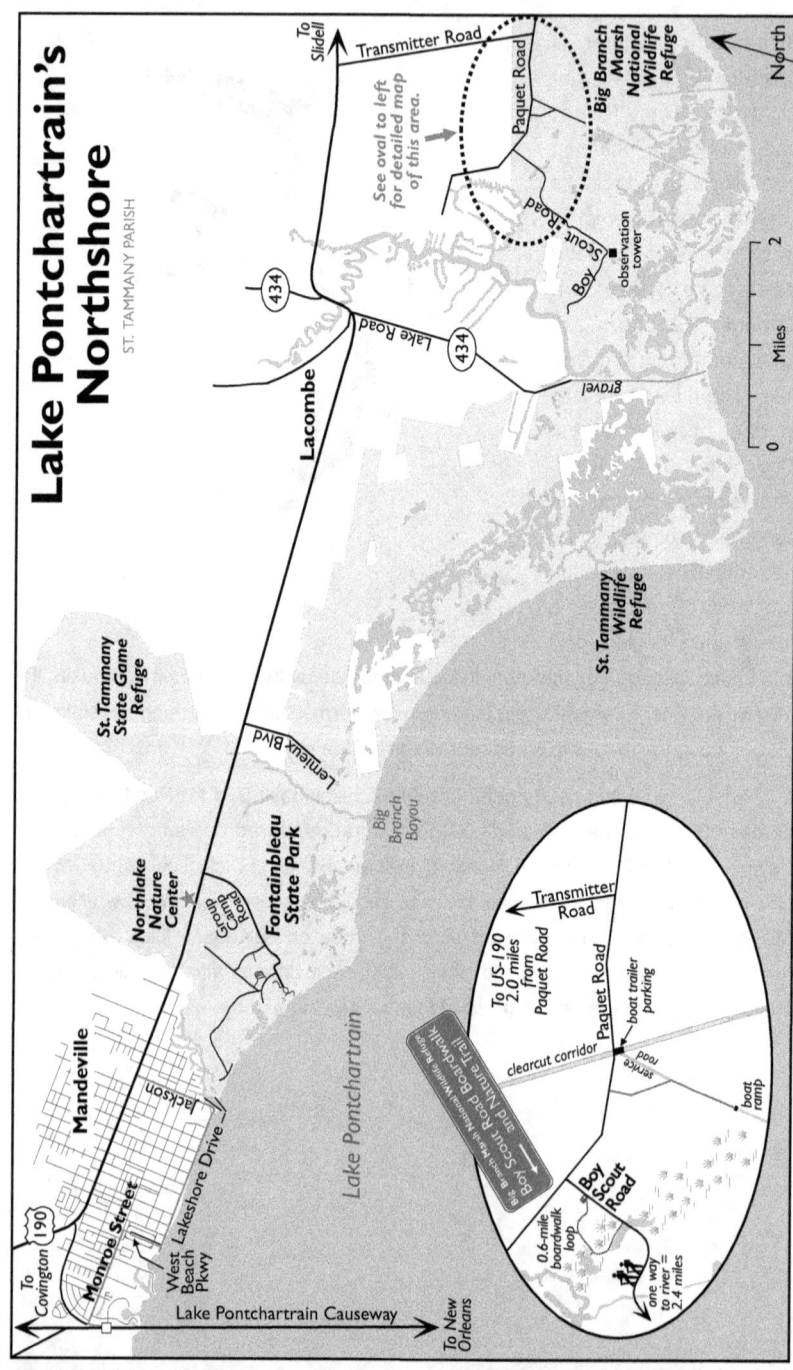

Fontainebleau State Park and Lake Pontchartrain's Northshore

To reach the Northshore from I-10 in Metairie, which is just west of New Orleans, take Exit 228 (Causeway Boulevard north). The toll across the 25-mile causeway is just $1, money well spent for the experience. On all but exceptionally clear days, land is beyond sight when you are halfway across the causeway. Gulls, terns, and the occasional Magnificent Frigatebird can be viewed only from the window of your vehicle because there is no stopping or parking along the causeway. Also, traffic is strictly monitored on the bridge, so drive the speed limit. At the north foot of the causeway, zero your odometer and at 0.1 mile, exit onto the service road. At 0.4 mile, turn right onto Monroe Street in Mandeville. Follow this narrow road for a mile and take another right onto West Beach Parkway. Head south until the road ends at Lakeshore Drive and turn left.

For the next 1.5 miles, the road parallels the north shore of the lake. The old oaks in the vicinity are of considerable interest in spring and fall, as migrants find them inviting. Vireos, warblers, tanagers, and orioles can all be found. Even so, this stretch of lakefront is most interesting during winter. The decades-old hardwoods protect the shoreline from northerly winds that tend to prevail at this season. The calmer water attracts ducks, loons, and grebes. There is plenty of parking near the shore and a scope is very helpful. The profile of the Common Loon can usually be found without great effort. Less common are Horned and Eared Grebes. Bufflehead and Common Goldeneye may join thousands of Lesser Scaup in the nearshore waters. The concrete pier at the east end of the road accommodates gulls and terns.

Turn left onto Jackson Avenue and head north. At 0.8 mile, turn right onto US-190 and drive east for 2 miles to Group Camp Road and turn right toward Fontainebleau State Park, another 0.8 mile ahead. Ask for a park map and the location of the 1.25-mile nature trail when you pay your $1 entrance fee. The birds of Fontainebleau are those of the piney woods. Red-cockaded Woodpecker nests here, and Brown-headed Nuthatch, Pine Warbler, and Bachman's Sparrow also are permanent residents. Bachman's Sparrow is somewhat shy except during the early breeding season in spring. During winter, the sparrow shares the understory in sparser areas with Henslow's Sparrow. Waterbirds can be seen in the park along the shore of a lake.

Back at the entrance to Fontainebleau, zero your odometer and turn right onto US-190. At 1.5 miles, just after crossing Big Branch Bayou, turn right (south) on Lemieux Boulevard. Park near some swamp habitat on the right at 0.6 mile.

After returning to US-190, turn right and drive 4.1 miles to the intersection with LA-434 (Lake Road) and turn right. At 2.5 miles, the blacktop ends at a small bridge where the road turns to gravel. Continue driving a mile or so for expansive views of the marsh bordering Lake Pontchartrain. Look for Least Bittern and Purple Gallinule in the pools during spring and summer. American Bittern is present during winter, and Marsh Wren is possible during all seasons.

Return to US-190 and take a right, traveling east. At 2.6 miles, turn right onto Transmitter Road and drive south for 2 miles to a T-intersection at Paquet Road. Turn right, and after 0.8 mile you reach a parking lot for Big Branch Marsh National Wildlife Refuge boat launch. Red-cockaded Woodpecker breeds here along with Brown-headed Nuthatch. Chuck-will's-widow can be heard after dark in spring and summer. Prairie Warbler breeds where the pines are thinnest and where clear-cuts are starting to regenerate. There is a parking facility at 1.2 miles near a nature trail.

Bachman's Sparrow　　　　　　　　　　　　Jim E. Johnson

JEAN LAFITTE NATIONAL HISTORIC PARK

This piece of prime Louisiana swampland is a short drive south of New Orleans. It is situated north of Barataria Bay and provides a convenient rest stop for migrating passerines. Although small as national parks go, it is well worth a visit, particularly during fall and spring. If conditions are favorable for migrants to stop over, you might find a colorful assortment of flycatchers, vireos, thrushes, warblers, grosbeaks, and orioles. Breeding songbirds include Acadian and Great Crested Flycatchers, Prothonotary Warbler, Northern Parula, and Yellow-throated Warbler.

The park has a visitors center and several trails, all of which are relatively flat and short. Some of the paths are boardwalks and at least one of them ends at a marsh. Herons and egrets are common. During fall, Groove-billed Ani (rare) might be found in the brushy areas near the visitors center parking lot. The park is always worth checking in spring and fall for migrants. To find the park, travel south on LA-45 (Barataria Boulevard) from its intersection with US-90 (West Bank Expressway) in Marrero for 7.2 miles. The parking lot is on the right a quarter mile past the levee.

Birding sites worth mentioning in addition to those covered in this chapter are:
- Lake Verret
- Vermilion Bay
- Cypremort State Park
- Mandalay National Wildlife Refuge
- Bayou Teche National Wildlife Refuge

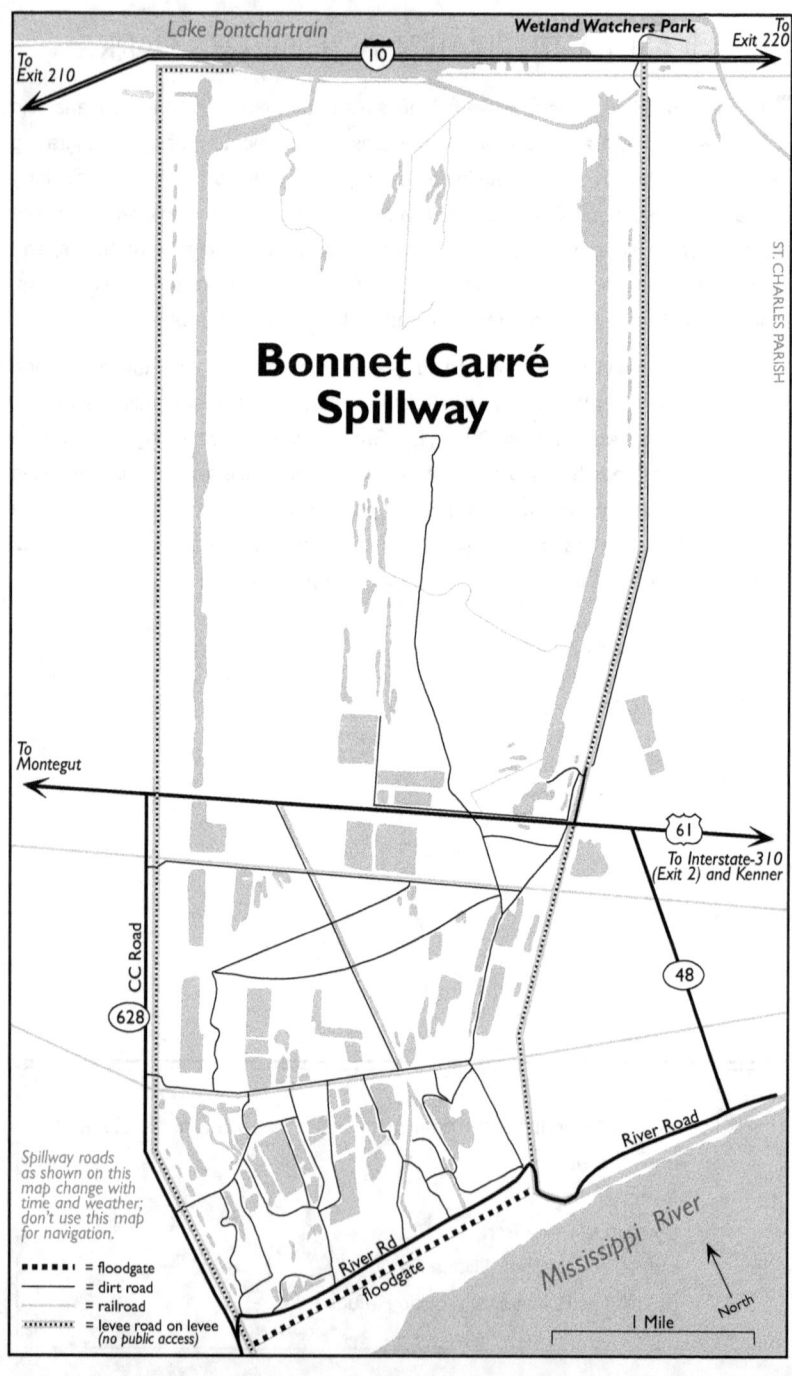

BONNET CARRÉ SPILLWAY

The Bonnet Carré Spillway (pronounced *Bonnie Caray*), about 10 miles west of New Orleans near the towns of Norco and Montz, stretches between the Mississippi River to the south and Lake Pontchartrain to the north. It was designed to divert the devastating floodwaters from the port town of New Orleans downriver. With over ten square miles of habitat crisscrossed with access roads, birding options are many. Habitats include mudflats, shallow ponds, and grassy areas near the river, and bottomland hardwoods and estuarine bay to the north. The eBird checklist for Bonnet Carré is well over 230 species—this is a major destination for area birders. The spillway is also the center of one of the longest running Christmas Bird Counts in Louisiana, the Reserve-Bonnet Carré CBC.

Several species of shorebirds use the spillway during migration, including peep and Upland, Pectoral, and Buff-breasted Sandpipers. Passerines forage in the woods during migration. Spring migration also lands Dickcissels and Bobolinks in the early successional habitats. The best birding is probably during the cooler months, with a rich mix of wrens, warblers, and sparrows. Of the sixteen sparrow species reported here, a healthy handful can be expected: Eastern Towhee, Field, Savannah, Le Conte's, Song, Swamp, and White-throated. Less common are Chipping, Vesper, Fox, and White-crowned. In winter, the spillway forests are a good place to find species less tolerant of urban encroachment, e.g., Rusty Blackbird and Purple Finch. The numerous wetland habitats provide ample habitat for the many herons and ibises so abundant in south Louisiana.

Although there are several ways to get to the spillway from New Orleans, the heavy city traffic makes all of them save one rather time-consuming. Interstate-10 crosses Bonnet Carré on the north, but there are no exits that allow direct access. So, head west from New Orleans on I-10. Just past Kenner and the airport, take I-310 south (Exit 220). At 2.3 miles, get off at Exit 2 and head north on US-61. (See map on page 99.) The east levee of the spillway is 6 miles ahead, just past the town of Norco, and the west levee is almost 2 miles farther. There are numerous dirt roads that cut across the spillway and all of these can be explored. The habitats include woodlots, grassland, short scrub, and marsh. Extra care should be exercised during winter when roads are muddy after it rains.

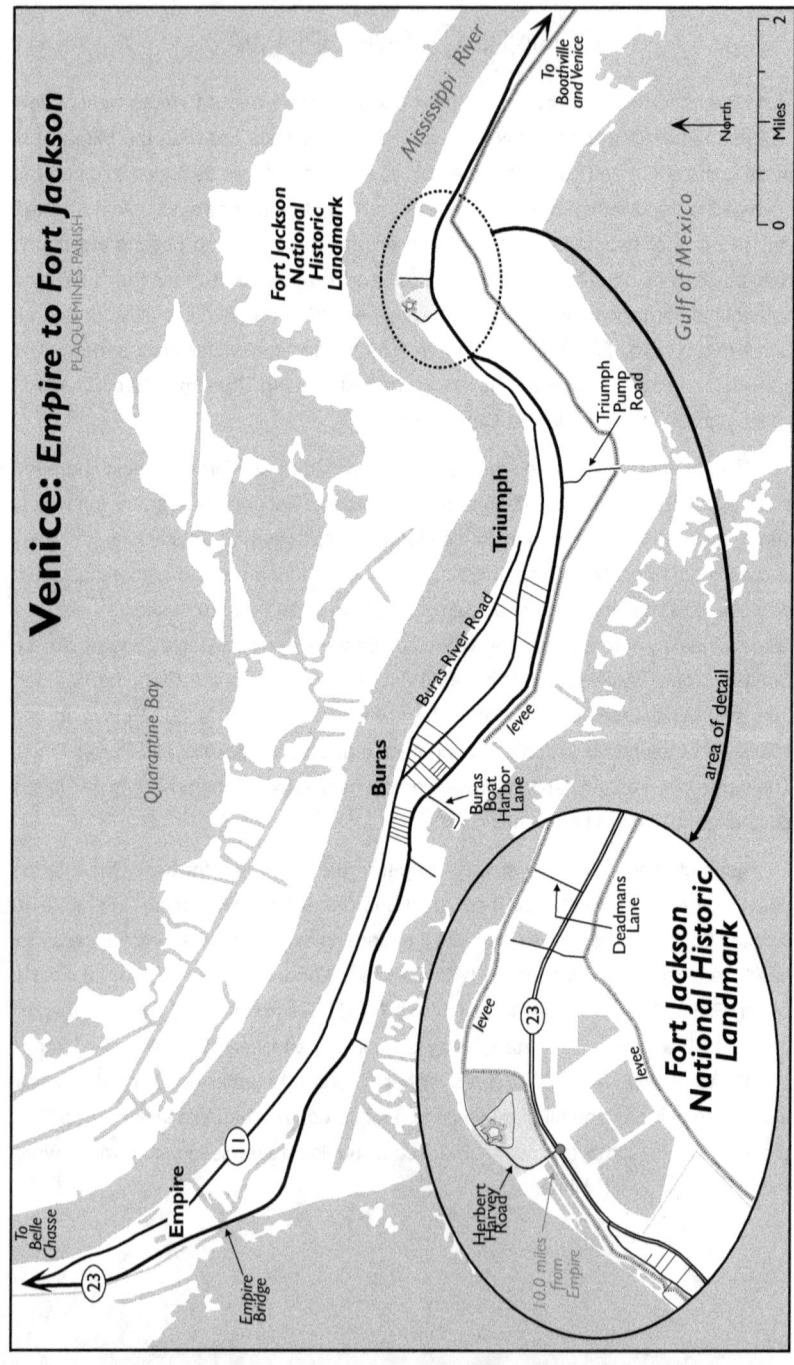

VENICE: EMPIRE TO FORT JACKSON

For birding purposes, the Venice area encompasses the woodlands that line both sides of LA-23 on the west bank of the Mississippi River in Plaquemines Parish from about Myrtle Grove to the end of the road at Venice (or Tidewater), which is about 25 miles upriver from its mouth in the "bird-foot" delta. There are a couple of ways to access LA-23 in Belle Chasse, by taking the Mississippi River bridge and exiting either at General DeGaulle or LA-23 itself. From Belle Chasse it is about 60 miles on a good road, often four-lane, to the Triumph / Boothville / Venice area. Often no more than a few hundred yards wide, and bounded by the river on one side and the flood protection levee on the west, the area is a narrow, somewhat meandering route with potential for vagrant raptors and flycatchers in winter and migration. Summer birding is challenging, but something of an open book.

On the other side of the river, LA-39 runs along the east bank for about 30 miles before ending below Pointe a la Hache, the seat of local government and the site of a ferry which crosses the river to the west bank at West Point a la Hache. It can be accessed via I-510 to LA-46. Although the west bank is generally of the greatest interest for birders, there is a lot of good habitat on the east bank as well, from St. Bernard State Park at the upper end to Bohemia at the lower.

Despite its proximity to New Orleans, Plaquemines Parish has a very low population density. Much of it is rural, much of the activity in its lower reaches is in support of the oil industry, with helicopter bases and so on. The 45-minute drive south from Belle Chasse to Empire, while not exactly pregnant with promise, is not without interest. Although the river is relatively inaccessible due to private holdings, you may catch a vagrant Scissor-tailed Flycatcher or Western Kingbird on a wire or a soaring raptor over the large fields that line the west side of the road below Myrtle Grove. White-tailed Kites are sometimes seen here, and a vagrant Swainson's Hawk is possible, though more likely farther downriver. Lake Hermitage Road, located on the right at 21.5 miles south of the Belle Chasse Tunnel and about half way to Empire, is a fairly interesting side trip. Offering live oaks, wooded swamps, Spanish moss, palmettos, marshes, dead timber stands, and a bayou, the road curls around for almost 5 miles before ending at the Hermitage Volunteer Fire Department. This road also provides an instructive introduction to the effects of subsidence and saltwater intrusion on the native ridge vegetation. The remaining live oaks can harbor northbound migrants in spring.

Just above Port Sulphur is the village of Diamond, where LA-23 goes from four-lane to two. About a half mile upriver on Foster Road is a public recreation facility with a baseball diamond and other facilities that has been a magnet for wintering flycatchers in recent years. Scissor-taileds and Western Kingbirds are almost regular, and there is often a Vermilion Flycatcher as well. A Green-tailed Towhee was present once. The woods to the south of the pipeline right-of-way is one of the best places to find Brown-crested Flycatcher in winter, and often an Ash-throated as well, but the woods are not public property. Observe the 35-mph speed limit as you drive through Port Sulphur.

Continuing south, crossing the high bridge at Empire, you will again see the effects of coastal erosion in the open bays to your right that were once productive marsh. At 4.4 miles below the bridge, a road leads to the right over the levee to the Buras Boat Harbor and marina (currently "Joshua's"), and a commercial fishing dock. There is good access to the salt marsh, with Nelson's and Seaside Sparrows, and Clapper and perhaps other rails. At the far end of the marina one can scope open water for ducks and other waterbirds.

Osprey   Ronnie Maum

As you drive south, look for raptors, which in winter may include Broad-winged or Swainson's Hawks. You will likely see an Osprey, though they are more common farther downriver.

Fort Jackson

One of the great treats during spring and fall migrations is provided by the majestic oaks that surround historic Fort Jackson, a landmark seen from Herbert Harvey Drive on the left 10 miles from the Empire bridge. The old fort provides a nice birding backdrop and the fort's moat often provides respite for Black-bellied Whistling-Duck and Common Gallinule. Unfortunately the understory is nonexistent and the birding suffers. Still, the walk around the fort can provide vantage into the trees where migrants may stop and a small wintering flock may take up residence. There is usually a wintering Yellow-throated Warbler or two, and perhaps other species, in the live oaks. The large open field south of the fort, if wet, can be good for migrating shorebirds such as Black-bellied Plover and American Golden-Plover, both yellowlegs, and Pectoral Sandpiper.

From fall to spring the impoundment adjacent to the fort can be checked for several duck species and for Spotted Sandpipers working the concrete shoreline. You can walk the Mississippi River levee and bird the batture, which is lined with willows and brushy habitat worth a check especially from fall to spring. Just below the fort is a large woodland which can best be entered at its downriver side where there is a good path into the woods. These woods, which belong to the parish, have yielded many excellent records over the years, including "Western" Flycatcher, Brown-crested Flycatcher, Townsend's Warbler, Black-throated Gray Warbler, and many records of winter warblers. Sometimes, of course, the woods may be dead. You can also bird the public habitat across the road from the fort, where there are some deep ponds, for various ducks and elderberry thickets which attract vagrant *Myiarchus* flycatchers.

As you drive south from Fort Jackson, either on LA-23 or the back road beside the river levee, there are many small woodlots. None are public, but they can be partly birded from the road. They often contain vagrants in late fall and winter. Wherever there are large stands of Roseau cane (*Phragmites*) you might check for Groove-billed Ani (now rather rare in fall and winter).

Fort Jackson   Mark Herse

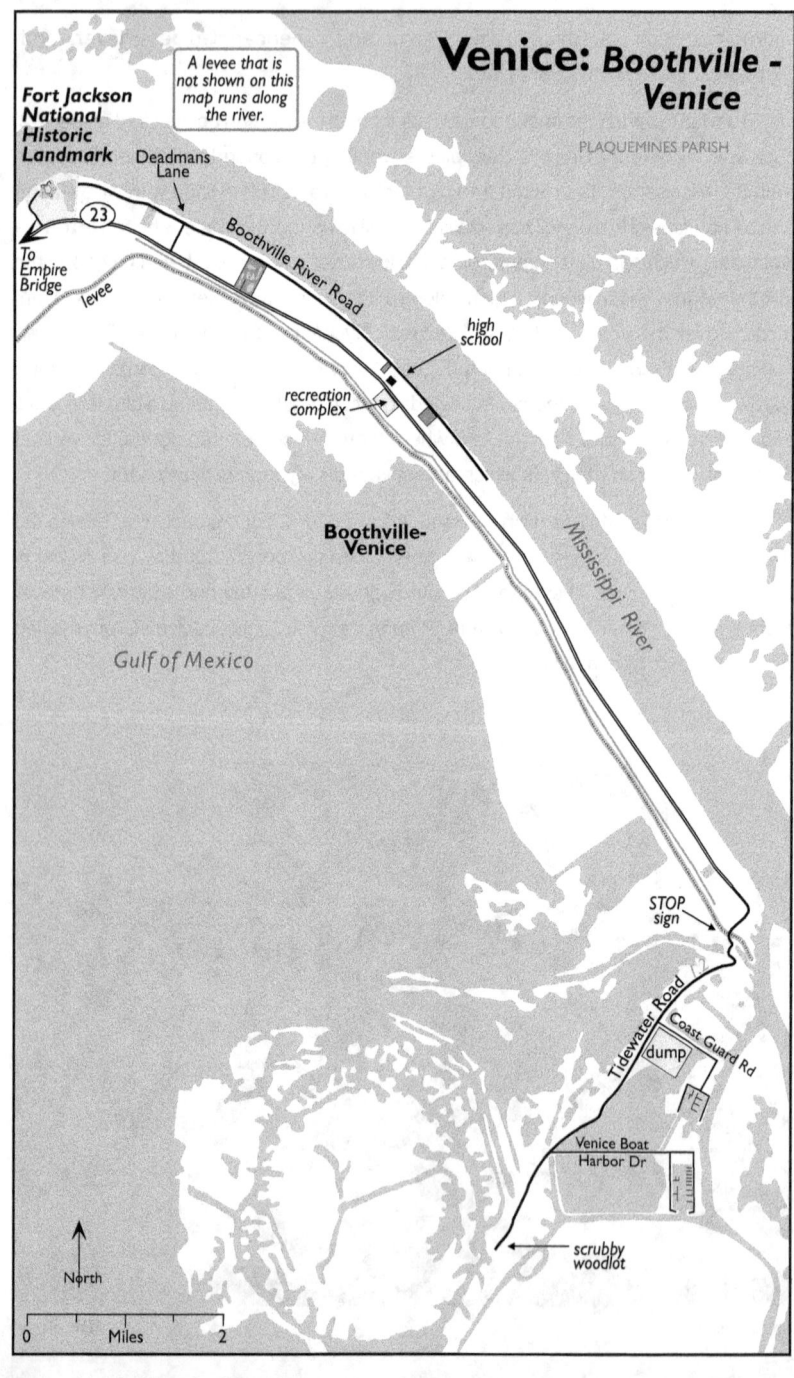

Venice: Boothville-Venice

This is the end of the line, where the big river starts to sprawl out into the dendritic bird's foot, depositing heavy sediment and nutrients. It is a rather bizarre outpost of bottomland hardwood forest where one can see cypress/tupelo swamp and armadas of Magnificent Frigatebirds in the same field of view. Because of the proximity to the open Gulf of Mexico, it is also a major deep-sea fishing center, where most pelagic boat trips leave port. You are 70 miles from New Orleans on a thin peninsula dominated by the Mississippi River. If for no other reason, visit this place for its unique geography. The birds found here can be an interesting blend of migrants that wandered down the peninsula refusing to correct or cross the Gulf, of coastal obligates, and of the ever-present flow of migrants heading in various directions.

About 8 miles south of Fort Jackson, LA-23 crosses the levee and ends at a stop sign. Turn right and drive toward the end of the road at Tidewater. The horizon opens up as you leave the protection and obstruction of the double levee system and leave the main artery of the Mississippi River. There are sometimes Shiny Cowbirds near the S-turn where the road turns toward Tidewater. Tidewater Road continues for almost 4 miles, meandering through marsh and wet willow woodlots. Several roads, mostly on the left, can be explored. The Coast Guard road leads to a landfill which may have up to 10,000 gulls feeding when the dump is active (never on Sunday) in winter. In addition to the regular Laughing, Ring-billed, and Herring Gulls, there are often a few Lesser Black-backeds present, and the potential exists for other rare gulls (e.g., Thayer's and Iceland have occurred). Gulls often rest on nearby rooftops and adjacent roads. The marina to the right near the end of the road may also harbor some gulls. Returning to Tidewater Road and continuing south, the road ribbons through open water and freshwater marsh. There are several pullouts on the road. The cypress trees on the left—which indicate fresh water—can provide nesting substrate for Anhingas, Tricolored Herons, and tens of night-herons. Ospreys are present year round and several nests can be seen from the road. In breeding season, Least Bitterns often can be seen crossing the road or heard calling from the *Phragmites* reed stands. Purple Gallinules are seen here regularly from late April to October, along with numerous Forster's and Sandwich Terns. The next left is pot-holed Venice Boat-Harbor Drive, which wanders back to the left toward the Venice marina. The open water, marshes, and willow woods on both sides are excellent for wintering and migrating species. Near the end of the road to the right is the marina, where a balconied restaurant provides a nice view of fishing catch. Return to Tidewater Road and continue southwest (left) to check a woodlot and scrubby field at approximately 0.8 mile where the road turns left. This is the end of the road, and as far south as one can drive in Louisiana.

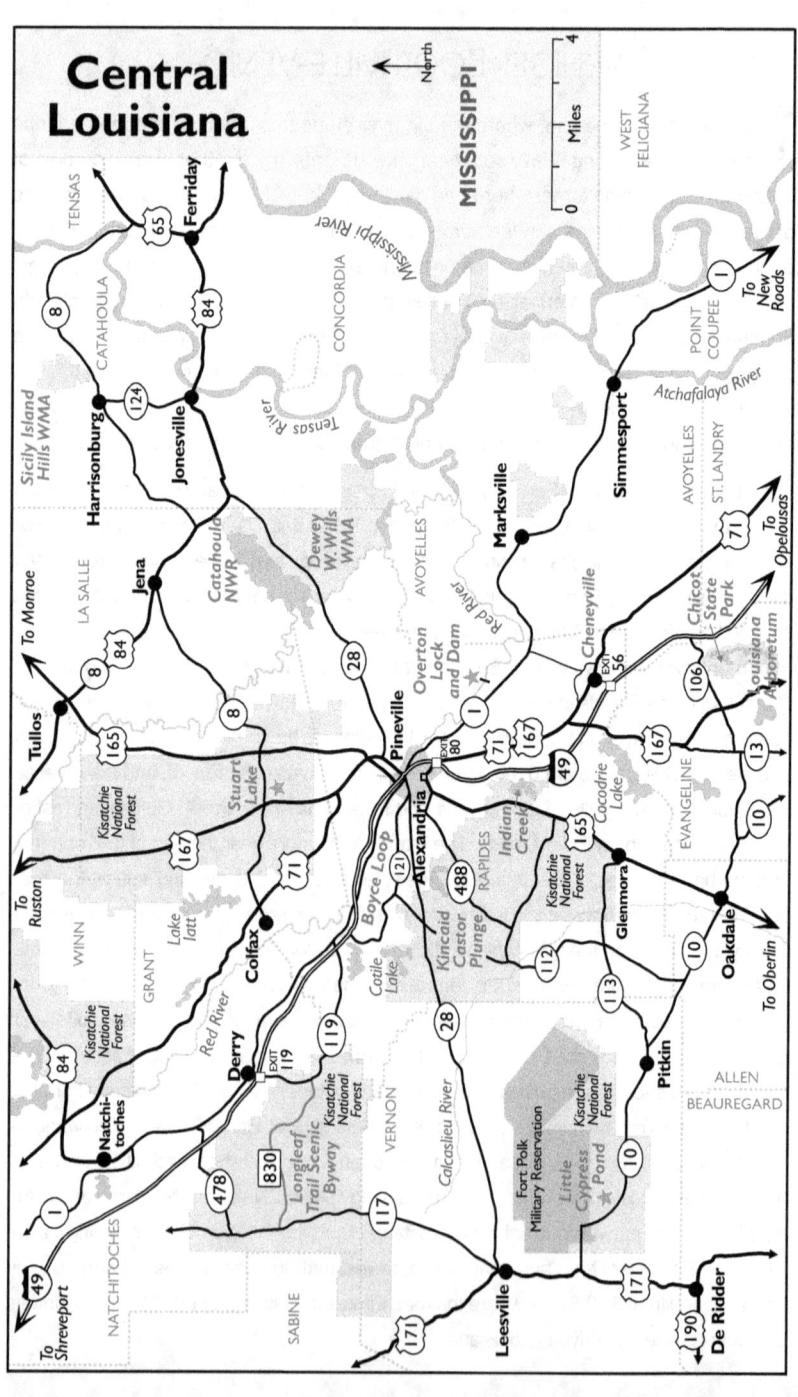

CENTRAL LOUISIANA

Central Louisiana, as treated here, is the region centered on Alexandria, including the convergent Red and Mississippi River floodplains, the vast pineywoods to the west, and a dash of coastal prairie to the south. The pineywoods offer gently rolling hills and pine specialists such as Red-cockaded Woodpecker and Bachman's and Henslow's Sparrows at sites such as Kisatchie National Forest and several wildlife management areas. To round out this mash-up, the coastal prairie reaches this section from the south where working wetlands (rice fields and crawfish impoundments) can be filled with ducks, spoonbills, shorebirds, and terns.

CHENEYVILLE

Due to its varied habitats, this is one of the most productive routes in the central part of the state. To start the Cheneyville route from Alexandria (Exit 80, I-49), drive south on combined US-71/167 for about 15 miles to Bayou Road, which is located 1.7 miles past the junction where US-167 splits off to the south while US-71 continues southeast. Turn left onto Bayou Road and follow it as it loops around the town of Cheneyville in a sort of semicircle before rejoining US-71 some 10.5 miles to the south of where it departed. (To reach the beginning of this route from the south, take US-71 into Cheneyville. From the traffic signal at Wadsworth Avenue, drive north on US-71 an additional 4.0 miles to a right turn onto Bayou Road.)

During winter, note the Red-tailed Hawks perched on the utility poles. Harlan's and Krider's forms can be found here, making it a great place to study the various types of Red-tailed. The fields to the left of the road should be scanned during winter for Horned Lark, American and Sprague's (rare) Pipits, and Lapland Longspur. During winter, the trees along the bayou harbor Hairy Woodpecker along with Yellow-bellied Sapsucker, Eastern Phoebe, Brown Creeper, House Wren, Ruby-crowned Kinglet, Cedar Waxwing, Orange-crowned Warbler, Chipping Sparrow, Purple Finch, Pine Siskin, and American Goldfinch. On drizzly winter afternoons, thousands of blackbirds congregate along the bayou under the trees. Rusty and Brewer's are generally among them. A lingering Yellow-headed Blackbird might be found mixed in with the flock.

130 Central Louisiana

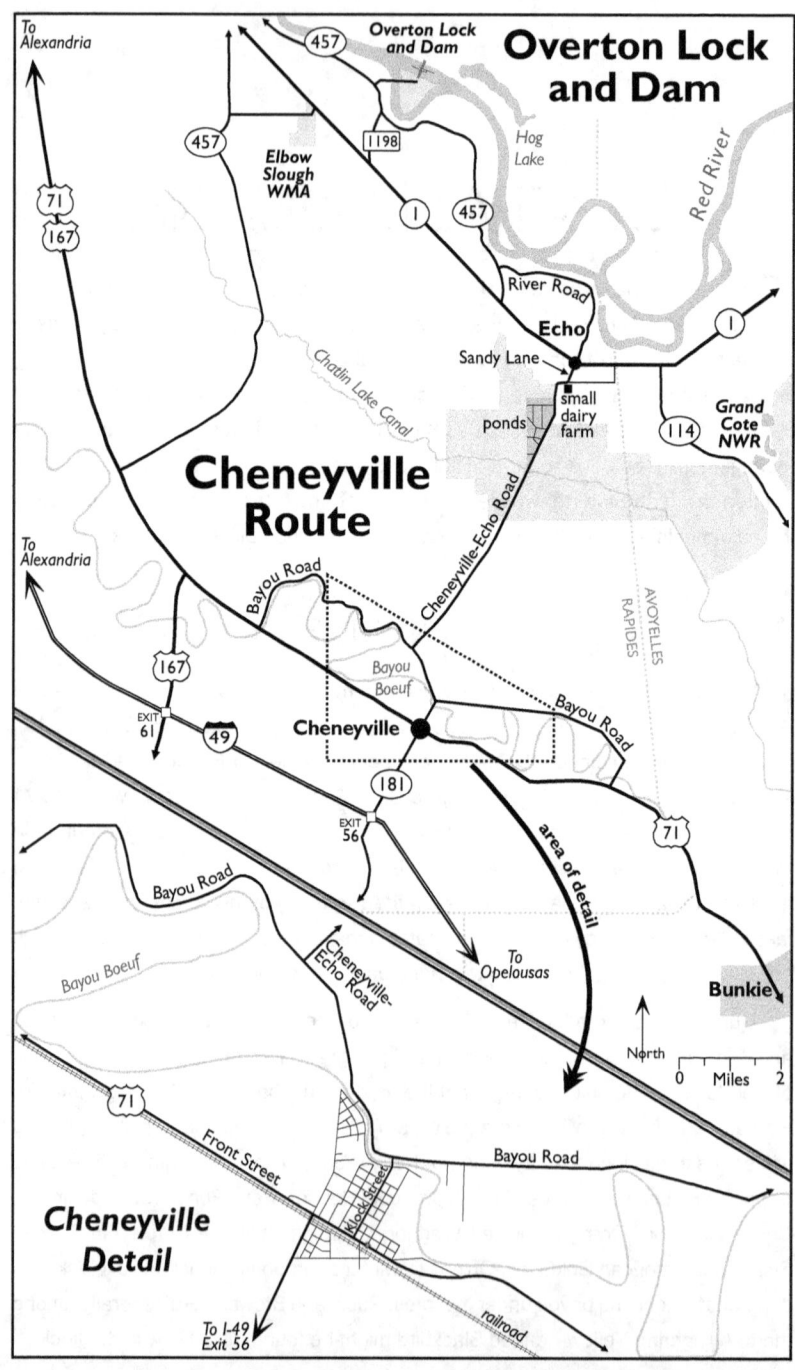

Permanent residents along Bayou Road include Wood Duck, Red-bellied and Downy Woodpeckers, Northern Flicker, Loggerhead Shrike, Carolina Chickadee, Tufted Titmouse, Eastern Bluebird, American Robin, Brown Thrasher, and Common Yellowthroat. A variety of neotropical migrants breed here, such as Yellow-throated and Red-eyed Vireos, Prothonotary Warbler, Northern Parula, Yellow-throated Warbler, Blue Grosbeak, Indigo and Painted Buntings, and Dickcissel.

During late spring and summer, the fields on the east side of the road bloom with cotton, soybeans, and sugarcane, but hold little of interest for the birder. However, in the colder months, these fields teem with birds. Northern Harriers patrol inches above the ground. American Kestrels by the dozen wait on the wires. The real attraction, however, is Louisiana's largest flock of Sandhill Cranes. A low, guttural "chortle" signals that a squadron of these stately creatures is on the wing.

Sandhill Cranes   Jim E. Johnson

Intersecting Bayou Road from the northeast at 4.6 miles south of its northern junction with US-71, Cheneyville-Echo Road should be explored. For the first couple of miles, the farms on both sides of the road are planted in row crops, which soon give way to rice fields and bayou bottoms. At about five miles, rice/crawfish impoundments, often on both sides of the road, deserve attention during winter for dabbling and diving ducks. The road in this area is, in fact, a levee with very narrow shoulders. Although traffic is light, extreme care must be practiced when birding in this area. Do not block exits to the farm buildings and fields. The owners tolerate birders, but do not drive or walk onto the adjacent property without permission.

During summer, the area is loaded with Fulvous Whistling- and Mottled Ducks, Anhinga, Tricolored and Green Herons, Yellow-crowned and Black-crowned Night-Herons, White Ibis, Mississippi Kite, Common Gallinule, Black-necked Stilt, Yellow-billed Cuckoo, Acadian Flycatcher, Eastern Kingbird, buntings, and Dickcissel. Less evident, but always present as breeders, are Black-bellied Whistling-Duck, Roseate

Spoonbill, Broad-winged Hawk, and Purple Gallinule. Wood Stork is a regular post-breeding visitor during late summer, as is White-faced Ibis.

During winter, the rice/crawfish fields are a haven for puddle ducks of every description. Gadwall, American Wigeon, Mallard, Northern Shoveler, Northern Pintail, and teal are numerous. Every so often, a very rare American Black Duck or Cinnamon Teal can be spotted. Short-eared Owl, Peregrine Falcon, and Western Meadowlark are outside possibilities. During late November, a build-up of Snow Geese and a few Ross's reaches its zenith. A Golden Eagle might be found. Spring and fall bring large flocks of mixed shorebirds including Semipalmated, Western, Least, and White-rumped (spring only) Sandpipers, Dunlin, Buff-breasted Sandpiper, and Long-billed Dowitcher. Canvasback, Redhead, Ring-necked Duck, Greater and Lesser Scaup, Bufflehead, Hooded Merganser, and Ruddy Duck have been seen at the ponds in winter, as well as Osprey and Bald Eagle. Vagrant Say's Phoebe and Vermilion Flycatcher have wintered in the area. The hedgerows during winter house a variety of sparrows, including Fox, Song, Lincoln's, Swamp, White-throated, and White-crowned.

Migration in the Cheneyville area is busy. Flocks of geese and ducks wing overhead or feed in the fields. Warblers swarm the bayou and hardwood bottoms. A variety of shorebirds seek sustenance on the expansive mudflats. Swallow flocks of Tree, Northern Rough-winged, Bank, Cliff, and Barn fly the fields and ponds, particularly during fall.

OVERTON LOCK AND DAM

Overton Lock and Dam is one of many such complexes constructed along the Red River to provide recreation and aid shipping. The entire area is an island, surrounded by an old oxbow. A few acres next to the road are mowed. The bulk is left to nature. The facility is all but deserted in winter, much to the delight of local birders. From late fall to spring, American Pipit is common and Sprague's Pipit can be seen with a little work. This is a great place to work wintering sparrows, with Vesper, Savannah, Grasshopper (occasional), Le Conte's, Fox, Song, Swamp, White-throated, and White-crowned possible. Northern Harrier and American Kestrel are common. Merlin is seen sporadically and there is at least one record of Rough-legged Hawk from the dam. Nesters arriving in spring include Mississippi Kite, Osprey, Broad-winged Hawk, Yellow-billed Cuckoo, Eastern Kingbird, Blue Grosbeak, Indigo and Painted Buntings, and Dickcissel. Late April and early May coincides with a fairly reliable passage of Bobolinks through the site.

Visiting the Overton complex can be a side trip to an outing in Cheneyville. To get to the locks from Cheneyville, take Cheneyville-Echo Road, then Sandy Lane north to the stop sign at LA-1 in Echo (6.5 miles). During winter, look for Rusty and Brewer's Blackbirds at the small dairy on the right, as you make the left turn onto Sandy Lane. Turn left onto LA-1, drive north for 1.8 miles, and turn right onto LA-457. From here, it is 5.8 miles to the unsigned Overton Lock entrance road on the right. In half a mile a road on the left leads to a boat launch with interesting riparian habitat and after a mile you reach a small parking lot with restrooms; only a few fishermen use the banks, casting into the tailrace.

From Alexandria, head south on LA-1 from its junction with US-167 near the Red River. At 9.0 miles, turn left onto LA-457 and travel 3.5 miles. The entrance road is on the left. This side of the unit is located adjacent to the highland overlooking the Red River Valley to the west. Given a choice, the west side of the facility offers better birding.

ELBOW SLOUGH WILDLIFE MANAGEMENT AREA

This site can be accessed from the Overton site. Return to the junction of LA-1198 and LA-1. Turn right (north) and drive 1.5 miles to LA-3170; turn left and go 0.3 mile. On your left is a small gravel road leading to Elbow Slough Wildlife Management Area. You must park near the check station at the gate and fill out a day-use form before proceeding, on foot, into the unit.

After several hundred yards, you will pass an office/equipment complex and reach a large 80+-acre impoundment with Elbow Slough on the left side of the impoundment. Most of the unit is taken up by the impoundment, which offers good walking on the levee. The impoundment is kept dry from May–October and grain crops are cultivated to attract doves for public hunting in September–October. After October, the drain is stopped and rain water is allowed to accumulate in the impoundment to provide shallow water/moist soil habitat for waterbirds.

Because of the nature of the unit, waterbirds—especially dabbling ducks, shorebirds, and waders—dominate the site. However, White-eyed Vireo, Common Yellowthroat, Yellow-breasted Chat, and Indigo and Painted Buntings nest there. There is a good mix of wintering sparrows—Field, Vesper, Savannah, Le Conte's, Song, Swamp, White-throated, and White-crowned. In the winter, Yellow-headed (very rare) and Rusty (occasional) Blackbirds have been found in association with Red-winged Blackbirds. There are occasionally fly-overs of Sandhill Cranes.

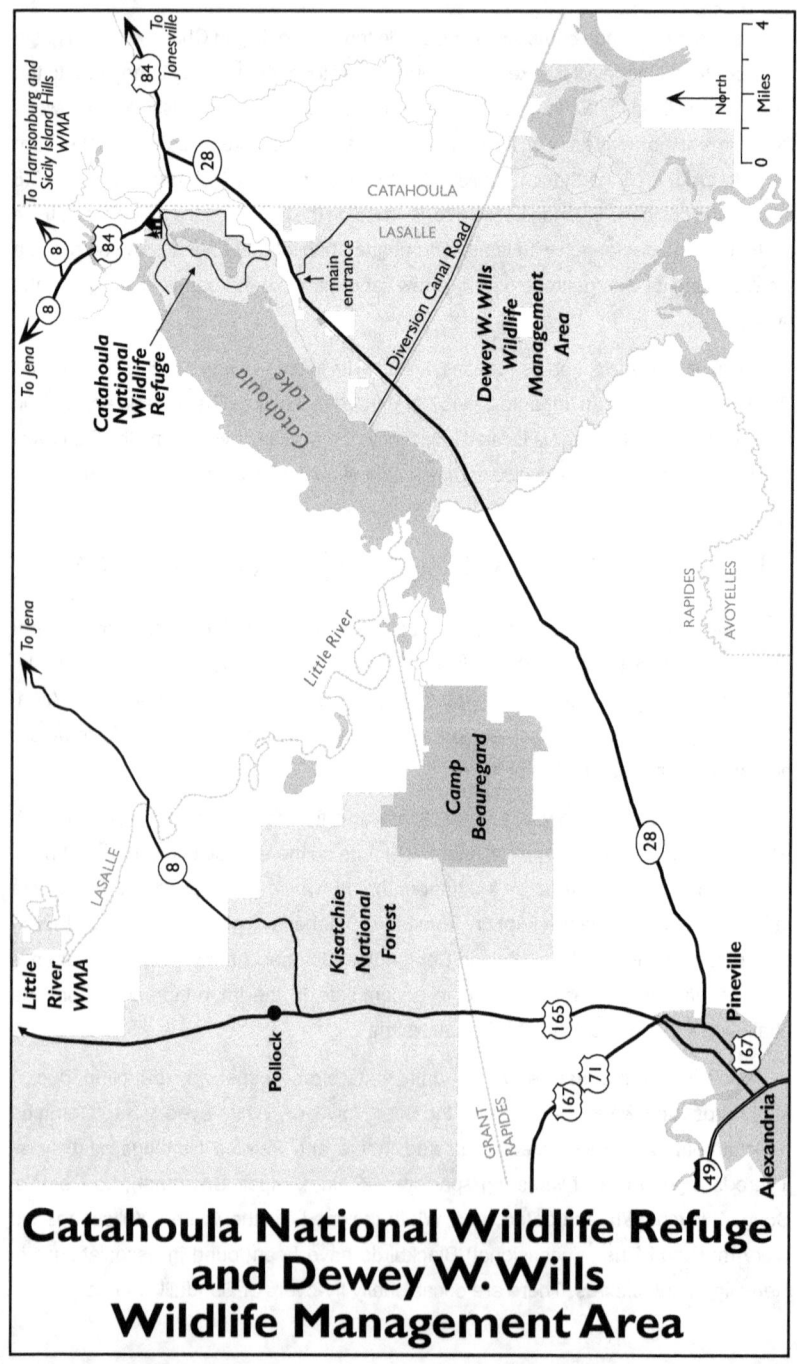

Catahoula National Wildlife Refuge and Dewey W. Wills Wildlife Management Area

CATAHOULA NATIONAL WILDLIFE REFUGE AND DEWEY W. WILLS WILDLIFE MANAGEMENT AREA

Catahoula National Wildlife Refuge was established in 1958 for wintering waterfowl. It has tens of thousands of acres managed for wetland birds, and restoration and creation of bottomland habitats continue. There are also several fallow fields where winter sparrow flocks can be searched. The refuge offers an auto tour and hiking trails.

To reach Catahoula National Wildlife Refuge from Pineville, head east on LA-28 from its junction with US-167. Zero your odometer here. Woodlands and pastures dominate the landscape for the first 17 miles or so. The road then passes through a vast drainage area, which has historically been a part of the Mississippi floodplain. Cypress swamps, sloughs, and hardwood bottoms typify the vegetation.

A diversion canal with a sluice was built to regulate the depth of Catahoula Lake for duck hunting. The road crosses this canal at 21.7 miles. The road atop the levee on the canal's east bank can be explored in both directions. To the west, the road leads to the sluice and the main lake. From here, thousands of ducks, American White Pelicans, and gulls are visible during winter. Catahoula Lake harbors the largest population of Canvasbacks in the United States and refuge staff keeps close tabs on their activity.

To the east, the levee road enters the Dewey W. Wills Wildlife Management Area where Red-headed Woodpecker, Gray Catbird, and Eastern Towhee reside year round. Winter visitors include American Woodcock, Blue-headed Vireo, Golden-crowned Kinglet, and Orange-crowned Warbler. Vesper Sparrow is fairly common during winter where short grasses border a creek or tree line. The well-signed main entrance to Dewey Wills is at 26.3 miles on LA-28. At 32 miles, LA-28 intersects with US-84. Turn left and proceed for 1.7 miles to a gravel road on the left, which leads to the brown-signed entrance to Catahoula National Wildlife Refuge.

A special amenity of this refuge is the Wildlife Drive, a 9-mile loop that features a nature trail leading to a lookout tower. From this tower, one or more Bald Eagles can usually be seen during fall and early winter. It's also an excellent perch from which to view the many species of puddle ducks found in the area. Also possible here are Osprey and Peregrine Falcon.

The cast of characters is dramatically enriched in late spring with the arrival of a host of breeders. During late winter and early spring, floodwaters generally make the loop impassable, but at other times, Catahoula is a delight.

SICILY ISLAND HILLS
WILDLIFE MANAGEMENT AREA

Sicily Island is the crown jewel of Louisiana's wildlife management system. It lies above the floodplains of the many bayous and rivers in the region and is an area of steep, forested slopes, winding brooks, and sylvan solitude. The deciduous woods of the innumerable ravines and hollows capture the imagination and transport the visitor to another time.

This intriguing location can be reached by traveling east on LA-28 for 32 miles from its intersection with US-167 in Pineville. (See map on page 128.) At this point, LA-28 empties onto US-84. Turn right and proceed for 10.2 miles to LA-124 in the town of

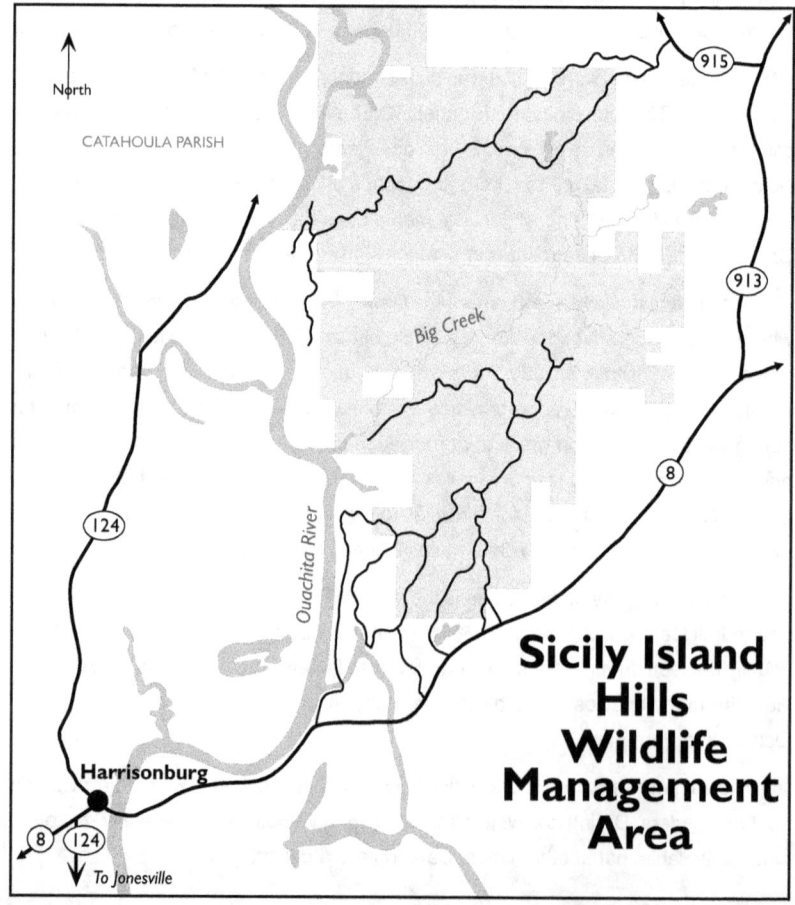

Jonesville. Turn left and continue north for 10 miles to LA-8. Turn right and follow this road through the quaint hillside town of Harrisonburg and across the Ouachita River. At the eastern end of the bridge, zero your odometer. At 4.5 miles, there is an opening on the left side of the highway that looks more like a poorly maintained private drive than a road. The road has no name, but is signed for the wildlife area. Turn left.

Upon entering the road, there are three ways to go. The right road leads up a hill and onto private property. The ruts on the left also wind into private property. Keep to the middle and the scarce-graveled path as it follows the left side of a slope. After a half mile or so, a sign on an old cattle gap announces that you have reached Sicily Island Hills Wildlife Management Area.

The road follows a ridge that meanders for several miles. At about the 3-mile mark, the Rock Falls Nature Trail on the right leads to Louisiana's highest waterfall. Although it's not a towering cascade, it is a pleasant location to spend a few reflective moments.

Louisiana Waterthrush nests along the stream above and below the falls. The nearby woods are a permanent home to the usual southeast deciduous forests species, including several warblers: Worm-eating, Black-and-white, Kentucky, Hooded, American Redstart, and Northern Parula. Flycatchers taking advantage of the long summer days are Eastern Wood-Pewee, Acadian, Great Crested, and Eastern Kingbird. Although a bit off the beaten path, the hour's drive is worthwhile just for the therapeutic value of the falls.

For more information: http://www.sicilyislandhills.com/nature-trails/.

Louisiana Waterthrush David Cagnolatti

138 CENTRAL LOUISIANA

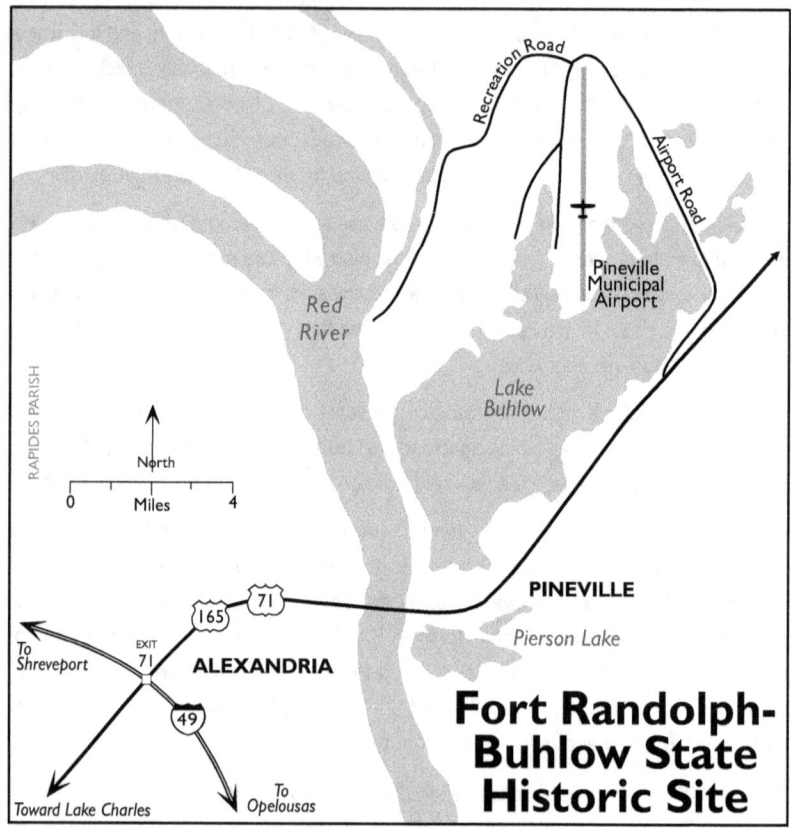

FORT RANDOLPH-BUHLOW STATE HISTORIC SITE

These Civil War earthen forts were built along the Red River by the Confederates to repel an attack that never came. The area, which includes Lake Buhlow and Buhlow airport, has since been developed into a recreation complex and is located within the city limits of Pineville. To get there, head north out of Alexandria on US-71 and cross the Red River. As you cross the river you will see Pierson Lake on the right and Lake Buhlow on the left. From the bottom of the bridge it is 0.9 mile to the Airport Road left turn.

Airport Road wraps around Lake Buhlow for a mile and then you can choose to continue on 0.3 mile toward the airport where a finger of the lake can be scanned or turn onto Recreation Road, which continues a mile to the Red River and provides access to a side channel of the Red River, open fields, and forest edge. The birding is pretty standard fare for Eastern deciduous forest and manicured fields. Substantial, mature mulberry trees line drainage ditches to the east of the road and also line the banks of the side channel. Search for migrating neotropical songbirds in April and May when these trees are heavy with mulberry fruits. Still, it is seldom crowded and is especially quiet during winter when wintering ducks, such as Northern Shoveler, Canvasback, Redhead, Ring-necked Duck, and perhaps a scaup or two, may be found.

Breeding season brings many new species to the park. Broad-winged Hawk, White-eyed Vireo, Northern Rough-winged Swallow, Gray Catbird, Blue Grosbeak, and Indigo and Painted Buntings nest in the vicinity. During spring, airports are often preferred habitat for grass-loving sandpipers. Upland and Buff-breasted Sandpipers may use the short grasses as stopover habitat around the perimeter of the airport on their journey north.

KISATCHIE NATIONAL FOREST

Louisiana is fortunate indeed to claim over 600,000 acres of forested uplands completely accessible to the public. Six separate ranger districts, five of which are located in the central portion of the state, provide recreational opportunities for birders, boaters, hikers, anglers, campers, and hunters. The Caney District, the only unit not in central Louisiana, has allowed the Red-cockaded Woodpecker to become extirpated within its confines. The remaining five, owing to the extensive efforts of dedicated wildlife biologists, still support a large number of active clusters (the term used to describe one or more family groups of woodpeckers occupying a group of roost trees), many of which are marked by two or three wide white bands painted on the trees.

The habitats included in Kisatchie National Forest are mature pine/oak stands, pine acreage managed for Red-cockaded Woodpecker, bottomland hardwoods, riparian, and the more ephemeral open tangles of cutovers. The variety of species generally found in the Kisatchie units is similar. In the central Louisiana districts, Red-cockaded Woodpecker is relatively easy to locate, particularly in late April and May when nesting takes place. So, too, are the species that enjoy the open understory provided by the controlled burns. Following are directions to five separate sites within the Kisatchie National Forest where Red-cockaded Woodpecker and other pine-associated species are easily found.

140 CENTRAL LOUISIANA

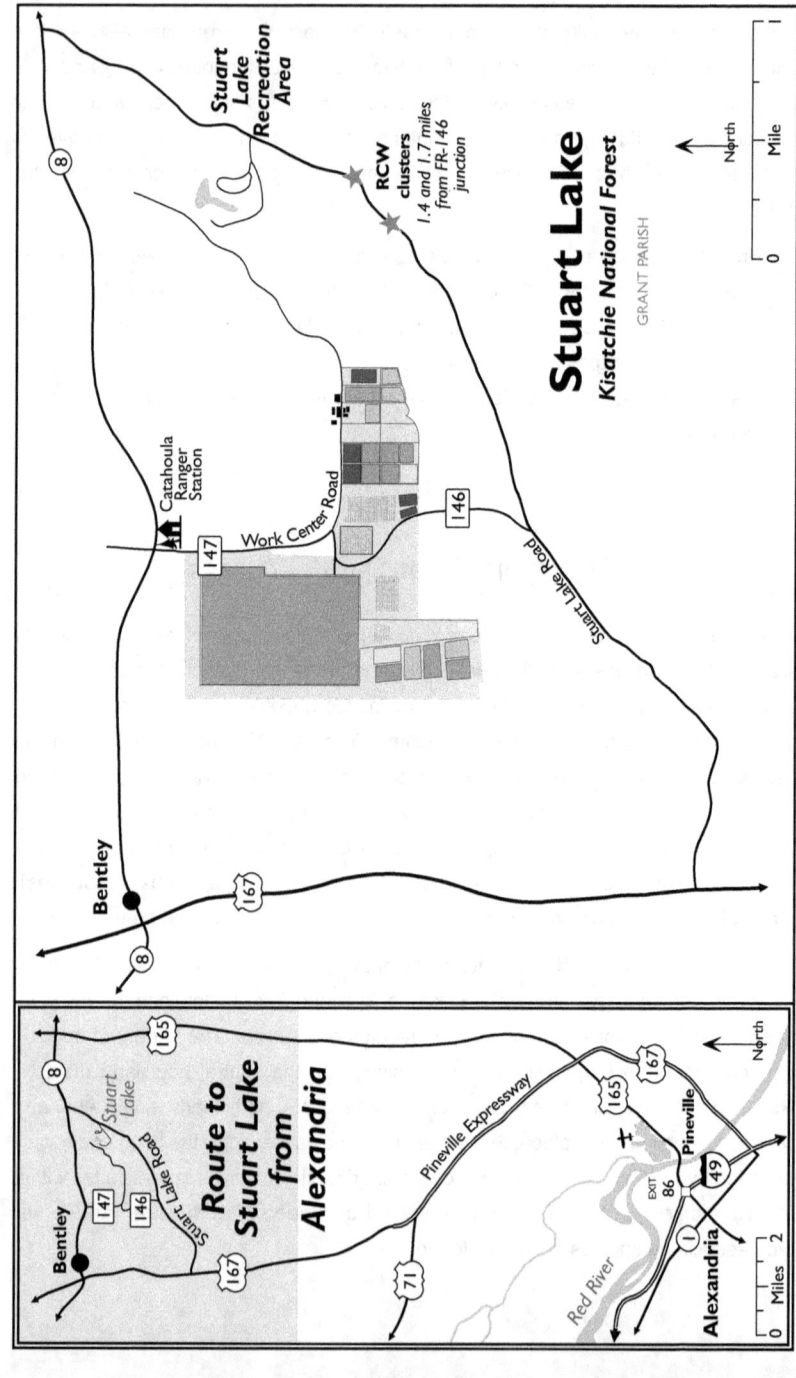

Stuart Lake

Located in the southern sector of Grant Parish, Stuart Lake lies in the Catahoula Ranger District of Kisatchie National Forest. The habitat is pine upland and the entire area could easily be traversed in a morning's hike. It should be pointed out that Stuart Lake is actually a pond covering no more than 15 total surface-acres. As a result, one should not expect to find a diversity of waterbirds at Stuart Lake.

To reach this sylvan delight, go north from Alexandria on US-167 for about 16 miles to the sleepy community of Bentley. Turn right (east) at the caution light onto LA-8 and proceed for 1.6 miles. Take another right onto FS-147, Work Center Road. This avenue passes a pine-seed orchard under which the grass is always mown, providing forage for many ground feeders. Follow this road for 0.8 mile. Take a right onto FR-146. Although only 1.1 miles in length, this gravel lane brushes shortgrass meadows and a tangle of mixed forest, the former good for Upland and Buff-breasted Sandpipers during spring. The meadows also support residents such as Eastern Bluebird and Eastern Meadowlark. During spring and summer, Eastern Kingbirds can be seen, as well as Eastern Wood-Pewee, Great Crested Flycatcher, Kentucky, Hooded, and Yellow-throated Warblers, and Summer Tanager.

Take a left when FR-146 intersects Stuart Lake Road. Proceed northeast on this winding asphalt for 1.4 miles. Here, several white-marked Longleaf Pines house a Red-cockaded Woodpecker cluster. Another active cluster can be found within yards of the road at 1.7 miles. The birds are most reliably found at cluster sites such as these very early and late in the day.

The open area beneath the pines is the result of controlled burns carried out in an attempt to approximate nature. Red-cockaded requires relatively mature longleaf pines, but it also insists that the area below its cluster site be open and without dense tangles.

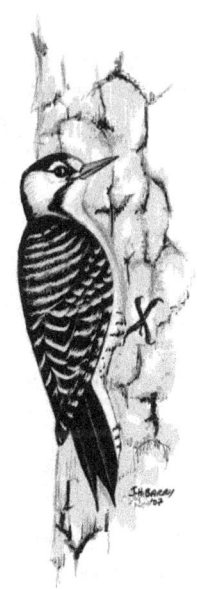

Red-cockaded Woodpecker Jessie Barry

Other species benefit from the burns. Bachman's Sparrow is a plentiful permanent resident here, although it's a skulker except during the early breeding season when singing. During winter, Henslow's Sparrow can be fairly numerous; however it often requires several flushes before it decides to perch and provide a good view.

Henslow's Sparrow   Erik I. Johnson

At 2.1 miles, another paved road leads to the left. This is the entrance to the Stuart Lake Recreation Area. Quiet during summer and abandoned during winter, Stuart Lake is a scenic spot where one can pause simply to enjoy the ambience or take a jaunt on the nature trail, along which one may hear the buzz of Worm-eating Warbler during spring and early summer. When you leave the recreation area, turn left onto Stuart Lake Road for a mile to LA-8; a left turn takes you back to US-167 in less than 4 miles.

LITTLE CYPRESS POND

Found within the largest concentration of Red-cockaded clusters west of the Mississippi, this marvelous locale in the Vernon District is somewhat out of the way, but worth the effort. It's also a great place for the other pine-associated species such as Chuck-will's-widow, Pine and Yellow-throated Warblers, and Bachman's Sparrow.

To get to Little Cypress Pond from Alexandria, drive south on US-165 for about 22 miles to the village of Glenmora and turn right, or west, on LA-113. (See map on page 128.) Stay on LA-113 for 21.6 miles until it intersects with LA-10 (Pitkin Highway) at the community of Pitkin. Turn right (west) onto LA-10 and drive another 16 miles. Turn right onto FR-400, a gravel road. In 0.3 mile turn left onto FR-471. In 0.5 mile you can

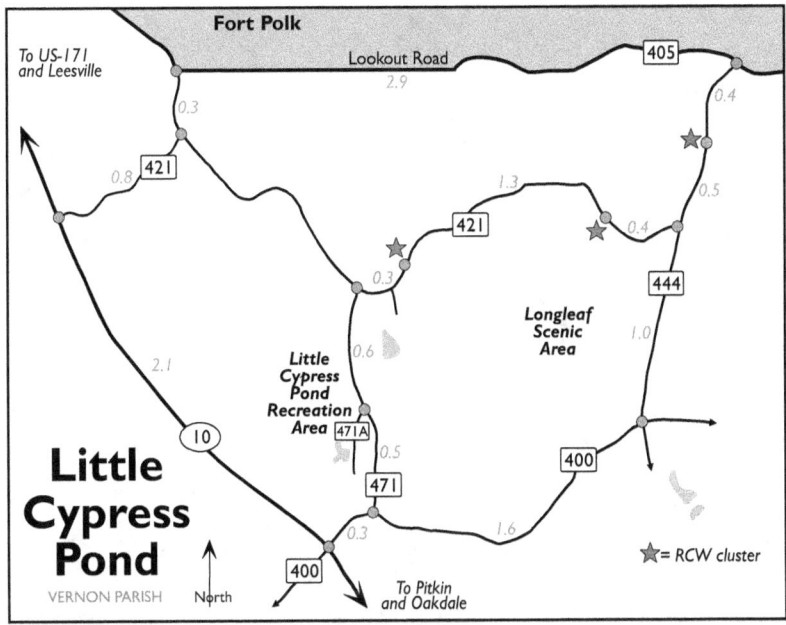

make a sharp left turn onto FR-471A to visit Little Cypress Pond Recreation Area. The birding in the immediate area is park-like.

Return to FR-471 and continue north 0.6 mile to a T-intersection with FR-421. Turn right. On the left in 0.3 mile is an active Red-cockaded Woodpecker cluster. Another cluster is located on the right 1.3 miles farther along. Continue on to a stop sign in 0.4 mile and turn left onto FR-444. There is another active woodpecker cluster ahead 0.5 mile from this intersection. Less than half a mile ahead, FR-444 intersects paved Lookout Road (FR-405) where you might encounter military traffic from nearby Fort Polk. There is no need to continue farther, so backtrack to LA-10. A possible diversion on your return route is a side trip departing from the stop sign at the FR-421/444 junction to visit the Longleaf Scenic Area. This is one the best areas in the state to find Greater Roadrunner.

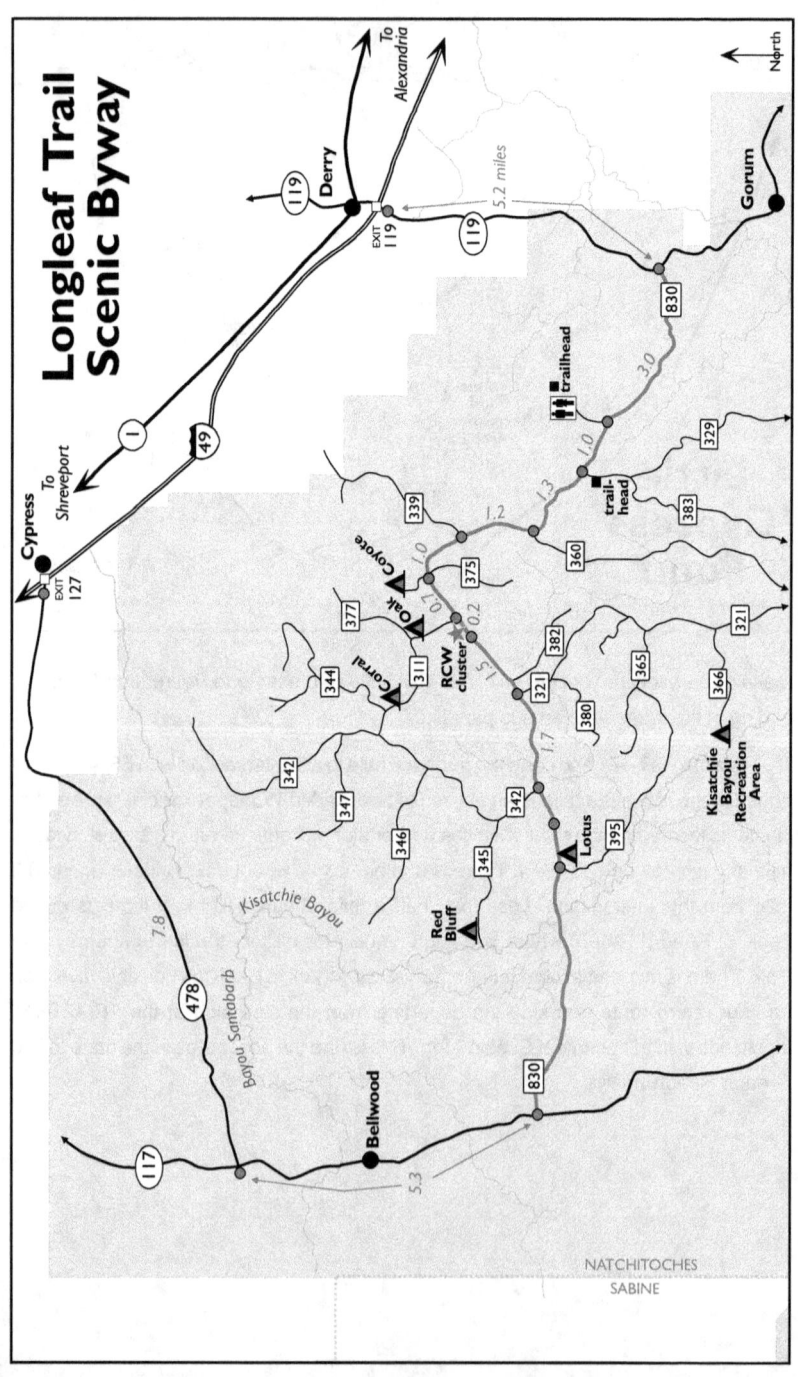

Longleaf Trail Scenic Byway

The vast expanse of forested hills makes this exotic locale a strong draw for serious backpackers as well as birders. Longleaf Trail is the heart of the Kisatchie Unit of Kisatchie National Forest. Pine/oak uplands, streams, and hardwood bottoms provide prime habitat for dozens of breeding, wintering, and resident species. Wild Turkey is an uncommon resident. Broad-winged Hawk nests in the hills. American Kestrel is a rare breeder, while Eastern Towhee is common at all seasons. Summer Tanager is "can't miss" in the nesting season. Acadian Flycatcher and Louisiana Waterthrush are uncommon during spring and early summer in the riparian areas and stream edges, respectively.

To find this spot, take I-49 northwest from Alexandria some 33 miles to Exit 119. Turn left (south) onto LA-119 and drive for 5.2 miles. Turn right onto PR-830, Longleaf Trail Scenic Byway. (Some maps show this road as FH-59.) At 3.0 miles a side road to the right leads 0.3 mile to restrooms and parking for a short nature trail to a scenic viewpoint. In another mile, Mora-Red Dirt Road (PR-329) also has trailhead parking—the 10.5-mile Caroline Dormon Trail departs from here for hikers, bikers, and equestrians. The other end of the trail is at Kisatchie Bayou Recreation Area (see map). Continue west on PR-830 for 1.3 miles to the junction with PR-360 coming in from the left (south). You should explore this road as well as PR-339 that intersects from the north in another 1.2 miles.

One mile farther along the byway (now 7.5 miles from LA-119) a road on the right leads to Coyote Camp primitive campground. Continue on PR-830, now headed southwest. At 0.7 mile PR-311 on the right leads to a pair of primitive campgrounds, Oak and Corral Camps. Just 0.2 mile past this junction, on the right, is a large and active Red-cockaded Woodpecker cluster.

Continue 1.5 miles to PR-321 on the left, which leads to Kisatchie Bayou Recreation Area, mentioned above. In another 1.7 miles, Red Bluff FR-342 is located on the right; Core Camp is also on the right 1.1 miles farther along. The last intersection before reaching the main highway is Lotus Camp. Prairie Warbler breeds here. Brown-headed Nuthatch and Pine Warbler are residents. The call of Northern Bobwhite, growing rather scarce throughout much of its range, often is heard here.

Unless you are inclined to retrace your route, turn right when PR-830 intersects LA-117 and drive north for 5.3 miles through the community of Bellwood to LA-478. Turn right—I-49 Exit 127 is ahead in 7.8 miles.

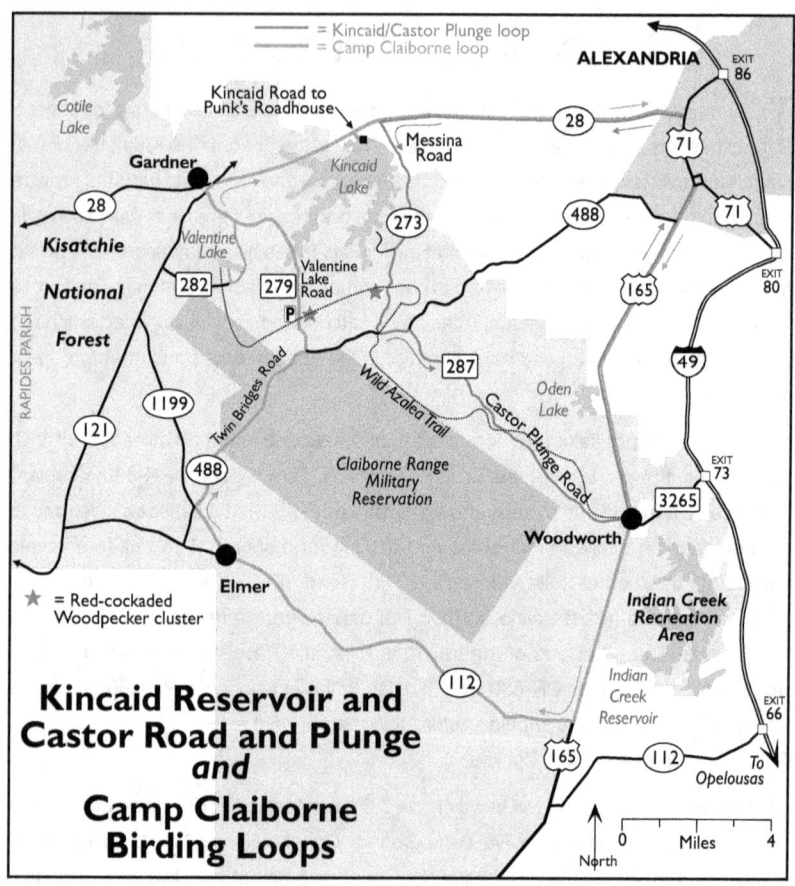

KINCAID RESERVOIR AND
CASTOR PLUNGE ROAD AND BOTTOMS

This elegant locale is found within a 15-minute drive of Alexandria and offers great hiking, camping, fishing, and birding. To find it, take LA-28 west (labeled Monroe Street in Alexandria, Coliseum Boulevard on the west side of town, and finally Leesville Highway outside of town) from its intersection with US-71, also called MacArthur Drive, for 8.0 miles to Messina Road (FR-273). This stretch of road is excellent during summer for Scissor-tailed Flycatcher.

Turn left onto Messina Road (FR-273) and travel about 2 miles, where it turns to gravel. Follow the gravel road for 2.8 miles to a parking area on the right. Here, the Wild Azalea Trail crosses the road and can be hiked in either direction. To the northwest,

Red-cockaded Woodpecker, Brown-headed Nuthatch, and Pine Warbler can be seen within the first quarter mile or so. The creek bottoms harbor Blue-gray Gnatcatcher and Louisiana Waterthrush during spring and summer, and the understory is a breeding site for Kentucky and Hooded Warblers. Golden-crowned Kinglet, Purple Finch, and American Goldfinch are regulars during winter. The grasses beneath the open woods are home to Henslow's Sparrow during winter and Bachman's Sparrow year round. The pine savannas often yield looks at Field Sparrow during fall and winter. The mixed hardwood habitats are good for wintering Blue-headed Vireo and Hermit Thrush. These same areas provide nesting spots for Eastern Wood-Pewee, Great Crested Flycatcher, Yellow-throated and Red-eyed Vireos, and Summer Tanager. And, during spring, the early riser can often be greeted by the gobble of a Wild Turkey on a distant ridge.

Continue along the gravel road for another 1.4 miles to LA-488 and take a left. Proceed for 0.8 mile and turn right onto FR-287—Castor Plunge Road—which winds through the Kisatchie for the next 7 miles or so, dipping into two extensive hardwood bottoms along the way. These bottoms, scarred by rills and creeks, are marvelous habitat for Winter Wren during the colder months. A bit of *pish*ing can often summon Hairy Woodpecker, Brown Creeper, House Wren, Ruby-crowned Kinglet, Orange-crowned Warbler, and Eastern Towhee. The bottoms are wonderful places to seek breeding neotropical songbirds including Wood Thrush, White-eyed, Red-eyed, and Yellow-throated Vireos, Northern Parula, Louisiana Waterthrush, and Prothonotary and Hooded Warblers. Castor Plunge Road intersects with US-165 about 1.5 miles beyond the village of Woodworth. Turn left onto US-165 to return to Alexandria.

White-eyed Vireo   Joseph Turner

Camp Claiborne Loop

This loop covers many of the same habitats as Kincaid Reservoir/Castor Road and Plunge Route and, therefore, many of the same birds can be found. This trip takes you to a camp that was once an army post and is now part of the Kisatchie National Forest.

To reach the camp, head south from Alexandria on US-165. From the traffic light in Woodworth, continue for 5.3 miles and turn right onto LA-112. The mixture of pine and hardwood habitat houses several resident species, including Greater Roadrunner. The tangled cutovers provide a summer home to Prairie Warbler, Indigo Bunting, and Orchard Oriole.

Follow LA-112 for 11 miles to the small community of Elmer and LA-1199. Most of the trip traverses national forest land and allows for excellent birding. The bulk of this property is accessible to the public. The spring morning chorus in cutover pine stands on nearby private property includes Northern Bobwhite, Eastern Kingbird, Scissor-tailed Flycatcher, Brown Thrasher, Prairie Warbler, Common Yellowthroat, Eastern Towhee, and Orchard Oriole. American Woodcock is fairly common during winter— and is best seen at dusk. Sparrow flocks in the winter can include Chipping, Field, Vesper, Fox, and Song.

At LA-1199, turn right, proceed 1.6 miles, and turn right onto LA-488. Continue on LA-488 (Twin Bridges Road) for 5.1 miles to the Forest Service's Evangeline Work Center, where you take a left onto FR-279. At 1 mile, there is a small parking area on the left where the Wild Azalea Trail cuts through. Across the road from this spot is an inactive Red-cockaded Woodpecker cluster, although an active site is just to the south, also on the east side of the road.

Prairie Warbler   Jim E. Johnson

At 2.7 miles, the road cuts through an arm of Kincaid Lake. From the bridge crossing this finger of water, Prothonotary Warbler can be found during spring and summer, along with Pied-billed Grebe, Anhinga, Green Heron, Blue Grosbeak, and Orchard Oriole. Wood Duck and Red-headed Woodpecker can be seen year round. This is often a good place for Osprey or Bald Eagle; the eagle nests in the Kincaid Lake Recreation Area day-use area and is accessible for viewing. (Also, much of the lake is visible from the day-use area, which is a good place to scope in winter for ducks and occasional Common Loons and American White Pelicans.) At 4.9 miles, the road leading to Valentine Lake comes in from the left (FR-282). The 2.6 miles of winding asphalt provides several options for birders, including cutovers, hardwood bottoms, sandy creeks, and a small lake.

Valentine Lake is a mildly popular recreation area during the more desirable camping weekends. During much of the remainder of the year, however, the place is mostly deserted. Red-eyed Vireos sing constantly through summer. Less evident, but a regular breeder, is Yellow-throated Vireo. Louisiana Waterthrush can be found in spring and early summer near the creek bottoms. Gray Catbird can be sought in the brush of the hardwoods, near the nesting spots of Acadian and Great Crested Flycatchers and Hooded and Kentucky Warblers. Alligators patrol the lake.

To return to Alexandria, go back to the intersection of FR-282 and FR-279. Bear to the left for 0.9 mile and turn right onto LA-121. After only 0.3 mile, this road intersects with LA-28 in the town of Gardner. Take a right here and travel 12 miles to Alexandria. This stretch of road is a good spot to find breeding Scissor-tailed Flycatchers.

Approximately 4 miles east of Gardner, you will find Kincaid Road. Turn right and travel 0.2 mile to the parking lot of Tunk's Cypress Inn restaurant. Park in the parking lot adjacent to a cove on Kincaid Reservoir near the dam. Walk across an emergency spillway, climb the forested hill, and proceed to the Kincaid Reservoir dam. The reservoir and associated riparian areas are excellent for birding at all times of the year. However, the period from October to April can be especially rewarding with respect to finding waterbirds, especially waterfowl. A rare White-winged Scoter and an equally rare Western Grebe were recorded at this location. This is also an area to visit for seabirds during hurricane and tropical storm passages during the hurricane season. Black Terns and Franklin's Gulls can be encountered during fall migration.

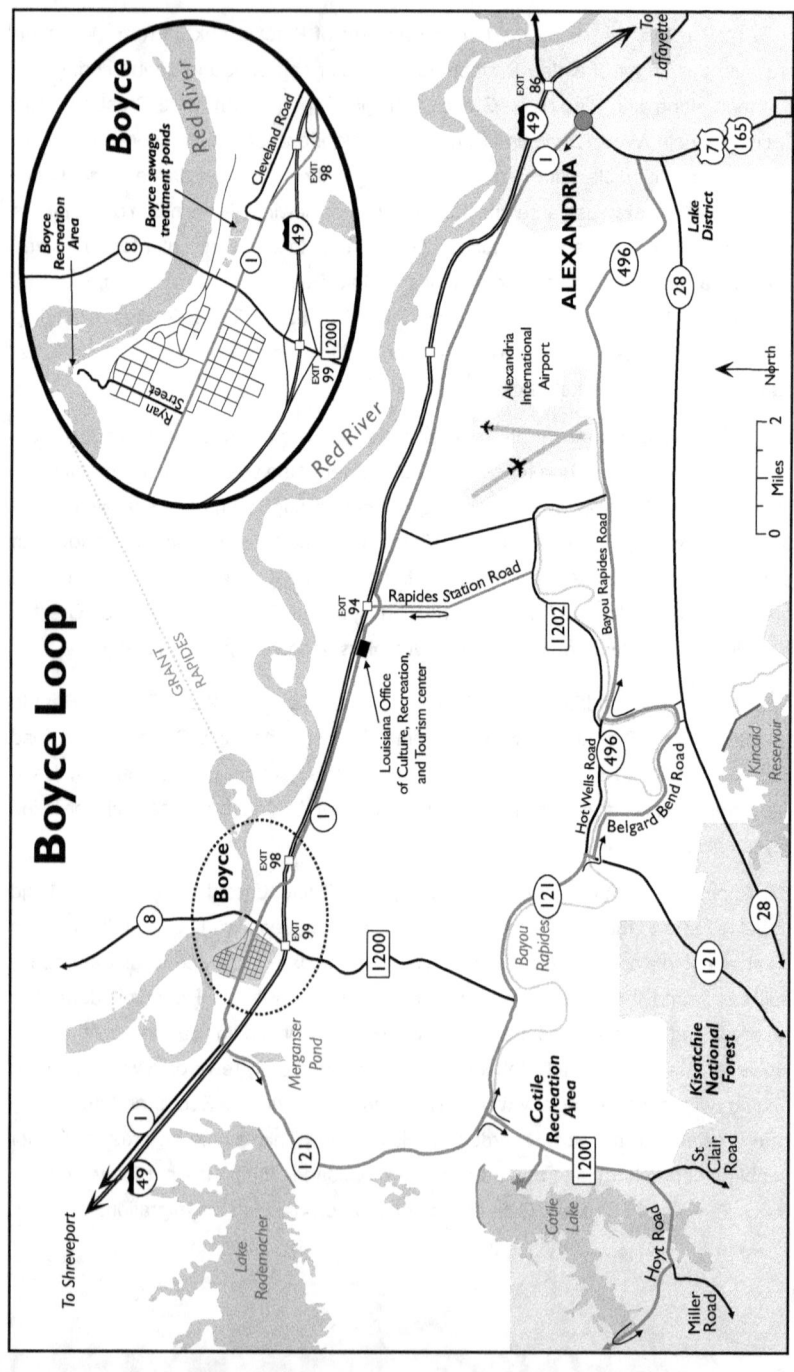

Boyce Loop

This area is just northwest of Alexandria. Most of this short route is through river-bottom farmland, but the few accessible hedgerows, Cotile Lake, and vast row-crop fields provide ample bird habitat. The best time to visit is during migration and winter. To get to Boyce Loop from the west side of Alexandria, start at the intersection of US-71 and LA-1.

A most interesting option before starting Boyce Loop is to take US-71 for 1.4 miles southwestward to the intersection of LA-28, go right 1.1 miles to Ansley Boulevard on your left, just past Menard High School. Turn left on Ansley Boulevard and enter the Lake District of Alexandria. Go 0.2 mile to the intersection of Provine Place and turn right, traveling less than 100 yards to the Alexandria South Side Library for parking. To the east, there is currently an open field that may eventually be developed. There are numerous water-retention ponds. A walking path on the east side of the Lake District leads to the east and is flanked by a diversion canal with decent riparian growth and retention ponds. Roughly half a mile from the library, the footpath passes through a 20-acre wooded area, where the retention pond is an undeveloped natural swamp slough with massive cypress trees. A potpourri of birds can be found along this walkway at any time of year. Wood Ducks are almost always present along with herons and egrets and sometimes ibises and spoonbills. The slough is a place to check blackbirds carefully in winter for Rusty Blackbirds.

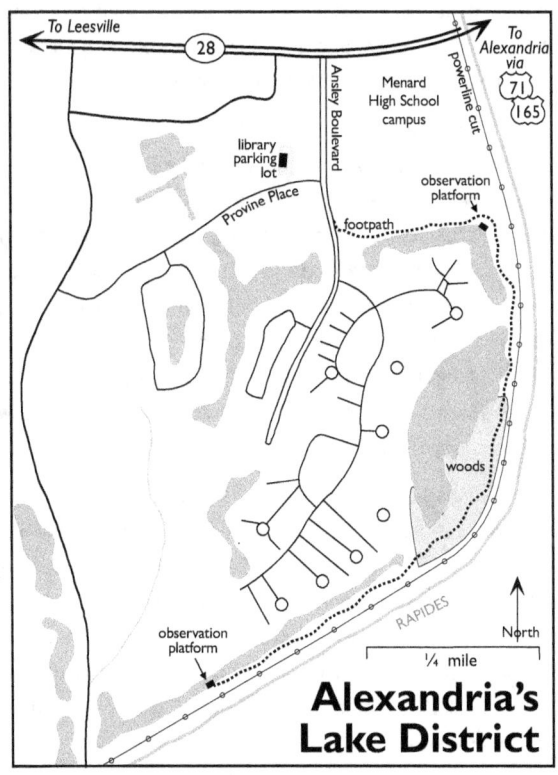

Alexandria's Lake District

Scissor-tailed Flycatchers are commonly encountered in spring and summer on power lines along Provine Boulevard.

If you choose not to visit the Lake District, travel northwest on LA-1 for 7.5 miles to Rapides Station Road, which can be explored for sparrows during winter and buntings during spring and summer. The Louisiana Office of Culture, Recreation and Tourism operates a tourist center at the Rapides Station junction that offers a good place for a break. Continuing northwest on LA-1, go 4.5 miles to the outskirts of Boyce. Immediately after crossing the I-49 overpass, look to your right for Cleveland Road; turn onto it. Immediately after crossing the railroad track, look left into the Boyce sewage treatment pond complex. This site can be good for Hooded Merganser during the winter and other ducks including shovelers and scaup.

Return to LA-1 and drive 1.1 miles through town to Ryan Street, turn right, and look for a sign directing you to the **Boyce Recreation Area**, 0.4 mile ahead at the Red River levee. Cross the levee onto the property, roughly 20 acres adjacent to an oxbow leading to the Red River. A picnic area and a free-standing restroom facility and boat launch make this a nice place to stop. Any number of birds may be expected to pass the area in fall and spring migrations. Two or three pairs of Baltimore Orioles nest in trees near the oxbow bank. Mississippi Kites nest in the immediate area.

Return to LA-1, turn right for 1.0 mile, and then turn left under the interstate onto LA-121. Cliff Swallows have established a small colony on the wall of the underpass. At 0.5 mile, Merganser Pond on the left is on private property, but it can be scoped from the side of the road. This is a dangerous area and stopping immediately adjacent to the pond is simply not safe. There is a turnout to agricultural fields just past the pond where one can safely pull off the road, being sure to park on the shoulder so as to not block access to the fields. Puddle and diving ducks are often abundant here and it's not unusual to find Gadwall, Northern Pintail, Green-winged Teal, Redhead, Bufflehead, Hooded Merganser, and Ruddy Duck swimming together in winter. A Long-tailed Duck was once reported accompanying a flock of Redheads.

From the pond, continue south on LA-121 for 4.6 miles. Turn right onto LA-1200 and continue for 0.9 mile to Cotile Lake Road and make another right. Cotile Lake Road leads to **Cotile Recreation Area**, a Rapides Parish-operated facility complete with campsites, boat launch, and picnic tables. A small fee is charged to enter. The forest mix here contains a greater percentage of deciduous trees than Kisatchie National Forest, making it more attractive to migrating warblers and other passerines. Yellow-bellied (uncommon) and Least Flycatchers can be seen during migration, particularly in fall, along with Warbling and Philadelphia (uncommon) Vireos. A small group of White-breasted Nuthatches occupies the park. Bald Eagles are present year round and are most easily viewed from the recreation area at the beach/boat launch area. Scoping the waters along the dam face during the winter can reveal an interesting potpourri of puddle and diving ducks and an occasional Common Loon or Horned Grebe may be observed. Tropical storm weather in summer and fall can bring in seabirds such as frigatebirds, Brown Pelicans, skimmers, and pelagic terns to this area. Black Terns may be found during fall migration.

Continue south on LA-1200 for 3.1 miles to **Hoyt Road** and turn right. Continue 1.1 miles to a causeway across the southwest arm of Cotile Lake. There is really no place to park unless one asks permission to park in a yard on either side of the causeway. There is little traffic on the causeway and careful drivers can search for birds by driving slowly and stopping. There is a major spring/summer rookery dominated by Cattle Egrets but also with Great and Snowy Egrets and Little Blue Herons and Anhingas. Purple Gallinules are seen regularly foraging on water lily pads from mid-April into mid-September.

To return to Alexandria, go back to the LA-1200/LA-121 junction and take a right onto LA-121. The fields on the left should be scanned during winter for Horned Lark, American Pipit, and Lapland Longspur. At 4.3 miles, LA-121 veers right to cross Bayou Rapides. Just after crossing the bridge, take a left onto Belgard Bend Road. Check the bayou for Belted Kingfisher and Rusty Blackbird during winter. During late February and March, American Golden-Plover can often be seen in the fields on the right. Rarely, a couple of individuals will hang on until early May, by which time they have donned their gorgeous nuptial plumage. You can return to Alexandria via LA-28 (see map) or complete the Belgard Bend Road loop to return via LA-496.

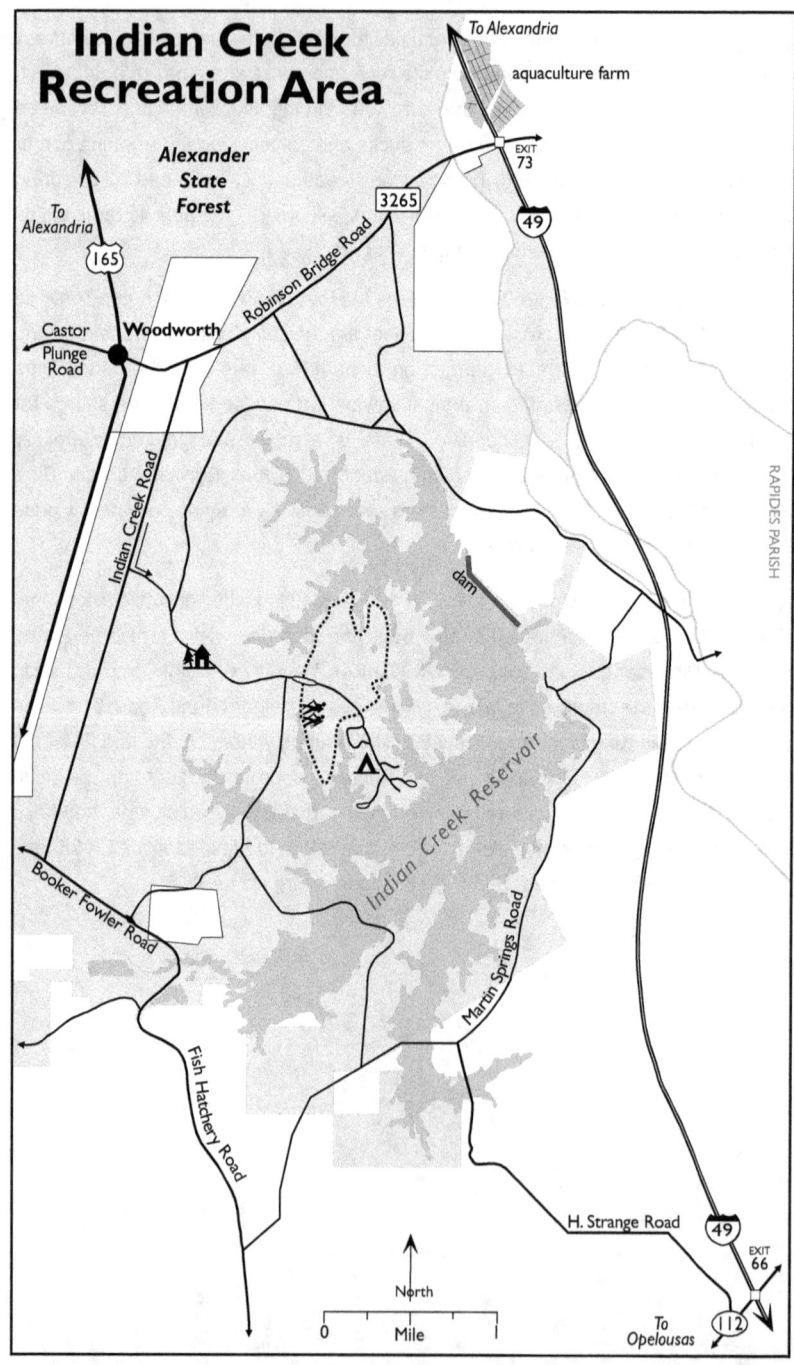

Indian Creek Recreation Area

The Indian Creek Recreation Area is part of Alexander State Forest and features a nature trail, primitive camping, boat launch, picnic tables, and full-hook-up RV sites. The woods just outside the park are nice, as well. To get to the park from Alexandria, take I-49 south for 6.3 miles from its intersection with US-71. Take Exit 73, Woodworth. Turn right onto PR-3265, also known as Robinson Bridge Road.

An aquaculture farm on the right near the Woodworth interchange can be checked out from the service road. Osprey and Bald Eagle may be seen here during winter, as well as American Wigeon, Canvasback, Redhead, Greater Scaup, American Avocet, and Bonaparte's Gull. Depending on water levels, sandpipers may be found during winter and during migration. Black Tern is a migrant here, along with most of the swallow species occurring in Louisiana. White and White-faced Ibises and Roseate Spoonbill are here during summer, as is Wood Stork.

Drive west on PR-3265 for 2.1 miles to Indian Creek Road and turn left. At 1.1 miles, the blacktop makes a 90-degree left turn and then winds about for another 1.3 miles until it reaches the park entrance. There is an entrance fee for automobiles, but walkers are generally not charged.

An alternate route from Alexandria can be taken by traveling south on US-165 from its intersection with Horseshoe Drive (LA-488). Go 8 miles to the traffic light in Woodworth and turn left onto PR-3265 (Robinson Bridge Road). Proceed for 0.4 mile and turn right onto Indian Creek Road. If you follow the US-165 route, half way between Alexandria and Woodworth, there is a low area on the right that might contain several acres of mudflats and crawfish ponds. During spring, shorebirds stop over and Wood Ducks with their young can be seen. Anhinga, Little Blue, Tricolored, and Green Herons, and Black-crowned Night-Heron also nest here. Check for Black-necked Stilt. And during late summer, an occasional Wood Stork from the south can be found, along with migrating yellowlegs and peep arriving from the north. This may be a good area for an assortment of ducks in winter.

At Indian Creek, trees that house active Red-cockaded Woodpecker clusters are marked with wide white bands. Spring is the best time to see them. In addition to the woodpecker, all of the expected pineywoods species can be found at Indian Creek. During summer, Yellow-throated Warbler frequents the mixed woodlands while Prairie Warbler sings in the new growth. Chuck-will's-widow, Eastern Wood-Pewee, Great Crested Flycatcher, Yellow-throated and Red-eyed Vireos, Kentucky and Hooded Warblers, Northern Parula, Yellow-breasted Chat, Summer

Tanager, Blue Grosbeak, and Indigo and Painted Buntings migrate here to nest. The reservoir at Indian Creek provides habitat for a few species of ducks each winter, along with an Osprey or two and perhaps a Bald Eagle (which may nest on the lake). Belted Kingfisher is common on the lake during winter and Ring-billed is the default gull. American Goldfinch is a fairly common winter visitor and Purple Finch might make an appearance. The open water near the dam usually hosts a pair of Common Loons during the colder months, as well as Horned Grebe. Overall, Indian Creek is well worth a look at any season.

Swainson's Warbler   Richard E. Gibbons

Boardwalk at Chicot State Park   Michael Harvey

CHICOT STATE PARK AND THE LOUISIANA STATE ARBORETUM

Chicot State Park was established in 1997 and quickly became a popular destination in central Louisiana. The park's location, only 45 miles south of Alexandria and 60 miles north of Lafayette, makes it an easy day-trip from either city. The 6,400-acre park has cabins and campsites to accommodate overnight visits. Chicot Lake is the main feature with canoe rentals and three boat ramps. Circling the lake are 22 miles of trails with primitive campsites and access to cypress/tupelo bottomlands and mature hickory/beech uplands.

To get to the park from Alexandria, take I-49 south for about 35 miles to Exit 46 (LA-106, St. Landry). The drive's birding opportunities vary with the season. After leaving the pine hills, the road passes through farms and wet woods. During late spring and summer, Swallow-tailed Kite is occasionally spotted. Mississippi Kite is fairly common, as is Black-necked Stilt and a variety of herons. (To get to the park from Lafayette, take I-49 north to Exit 46, St. Landry.)

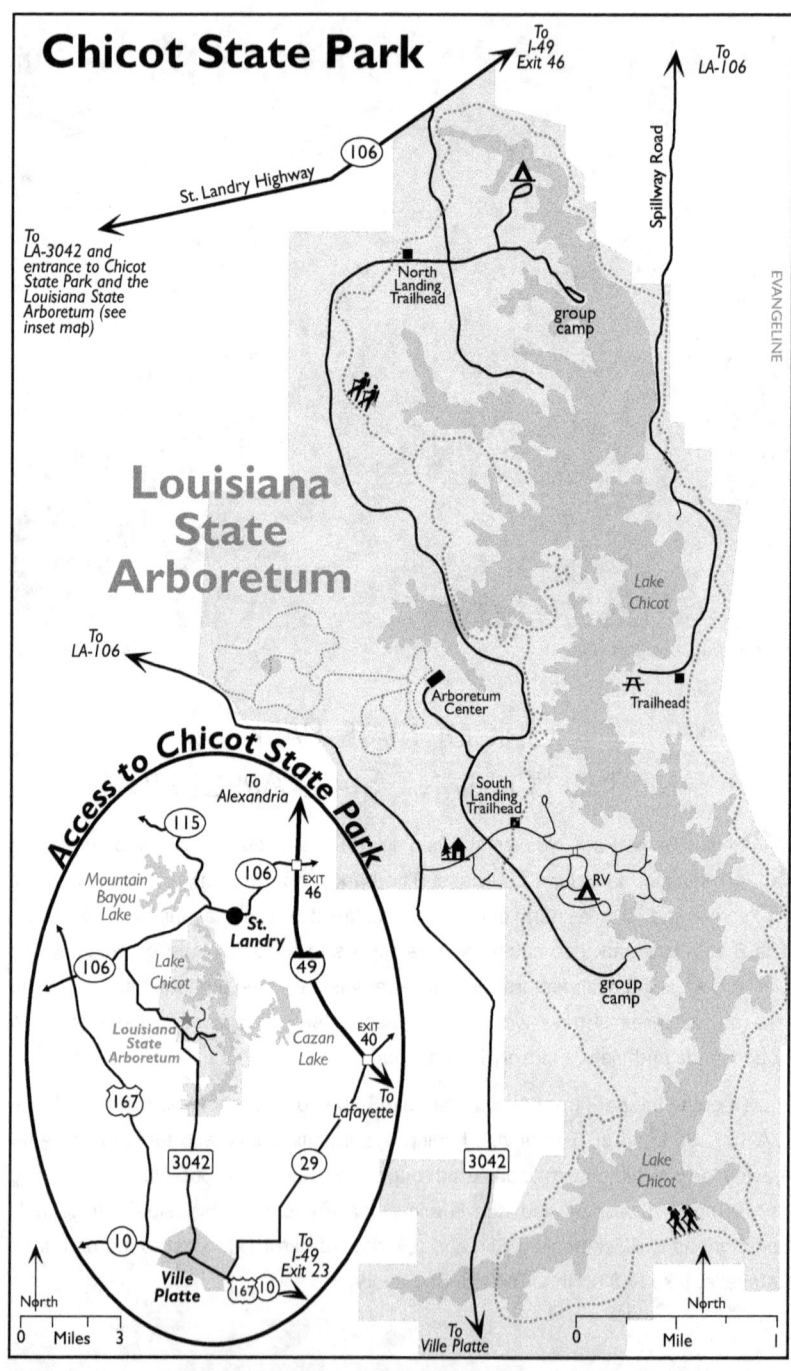

To get to the park from the north, turn right at I-49, Exit 46 and travel 3.2 miles to Spillway Road, a paved avenue just past the power plant on the left. Turn left and go 1.9 miles to a parking lot for the spillway. At 2.1 miles, there is parking for a trailhead. At 2.4 miles the road basically ends in a parking lot for a self-pay station and a boat launch. Rusty Blackbirds can be found here during winter.

After a thorough examination of this venue, return to LA-106 and turn left. Proceed for 3.6 miles to LA-3042, turn left, and head south on this road for 4 miles to the entrance to Chicot State Park. Turn left into the park and go 0.3 mile to the fee station where there is a charge of $2 per vehicle. The park has many amenities including cabins, primitive and established camp sites, boat launches, summertime swimming pool, and canoe rentals ($20). Beyond the fee station, the main park road continues for 1.1 miles. The swimming, picnicking, and camping areas are crowded during summer, but there are a number of side roads that lead to more secluded parts of the park, including a lake inlet to the north that can harbor Neotropic Cormorant and Anhinga year round. Wood Ducks and Belted Kingfishers are common. Black-bellied Whistling-Ducks and Roseate Spoonbills can be found during spring and summer. A bird checklist for the park is available at either the arboretum (see below) or the park fee station.

The 22-mile lake loop trail offers peaceful birding with occasional bottomland swamp overlooks where Wood Duck, Pileated Woodpecker, Blue-headed Vireo, Brown Creeper, Winter Wren, both kinglets, Hermit Thrush, and Yellow-rumped Warbler are winter mainstays. Late spring and early summer are best to see breeding visitors. The possibilities include Mississippi Kite, Broad-winged Hawk, Acadian and Great Crested Flycatchers, Worm-eating, Prothonotary, and Swainson's Warblers, Louisiana Waterthrush, Yellow-throated Warbler, and Summer Tanager. Even Warbling Vireo has reared young here. The trail can be accessed from the main entrance road and several locations along the park roads.

The Louisiana State Arboretum is accessed from within Chicot State Park. From the entrance/fee booth, travel 0.1 mile and take your first left, then 0.4 mile to a second left—both are well signed. From here it is one-half mile to the visitors center. Rather large for an arboretum, this state preservation area encompasses more than 300 acres with several miles of walking paths through centuries-old beech/hickory-forested slopes and swampy backwaters. This place is especially nice to visit if you appreciate trees identified with signage. The staff is a birder-friendly bunch and can often provide good information on what is being reported. Sign in and let them know you're a birder—they might have some birding tips for you.

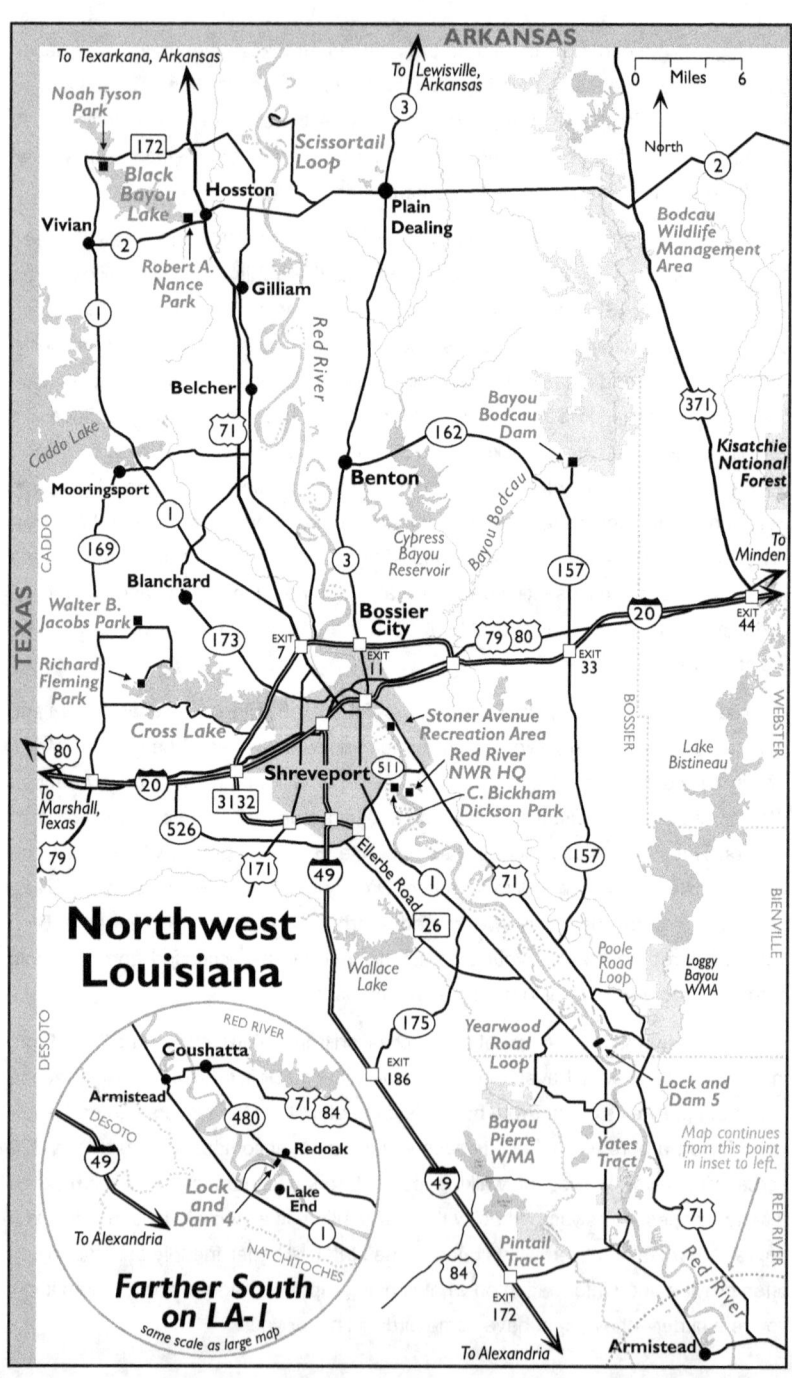

NORTHWEST LOUISIANA

This is the Louisiana region where, for well over half a century, the legendary Horace Jeter and his disciples meticulously and painstakingly documented so many marvelous records. Although there are a number of wooded regions accessible to birders, the northwestern portion of Louisiana contains what may well be the best open country birding in the state. The area reservoirs, particularly Cross Lake, have had several important sightings.

Black Bayou Lake Richard E. Gibbons

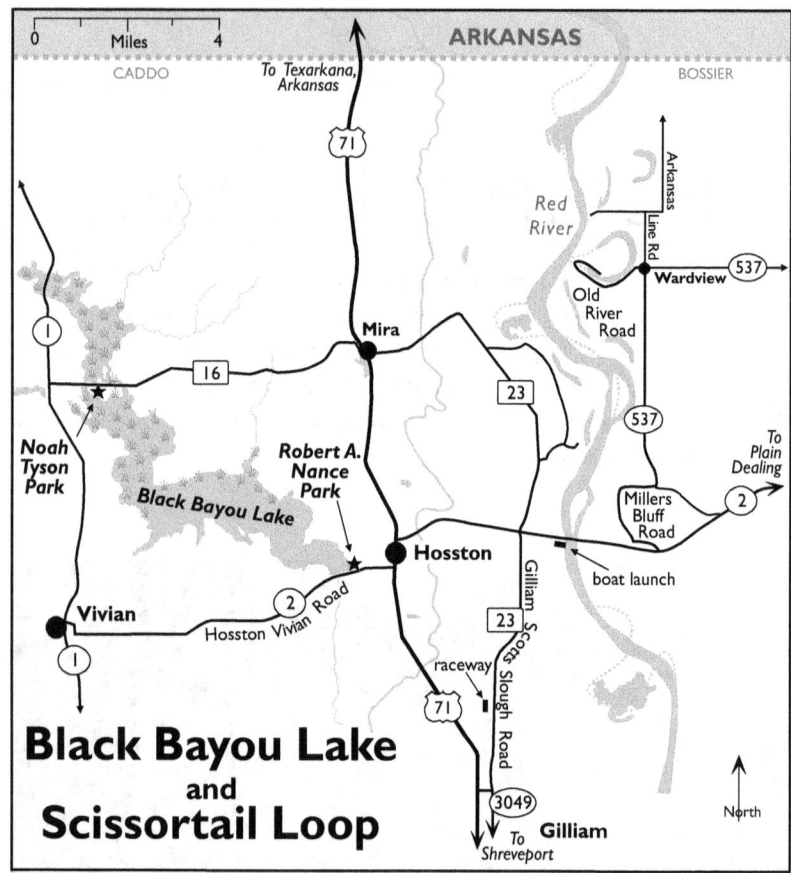

BLACK BAYOU LAKE

Not to be confused with the national wildlife refuge north of Monroe, this lake is in the farthest reaches of northwest Louisiana near the Arkansas and Texas state lines. Black Bayou Lake is a mixture of open water and cypress/tupelo flooded forest. It is most popular with anglers, and an early morning visit to **Robert A. Nance Park** just west of Hosston would likely provide the spectacle of trucks and trailers queuing up at the boat launch, anglers anxious to blast off for their favorite fishing holes. After the morning rush or during the week, this vantage can be quite peaceful and a small observation deck provides a scan of the deeper parts of the lake. The best time to bird this parish park is winter. Common Goldeneye is a regular winter find along with Mallard, Ring-necked Duck, Pied-billed Grebe, Osprey, Bald Eagle, Ring-billed Gull, Forster's Tern, and Belted Kingfisher.

To get to Robert A. Nance from Shreveport, take LA-71 for 24 miles north to the south side of Hosston, where the Hosston Vivian Road (LA-2) turns to the west. Take this road 0.8 mile west to the entrance to this pocket park on the edge of Hosston. A roadside pullout 0.2 mile farther down gives a different view of the lake. Common Yellowthroat, and Swamp and White-throated Sparrows may be heard along the lake-edge habitat.

Black Bayou Lake is surrounded by agriculture, mixed hardwoods, and pine stands. Most of the shoreline is private, so lake views are at a premium. You can explore the many side roads off Hosston Vivian Road as you head west toward the town of Vivian. Eastern Phoebe and Eastern Bluebird are conspicuous roadside birds.

Noah Tyson Park is a public park five miles north of Vivian. This quiet parish park sits on the flooded forest banks of Black Bayou Lake. Red-bellied, Downy, and Pileated Woodpeckers can be found here, and a spring visit provides a cacophony of Yellow-throated and Red-eyed Vireos and Prothonotary Warblers, to name a few. This is a great place for Rusty Blackbird in winter along with Common Grackle and the usual mix of wintering passerines such as Brown Creeper, Golden-crowned and Ruby-crowned Kinglets, Hermit Thrush, and Orange-crowned and Yellow-rumped Warblers. The few pine trees are visited by Brown-headed Nuthatches year round.

To reach Noah Tyson Park, travel north from Vivian on LA-1 for 4.5 miles to PR-16 (Mira Myrtis Road). Turn right (east) and continue 0.9 mile to the well-signed park entrance on the right. Facilities include toilets, a pavilion, and boat launch.

Brown-headed Nuthatch　　　　　　　　　　　　　　　Dan Lane

Scissortail Loop

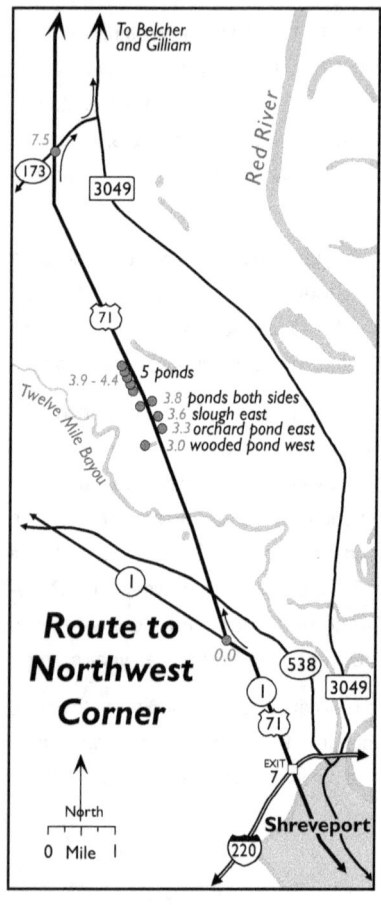

This route through the Red River floodplain near the Arkansas state line is interesting at any season. A variety of ducks, Merlin, Horned Lark, Bewick's Wren, Sprague's Pipit, longspurs, Vesper Sparrow, and Western Meadowlark are found during the colder months, while Bell's Vireo (rare), Grasshopper Sparrow (rare), Blue Grosbeak, Painted Bunting, and Orchard Oriole nest here. The real summer draw is the loop's namesake—huge numbers of Scissor-tailed Flycatchers. In recent years, Western Kingbird has been documented as a breeder.

Drive north from Shreveport on combined US-71/LA-1 for several miles to where the highways diverge. At the split, stay to the right on US-71 toward Texarkana and zero your odometer. In winter, pause at a wooded pond at 3.0 miles on the west side of the road to check for Hooded Merganser and other ducks. At 3.3 miles, a pond on the right (east) in a pecan orchard deserves a glance—you might just find a wintering Bewick's Wren in the thickets there or Rusty Blackbird at the pond's edge. The 3.6-mile mark is a slough on the right, while 3.8 on the odometer offers you ponds on both sides. The one on the left is so predictable that it's dubbed Merganser Pond by local birders. On the right, Wilson's Snipe is often seen when there has been ample rainfall. A series of small ponds on the left are seen at 3.9, 4.1, 4.2, 4.25, and 4.4 miles. Look for Rusty and Brewer's Blackbirds along this entire section in winter. US-71 intersects the Dixie Blanchard Road (LA-173) at 7.5 miles. Turn right (east). At 8.2 miles, LA-173 meets LA-3049. Turn left (north) and check the fields along the way for upland shorebirds during migration. The road forks in the small community of Belcher at 12.8 miles. Stay to the right as LA-3049 continues north to Gilliam. (Now, follow map on page 162.)

Scissor-tailed Flycatcher Dan Lane

When LA-3049 turns left (west) at 18 miles, zero your odometer and continue north on Main Street. This becomes Gilliam Scotts Slough Road (PR-23). At 1.5 miles, check the fields in front of the Red River Raceway in winter for Sprague's Pipit and listen for the beautiful song of Western Meadowlark. Lapland Longspurs may be heard giving their distinctive calls in the bare fields to the east. Gilliam Scotts Slough Road intersects LA-2 at 4.9 miles. Turn right (east) and at 5.5 miles, check the boat launch on the west side of the Red River.

Zero your odometer when leaving, and turn east again on LA-2. Cross the river, and at 2.0, Millers Bluff Road (gravel) meets LA-2 from the left. Turn left (north), and at 3.8 miles, the road becomes blacktop. At 4.4 miles, LA-537 enters from the left (north). Take this left and travel north. At 8.5 miles, there is an intersection where LA-537 turns east. Old River Road comes in from the west and Arkansas Line Road continues on to the north. Turn left onto Old River Road to explore its reaches. In summer, listen for the thin whistle of the Grasshopper Sparrow in the fields.

To return to Shreveport, retrace your route on LA-537 to LA-2 and then right (west). Until new I-49 is completed, take LA-2 into Hosston and get on southbound US-71 to return to Shreveport.

BAYOU BODCAU WILDLIFE MANAGEMENT AREA

This WMA contains a bevy of habitats in a relatively limited area. Although it extends northward for well over 20 miles to the Arkansas state line, the boundaries are generally very narrow, often only a few hundred yards wide. Even so, good birding venues from swamps to pine uplands are found in the WMA's 32,000+ acres. Bayou Bodcau rivals Yearwood Road as *the* place to bird in northwest Louisiana, although it is probably of more year-round interest, while Yearwood is *primo* in winter.

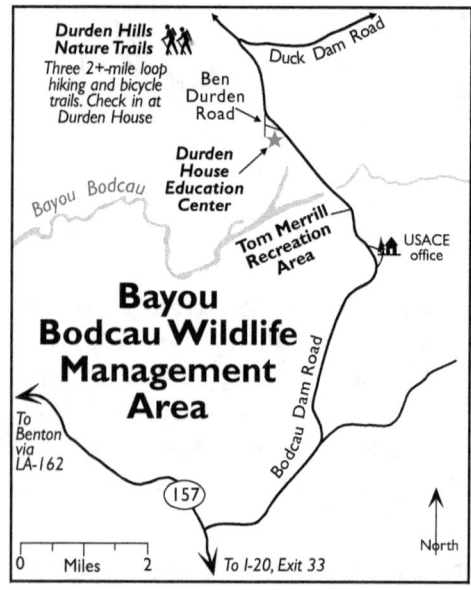

Head east from Shreveport on I-20. Travel approximately 13 miles to the intersection with LA-157 (Exit 33) and turn left (north). After about 8.5 miles, Bodcau Dam Road intersects LA-157 from the east, marked by a sign that announces a recreation area at 3 miles. Take this right turn, and at 2.2 miles, a sign proclaims the Bodcau Dam and Reservoir are to the right down a very short lane. At 2.5 miles, a short road to the left leads to the Tom Merrill Recreation Area. This spot is excellent for Wild Turkey, various herons, Belted Kingfisher, Sedge Wren, Black-and-white, Prothonotary, Kentucky, Hooded, and Yellow-throated Warblers, Eastern Towhee, and Chipping Sparrow. It is also an excellent place to look for Yellow-throated and Red-eyed Vireos, White-breasted Nuthatch, and Northern Parula.

Ben Durden Road (at 3.3 miles on the left) should be explored. The John Haygood Nature Trail, a 0.75-mile paved hike, starts next to the Durden House Education Center on Ben Durden Road. The pine upland habitat of the trail is home to Eastern Bluebird and Pine Warbler at all seasons, while in winter the residents are joined by Golden-crowned and Ruby-crowned Kinglets, Hermit Thrush, the Slate-colored form of the Dark-eyed Junco, and American Goldfinch. At 3.8 miles, Duck Dam Road on the right should also be explored. At about 4.2 miles, the fields on both sides of the road should be checked in winter for Sedge Wren, longspurs, and Henslow's and Le Conte's Sparrows.

CROSS LAKE

Although not an exceptionally large impoundment, this over-8,000-acre open body of shallow water has produced a surprising number of rarities, particularly in winter and during migration. A few examples are Surf, White-winged, and Black Scoters, Common Merganser, Red-throated Loon, Red-necked and Western Grebes, Sabine's Gull, Black-legged Kittiwake, Pomarine and Parasitic Jaegers, and Ringed Kingfisher. The lake is just large enough so that Bald Eagle is not unexpected during the colder months. Wintering ducks run the gamut and include the entire *Anas* spectrum, Canvasback, Redhead, scaup, Bufflehead, Common Goldeneye, and Ruddy Duck. A male Cape May Warbler spent a recent winter along the lakeshore, and a year or so later a male Tropical Parula did so, as well.

While Cross Lake may well be Louisiana's number one inland lake for rarity sightings, the bad news is that development along the shores has severely limited the chances for birders to use a spotting scope to search for them. In fact, a large portion of the water's surface cannot be scrutinized from the few spots along the banks that allow public access. Added to the problem is the lack of adequate parking, as the narrow shoulders and the law prohibit pulling off the road except in emergency situations. Nevertheless, the reward-to-risk ratio is great enough to warrant a visit by birders during the winter. This is particularly true if it is combined with a side trip to one of the nearby parks or nature areas.

To begin a tour of Cross Lake, take the northbound I-220 bypass from its junction with I-20 west of Shreveport and exit west onto Lakeshore Drive (Exit 2). At 0.9 mile, the road Ts at South Lakeshore Drive. Turn left and drive 0.4 mile to the entrance to Ford Park. Ford Park occupies property on both sides of the road; however, the small segment of the park on the lake side can be more interesting to birders and is worth a look. In addition to a good view of the lake, resident White-breasted and Brown-headed Nuthatches can be seen and heard here. Red-breasted Nuthatch joins them during irruption winters. Also in winter, Winter Wrens and Rusty Blackbirds work the lake edges where cypress and tupelo occur.

A public boat launch operated by Shreveport Parks and Recreation is on the right 0.2 mile past the parking lot entrance, one of the very few sites from which a scope gives you a good look across an expanse of open water. Visible from here is an island rookery used by Double-crested Cormorants, herons, egrets, and perhaps even a Bald Eagle. During post-breeding-dispersal season, the roosting birds number in the tens of thousands.

168 Northwest Louisiana

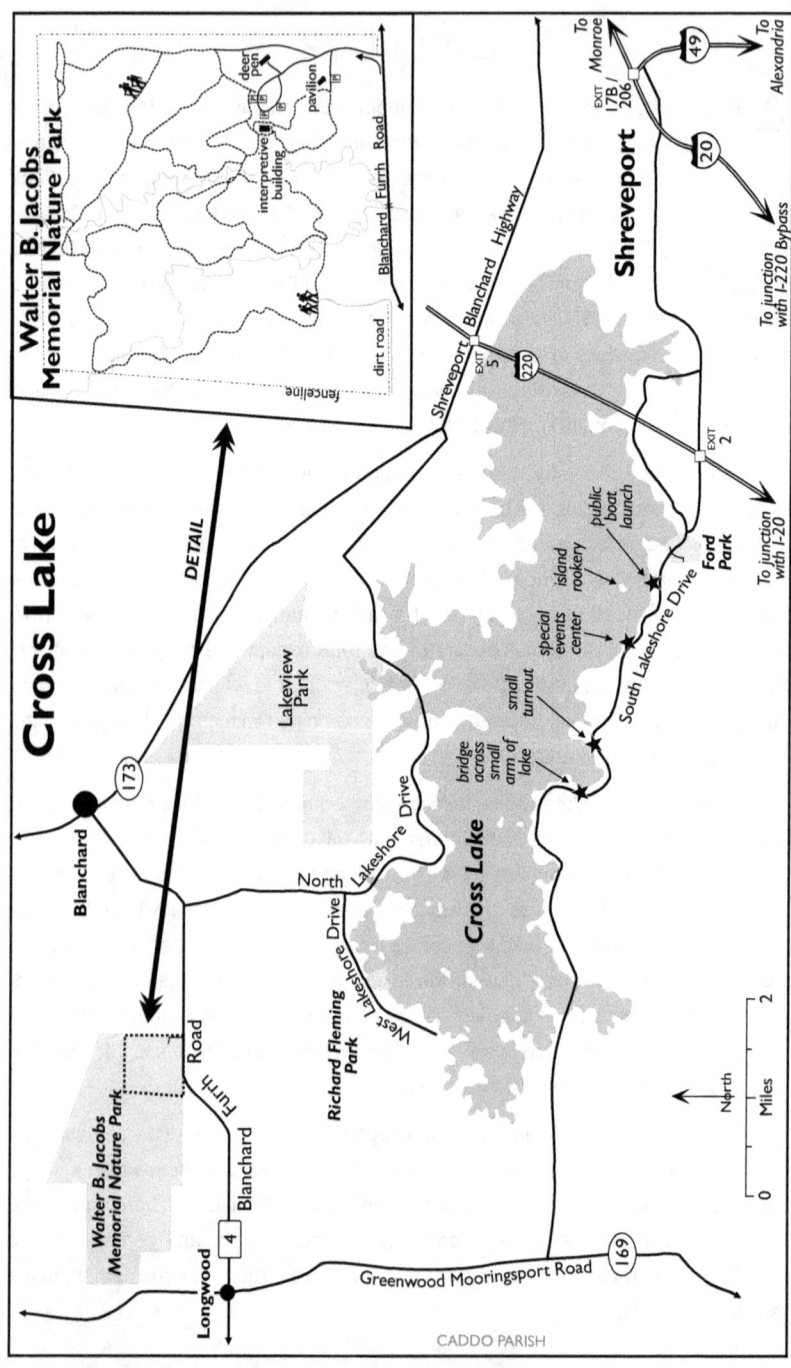

At 0.7 mile farther, the Valencia On Cross Lake special event center has a parking lot with great view across the lake. The next opportunity to use a scope doesn't come for 1.4 miles. Here, a small turnout at a grocery and boat dock offers a limited view of the lake. One of the lake's heron roosts may be observed off to the right. A half mile ahead you may legally park on the right just prior to crossing a bridge that spans a very small arm of the lake. Continue west on South Lakeshore Drive for an additional 5.5 miles to LA-169 (Greenwood Mooringsport Road), and access to the next birding site.

Walter B. Jacobs Memorial Nature Park

This park is best reached as a side trip from the south lakeshore trip detailed above. Travel north on LA-169 (Greenwood Mooringsport Road) for about 3.5 miles into the small community of Longwood. Here, LA-169 meets Blanchard-Furrh Road, which is marked by a caution light. Turn right and drive east for 2.7 miles to the entrance to Walter Jacobs Park located on the north (left) side of the road.

This nature center, complete with exhibits, feeders, and birding trails, is always a joy to visit. In winter, the patient birder may see Blue-headed Vireo, Red-breasted Nuthatch, Golden-crowned Kinglet, Fox Sparrow, Pine Siskin, and Purple Finch. A late-spring walk along the trails may yield a glimpse of Red-shouldered Hawk, Eastern Wood-Pewee, Blue-gray Gnatcatcher, White-eyed Vireo, Louisiana Waterthrush, Swainson's (rare) and Yellow-throated Warblers, and Summer Tanager.

Richard Fleming Park

From the entrance to Walter Jacobs Park, turn left (east) toward Blanchard and drive 1.4 miles to North Lakeshore Drive. Turn right (south) and proceed for 1.8 miles and turn right onto West Lakeshore Drive. From this intersection, it is 1 mile to the Richard Fleming Park entrance on the left. The park, rimmed by a 0.4-mile loop trail, is small enough to walk. This small stopover for migrants attracts Warbling and Philadelphia (uncommon) Vireos, Blue-winged, Mourning (uncommon), Magnolia, Yellow, and Black-throated Green Warblers and American Redstart. White-breasted Nuthatch is almost always found, along with Barred Owl.

Winter species include Blue-headed Vireo and Orange-crowned and Yellow-rumped Warblers. Some of the common breeders are Prothonotary Warbler, Northern Parula, and Yellow-throated Warbler. Be certain to walk the trail that parallels the bayou leading to the lake from the boat ramp. In many years, Winter Wren is one of the most numerous species encountered along this peninsula during the colder months. This area serves as an excellent migrant trap, as well.

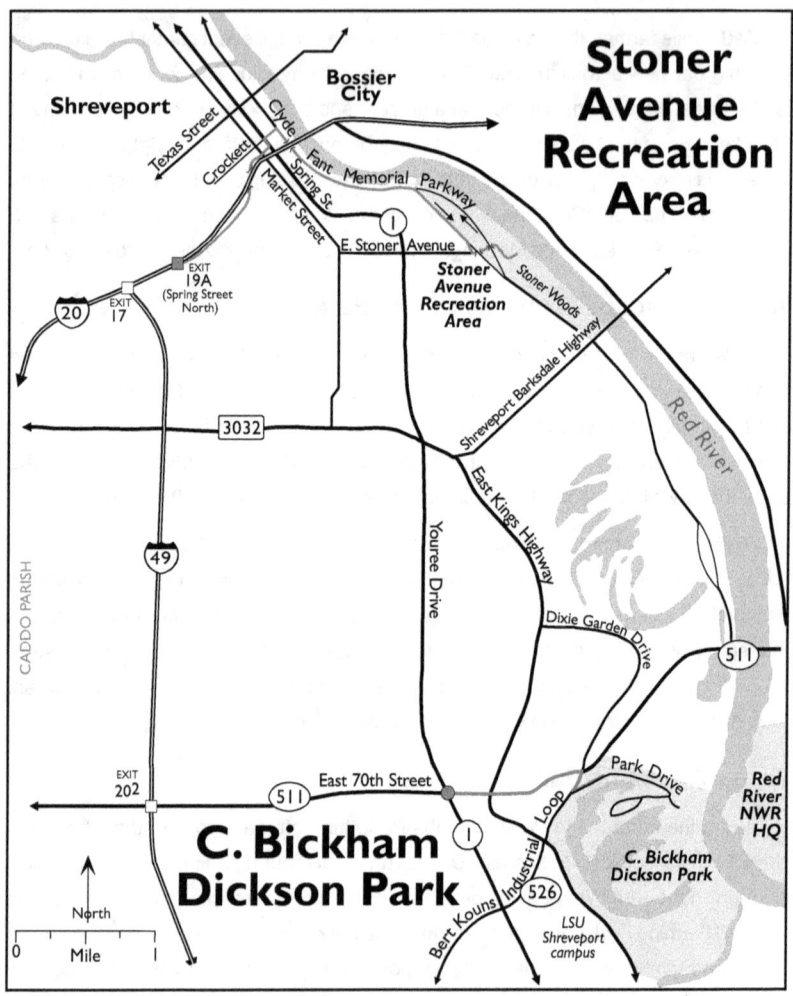

C. BICKHAM DICKSON PARK

Along the northern shore of the Gulf of Mexico there is a rather interesting phenomenon known to the birding community as the coastal hiatus (see page 73 also). It refers to the periodic scarcity of trans-Gulf migrants in spring along the wooded *cheniers*. While radar may show vast clouds of birds aloft, prevailing south winds aid their efforts to the extent that, normally, most of them overfly the coast and set down farther inland. It seems that Shreveport is located where they are inclined to seek food, water, and rest. Migratory songbirds abound here from late March through early May.

NORTHWEST LOUISIANA   171

Inasmuch as the greater Shreveport area is becoming urban/industrialized, the few areas along the Red River with mature trees form small habitat pockets, which birders refer to as migrant traps.

C. Bickham Dickson Park is such a pocket of habitat. Despite its diminutive size, it boasts a large number of migrants and rarities yearly. The species list for the park is an incredible 216, over 30 of which are wood-warblers. The varied habitats include hardwoods, fields, and the levees of the Red River. Bickham Dickson is good for a variety of migrating and wintering ducks and shorebirds in the fall. This site is accessible via an auto loop and trails leading from the old equestrian center. Pay no heed if the gate is locked. Birders are welcome to climb the gate to access the best birding. Every trail in the park should be explored as each provides a different set of habitats.

To reach this site, begin at the intersection of LA-1 and East 70th Street (LA-511). Go east (toward the river) on East 70th Street until LA-526 (East Bert Kouns Industrial Loop) comes in from the right at 0.9 mile. Turn right (south) onto LA-526 and you will quickly encounter the signs for the park, to the left on Park Drive in an old oxbow.

The migrant fare includes many of the *Empidonax* clan and loads of warblers such as Worm-eating, Golden-winged (rare), Swainson's (scarce), and Cerulean (scarce). You may also find Western Kingbird, Warbling Vireo, Sedge Wren, Nashville Warbler, shorebirds in the fields, gulls and terns over the waterway, and swallows in all areas. All of the state's woodpeckers (except Red-cockaded) can be found in the park. Breeders include Eastern Wood-Pewee and Summer Tanager in the woodlots, Prothonotary Warbler in the moist woods near the riverbanks, Baltimore Oriole in the cottonwoods, and Indigo Bunting at the edges.

Birding sites worth mentioning in addition to those covered in this chapter are:
    Lake Ophelia
    Grand Cote National Wildlife Refuge
    Grassy Lake
    Pomme de Terre Wildlife Management Area
    Spring Bayou Wildlife Management Area

Stoner Avenue Recreation Area

Known to locals as Stoner Woods, this public patch of riparian forest is minutes from downtown Shreveport. Like many urban forests, security issues are not to be taken lightly. Although encounters are more likely to be with mountain bikers than muggers, visitors should be aware of the dangers. Birding this patch alone is not recommended.

That being said, local birder Terry Davis has worked this block of batture land more than any other and his dedication and keen ear have proven the worth of a visit, especially during migration. Shreveport's Bird Study Group has reported 210 species for the Clyde Fant Parkway area, which includes Stoner Woods.

To get there from the intersection of I-20 and I-49 in Shreveport, travel 0.7 mile east on I-20 and exit right on Spring Street, Exit 19A. Stay to the left and take Spring Street northbound. When you are finally on Spring Street, get over to the right as soon as you can. In two blocks, at a traffic light, turn right onto Crockett Street and drive two more blocks toward the riverfront. Turn right (south) onto Clyde Fant Memorial Parkway and travel 2.2 miles to East Stoner Avenue, a right-side exit ramp. At the stop sign at the end of the exit ramp turn left (east) onto Stoner Avenue and drive under the two overpasses to the riverfront. At the stop sign turn right to park in the lot.

Scan the Red River for Least Terns during the warmer months. This declining interior-breeding population has nested on nearby river sandbars in the past. The mountain bikers help maintain the many trails through the woods, so be on the lookout for them on blind curves.

The birds of Stoner Woods are similar to those of C. Bickham Dickson Park, with flycatchers, thrushes, warblers, tanagers, grosbeaks, and orioles during migration and breeding season, and kinglets, nuthatches, creepers, and sparrows during the winter months.

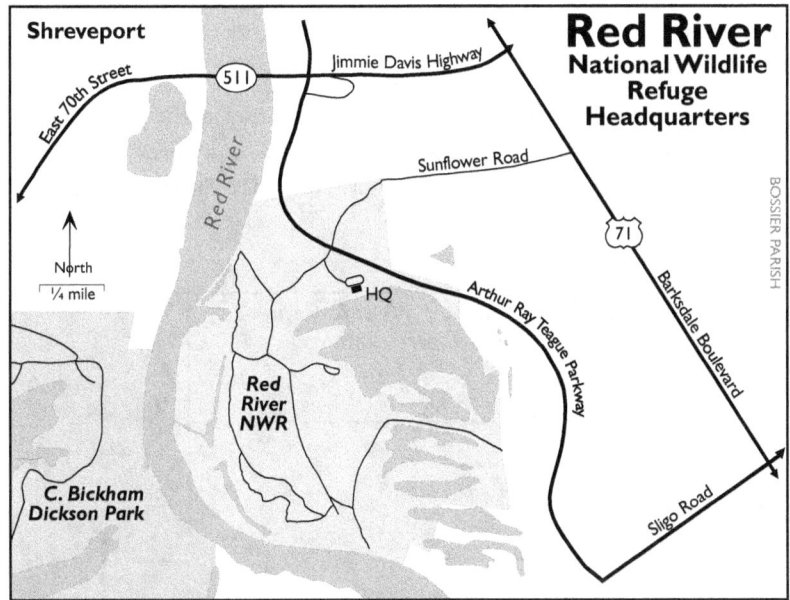

RED RIVER NATIONAL WILDLIFE REFUGE

Red River National Wildlife Refuge was dedicated in August 2002. A visitors center at the headquarters opened in early 2012. The refuge is a critical stopover point for over 200 species of migratory songbirds and shorebirds and provides wintering grounds for waterfowl and wading birds. Over 80,000 waterfowl used the refuge in 2008.

There are four units of the refuge: Headquarters (Bossier Parish), Bayou Pierre Floodplain (Red River and Desoto Parishes), Spanish Lake Lowlands (Natchitoches Parish), and Lower Cane River (Natchitoches Parish). Although all of the units are technically open to the public, there are only three areas with easy access at this time.

The **refuge headquarters and visitors center** are accessed via a dedicated exit from the new Arthur Ray Teague Parkway. If coming from Shreveport, go over the Jimmie Davis/70th Street Bridge and take the A.R. Teague Parkway ramp on the Bossier Parish side, drive south about 0.6 mile to the refuge entrance. Coming from the south in Bossier City, take Barksdale Boulevard/LA-71 to the stop light intersection with Sligo Road by Parkway High School. Turn west onto the A. R. Teague Parkway extension and drive approximately 2.6 miles to the entrance of Red River National

Wildlife Refuge (on the left). If you are coming from Bossier City, take the A. R. Teague Parkway to the refuge.

This area has access to the Red River, an oxbow lake, sandbars, and typical bottomland hardwood forest with pecan, oak, pine, hackberry, dense shrubs/scrub swamps, and is good for many migrants as well as nesting Prothonotary Warbler and Northern Parula.

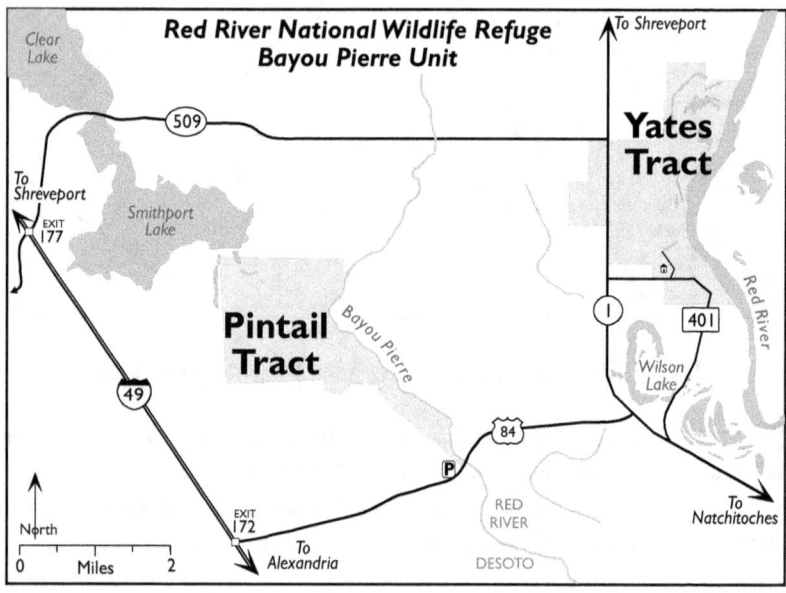

Bayou Pierre Unit, Yates Tract

This site is located off LA-1 in Red River Parish just north of Grand Bayou. From Shreveport go south on LA-1 for about 25 miles to a blinking caution light at the intersection of LA-1 and LA-509 in Red River Parish. Continue south on LA-1 for 1.6 miles. Turn left (east) on Grand Bayou Loop/PR-401 and proceed 0.7 mile. On your left you will see the Red River National Wildlife Refuge sign and a white house behind it. You may park at the house, or go past the house driveway and turn in at the gate nearest the barn to enter the refuge and then park in the gravel parking lot. The refuge manages approximately 1,500 acres of moist-soil impoundments for wintering waterfowl and migrant shorebirds. Various stages of reforested agricultural lands and open fields are good for sparrows. American Bittern and Yellow Rail (rare) have been found here in migration.

Le Conte's Sparrow   Richard E. Gibbons

Bayou Pierre Unit, Pintail Tract

This tract is located in DeSoto Parish and is not far from the Yates Tract. From the intersection of US-84 and LA-1 in Red River Parish, go west on US-84 for 2.4 miles to the bridge crossing over Bayou Pierre. Immediately after the bridge, turn right into the parking lot of the Bayou Pierre Unit Pintail Tract. (The LA-1/US-84 intersection is 3.5 miles south of the intersection of LA-1 and LA-509.) Or, from I-49, take Exit 172 and head east on US-84 for 3.2 miles; just before the bridge crossing over Bayou Pierre, turn left into the parking lot of the Bayou Pierre Unit Pintail Tract. The area contains bayous and riparian woodlands along with mature cypress swamp forest habitat.

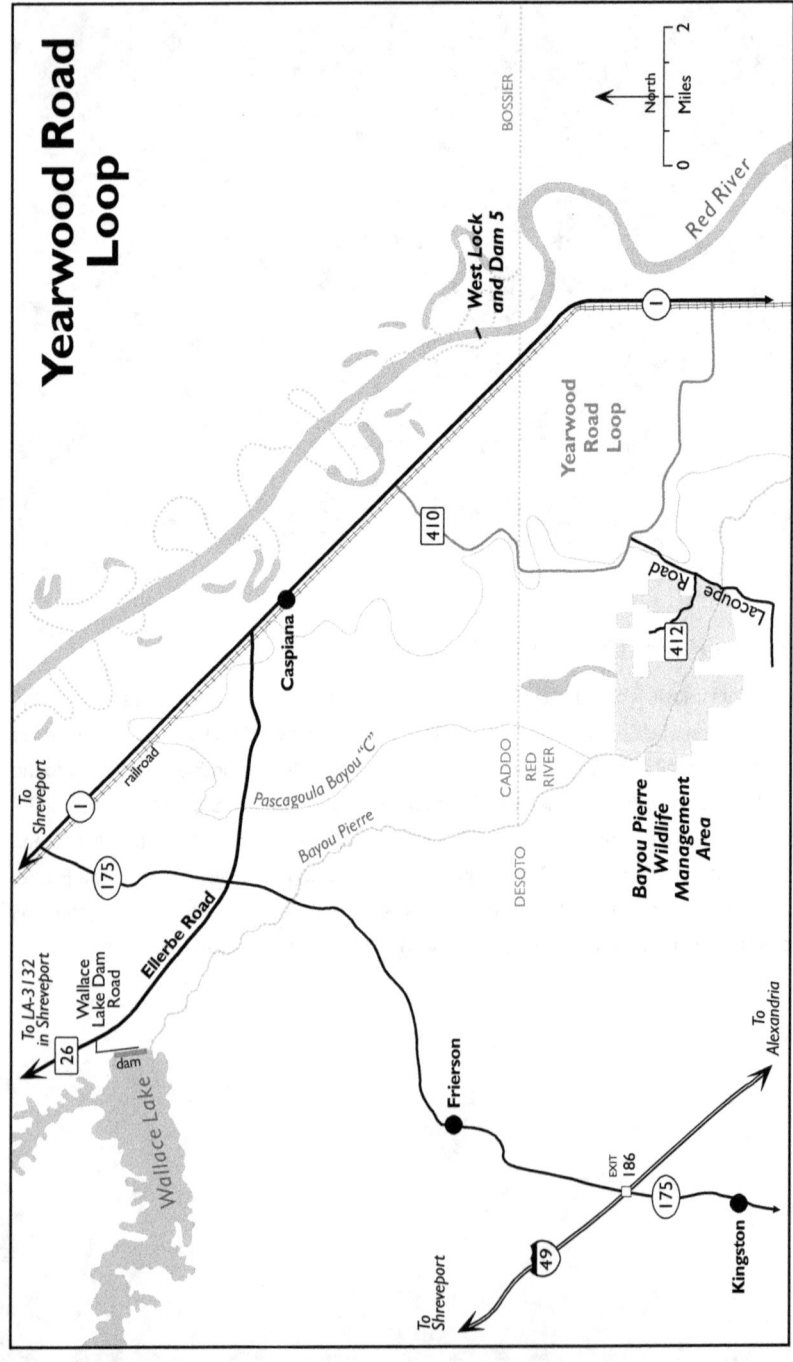

YEARWOOD ROAD LOOP

This riverbottom route mostly through farmland can be exciting in winter. At other seasons, especially during migration, the area can still claim certain attractions. To reach it, travel south on Ellerbe Road (PR-26) from its junction with LA-3132 in southeast Shreveport. After about 7 miles, the low hills of suburbia yield to the floodplains of the Red River. The fields on both sides are good for upland species including Eastern Kingbird and Scissor-tailed Flycatcher in spring and summer. During migration, American Golden-Plover, Upland and Buff-breasted Sandpipers, and grassland sparrows such as Grasshopper may be found. In winter, the density of raptors can be astounding. Northern Harriers are common in open habitats, which are occasionally shared with Short-eared Owl. Harlan's, Krider's, and Fuertes' forms of Red-tailed Hawk are seen annually. Merlin is an uncommon visitor, and more American Kestrels than one might want to count are along the roadways.

At 7.8 miles, Wallace Lake Dam Road wanders off to the right and may be checked for raptors and hedgerow birds. A Peregrine Falcon would not be out of the question near the lake's dam. At 10.7 miles, left of the intersection with LA-175, a number of fields should be checked in winter for Horned Lark, American Pipit, and Lapland Longspur. At 14.6 miles, after crossing a railroad track, Ellerbe Road empties into LA-1. Turn right and zero your odometer. In 3.1 miles, turn right onto Yearwood Road (PR-410) as it winds off across the tracks to the right. Two miles from LA-1, in the middle of a right curve, a bayou on the right along with its attendant grasses and shrubs should be examined at any season. In summer, you may find Green Heron, Indigo and Painted Buntings, and Dickcissel. Northern Rough-winged Swallows nest in the area.

The habitats here are excellent for wintering sparrows and other birds that prefer open fields. At 2.5 miles, hedgerows on both sides harbor Bewick's Wren (uncommon) and White-throated and White-crowned Sparrows during the colder months. This is also one of the most reliable spots in the state for the marvelous Harris's Sparrow, a winter visitor. At 4.6 miles, turn right (west) onto Lacoupe Road. Check the fields and hedgerows on both sides—Le Conte's Sparrow is occasionally seen here in winter, as are Chipping, Song, and Swamp Sparrows. At 5.8 miles, a gravel road comes in from the right (Red River PR-412). Turn here and enter the relatively new **Bayou Pierre Wildlife Management Area**. At 6.3 miles, a group of silos on the left, along with the remnants of an old stable, are the haunt of Barn Owl and Bewick's Wren. From this point, the fields on both sides are becoming quite overgrown in an effort by state officials to increase deer habitat. Historically, they were the winter hunting grounds of Short-eared Owl. Among the present breeders are White-eyed Vireo, Blue-gray

Field Sparrow   Richard E. Gibbons

Gnatcatcher, Gray Catbird, Yellow-breasted Chat, Eastern Towhee, Blue Grosbeak, and Orchard Oriole. Winter visitors to this scrub include House Wren, Orange-crowned and Yellow-rumped Warblers, and Field, Fox, and Song Sparrows. At 6.8 miles, use the turnout on the left to turn around as the road reaches an end within a few hundred yards at a private residence.

Return to Yearwood Road and turn right. Zero your odometer again. From this point, there are bayou crossings, at 2.4 and 3.6 miles, which form corridors for nesting and migrant passerines. Watch the shortgrass habitat on both sides of the road in summer as Lark Sparrow nests along the southern end of Yearwood Road. At 3.8 miles, hedgerows and pastures appear on both sides, good for sparrows and field birds. At 4.5 miles, cross the tracks yet again and take a left on LA-1 to return to Shreveport.

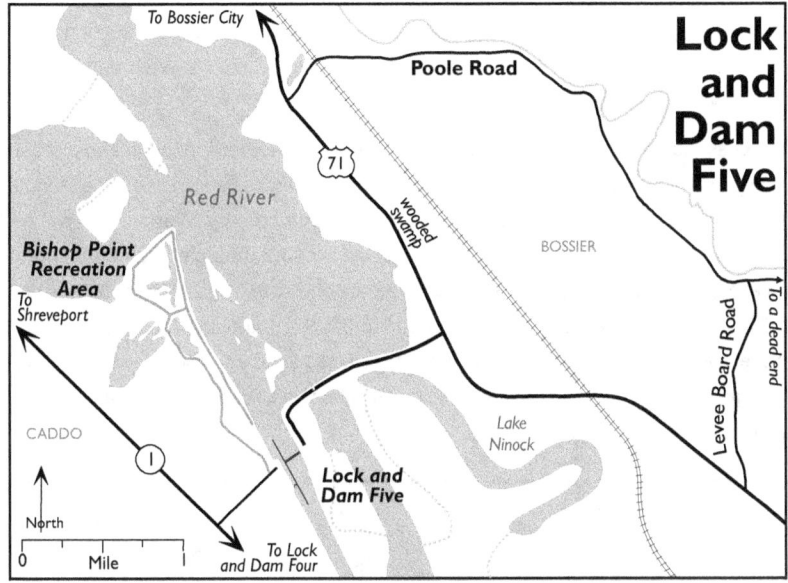

RED RIVER LOCKS AND DAMS

The development of the Red River into a navigable waterway supported by a series of transference locks was met with as many boos and hisses as it was with applause. Nevertheless, the project provides new birding opportunities for the birding community. There are now countless tons of rocks and boulders lining the banks, along with meadows, fields, and thickets.

East (North) Lock and Dam Five

The Red River of the South rises disputably in northeastern New Mexico or the Panhandle of Texas, depending upon which tourist commission is to be believed. It flows, thereafter, generally eastward, although at times references may be made to the *east* or *west* banks. This is because it often takes a southerly course, particularly in North Louisiana.

To reach Lock and Dam #5 on its eastern shore, begin on the east side of the river (Bossier City) at the intersection of LA-511 (the extension of East 70th Street after it crosses the river) and US-71 South. Go south on US-71. At 15.7 miles Poole Road intersects LA-71 from the left. This 5¼-mile-long lane passes through hardwood bottomlands, fields, and waterways before reaching a dead end. Once the entire venue has been surveyed, retrace your route back to the Poole Road intersection with the main highway. In summer, edge-dwellers such as Blue Grosbeak, buntings, and Orchard Oriole are possible. In winter, the uncommon Bewick's Wren and Harris's Sparrow may be seen.

Less than a mile south of the Poole Road/US-71 intersection, on the right (east) side of the highway is a wooded swamp that is worth an inspection in any season. In summer, listen for the repeated whistles of Prothonotary Warbler. In winter, Blue-headed Vireo, Brown Creeper, and Golden-crowned Kinglet may be found. A mile farther along, the road to the lock is indicated on a brown sign. Turn right here and drive toward the river. This 1.5-mile stretch of blacktop should be examined rather closely; feel free to walk the levees. The cattails along the road should be examined for Marsh Wren and rails in winter. The fields often host Horned Lark and Lapland Longspur in the winter as well.

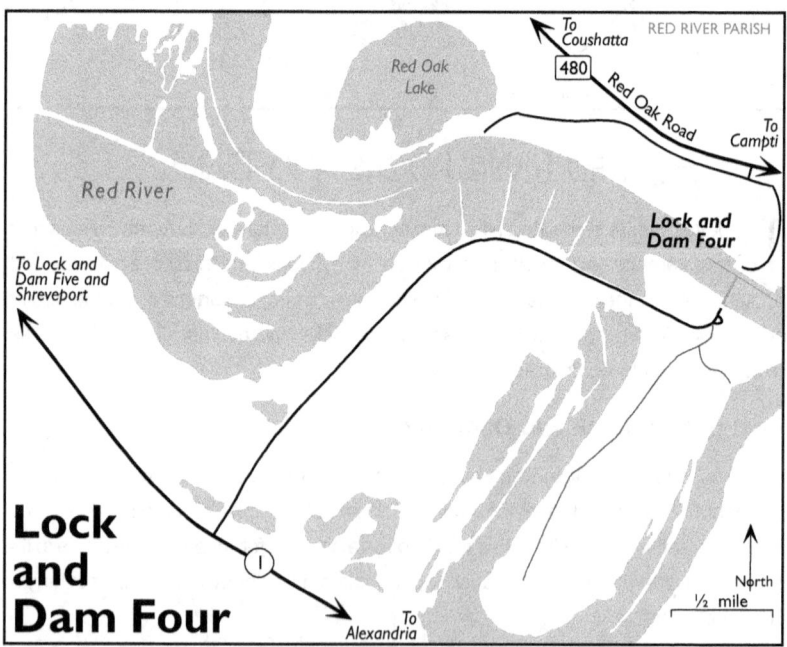

West (South) Lock and Dam Five and Lock and Dam Four

Getting to the west shore is also a rather straightforward affair. Begin in southeast Shreveport at the intersection of LA-526 and LA-1. Go south on LA-1 through prime Louisiana farmland. At 3.2 miles, a slough on the left warrants a scan. Harts Island Road can be explored. At 7.5 miles a stock pond on the left sometimes harbors a few species of dabbling ducks in winter. There is a stock pond in a woodlot at 9.5 miles. Flooded fields on the right and a pond on the left at 14.1 miles should be surveyed for ducks, waders, and shorebirds. A second slough is found at 14.4 miles, also on the left. At 15.6 miles, the road to Lock & Dam 5 is on the left. Turn here (east) at the old store, and at 16.1 miles, turn right at the stop sign and park. Sprague's Pipit may sometimes be flushed from the short grasses beyond the parking area in winter. Also in late fall and winter, be alert for Osprey, Bald Eagle, and the occasional Peregrine Falcon as they patrol the river.

Just prior to reaching the control facility for the lock, a sign points to **Bishop Point Recreation Area**, which lies to the left (north) down a gravel road that parallels the river. Western Kingbird has nested at this site. The 1.7 miles to the boat ramp traverse lands studded by ponds, grasses, and hardwoods. Several species of sparrows should be found here in winter. This area might very well be a productive stop during migration. Large river courses are natural byways for migrants and the Red is certainly no exception. The varied habitats provide foraging for a wide range of species. Scope the fields on the left for migrant shorebirds. The drowned timber (as in other places) is excellent for Red-headed Woodpecker. American White Pelicans visit the lock in winter. Large numbers of Bonaparte's Gulls are not uncommon in winter.

To continue on to Lock #4, backtrack to LA-1 and zero your odometer and refer to the map on page 160 to get your bearings. Turn south (left) and travel through the river's floodplain as the levees usher the Red toward its eventual confluence with the Mississippi. At 19.6 miles, the crossroads at Armistead is reached (see inset map). Continue south on LA-1 and at 26.8 miles, a brown road sign points to the lock. Turn left (east). The asphalt lane traverses some 2.8 miles of excellent habitat—watercourses, flooded timber, fields, and mudflats flank the road on both sides. Anhinga, Green Heron, Common Gallinule, Red-headed Woodpecker, Eastern Kingbird, Common Yellowthroat, and Painted Bunting breed here. In winter, look for American Wigeon, Green-winged Teal, Hooded Merganser, American White Pelican, Bald Eagle, Virginia Rail, Sora, and Peregrine Falcon. Huge flocks of Eastern Kingbirds are seen during the early autumn. The oxbow on the right at the dam approach should be examined for shorebirds. Migrant Caspian Terns are seen here regularly.

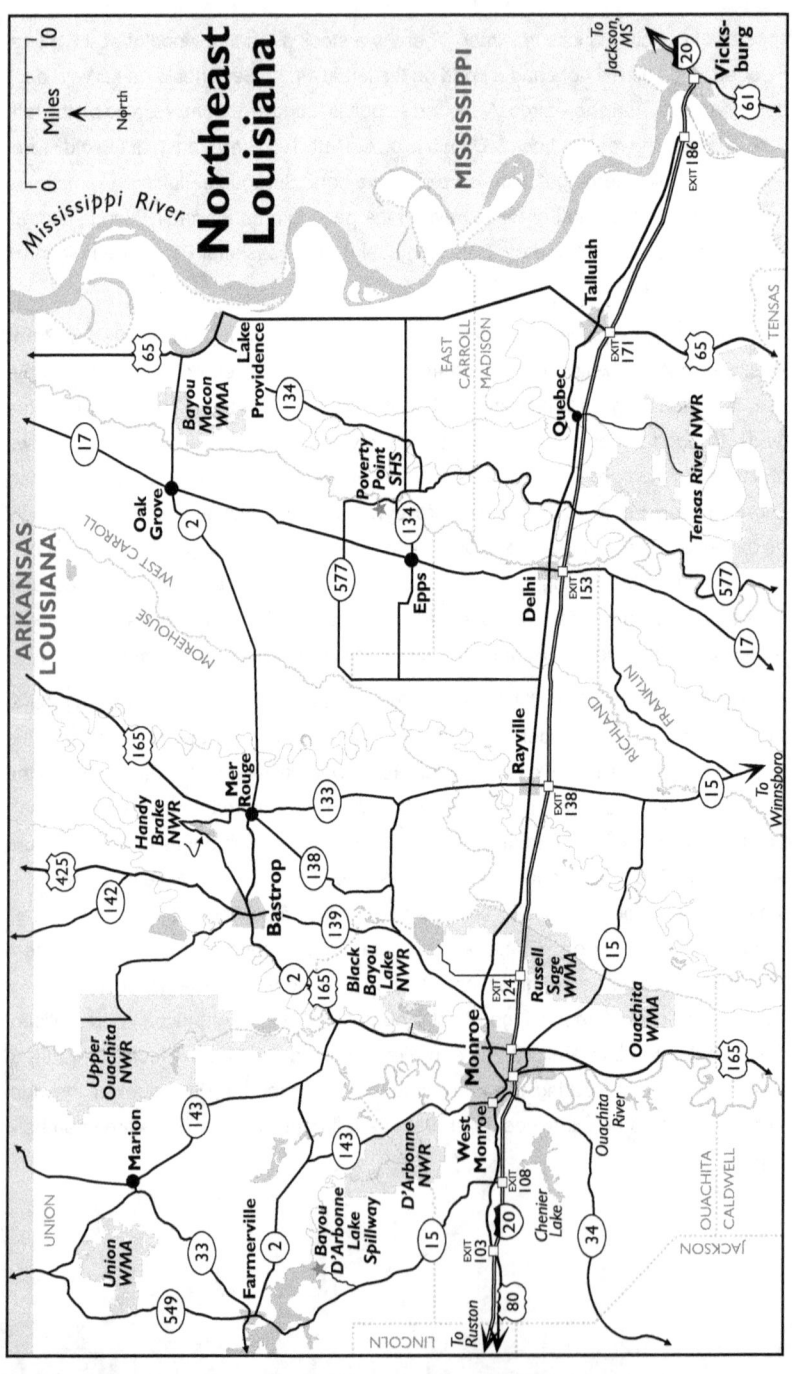

Northeast Louisiana

Worn down and maintained by the ancient annual floods of the Mississippi River, the fields, streams, and bottomlands of Louisiana's delta region support a rich array of habitats. Birds such as American Black Duck and Golden Eagle, very rare in other parts of the state, are seen here virtually every year—at least until recent years in the case of the duck. This region supported the last confirmed breeding area of the Ivory-billed Woodpecker and remains remote and off the beaten path for most birders. However, a handful of hardy birders know and work the area well and contribute more than their fair share during Christmas Bird Counts, bird atlases, and breeding bird surveys.

A network of wildlife management areas and national wildlife refuges covers the region. Because the delta region is large and is home to so few birders, there is great potential for discovering new birding sites and refining what is known about the birdlife here. This is the place in Louisiana where Cerulean Warbler, Scarlet Tanager, and American Goldfinch are suspected to breed. You could be the first to confirm this.

Yellow-billed Cuckoo   Dan Lane

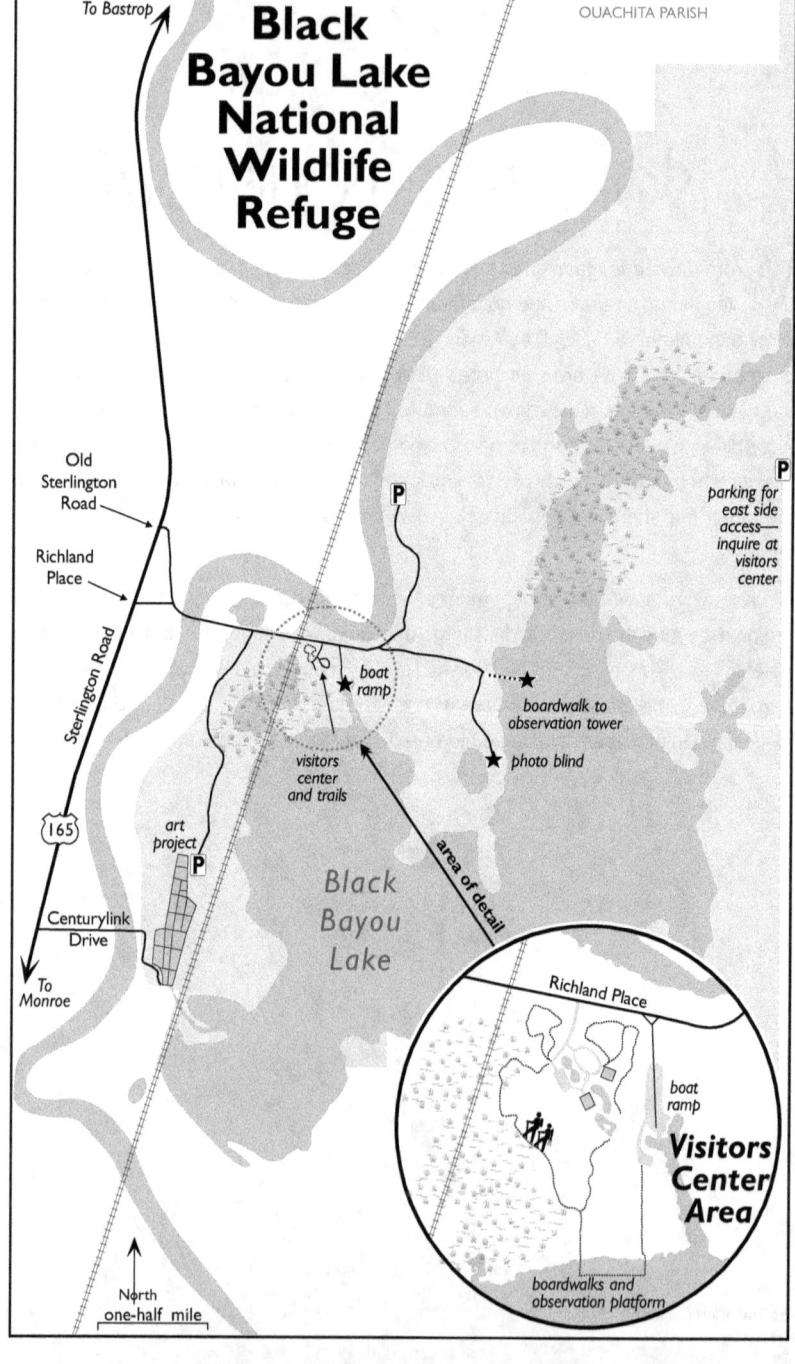

BLACK BAYOU LAKE NATIONAL WILDLIFE REFUGE

This relatively new, yet exceedingly interesting, refuge lies within a few short miles of Monroe. The U.S. Fish and Wildlife Service partnered with the city to establish the reserve. With more than 4,200 acres, it not only protects most of the lake, but also contains the full spectrum of the region's habitats, from cypress/tupelo swamp and bottomland hardwoods to upland mixed pine/hardwoods.

The small upland area on the east side of the refuge is home to a cluster of endangered Red-cockaded Woodpeckers. Check with the refuge staff for recent sightings. White-breasted and Brown-headed Nuthatches, Prothonotary Warbler, and Bachman's and Chipping Sparrows also can be found.

The observation tower beyond the visitors center overlooks flooded hardwoods and the pier offers a view of Black Bayou Lake. Covering roughly 2,000 acres, this cypress lake provides a thriving habitat for an array of species during all seasons. Green Heron, Yellow-billed Cuckoo, Great Crested Flycatcher, Prothonotary Warbler, Northern Parula, Yellow-throated Warbler, Summer Tanager, Indigo and Painted Buntings, and Baltimore Oriole are representative breeders.

Waterfowl enthusiasts visiting in January, when the refuge is full of resident and wintering birds, can see the majority of the refuge's 20 documented duck species. Refuge employees provide nest boxes for Wood Ducks, which are banded on the refuge each year.

To reach the refuge from Monroe, head north on US-165 (Sterlington Road) from its intersection with US-80. After 6 miles, turn right (east) at Richland Place. At 0.2 mile, check out the bayou on both sides, but don't park on the bridge. At 0.6 mile, you reach a visitors center with interactive exhibits. Farther along are a nature trail, meadows, woods, an observation deck, wildlife pier, and a boat ramp. Follow refuge signage to other features.

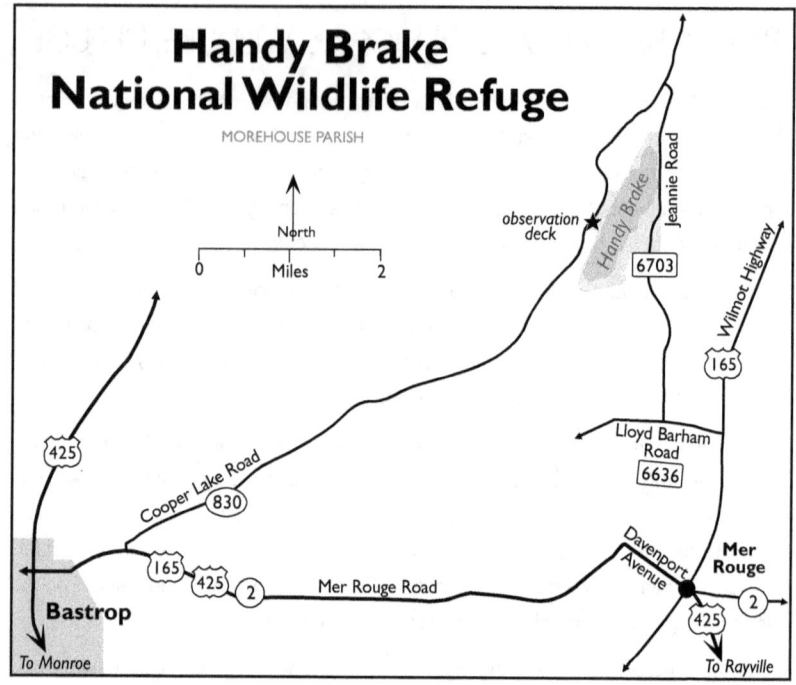

HANDY BRAKE NATIONAL WILDLIFE REFUGE

Handy Brake was established in 1990 and comprises 490 acres of early bottomland hardwood forest. It can be a good place to stop for waterfowl, raptors, and shorebirds during winter and migration.

Year-round residents include Great Blue Heron, Great Egret, and Black-crowned Night-Heron. During summer, Snowy Egret, Little Blue, Tricolored, and Green Herons, and Yellow-crowned Night-Heron are seen. Anhingas are seen here in late spring, summer, and early fall as they dry their wings or swim along between dives with only their heads above water. Breeding songbirds include most, if not all, of the warblers that regularly nest in Louisiana.

To reach the refuge from the town of Bastrop, go east 1 mile on US-165 from its junction with US-465 in the center of town. Turn left onto Cooper Lake Road (LA-830). Zero your odometer and travel northeast for 6.2 miles to an observation deck from which you can scope the lake or walk down to its shore. Wood Duck and Pied-billed Grebe are permanent residents and share their habitat during winter with dabbling and diving ducks.

Continue on Cooper Lake Road and at 8.1 miles, turn right onto gravel-surfaced Jeannie Road (PR-6703). Exercise caution on this road during winter or after a heavy rain as the mud might make it impassable. After about 800 yards, all the land on the right for the next 2 miles or so is refuge land. This road intersects Lloyd Barham Road (PR-6636) at 11.8 miles. Turn left to meet US-165 at 12.4 miles. A right turn takes you back to Monroe.

Observation tower at Mollicy Unit of Upper Ouchita NWR   USFWS

UPPER OUACHITA NATIONAL WILDLIFE REFUGE

The Upper Ouachita NWR is massive, with more than 40,000 acres of open water, bottomland hardwoods, wooded swamp, and uplands. Bald Eagles nest here and can sometimes be seen from the new observation tower at the Mollicy Unit. There are ample opportunities to observe wading birds, raptors, and songbirds at this relatively new refuge. A checklist for the North Louisiana National Wildlife Refuges can be found online at their website: *http://www.fws.gov/northlouisiana/*.

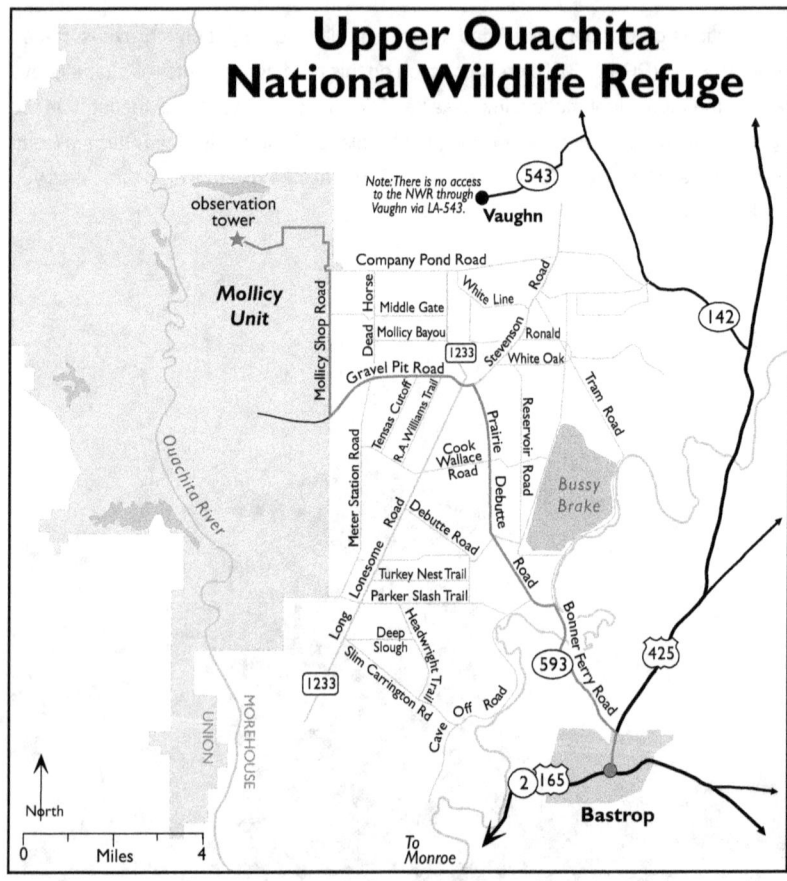

From Monroe, travel north on US-165 to the town of Bastrop. At the town square, take a left onto US-425 north. In 0.9 mile turn left onto LA-593, Bonner Ferry Road, and follow it for 3.3 miles to Prairie Debutte Road on the left. Turn left here and in half a mile stay right at a fork, still on Prairie Debutte Road. There are many side roads you may explore given the right weather conditions, or you can head straight to the new observation tower on the Mollicy Unit. To do this, keep driving north on Prairie Debutte Road for 4.8 miles until it ends at Stevenson Road. Turn left and keep straight ahead onto Gravel Pit Road, which you follow for 3.5 miles to Mollicy Shop Road. This road follows the boundary of the Upper Ouachita NWR Mollicy Unit. Turn right (north) here for 3.0 miles to reach Company Pond Road. (*Note:* Direct access to the refuge from LA-142 via LA-543 and Vaughn is no longer permitted.) Turn left, then right, then left and right again, following signage to reach the observation tower.

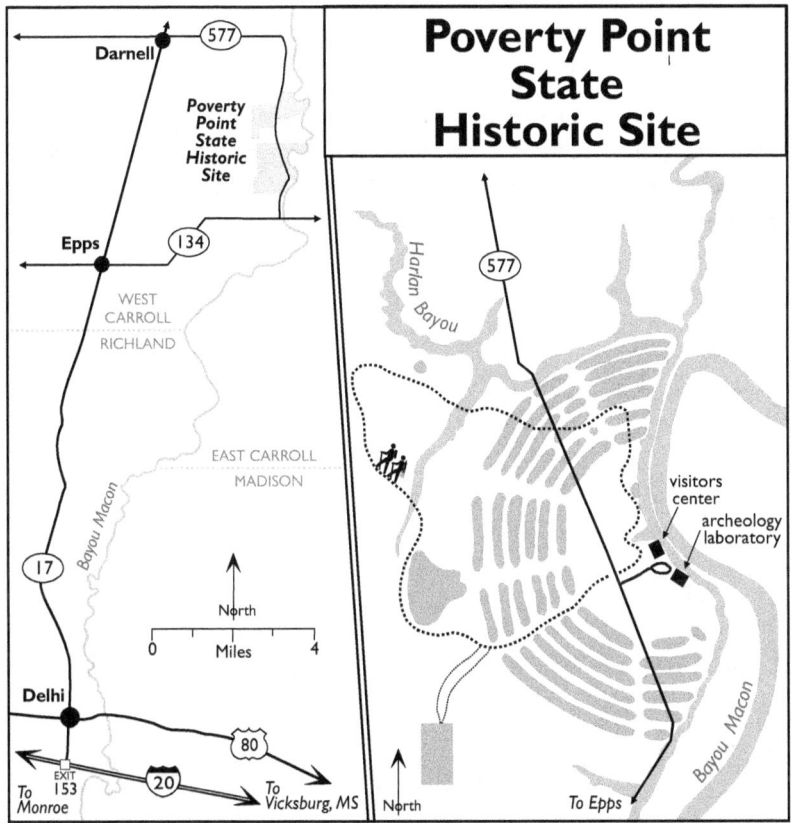

POVERTY POINT STATE HISTORIC SITE

An extremely important prehistoric archaeological site, Poverty Point was created by mound builders more than 3,000 years ago and is comprised of more than 400 acres of habitat including meadows, streams, and woods. Bayou Macon borders the park to the east and Harlan Bayou bisects much of the northern section of the park. The many species of trees, shrubs, and vines provide habitat for the numerous songbirds that nest and spend the winter here. Eastern Wood-Pewee, Great Crested Flycatcher, Eastern Kingbird, Wood Thrush, Hooded Warbler, Northern Parula, Summer Tanager, Dickcissel, and Orchard Oriole are representative nesters. Wood Duck, Barred Owl, Red-headed Woodpecker, Eastern Bluebird, and Brown Thrasher are examples of permanent residents; while American Kestrel, Brown Creeper, Winter Wren, both kinglets, American Pipit, and Orange-crowned Warbler are some of the many wintering birds. The entire park can be traversed along a 2.5-mile interpretive walkway.

To reach this ancient wonder, go north from the town of Delhi on LA-17 from its intersection with US-80 for 10.5 miles to Epps. At Epps, turn right onto LA-134 and travel east for 4.6 miles. Turn left onto LA-577. Take this road for 1.1 miles to the park entrance, which is on the right.

Yellow-throated Warbler Dan Lane

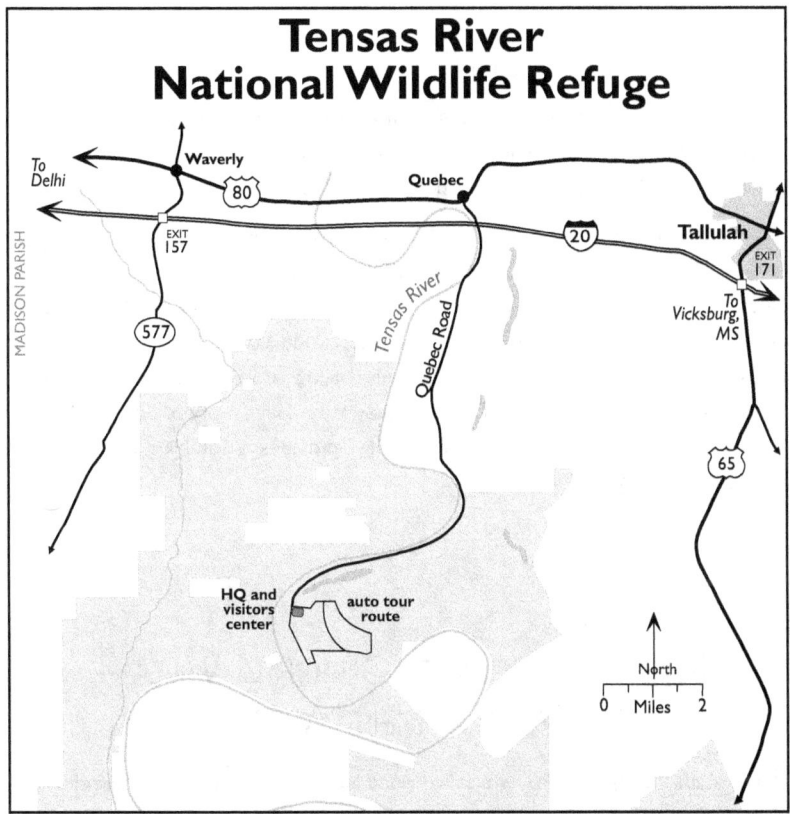

TENSAS RIVER NATIONAL WILDLIFE REFUGE

This extensive hardwood bottomland was one of the last known nesting sites of Ivory-billed Woodpecker and Bachman's Warbler. Lying in the alluvial flats created by prehistoric Mississippi River floods, the preserve encompasses more than 66,000 acres. It is a large, wild place as evidenced by the concentration of an estimated 250 Black Bears found here. The birding opportunities at the refuge rival those of any inland Louisiana locale.

A sampling of the common nesting species includes Wood Duck, Wild Turkey, Yellow-crowned Night-Heron, Mississippi Kite, Pileated Woodpecker, Horned Lark, Yellow-throated and Red-eyed Vireos, White-breasted Nuthatch, Blue-gray Gnatcatcher, Black-and-white, Swainson's, Kentucky, and Hooded Warblers, American Redstart, Yellow-throated Warbler, Yellow-breasted Chat, and Eastern Towhee.

Cerulean Warbler has been reported here during summer, although it has yet to be confirmed as a breeder in Louisiana.

Spring and fall produce migrants such as Tree Swallow, Veery, Gray-cheeked Thrush, Ovenbird, and Golden-winged (scarce), Blue-winged, Bay-breasted, Blackburnian, Chestnut-sided, Blackpoll, and Canada Warblers.

Finding this wonderful area is fairly straightforward. From the town of Delhi, go east on US-80 from its junction with LA-17 for 11.3 miles to the small crossroad of Quebec. Turn right on Fred Morgan Sr. Road and travel south for 5.9 miles to the refuge. The road becomes paved on the refuge and boasts ample shoulders for parking. At 9.8 miles, 4-mile-long Rainey Lake Hiking Trail is to the left. At 10.4 miles, a visitors center is on the left. The extremely informative Ivory-billed Woodpecker display is a "must see." A 0.3-mile nature trail provides a sampling of the forest's deciduous majesty.

RUSSELL SAGE AND OUACHITA WILDLIFE MANAGEMENT AREAS

The Russell Sage complex, which is divided into northern and southern portions, is comprised of more than 17,000 acres of prime alluvial properties. Although non-game species receive short shrift at WMAs, many birds and mammals benefit from the money and attention paid to White-tailed Deer. The many and varied habitats provide yearlong foraging for a great number of birds. But, keep in mind the hunting seasons (generally mid-October through January; check the Louisiana Department of Wildlife and Fisheries website for local details) and make certain if you are walking around in the woods during those times that you are wearing something bright, preferably in blaze orange.

To reach the northern part of the wildlife management area, go east from Monroe on I-20 for about 5 miles and take Exit 124. Turn left and head north on LA-594 for 5.4 miles to Stubbs Ritchie Road. Take a right and head east for 0.6 mile to Stubbs Vinson Road. Turn left and travel north 0.5 mile to Buckley Hill Road. Make a right and head east for a mile until the road ends at Russell Sage. Park on the left side of the road at the yellow gates.

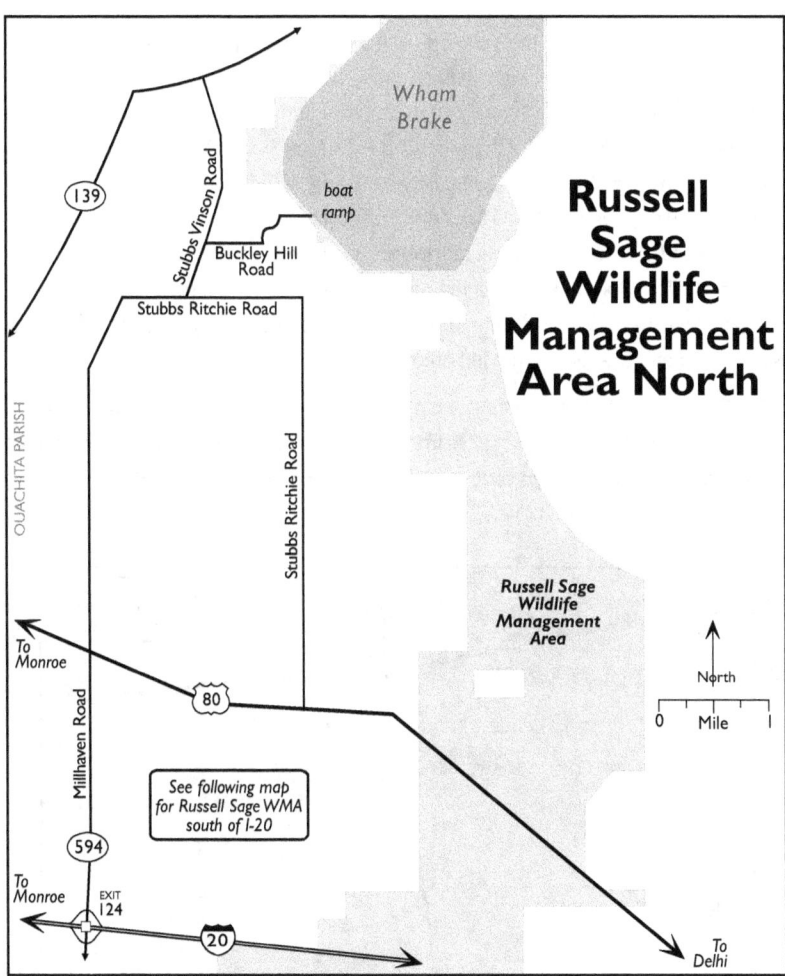

Beyond the levee, Wham Brake should be scoped during winter for ducks. During summer, look for Anhinga and large waders. Walk the levee during winter to stir up wrens, kinglets, pipits, warblers, and sparrows. Summer and migration fare are the expected flycatchers, vireos, thrushes, warblers, tanagers, grosbeaks, and orioles.

194 NORTHEAST LOUISIANA

The southern portion of the WMA is called Ouachita and is comprised of 26,000 acres. To reach this part from Monroe, take I-20 east for roughly 5 miles to Exit 124 and turn right onto Russell Sage Road. In 0.5 mile turn right onto the gravel road just past the entrance driveway of the Magnolia Recycling Plant. Follow this road for 5.3 miles through Russell Sage to Gourd Bayou Road, exploring along the way. Turn left onto Gourd Bayou and go 1 mile to LA-15. Turn right and take this highway for 0.8 mile to Miller Road. At this intersection, turn left and go 1.6 miles to Bud Smith Road. Follow Bud Smith Road for 0.5 mile until the pavement ends. From here, Ouachita may be examined via the gravel roads ahead. To return to Monroe, backtrack to the junction of Miller Road and LA-15 and turn left onto LA-15.

If Russell Sage Road is impassable, which can sometimes occur during winter, access to Ouachita might be possible from Monroe as follows: From the intersection of LA-15 and US-165 South, go southeast on LA-15 for 5 miles to Miller Road. Turn right and proceed as outlined above.

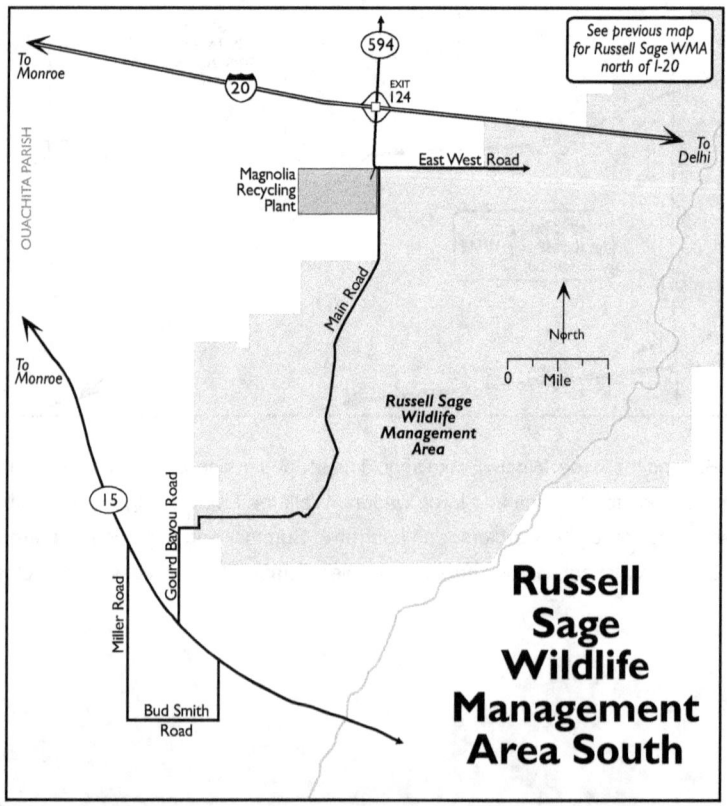

Russell Sage Wildlife Management Area South

D'ARBONNE NATIONAL WILDLIFE REFUGE

Red-cockaded Woodpecker Jim E. Johnson

Located just northwest of Monroe, this refuge represents the only viable Red-cockaded Woodpecker habitat in the northeast region of the state that is easily accessible. Although it's mostly lowland, the refuge contains pine uplands at its eastern and western boundaries. The 17,415-acre NWR is a haven during winter for waterfowl. Divided north to south by Bayou D'Arbonne, the area represents the eastern extent of Greater Roadrunner's range, as well as that of the core of nesting Scissor-tailed Flycatchers.

To get to the refuge, drive north on LA-143 (North 7th Street) from its intersection with US-80 (Cypress Street) in West Monroe. The highway becomes the eastern boundary of the refuge at about 6 miles. At about 8.4 miles you pass New Wall Lake Road on the right. To find the principal Red-cockaded Woodpecker area, drive 0.45 mile past this junction to a parking lot on the left (west) side of the road. Park there and walk toward the west into the refuge on an old woods road. After about a hundred yards, look south into a mature pine area where some trees are painted with white bands. From that point south—and even to the west—you will find more banded cavity trees.

Back on LA-143, in 1.1 miles, well-maintained Holland Bluff Road leads through the reserve to a boat ramp. Also on this road is the NWR's headquarters.

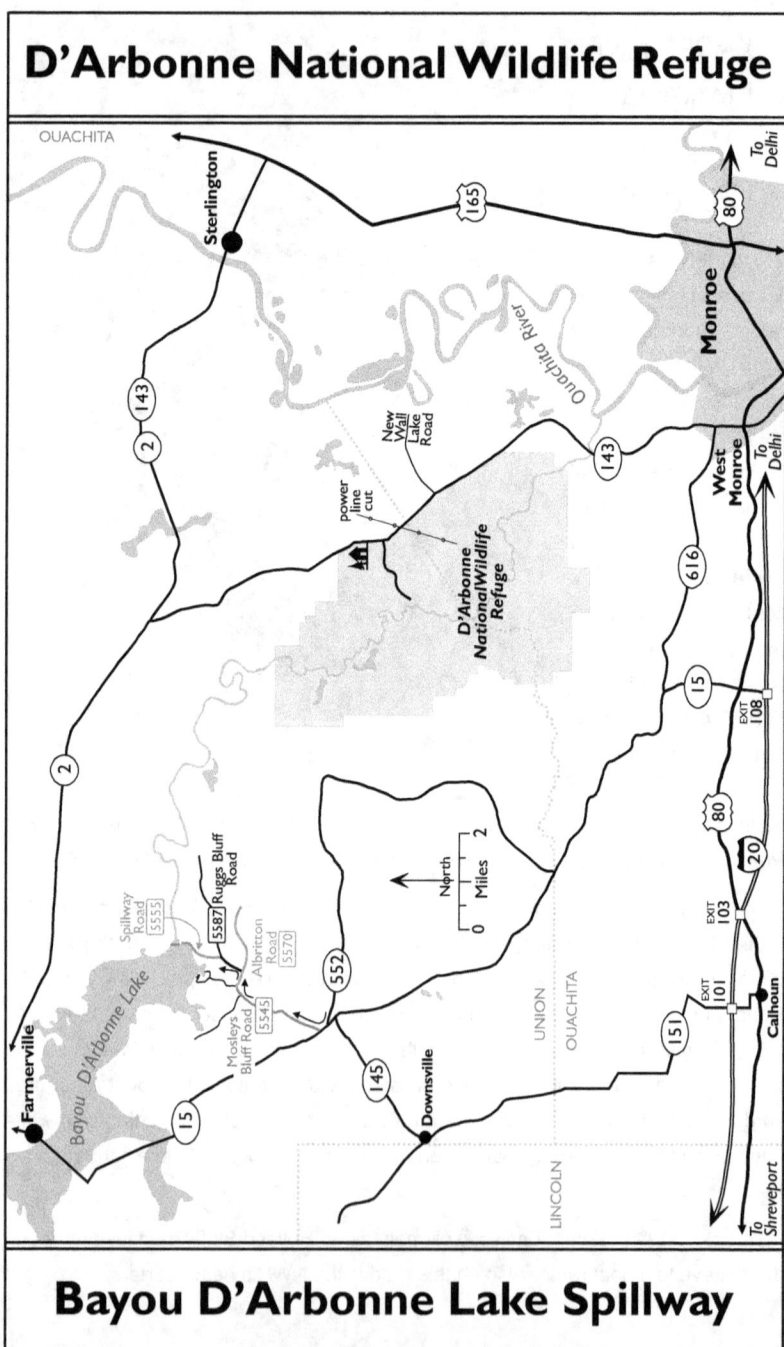

A few of the usual suspects seen on the refuge during winter include House, Winter, Sedge, and Marsh Wrens, Golden-crowned and Ruby-crowned Kinglets, Hermit Thrush, and Orange-crowned and Yellow-rumped Warblers. A few of the many nesting birds include Eastern Wood-Pewee, Acadian and Great Crested Flycatchers, and Worm-eating, Black-and-white, Kentucky, Hooded, and Pine Warblers.

BAYOU D'ARBONNE LAKE SPILLWAY

This relatively short loop through pine uplands and farms holds far more interest for the winter birder. Nonetheless, the prudent observer will always keep a watchful eye for migrants during spring and fall.

To find the spillway, go west from Monroe on I-20. Take Exit 108 and turn right (north) onto LA-15. At about 13 miles, LA-15 intersects first with LA-145 on the left, then LA-552 on the right. Take the next right onto Moseleys Bluff Road (PR-5545). After 2.2 miles, bear right onto Albritton Road (PR-5570). Stay right again at 2.4 miles, following PR-5570. At 2.7 miles, turn left on Ruggs Bluff Road (PR-5587). Follow this lane for 0.6 mile and turn left onto Spillway Road (PR-5555). You reach the dam in 0.7 mile. Park anywhere near the boat launch and walk up to the levee to scope the open water. This is an excellent cold-weather spot for both scaup, Common Goldeneye, Ruddy Duck, Common Loon, Osprey, Bald Eagle, Bonaparte's and Ring-billed Gulls, and massive rafts of Double-crested Cormorants.

To bird a 4.5-mile bridged arm of the lake, return to the intersection of Moseleys Bluff Road and LA-15 and turn right. At 6.6 miles, turn right onto LA-33 toward Farmerville. Here there will be opportunities to scope the lake from both sides of the short causeway.

ABUNDANCE AND STATUS OF LOUISIANA BIRDS

These bar graphs estimate the likelihood of detecting bird species by week within Louisiana. For purposes of this guide, the state is divided into two sections. The North is generally the area north of I-10. The South is the area south of I-10. There are certainly exceptions, with some habitats occurring north of I-10 that are more similar to the coastal prairie and *vice versa*. However imperfect, we inflict this typology on the reader with hope that it provides useful refinement. Species that are, overall, only of casual or accidental occurrence in Louisiana are not included, though casual and accidental designations are given for seasonal rarity.

The key to finding your "target" birds is to be in the right place at the right time. In other words, arrange to be in proper habitat in the appropriate season(s). Use these bar graphs for seasonal abundance, particularly useful for noting the comings and goings of seasonal migrants, but also for the overall abundance of resident species. Use the annotated checklist (page 221) for learning details about habitat preferences and best sites to find many of the more-sought-after species.

If you locate a bird which you believe is noteworthy due to its overall rarity in the region, or because of its seasonal rarity, or you find it in particularly unusual numbers, take careful notes and/or photos and report your observation promptly to the regional editor(s) of the Arkansas & Louisiana Region of the journal *North American Birds* http://www.aba.org/nab and to the LABIRD website. (See also page 13.)

The American Birding Association adopted the following standardized abundance definitions below in 2001.

ABUNDANCE AND STATUS OF LOUISIANA BIRDS 199

COMMON: Present in moderate to large numbers, and easily found in appropriate habitat at the right time of year.

FAIRLY COMMON: Present in small to moderate numbers, and usually can be found in appropriate habitat at the right time of year.

UNCOMMON: Present in small numbers, and sometimes—but not always—found with some effort in appropriate habitat at the right time of year.

RARE: Occurs annually in very small numbers. Not to be expected on any given day, but some species might be found with extended effort over the course of the appropriate season(s).

CASUAL: Occurs less than annually, but there tends to be a pattern over time at the right time of year in appropriate habitat; usually 4 or more records in last 10 years. Single, accidental seasonal occurrences are not shown.

COMMON: Occurs in moderate to large numbers, and easily found in appropriate habitat at the right time of year.

FAIRLY COMMON: Occurs in small to moderate numbers, and usually easy to find in appropriate habitat at the right time of year.

UNCOMMON: Occurs in small numbers, and usually—but not always—found with some effort in appropriate habitat at the right time of year.

RARE: Occurs annually in very small numbers. Not to be expected on any given day, but may be found with extended effort over the course of the appropriate season(s).

CASUAL: Occurs less than annually, but there tends to be a pattern over time at the right time of year in appropriate habitat; 4 or more records in last 10 years.

IRREGULAR: Represents an irruptive species whose numbers are highly variable from year to year. There may be small to even large numbers present in one year, while in another year it may be absent altogether

200 ABUNDANCE AND STATUS OF LOUISIANA BIRDS

		January	February	March	April	May	June	July	August	September	October	November	December
☐ Black-bellied Whistling-Duck	N												
	S												
☐ Fulvous Whistling-Duck	N												
	S												
☐ Greater White-fronted Goose	N												
	S												
☐ Snow Goose	N												
	S												
☐ Ross's Goose	N												
	S												
☐ Cackling Goose	N												
	S												
☐ Wood Duck	N												
	S												
☐ Gadwall	N												
	S												
☐ American Wigeon	N												
	S												
☐ Mallard	N												
	S												
☐ Mottled Duck	N												
	S												
☐ Blue-winged Teal	N												
	S												
☐ Cinnamon Teal	N												
	S												
☐ Northern Shoveler	N												
	S												
☐ Northern Pintail	N												
	S												
☐ Green-winged Teal	N												
	S												

ABUNDANCE AND STATUS OF LOUISIANA BIRDS 201

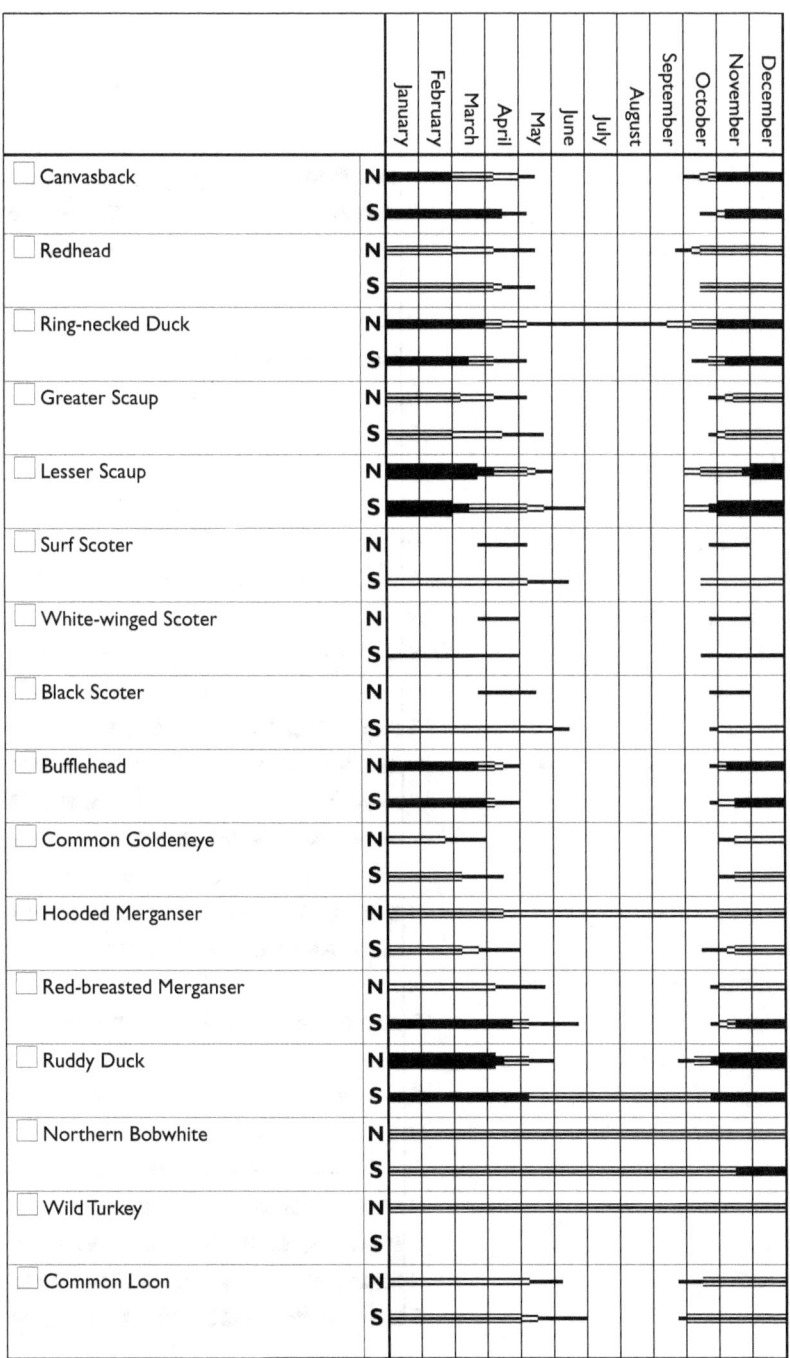

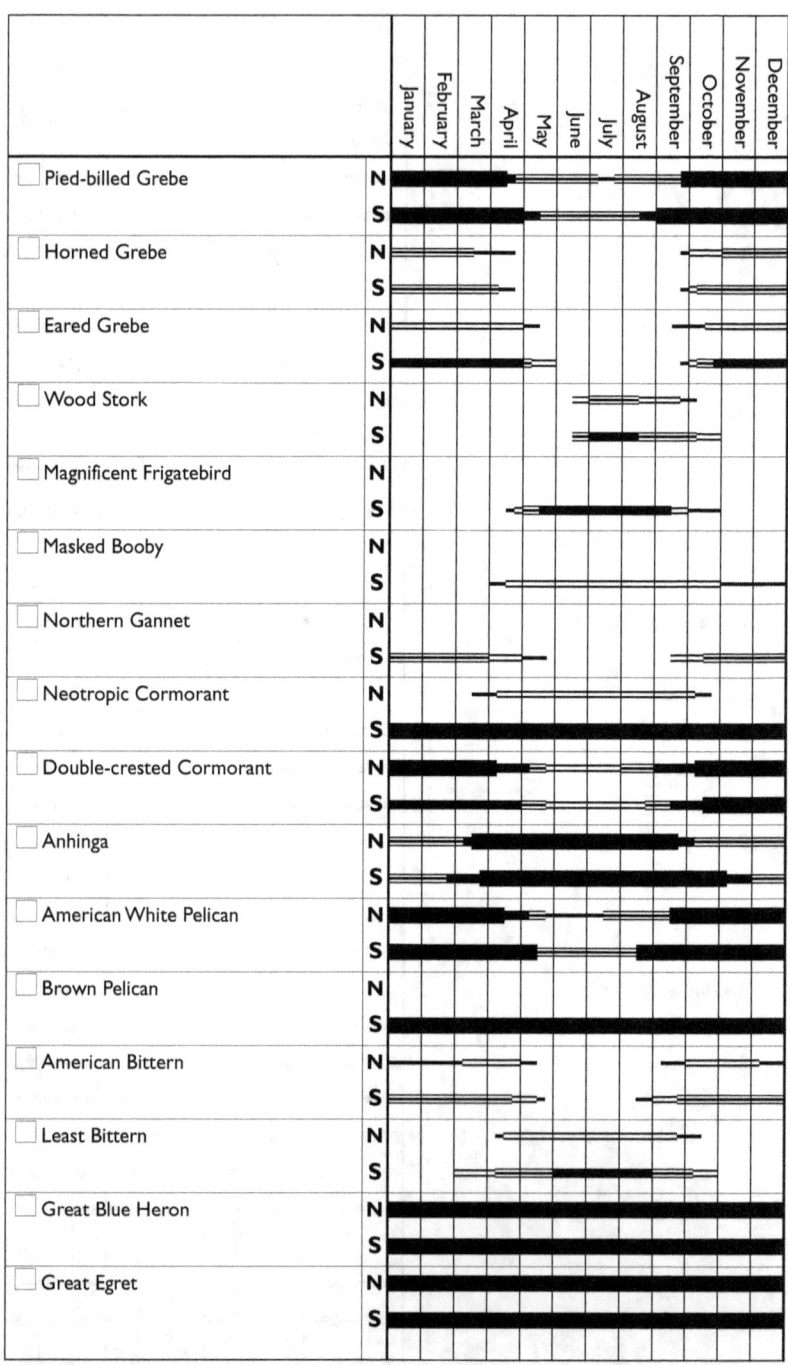

Abundance and Status of Louisiana Birds

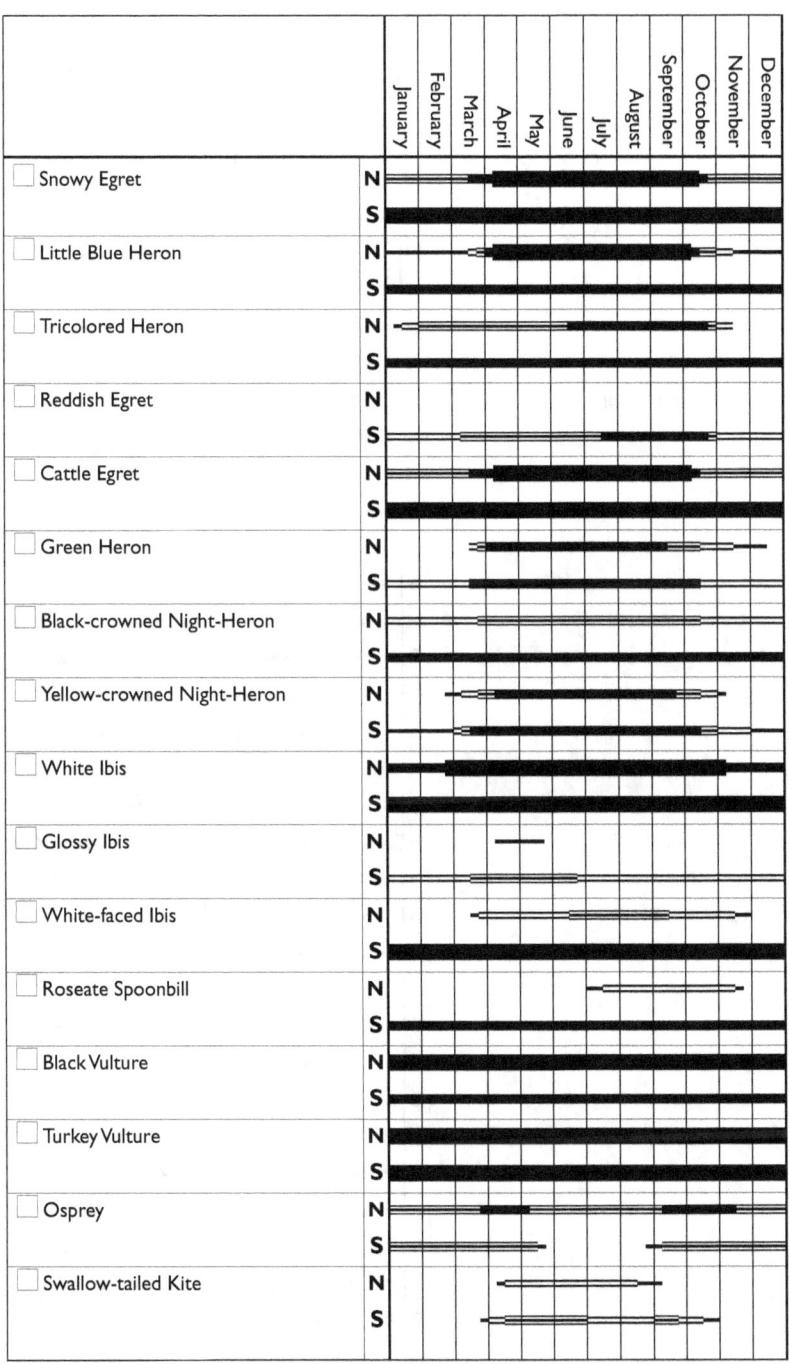

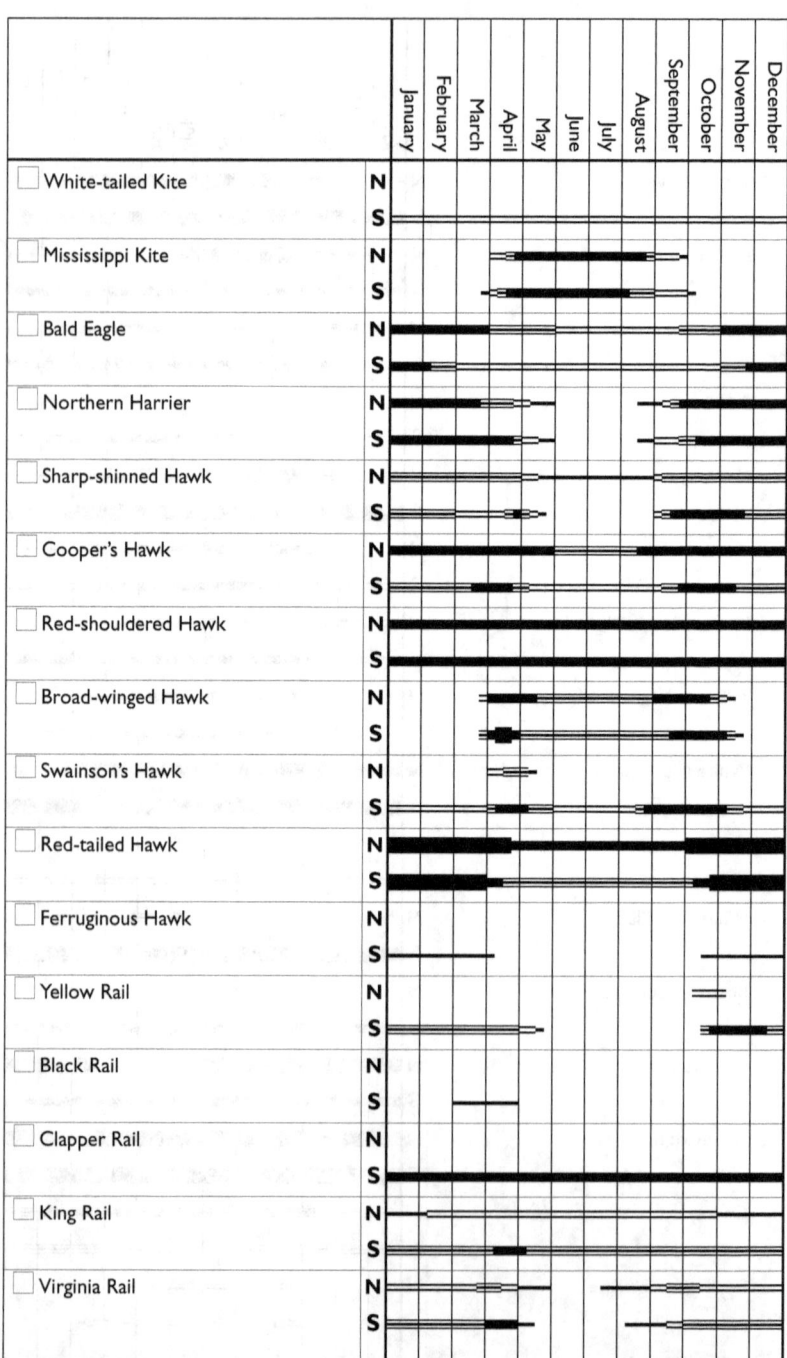

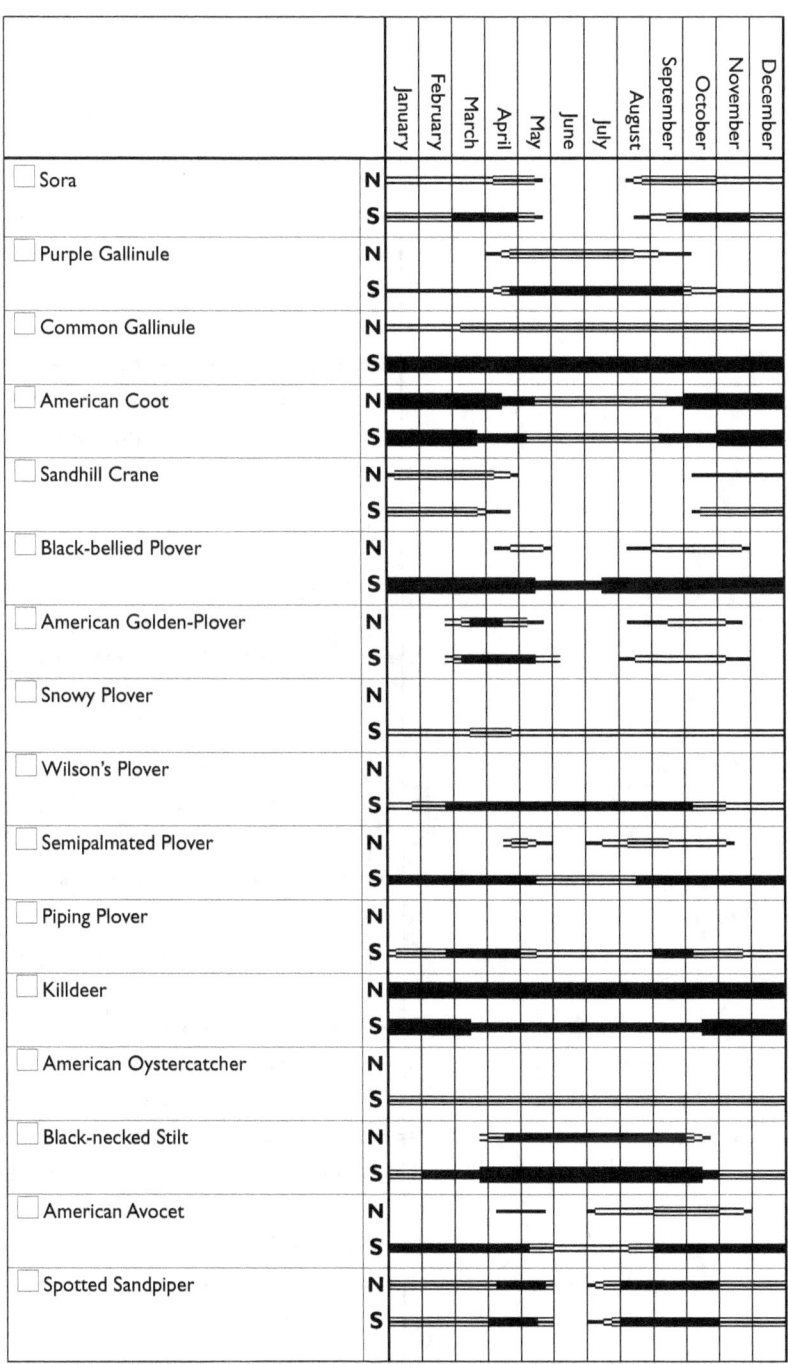

206 Abundance and Status of Louisiana Birds

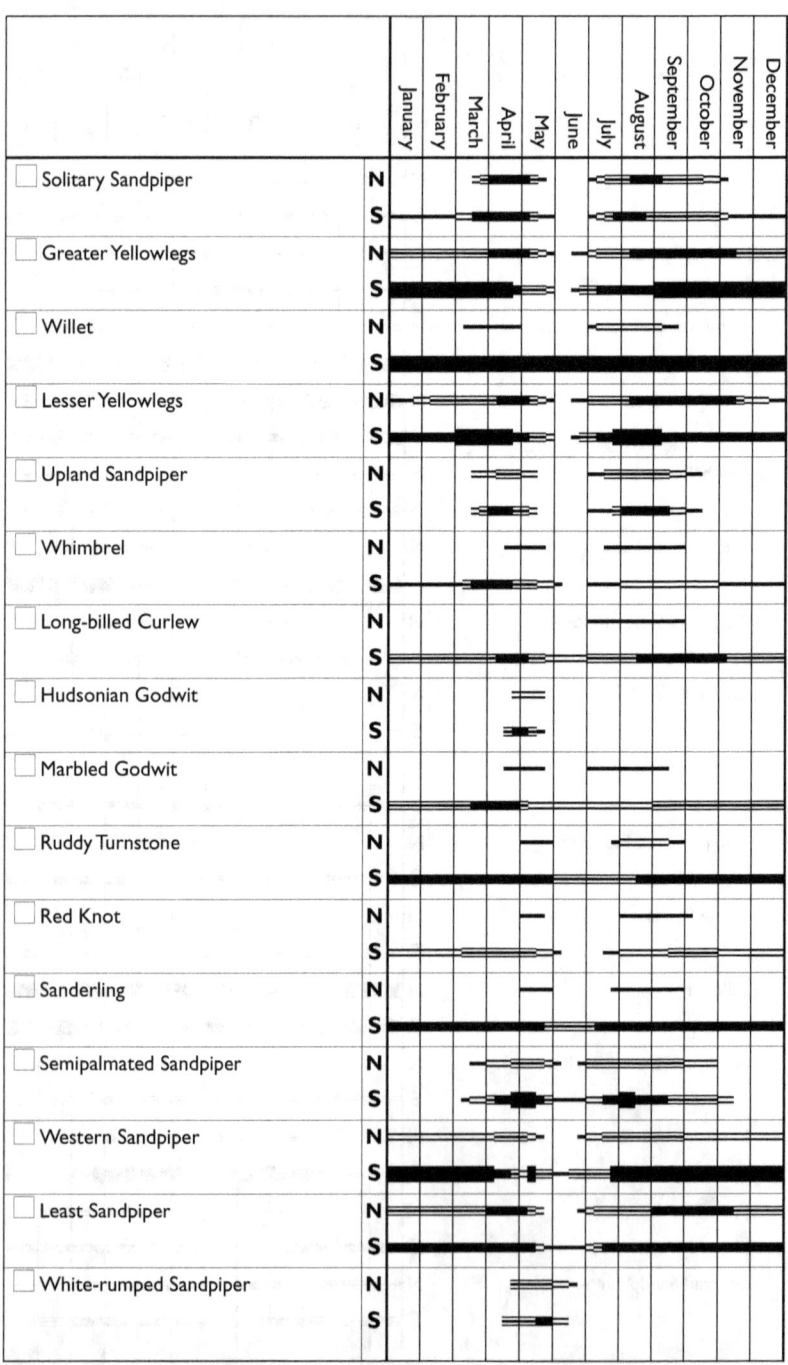

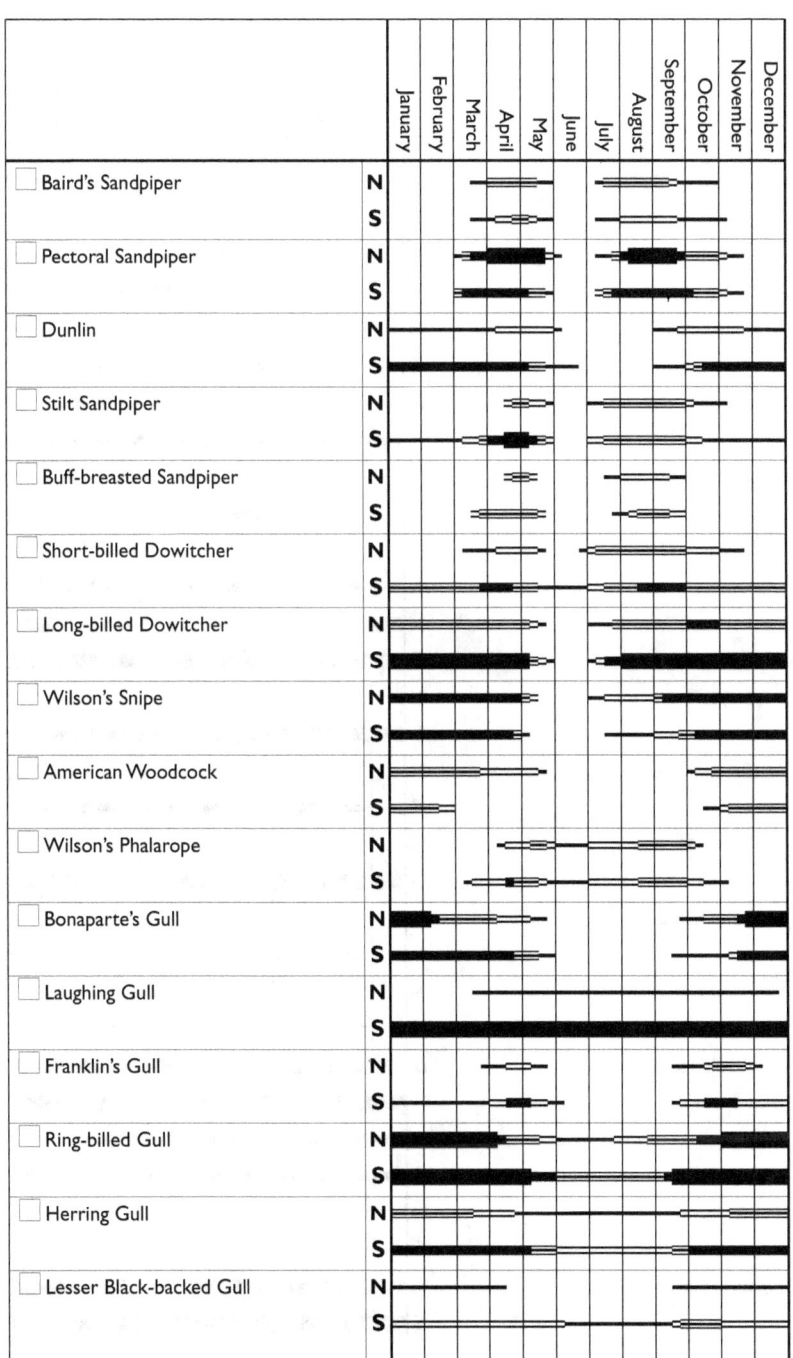

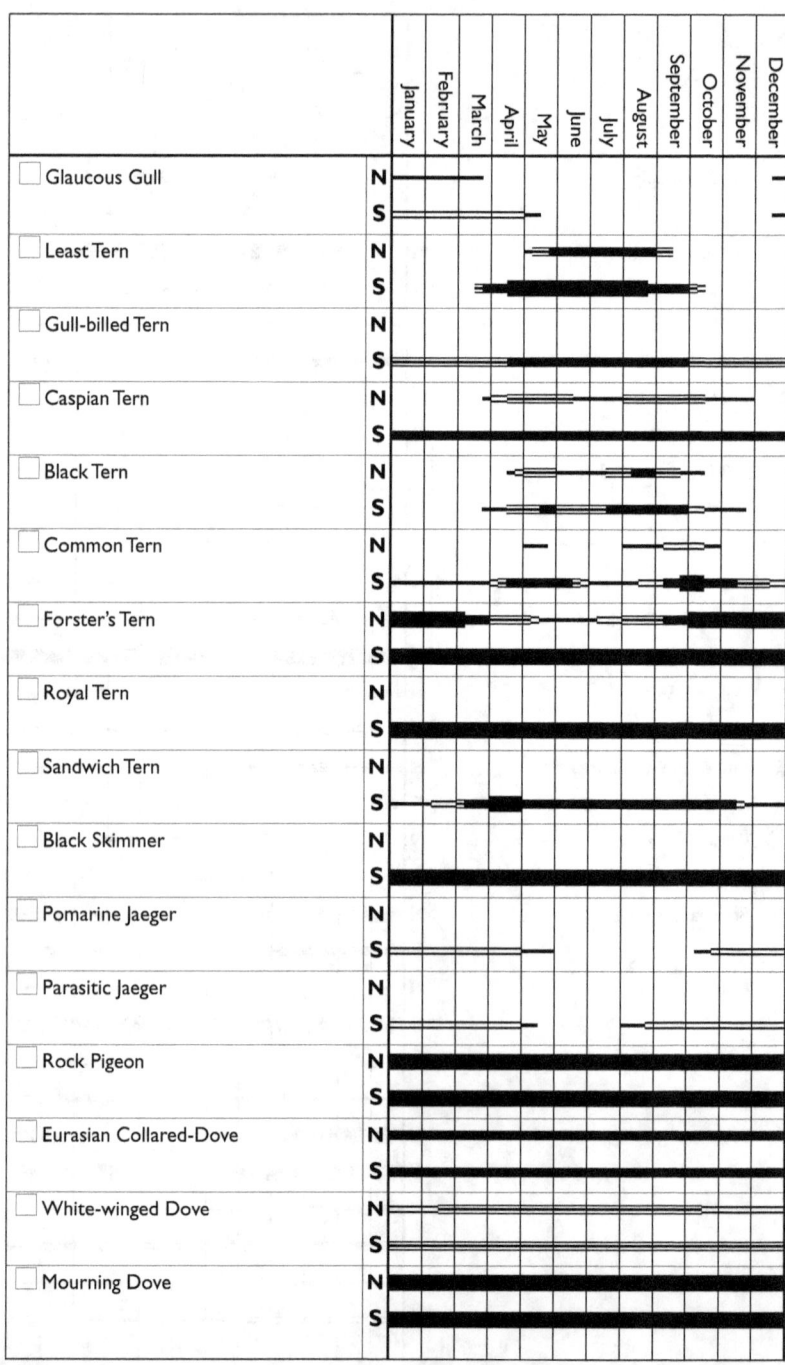

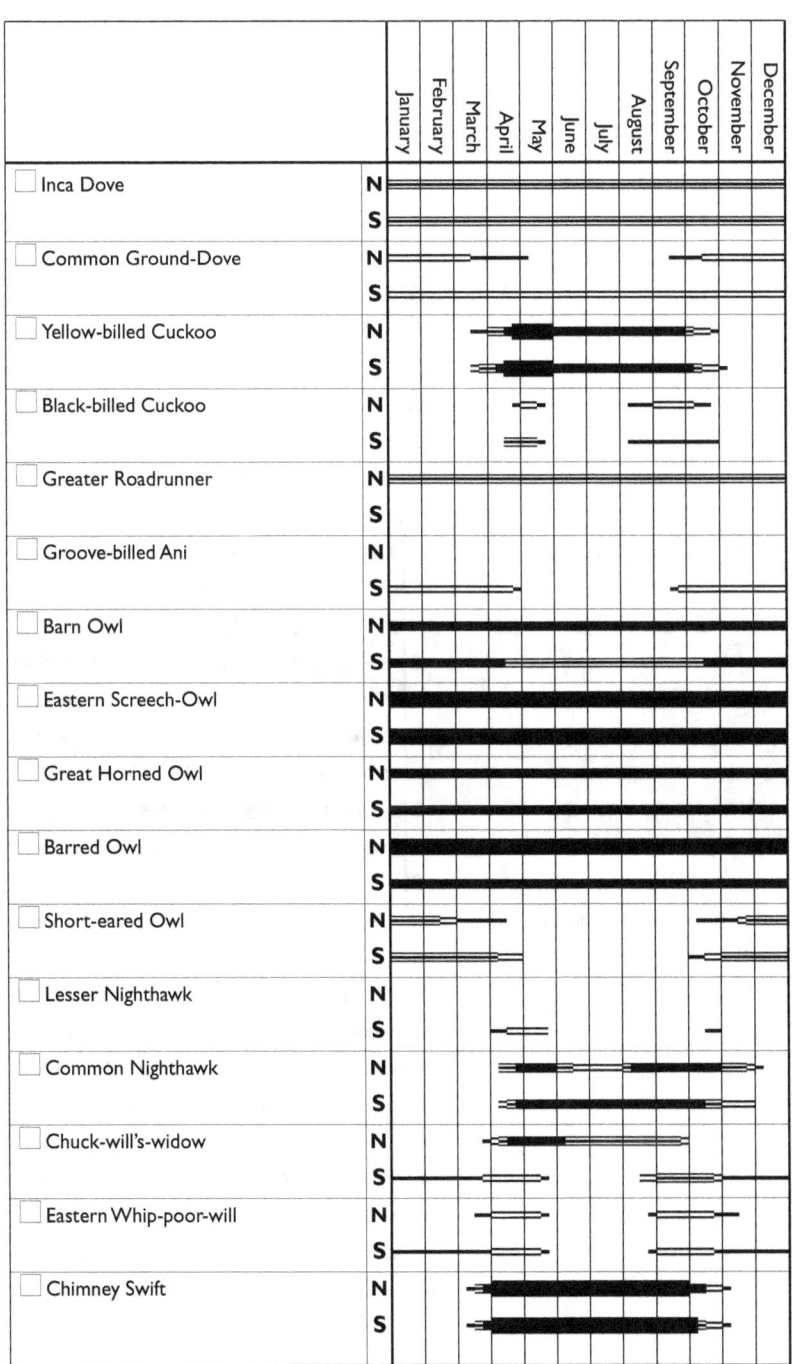

ABUNDANCE AND STATUS OF LOUISIANA BIRDS 211

Species		Jan	Feb	Mar	Apr	May	Jun	Jul	Aug	Sep	Oct	Nov	Dec
☐ Peregrine Falcon	N												
	S												
☐ Olive-sided Flycatcher	N												
	S												
☐ Eastern Wood-Pewee	N												
	S												
☐ Yellow-bellied Flycatcher	N												
	S												
☐ Acadian Flycatcher	N												
	S												
☐ Alder Flycatcher	N												
	S												
☐ Willow Flycatcher	N												
	S												
☐ Least Flycatcher	N												
	S												
☐ Eastern Phoebe	N												
	S												
☐ Vermilion Flycatcher	N												
	S												
☐ Ash-throated Flycatcher	N												
	S												
☐ Great Crested Flycatcher	N												
	S												
☐ Western Kingbird	N												
	S												
☐ Eastern Kingbird	N												
	S												
☐ Gray Kingbird	N												
	S												
☐ Scissor-tailed Flycatcher	N												
	S												

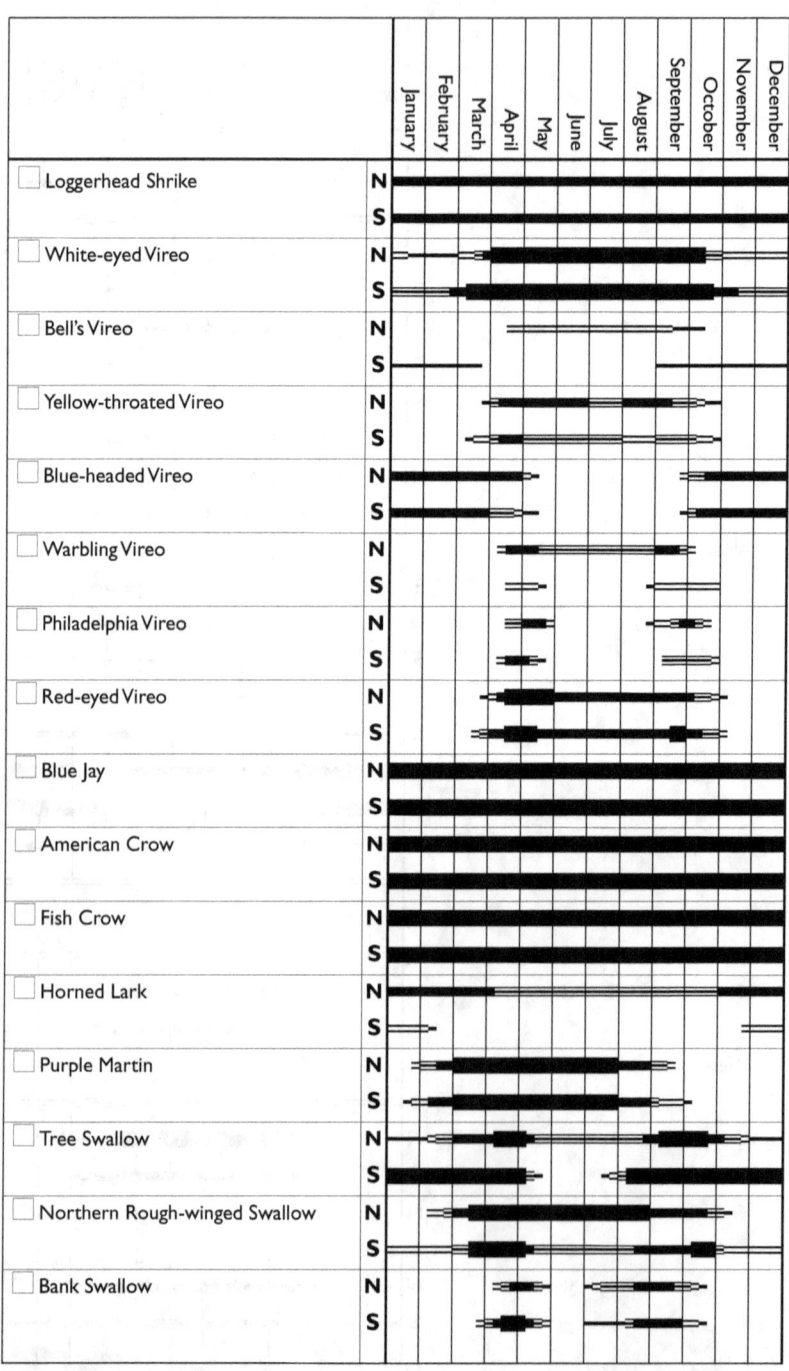

ABUNDANCE AND STATUS OF LOUISIANA BIRDS 213

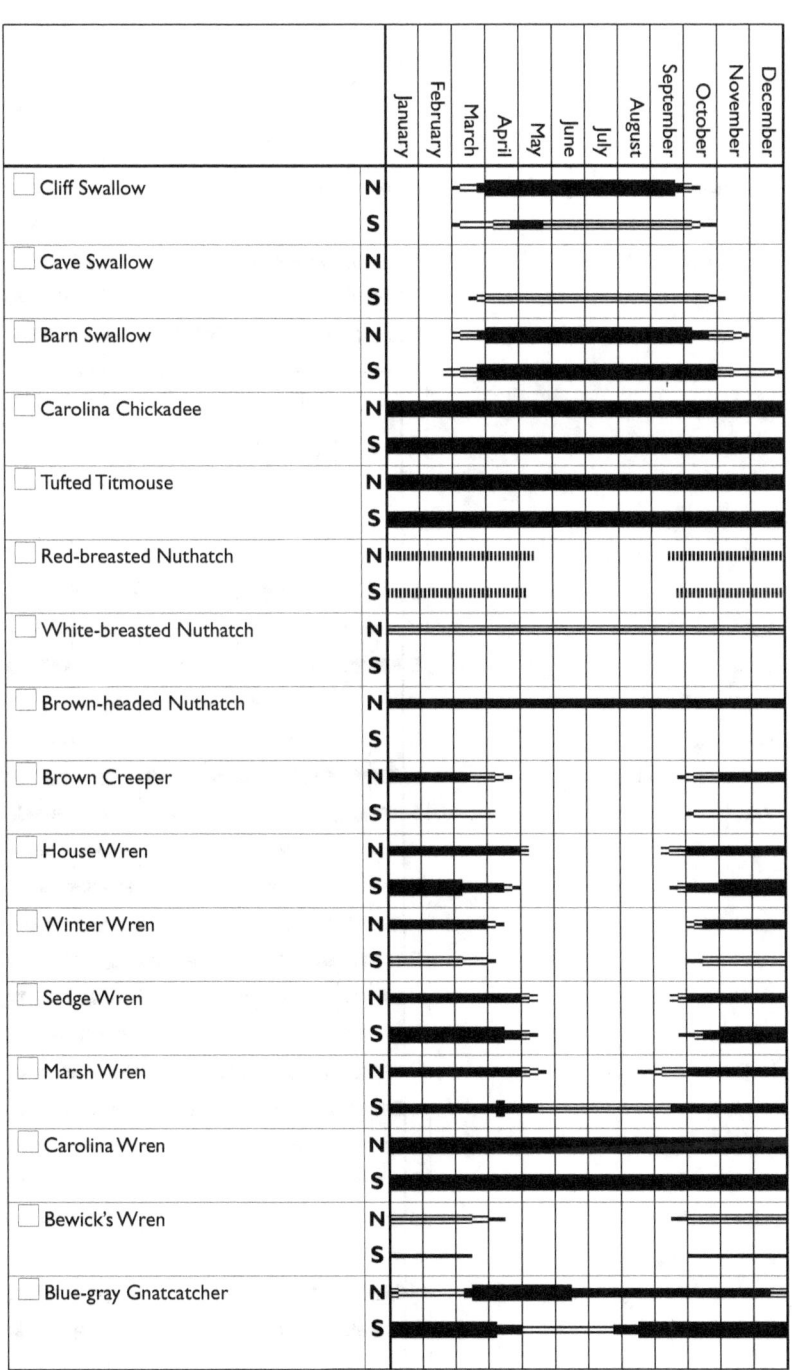

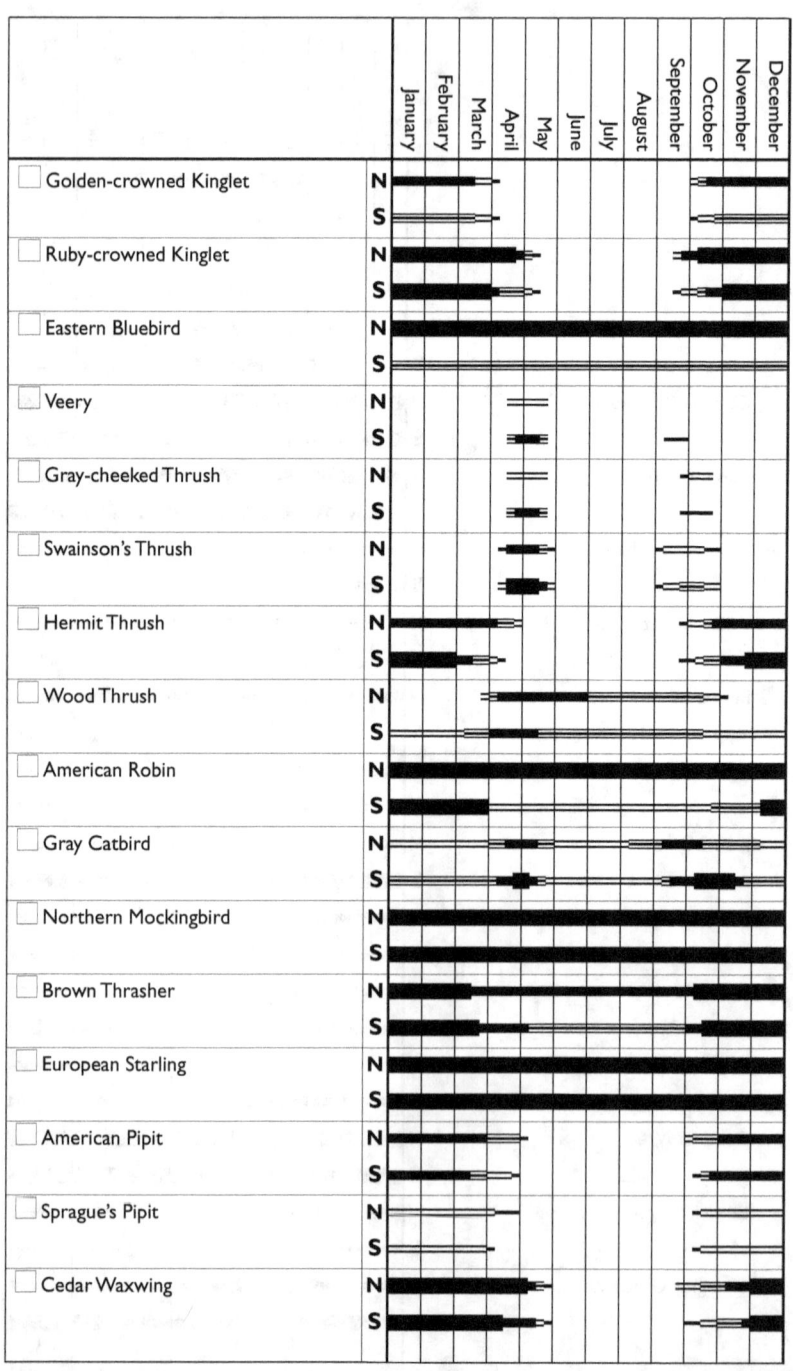

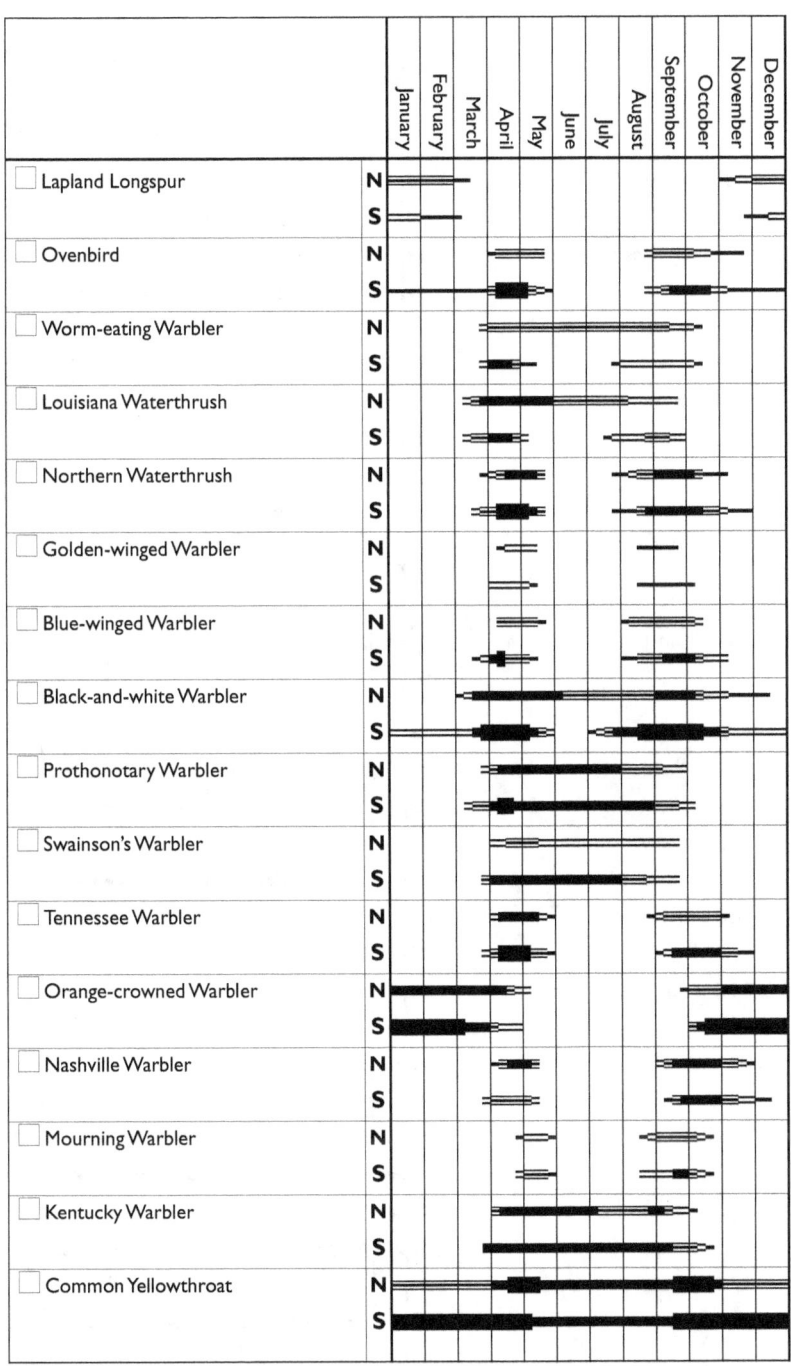

216 ABUNDANCE AND STATUS OF LOUISIANA BIRDS

		Jan	Feb	Mar	Apr	May	Jun	Jul	Aug	Sep	Oct	Nov	Dec
Hooded Warbler	N												
	S												
American Redstart	N												
	S												
Cape May Warbler	N												
	S												
Cerulean Warbler	N												
	S												
Northern Parula	N												
	S												
Magnolia Warbler	N												
	S												
Bay-breasted Warbler	N												
	S												
Blackburnian Warbler	N												
	S												
Yellow Warbler	N												
	S												
Chestnut-sided Warbler	N												
	S												
Blackpoll Warbler	N												
	S												
Black-throated Blue Warbler	N												
	S												
Palm Warbler	N												
	S												
Pine Warbler	N												
	S												
Yellow-rumped Warbler	N												
	S												
Yellow-throated Warbler	N												
	S												

ABUNDANCE AND STATUS OF LOUISIANA BIRDS 217

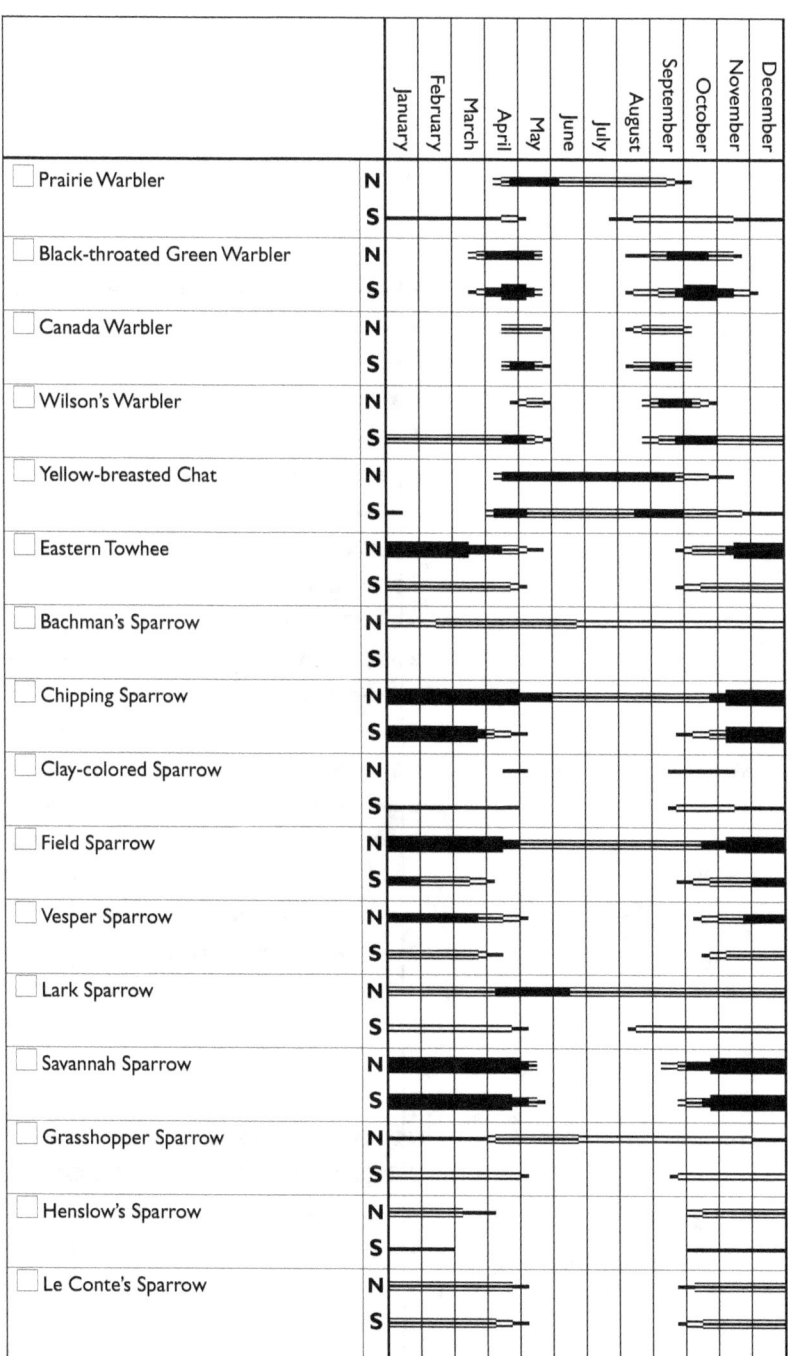

218 ABUNDANCE AND STATUS OF LOUISIANA BIRDS

		Jan	Feb	Mar	Apr	May	Jun	Jul	Aug	Sep	Oct	Nov	Dec
Nelson's Sparrow	N					—							
	S												
Seaside Sparrow	N												
	S												
Fox Sparrow	N												
	S												
Song Sparrow	N												
	S												
Lincoln's Sparrow	N												
	S												
Swamp Sparrow	N												
	S												
White-throated Sparrow	N												
	S												
Harris's Sparrow	N												
	S												
White-crowned Sparrow	N												
	S												
Dark-eyed Junco	N												
	S												
Summer Tanager	N												
	S												
Scarlet Tanager	N												
	S												
Western Tanager	N												
	S												
Northern Cardinal	N												
	S												
Rose-breasted Grosbeak	N												
	S												
Black-headed Grosbeak	N												
	S												

Abundance and Status of Louisiana Birds 219

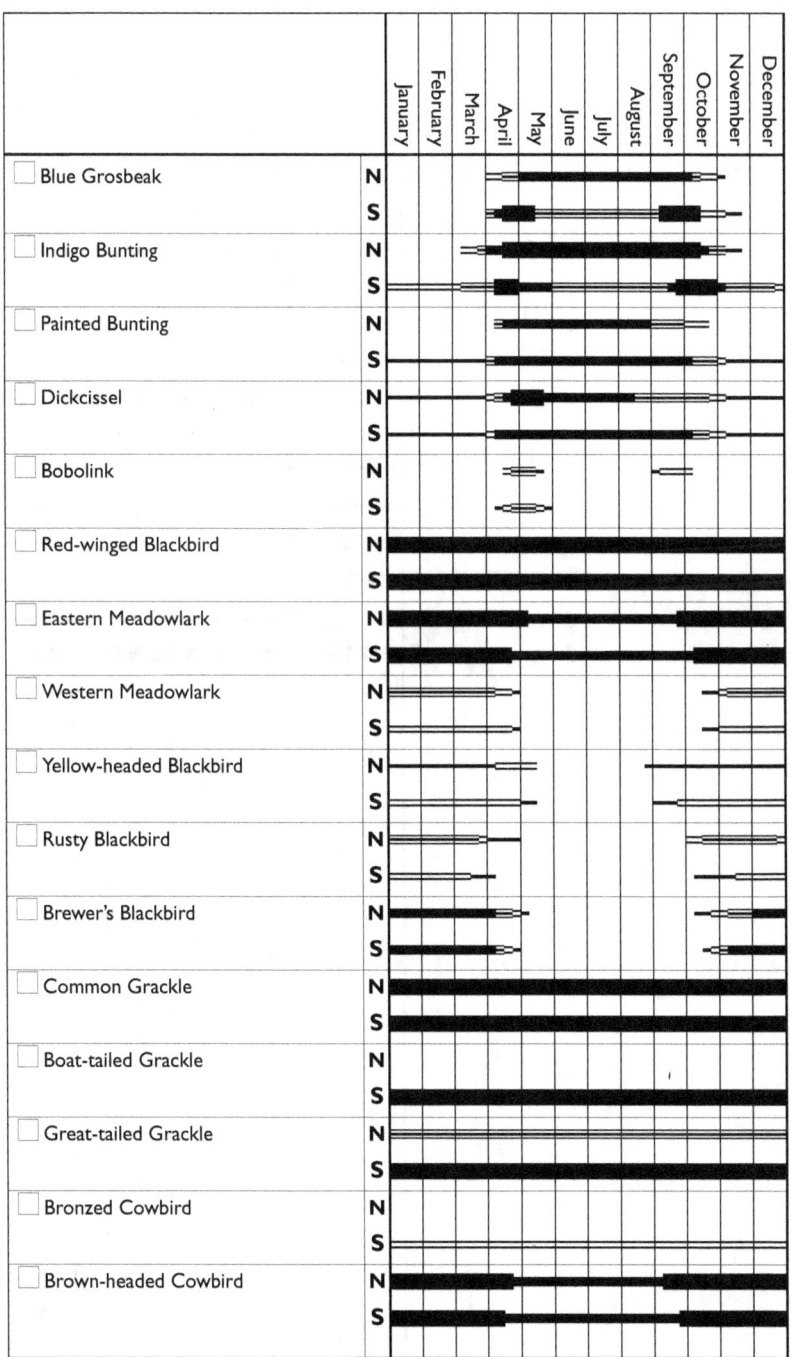

		January	February	March	April	May	June	July	August	September	October	November	December
☐ Orchard Oriole	N												
	S												
☐ Baltimore Oriole	N												
	S												
☐ Purple Finch	N												
	S												
☐ House Finch	N												
	S												
☐ Pine Siskin	N												
	S												
☐ American Goldfinch	N												
	S												
☐ House Sparrow	N												
	S												

SPECIALTIES OF LOUISIANA

Black-bellied Whistling-Duck: This permanent resident can be found at many places along the coast where concentrations may reach into the hundreds in New Orleans and south of Lafayette. It occasionally breeds as far north as Caddo Parish in the Red River Waterway. Formerly solely a tree or nest-box nester, this bird will now also rear young in the rice fields.

Fulvous Whistling-Duck: Seen in summer, primarily throughout the Rice Country of the southwest. Very small populations nest in central Louisiana around Cheneyville and in northeast Louisiana in rice fields. Only the Mottled Duck (of waterfowl) enjoys a greater density as a breeder in the southwestern portion of the state.

Mottled Duck: Permanent resident in the marshes along the coast. This "Summer Mallard" breeds northward into the rice fields. A few birds nest in the extreme northeast in the Upper Ouachita NWR and adjacent rice fields.

Wood Stork: Found in freshwater wetlands in summer during a post-breeding dispersal from its native Mexico. The Morganza Floodway on LA-1 between Marksville and False River is an excellent place to find this species (page 92). It may also be located in the Rice Country, crawfish farms, swamps, and riverbottoms. A fairly reliable day-roost (July–September) is located just north of I-10 at Crowley (Exit 80, LA-13).

Magnificent Frigatebird: Seen along the coast (very notably at Grand Isle) during the summer months, sometimes in spring.

Neotropic Cormorant: Permanent resident along the coast in inland waterways of Cameron Parish in the southwest, but extending its range eastward and northward to the inland parishes.

Anhinga: Enjoys freshwater habitats statewide during breeding, mostly withdraws to just behind the coast in winter. Lake Martin, freshwater swamps, Red River Waterway, and the Atchafalaya/Mississippi River systems are reliable places to look.

Reddish Egret: Rare breeder on barrier islands, uncommon along the coast year round. Best places to look are Grand Isle/Port Fourchon and near the East Jetty in Cameron Parish (page 36).

Roseate Spoonbill: Relatively common in the coastal marshes, especially of the southwest. The "Cajun Flamingo" has expanded its range in recent years to the north and east. It is a colonial breeder at Lake Martin/Cypress Island Preserve (page 62) and hard to miss in Cameron Parish. Rather nomadic during its post-breeding dispersal, though not as far flung as the Wood Stork.

Swallow-tailed Kite: Most easily found in the swamps of the Atchafalaya and Pearl River (Honey Island) systems, but breeds sporadically as well into the central region and into the Sabine and Red River drainages. Sherburne WMA is the most accessible site. There is a turnoff into north Sherburne on US-190 just east of the Atchafalaya River near the village of Krotz Springs. From the levee road just south of the bridge, this species may be seen soaring in the spring and summer sky after mid-morning (page 70).

Mississippi Kite: Common in most of the state from late April to August. Greatest abundance is in deciduous broadleaf forests in riverbottoms. This insectivore appears comfortable in suburban areas. The Bonnet Carré Spillway (page 120) and LSU campus (page 76) are excellent places to see this bird, but the Sherburne WMA (page 70) is the absolute best spot, a "can't miss" site.

Swainson's Hawk: Historically, a very rare but regular migrant in the west. It is known to have nested sporadically—yet increasingly—east of Lake Charles. It is found every winter (in growing numbers) in the southwest. This appears to be another species whose range continues to expand to the north and east. The easiest way to see this bird is to locate a farmer around the town of Thornwell (page 49) operating a tractor in a dry field. The birds will follow the implement in hopes of an easy meal. Also seen during active plowing, groupings of anywhere from 550+ Swainson's Hawks now seem to be a fairly regular occurrence—depending on the individual year and plowing schedules of farmers—during April and early May in the region between Dixie and Gilliam in northeast Caddo Parish.

Yellow Rail: Yellow Rail is a very secretive non-breeding denizen of the rice fields and shallow marshes in the southern sector of the state. It is most easily seen if you have permission to ride along on the combines of rice farmers during their second harvest, usually in late October and early November. The Yellow Rails and Rice Festival (October; page 46) provides an unrivaled opportunity to see these birds from the deck of a rice combine. Observers not so fortunate can spot Yellow Rails by watching just in front of the reaper from a nearby roadway. Be mindful of the vehicle traffic, as always.

Purple Gallinule: Common in spring and summer (very rare in winter) in freshwater marsh and water-lily-choked backwaters throughout the state. Little Chenier Road (page 41), Bayou Sauvage NWR (page 113), Venice (page 126), Lacassine NWR (page 46), Sabine NWR (page 31), and Cameron Prairie NWR (page 41) are excellent locales.

Snowy and **Piping Plovers**: Uncommon on beaches and mud flats of the Gulf during the non-breeding season. There is a breeding record for Snowy in Cameron Parish.

Wilson's Plover: Uncommon as a breeder on shoreline mudflats, and not to be expected away from the immediate coast. Look for it along the beach at the East Jetty and along Holly Beach (page 31) in Cameron Parish and at Grand Isle/Port Fourchon (page 101, 104). A small number of birds overwinter.

Long-billed Curlew: Seen every winter in wet fields near the Gulf, with most sightings coming from Cameron and Vermilion Parishes. "Winter," for purposes of this species, means September to May. Every so often, a non-breeder or early arrival will be spotted during the early summer.

Buff-breasted Sandpiper: Uncommon migrant in areas of short grass (turf farms, back beaches, golf courses, etc.). If a rice field with ample dry short growth can be located, it becomes a suitable venue as well. One of the best places to look is along the Red River Waterway in the newly acquired Red River NWR near the village of Powhatan. Check the turf farm here, also along LA-485. Also, Turf Grass Road just east of Lake Charles is a reliable spot (page 25).

Gull-billed Tern: Uncommon in winter along waterways near the coast. It occasionally breeds on flat roofs in the greater New Orleans area. In late spring and summer, it is surprisingly easy to see at the southern golf fairways of New Orleans' Audubon Park (page 108).

White-winged Dove: Increasingly common resident in the southwest and Baton Rouge area. The range appears to be expanding, overall, to the north and east, as there are records from Shreveport.

Common Ground-Dove: Rare but regular in winter from Alexandria south in old cane fields and hedgerows adjacent to clearings. Records are increasing in the north. It seems that the few reports from parishes in the northwest likely involve a different subspecies from those in the south. Although nesting has been documented, this species is not to be expected during the summer.

Red-cockaded Woodpecker: Uncommon to common locally in protected national forest lands where they are permanent residents of mature Longleaf Pines. It also exists in a few other protected locales where the understory is burned to simulate the natural wildfires that once were prevalent. This endangered species is most easily observed at Indian Creek (Alexander State Forest; page 154), D'Arbonne NWR, Big Branch Marsh NWR, and at Fountainebleau State Park. The Vernon and Evangeline Units of the Calcasieu, and the Catahoula, Winn, and Kisatchie Ranger Districts of the Kisatchie National Forest all contain active clusters. The largest concentration of clusters west of the Mississippi is at the Vernon Unit of the Calcasieu Ranger District north of LA-10 in Vernon Parish. Birds are most reliably seen at the clusters very early and late in the day.

Crested Caracara: A population exists southwest of Lake Charles (see LA-108 Loop, page 28) and east to Jennings. In winter, birds may forage eastward as far as Avery Island on the coast. A few records farther east may forebode of continued range expansion.

Ash-throated Flycatcher: Regular late fall and winter visitor to the brush country of the coastal parishes. It is most reliable across the road from Fort Jackson north of Venice (page 125).

Gray Kingbird: Rare spring migrant to Grand Isle. This bird nested several years in the greater New Orleans area; look along Lakeshore Drive (south of Lake Pontchartrain) just east of the Southern University of New Orleans campus.

Brown-headed Nuthatch: Common in the pine uplands away from the Gulf. This species is best located by its "squeaky duck" call. Hard to miss in the areas inhabited by Red-cockaded Woodpecker if dialed in to the vocalization.

Sprague's Pipit: Very uncommon in winter in the grassy areas and back beaches of the western portion of the state. It prefers short grasses and usually must be "walked up" in suitable habitat. When flushed it flies in a stair-step fashion before dropping back to the ground some distance away. The Red River Raceway north of Gilliam near the Scissor-tailed Loop (page 165) and the mown fields of the Overton Lock & Dam Recreation Area (page 180) southeast of Alexandria are excellent places to look. Listen for the distinct *squeet!* call note. Does *not* flock with American Pipits.

Prothonotary Warbler: The "Golden Swamp Warbler" is a common spring and summer nester in bottomland backwaters and swamps throughout the state. Also a fairly common migrant.

Swainson's Warbler: A dead-leaf specialist found in spring and summer, mainly in swamps and backwaters. Even so, it does occur in pine uplands in riparian areas. Uncommon, it is easily missed because of its furtive behavior. The most accessible locale is Sherburne WMA (page 70) and Pearl River's Honey Island Swamp (page 115). It may be found where streams and waterways cross the gravel road east of the Whiskey Bay bridge (I-10 Exit 127 west from Baton Rouge or east from Lafayette). Also found at Palmetto Island State Park near Abbeville (page 58). It may also be located in Tensas River NWR south of Delhi (page 191). Also a scarce migrant at coastal migrant traps.

Hooded Warbler: Another common nester, found in most any wooded habitat with ample understory. Also a fairly common migrant.

Bachman's Sparrow: Locally fairly common permanent resident of pine uplands, often in association with the artificially maintained grassy (with little or no brush) understories near Red-cockaded clusters. It is secretive in winter, but vociferous from an open perch during spring.

Henslow's Sparrow: Found during winter in pine savanna and in the grasses often associated with Red-cockaded Woodpecker clusters. Fairly secretive. Indian Creek (Alexander State Forest; page 154) and the Vernon Unit of the Calcasieu Ranger District of Kisatchie National Forest (page 146) are excellent sites.

Painted Bunting: Fairly common breeder in open thickets and brush, fairly common migrant, and rarely spends the winter on the coast. Look carefully during the breeding season around the levee at Sherburne WMA (page 70) and Bonnet Carré Spillway (page 120). It nests across the entire state, but population density increases in the river systems.

Shiny Cowbird: A very rare spring and summer visitor to the coastal parishes. Look for this bird around the Coast Guard station at the eastern end of Grand Isle (page 106). Also may be seen in winter at Port Fourchon (page 101) and the Venice area at the big bend of Tidewater Road near the rooster cages and pigeon coop (page 126).

Bronzed Cowbird: Uncommon in the southern tier of parishes. Seen often along the Lake Pontchartrain levee in Metairie and always at Lafreniere Park, just off Veterans Boulevard, also in Metairie.

CHECKLIST OF LOUISIANA BIRDS

Official Louisiana Check-list compiled by the Louisiana Bird Records Committee, Donna L. Dittmann, Secretary, LBRC (May 2013).

Species order follows the taxonomic sequence presented in the *A.O.U.Check-list of North American Birds* 7th edition (1998) and as modified through its 53rd Supplement (2012).

Species in **BOLD** type are on the Review List of the Louisiana Bird Records Committee (LBRC). For information on the Committee and about submission of documentation for review species visit the LBRC website *http://losbird.org/lbrc/lbrc.htm*.

(E) = extinct
(e) = formerly present but now extirpated in Louisiana
(Q) = status in question
(I) = established introduced population,
or records originate from established introduced population

DUCKS, GEESE, and SWANS
____Black-bellied Whistling-Duck *Dendrocygna autumnalis*
____Fulvous Whistling-Duck *Dendrocygna bicolor*
____Greater White-fronted Goose *Anser albifrons*
____Snow Goose *Chen caerulescens*
____Ross's Goose *Chen rossii*
____**Brant** *Branta bernicla*
____Cackling Goose *Branta hutchinsii*
____**Canada Goose** *Branta canadensis*

___ **Trumpeter Swan (Q)** *Cygnus buccinator*
___ **Tundra Swan** *Cygnus columbianus*
___ Wood Duck *Aix sponsa*
___ Gadwall *Anas strepera*
___ **Eurasian Wigeon** *Anas penelope*
___ American Wigeon *Anas americana*
___ **American Black Duck** *Anas rubripes*
___ Mallard *Anas platyrhynchos*
___ Mottled Duck *Anas fulvigula*
___ Blue-winged Teal *Anas discors*
___ **Cinnamon Teal** *Anas cyanoptera*
___ Northern Shoveler *Anas clypeata*
___ Northern Pintail *Anas acuta*
___ Green-winged Teal *Anas crecca*
___ Canvasback *Aythya valisineria*
___ Redhead *Aythya americana*
___ Ring-necked Duck *Aythya collaris*
___ Greater Scaup *Aythya marila*
___ Lesser Scaup *Aythya affinis*
___ **King Eider** *Somateria spectabilis*
___ Surf Scoter *Melanitta perspicillata*
___ **White-winged Scoter** *Melanitta fusca*
___ Black Scoter *Melanitta americana*
___ **Long-tailed Duck** *Clangula hyemalis*
___ Bufflehead *Bucephala albeola*
___ Common Goldeneye *Bucephala clangula*
___ Hooded Merganser *Lophodytes cucullatus*
___ Common Merganser *Mergus merganser*
___ Red-breasted Merganser *Mergus serrator*
___ **Masked Duck** *Nomonyx dominicus*
___ Ruddy Duck *Oxyura jamaicensis*

NEW WORLD QUAIL
___ Northern Bobwhite *Colinus virginianus*

GROUSE and TURKEYS
___ **Greater Prairie-Chicken (e)** *Tympanuchus cupido*

____Wild Turkey *Meleagris gallopavo*

LOONS
____**Red-throated Loon** *Gavia stellata*
____**Pacific Loon** *Gavia pacifica*
____Common Loon *Gavia immer*

GREBES
____**Least Grebe** *Tachybaptus dominicus*
____Pied-billed Grebe *Podilymbus podiceps*
____Horned Grebe *Podiceps auritus*
____**Red-necked Grebe** *Podiceps grisegena*
____Eared Grebe *Podiceps nigricollis*
____**Western Grebe** *Aechmophorus occidentalis*

FLAMINGOS
____**American Flamingo** *Phoenicopterus ruber*

ALBATROSSES
____**Yellow-nosed Albatross** *Thalassarche chlororhynchos*

SHEARWATERS and PETRELS
____**Cory's Shearwater** *Calonectris diomedea*
____**Great Shearwater** *Puffinus gravis*
____**Manx Shearwater** *Puffinus puffinus*
____**Audubon's Shearwater** *Puffinus lherminieri*

STORM-PETRELS
____Wilson's Storm-Petrel *Oceanites oceanicus*
____**Leach's Storm-Petrel** *Oceanodroma leucorhoa*
____Band-rumped Storm-Petrel *Oceanodroma castro*

TROPICBIRDS
____**Red-billed Tropicbird** *Phaethon aethereus*

STORKS
____**Jabiru** *Jabiru mycteria*
____Wood Stork *Mycteria americana*

FRIGATEBIRDS
____Magnificent Frigatebird *Fregata magnificens*

BOOBIES and GANNETS
____Masked Booby *Sula dactylatra*
____**Brown Booby** *Sula leucogaster*
____**Red-footed Booby** *Sula sula*
____Northern Gannet *Morus bassanus*

CORMORANTS
____Neotropic Cormorant *Phalacrocorax brasilianus*
____Double-crested Cormorant *Phalacrocorax auritus*

DARTERS
____Anhinga *Anhinga anhinga*

PELICANS
____American White Pelican *Pelecanus erythrorhynchos*
____Brown Pelican *Pelecanus occidentalis*

BITTERNS, HERONS, and ALLIES
____American Bittern *Botaurus lentiginosus*
____Least Bittern *Ixobrychus exilis*
____Great Blue Heron *Ardea herodias*
____Great Egret *Ardea alba*
____Snowy Egret *Egretta thula*
____Little Blue Heron *Egretta caerulea*
____Tricolored Heron *Egretta tricolor*
____Reddish Egret *Egretta rufescens*
____Cattle Egret *Bubulcus ibis*
____Green Heron *Butorides virescens*
____Black-crowned Night-Heron *Nycticorax nycticorax*
____Yellow-crowned Night-Heron *Nyctanassa violacea*
____White Ibis *Eudocimus albus*

IBISES and SPOONBILLS
____Glossy Ibis *Plegadis falcinellus*
____White-faced Ibis *Plegadis chihi*
____Roseate Spoonbill *Platalea ajaja*

NEW WORLD VULTURES
____Black Vulture *Coragyps atratus*
____Turkey Vulture *Cathartes aura*

HAWKS, KITES, EAGLES, and ALLIES
____ Osprey *Pandion haliaetus*
____ Swallow-tailed Kite *Elanoides forficatus*
____ White-tailed Kite *Elanus leucurus*
____ Mississippi Kite *Ictinia mississippiensis*
____ Bald Eagle *Haliaeetus leucocephalus*
____ Northern Harrier *Circus cyaneus*
____ Sharp-shinned Hawk *Accipiter striatus*
____ Cooper's Hawk *Accipiter cooperii*
____ **Northern Goshawk** *Accipiter gentilis*
____ **Harris's Hawk** *Parabuteo unicinctus*
____ Red-shouldered Hawk *Buteo lineatus*
____ Broad-winged Hawk *Buteo platypterus*
____ Swainson's Hawk *Buteo swainsoni*
____ **White-tailed Hawk** *Buteo albicaudatus*
____ **Zone-tailed Hawk** *Buteo albonotatus*
____ Red-tailed Hawk *Buteo jamaicensis*
____ **Ferruginous Hawk** *Buteo regalis*
____ **Rough-legged Hawk** *Buteo lagopus*
____ **Golden Eagle** *Aquila chrysaetos*

RAILS, GALLINULES, and COOTS
____ Yellow Rail *Coturnicops noveboracensis*
____ **Black Rail** *Laterallus jamaicensis*
____ Clapper Rail *Rallus longirostris*
____ King Rail *Rallus elegans*
____ Virginia Rail *Rallus limicola*
____ Sora *Porzana carolina*
____ Purple Gallinule *Porphyrio martinicus*
____ Common Gallinule *Gallinula galeata*
____ American Coot *Fulica americana*

CRANES
____ Sandhill Crane *Grus canadensis*
____ **Whooping Crane (e)** *Grus americana*

LAPWINGS and PLOVERS
____ Black-bellied Plover *Pluvialis squatarola*

____American Golden-Plover *Pluvialis dominica*
____**Lesser Sand-Plover** *Charadrius mongolus*
____Snowy Plover *Charadrius nivosus*
____Wilson's Plover *Charadrius wilsonia*
____Semipalmated Plover *Charadrius semipalmatus*
____Piping Plover *Charadrius melodus*
____Killdeer *Charadrius vociferus*
____**Mountain Plover** *Charadrius montanus*

OYSTERCATCHERS
____American Oystercatcher *Haematopus palliatus*

STILTS and AVOCETS
____Black-necked Stilt *Himantopus mexicanus*
____American Avocet *Recurvirostra americana*

SANDPIPERS, PHALAROPES, and ALLIES
____Spotted Sandpiper *Actitis macularius*
____Solitary Sandpiper *Tringa solitaria*
____Greater Yellowlegs *Tringa melanoleuca*
____Willet *Tringa semipalmata*
____Lesser Yellowlegs *Tringa flavipes*
____Upland Sandpiper *Bartramia longicauda*
____**Eskimo Curlew** *Numenius borealis*
____Whimbrel *Numenius phaeopus*
____Long-billed Curlew *Numenius americanus*
____**Black-tailed Godwit** *Limosa limosa*
____Hudsonian Godwit *Limosa haemastica*
____Marbled Godwit *Limosa fedoa*
____Ruddy Turnstone *Arenaria interpres*
____Red Knot *Calidris canutus*
____Sanderling *Calidris alba*
____Semipalmated Sandpiper *Calidris pusilla*
____Western Sandpiper *Calidris mauri*
____Least Sandpiper *Calidris minutilla*
____White-rumped Sandpiper *Calidris fuscicollis*
____Baird's Sandpiper *Calidris bairdii*
____Pectoral Sandpiper *Calidris melanotos*

___Purple Sandpiper *Calidris maritima*
___Dunlin *Calidris alpina*
___**Curlew Sandpiper** *Calidris ferruginea*
___Stilt Sandpiper *Calidris himantopus*
___Buff-breasted Sandpiper *Tryngites subruficollis*
___**Ruff** *Philomachus pugnax*
___Short-billed Dowitcher *Limnodromus griseus*
___Long-billed Dowitcher *Limnodromus scolopaceus*
___Wilson's Snipe *Gallinago delicata*
___American Woodcock *Scolopax minor*
___Wilson's Phalarope *Phalaropus tricolor*
___**Red-necked Phalarope** *Phalaropus lobatus*
___**Red Phalarope** *Phalaropus fulicarius*

GULLS, TERNS, and SKIMMERS
___**Black-legged Kittiwake** *Rissa tridactyla*
___**Sabine's Gull** *Xema sabini*
___Bonaparte's Gull *Chroicocephalus philadelphia*
___**Black-headed Gull** *Chroicocephalus ridibundus*
___**Little Gull** *Hydrocoloeus minutus*
___Laughing Gull *Leucophaeus atricilla*
___Franklin's Gull *Leucophaeus pipixcan*
___Ring-billed Gull *Larus delawarensis*
___**Western Gull** *Larus occidentalis*
___**California Gull** *Larus californicus*
___Herring Gull *Larus argentatus*
___**Thayer's Gull** *Larus thayeri*
___**Iceland Gull** *Larus glaucoides*
___Lesser Black-backed Gull *Larus fuscus*
___**Glaucous Gull** *Larus hyperboreus*
___**Great Black-backed Gull** *Larus marinus*
___**Kelp Gull** *Larus dominicanus*
___**Brown Noddy** *Anous stolidus*
___Sooty Tern *Onychoprion fuscatus*
___Bridled Tern *Onychoprion anaethetus*
___Least Tern *Sternula antillarum*
___Gull-billed Tern *Gelochelidon nilotica*

____Caspian Tern *Hydroprogne caspia*
____Black Tern *Chlidonias niger*
____Common Tern *Sterna hirundo*
____**Arctic Tern** *Sterna paradisaea*
____Forster's Tern *Sterna forsteri*
____Royal Tern *Thalasseus maximus*
____Sandwich Tern *Thalasseus sandvicensis*
____Black Skimmer *Rynchops niger*

SKUAS and JAEGERS
____Pomarine Jaeger *Stercorarius pomarinus*
____Parasitic Jaeger *Stercorarius parasiticus*
____**Long-tailed Jaeger** *Stercorarius longicaudus*

AUKS, MURRES, and PUFFINS
____**Razorbill** *Alca torda*
____**Ancient Murrelet** *Synthliboramphus antiquus*

PIGEONS and DOVES
____Rock Pigeon (I) *Columba livia*
____**Band-tailed Pigeon** *Patagioenas fasciata*
____Eurasian Collared-Dove (I) *Streptopelia decaocto*
____White-winged Dove *Zenaida asiatica*
____Mourning Dove *Zenaida macroura*
____Passenger Pigeon (E) *Ectopistes migratorius*
____Inca Dove *Columbina inca*
____Common Ground-Dove *Columbina passerina*

CUCKOOS, ROADRUNNERS, and ANIS
____Yellow-billed Cuckoo *Coccyzus americanus*
____**Mangrove Cuckoo** *Coccyzus minor*
____Black-billed Cuckoo *Coccyzus erythropthalmus*
____Greater Roadrunner *Geococcyx californianus*
____**Smooth-billed Ani** *Crotophaga ani*
____Groove-billed Ani *Crotophaga sulcirostris*

BARN OWLS
____Barn Owl *Tyto alba*

TYPICAL OWLS
____**Flammulated Owl** *Otus flammeolus*
____Eastern Screech-Owl *Megascops asio*
____Great Horned Owl *Bubo virginianus*
____Snowy Owl *Bubo scandiacus*
____Burrowing Owl *Athene cunicularia*
____Barred Owl *Strix varia*
____Long-eared Owl *Asio otus*
____Short-eared Owl *Asio flammeus*
____Northern Saw-whet Owl *Aegolius acadicus*

GOATSUCKERS and NIGHTJARS
____**Lesser Nighthawk** *Chordeiles acutipennis*
____Common Nighthawk *Chordeiles minor*
____**Antillean Nighthawk** *Chordeiles gundlachii*
____Chuck-will's-widow *Antrostomus carolinensis*
____Eastern Whip-poor-will *Antrostomus vociferus*
____Chimney Swift *Chaetura pelagica*
____**Vaux's Swift** *Chaetura vauxi*

HUMMINGBIRDS
____**Green Violetear** *Colibri thalassinus*
____**Green-breasted Mango** *Anthracothorax prevostii*
____**Magnificent Hummingbird** *Eugenes fulgens*
____**Blue-throated Hummingbird** *Lampornis clemenciae*
____Ruby-throated Hummingbird *Archilochus colubris*
____Black-chinned Hummingbird *Archilochus alexandri*
____**Anna's Hummingbird** *Calypte anna*
____Broad-tailed Hummingbird *Selasphorus platycercus*
____Rufous Hummingbird *Selasphorus rufus*
____Allen's Hummingbird *Selasphorus sasin*
____Calliope Hummingbird *Selasphorus calliope*
____**Broad-billed Hummingbird** *Cynanthus latirostris*
____Buff-bellied Hummingbird *Amazilia yucatanensis*

KINGFISHERS
____**Ringed Kingfisher** *Megaceryle torquata*
____Belted Kingfisher *Megaceryle alcyon*

WOODPECKERS and ALLIES
____Red-headed Woodpecker *Melanerpes erythrocephalus*
____Red-bellied Woodpecker *Melanerpes carolinus*
____**Williamson's Sapsucker** *Sphyrapicus thyroideus*
____Yellow-bellied Sapsucker *Sphyrapicus varius*
____**Red-naped Sapsucker** *Sphyrapicus nuchalis*
____**Ladder-backed Woodpecker** *Picoides scalaris*
____Downy Woodpecker *Picoides pubescens*
____Hairy Woodpecker *Picoides villosus*
____Red-cockaded Woodpecker *Picoides borealis*
____Northern Flicker *Colaptes auratus*
____Pileated Woodpecker *Dryocopus pileatus*
____**Ivory-billed Woodpecker (E?)** *Campephilus principalis*

CARACARAS and FALCONS
____Crested Caracara *Caracara cheriway*
____American Kestrel *Falco sparverius*
____Merlin *Falco columbarius*
____Peregrine Falcon *Falco peregrinus*
____**Prairie Falcon** *Falco mexicanus*

LORIES, PARAKEETS, MACAWS, and PARROTS
____Carolina Parakeet (E) *Conuropsis carolinensis*

TYRANT FLYCATCHERS
____Olive-sided Flycatcher *Contopus cooperi*
____**Western Wood-Pewee** *Contopus sordidulus*
____Eastern Wood-Pewee *Contopus virens*
____Yellow-bellied Flycatcher *Empidonax flaviventris*
____Acadian Flycatcher *Empidonax virescens*
____Alder Flycatcher *Empidonax alnorum*
____**Willow Flycatcher** *Empidonax traillii*
____Least Flycatcher *Empidonax minimus*
____**Hammond's Flycatcher** *Empidonax hammondii*
____**Gray Flycatcher** *Empidonax wrightii*
____**Pacific-slope Flycatcher** *Empidonax difficilis*
____**Cordilleran Flycatcher** *Empidonax occidentalis*
____Eastern Phoebe *Sayornis phoebe*

____Say's Phoebe *Sayornis saya*
____Vermilion Flycatcher *Pyrocephalus rubinus*
____**Dusky-capped Flycatcher** *Myiarchus tuberculifer*
____Ash-throated Flycatcher *Myiarchus cinerascens*
____Great Crested Flycatcher *Myiarchus crinitus*
____**Brown-crested Flycatcher** *Myiarchus tyrannulus*
____**Great Kiskadee** *Pitangus sulphuratus*
____**Sulphur-bellied Flycatcher** *Myiodynastes luteiventris*
____**Crowned Slaty Flycatcher** *Empidonomus aurantioatrocristatus*
____**Tropical Kingbird** *Tyrannus melancholicus*
____**Couch's Kingbird** *Tyrannus couchii*
____**Cassin's Kingbird** *Tyrannus vociferans*
____Western Kingbird *Tyrannus verticalis*
____Eastern Kingbird *Tyrannus tyrannus*
____**Gray Kingbird** *Tyrannus dominicensis*
____Scissor-tailed Flycatcher *Tyrannus forficatus*
____**Fork-tailed Flycatcher** *Tyrannus savana*

SHRIKES
____Loggerhead Shrike *Lanius ludovicianus*

VIREOS
____White-eyed Vireo *Vireo griseus*
____**Bell's Vireo** *Vireo bellii*
____Yellow-throated Vireo *Vireo flavifrons*
____Plumbeous Vireo *Vireo plumbeus*
____Cassin's Vireo *Vireo cassinii*
____Blue-headed Vireo *Vireo solitarius*
____Warbling Vireo *Vireo gilvus*
____Philadelphia Vireo *Vireo philadelphicus*
____Red-eyed Vireo *Vireo olivaceus*
____**Yellow-green Vireo** *Vireo flavoviridis*
____**Black-whiskered Vireo** *Vireo altiloquus*

JAYS and CROWS
____Blue Jay *Cyanocitta cristata*
____**Clark's Nutcracker** *Nucifraga columbiana*
____American Crow *Corvus brachyrhynchos*

____Fish Crow *Corvus ossifragus*
____**Chihuahuan Raven** *Corvus cryptoleucus*

LARKS
____Horned Lark *Eremophila alpestris*

SWALLOWS
____Purple Martin *Progne subis*
____**Brown-chested Martin** *Progne tapera*
____Tree Swallow *Tachycineta bicolor*
____Northern Rough-winged Swallow *Stelgidopteryx serripennis*
____Bank Swallow *Riparia riparia*
____Cliff Swallow *Petrochelidon pyrrhonota*
____Cave Swallow *Petrochelidon fulva*
____Barn Swallow *Hirundo rustica*

CHICKADEES and TITMICE
____Carolina Chickadee *Poecile carolinensis*
____Tufted Titmouse *Baeolophus bicolor*

NUTHATCHES
____Red-breasted Nuthatch *Sitta canadensis*
____White-breasted Nuthatch *Sitta carolinensis*
____Brown-headed Nuthatch *Sitta pusilla*

CREEPERS
____Brown Creeper *Certhia americana*

WRENS
____**Rock Wren** *Salpinctes obsoletus*
____House Wren *Troglodytes aedon*
____Winter Wren *Troglodytes hiemalis*
____Sedge Wren *Cistothorus platensis*
____Marsh Wren *Cistothorus palustris*
____Carolina Wren *Thryothorus ludovicianus*
____Bewick's Wren *Thryomanes bewickii*

OLD WORLD WARBLERS and GNATCATCHERS
____Blue-gray Gnatcatcher *Polioptila caerulea*

KINGLETS
____Golden-crowned Kinglet *Regulus satrapa*
____Ruby-crowned Kinglet *Regulus calendula*

THRUSHES
____**Northern Wheatear** *Oenanthe oenanthe*
____Eastern Bluebird *Sialia sialis*
____**Mountain Bluebird** *Sialia currucoides*
____**Townsend's Solitaire** *Myadestes townsendi*
____Veery *Catharus fuscescens*
____Gray-cheeked Thrush *Catharus minimus*
____Swainson's Thrush *Catharus ustulatus*
____Hermit Thrush *Catharus guttatus*
____Wood Thrush *Hylocichla mustelina*
____American Robin *Turdus migratorius*
____**Varied Thrush** *Ixoreus naevius*

MOCKINGBIRDS and THRASHERS
____Gray Catbird *Dumetella carolinensis*
____Northern Mockingbird *Mimus polyglottos*
____**Sage Thrasher** *Oreoscoptes montanus*
____Brown Thrasher *Toxostoma rufum*
____**Curve-billed Thrasher** *Toxostoma curvirostre*

STARLINGS
____European Starling (I) *Sturnus vulgaris*

WAGTAILS and PIPITS
____**White Wagtail** *Motacilla alba*
____American Pipit *Anthus rubescens*
____Sprague's Pipit *Anthus spragueii*

WAXWINGS
____Cedar Waxwing *Bombycilla cedrorum*

LONGSPURS
____Lapland Longspur *Calcarius lapponicus*
____**Chestnut-collared Longspur** *Calcarius ornatus*
____**Smith's Longspur** *Calcarius pictus*
____**McCown's Longspur** *Rhynchophanes mccownii*

WOOD-WARBLERS

___Ovenbird *Seiurus aurocapilla*
___Worm-eating Warbler *Helmitheros vermivorum*
___Louisiana Waterthrush *Parkesia motacilla*
___Northern Waterthrush *Parkesia noveboracensis*
___**Bachman's Warbler (E?)** *Vermivora bachmanii*
___Golden-winged Warbler *Vermivora chrysoptera*
___Blue-winged Warbler *Vermivora cyanoptera*
___Black-and-white Warbler *Mniotilta varia*
___Prothonotary Warbler *Protonotaria citrea*
___Swainson's Warbler *Limnothlypis swainsonii*
___Tennessee Warbler *Oreothlypis peregrina*
___Orange-crowned Warbler *Oreothlypis celata*
___**Lucy's Warbler** *Oreothlypis luciae*
___Nashville Warbler *Oreothlypis ruficapilla*
___**Virginia's Warbler** *Oreothlypis virginiae*
___**Connecticut Warbler** *Oporornis agilis*
___**MacGillivray's Warbler** *Geothlypis tolmiei*
___Mourning Warbler *Geothlypis philadelphia*
___Kentucky Warbler *Geothlypis formosa*
___Common Yellowthroat *Geothlypis trichas*
___Hooded Warbler *Setophaga citrina*
___American Redstart *Setophaga ruticilla*
___Cape May Warbler *Setophaga tigrina*
___Cerulean Warbler *Setophaga cerulea*
___Northern Parula *Setophaga americana*
___**Tropical Parula** *Setophaga pitiayumi*
___Magnolia Warbler *Setophaga magnolia*
___Bay-breasted Warbler *Setophaga castanea*
___Blackburnian Warbler *Setophaga fusca*
___Yellow Warbler *Setophaga petechia*
___Chestnut-sided Warbler *Setophaga pensylvanica*
___Blackpoll Warbler *Setophaga striata*
___Black-throated Blue Warbler *Setophaga caerulescens*
___Palm Warbler *Setophaga palmarum*
___Pine Warbler *Setophaga pinus*

____Yellow-rumped Warbler *Setophaga coronata*
____Prairie Warbler *Setophaga discolor*
____**Black-throated Gray Warbler** *Setophaga nigrescens*
____**Townsend's Warbler** *Setophaga townsendi*
____**Hermit Warbler** *Setophaga occidentalis*
____Black-throated Green Warbler *Setophaga virens*
____Canada Warbler *Cardellina canadensis*
____Wilson's Warbler *Cardellina pusilla*
____**Red-faced Warbler** *Cardellina rubrifrons*
____**Painted Redstart** *Myioborus pictus*
____Yellow-breasted Chat *Icteria virens*

EMBERIZIDS
____**Green-tailed Towhee** *Pipilo chlorurus*
____**Spotted Towhee** *Pipilo maculatus*
____Eastern Towhee *Pipilo erythrophthalmus*
____**Cassin's Sparrow** *Peucaea cassinii*
____Bachman's Sparrow *Peucaea aestivalis*
____**American Tree Sparrow** *Spizella arborea*
____Chipping Sparrow *Spizella passerina*
____Clay-colored Sparrow *Spizella pallida*
____**Brewer's Sparrow** *Spizella breweri*
____Field Sparrow *Spizella pusilla*
____Vesper Sparrow *Pooecetes gramineus*
____Lark Sparrow *Chondestes grammacus*
____**Lark Bunting** *Calamospiza melanocorys*
____Savannah Sparrow *Passerculus sandwichensis*
____Grasshopper Sparrow *Ammodramus savannarum*
____**Baird's Sparrow** *Ammodramus bairdii*
____Henslow's Sparrow *Ammodramus henslowii*
____Le Conte's Sparrow *Ammodramus leconteii*
____Nelson's Sparrow *Ammodramus nelsoni*
____Seaside Sparrow *Ammodramus maritimus*
____Fox Sparrow *Passerella iliaca*
____Song Sparrow *Melospiza melodia*
____Lincoln's Sparrow *Melospiza lincolnii*
____Swamp Sparrow *Melospiza georgiana*

___White-throated Sparrow *Zonotrichia albicollis*
___Harris's Sparrow *Zonotrichia querula*
___White-crowned Sparrow *Zonotrichia leucophrys*
___**Golden-crowned Sparrow** *Zonotrichia atricapilla*
___Dark-eyed Junco *Junco hyemalis*

TANAGERS
___**Hepatic Tanager** *Piranga flava*
___Summer Tanager *Piranga rubra*
___Scarlet Tanager *Piranga olivacea*
___Western Tanager *Piranga ludoviciana*

CARDINALS and ALLIES
___Northern Cardinal *Cardinalis cardinalis*
___Rose-breasted Grosbeak *Pheucticus ludovicianus*
___**Black-headed Grosbeak** *Pheucticus melanocephalus*
___**Blue Bunting** *Cyanocompsa parellina*
___Blue Grosbeak *Passerina caerulea*
___**Lazuli Bunting** *Passerina amoena*
___Indigo Bunting *Passerina cyanea*
___**Varied Bunting** *Passerina versicolor*
___Painted Bunting *Passerina ciris*
___Dickcissel *Spiza americana*

BLACKBIRDS
___Bobolink *Dolichonyx oryzivorus*
___Red-winged Blackbird *Agelaius phoeniceus*
___Eastern Meadowlark *Sturnella magna*
___Western Meadowlark *Sturnella neglecta*
___Yellow-headed Blackbird *Xanthocephalus xanthocephalus*
___Rusty Blackbird *Euphagus carolinus*
___Brewer's Blackbird *Euphagus cyanocephalus*
___Common Grackle *Quiscalus quiscula*
___Boat-tailed Grackle *Quiscalus major*
___Great-tailed Grackle *Quiscalus mexicanus*
___**Shiny Cowbird** *Molothrus bonariensis*
___Bronzed Cowbird *Molothrus aeneus*
___Brown-headed Cowbird *Molothrus ater*

____Orchard Oriole *Icterus spurius*
____**Hooded Oriole** *Icterus cucullatus*
____**Bullock's Oriole** *Icterus bullockii*
____Baltimore Oriole *Icterus galbula*
____**Scott's Oriole** *Icterus parisorum*

FRINGILLINE and CARDUELINE FINCHES and ALLIES
____Purple Finch *Haemorhous purpureus*
____House Finch (I) *Haemorhous mexicanus*
____**Red Crossbill** *Loxia curvirostra*
____Pine Siskin *Spinus pinus*
____**Lesser Goldfinch** *Spinus psaltria*
____American Goldfinch *Spinus tristis*
____**Evening Grosbeak** *Coccothraustes vespertinus*

OLD WORLD SPARROWS
____House Sparrow (I) *Passer domesticus*

Mammals of Louisiana

See: http://www.wlf.louisiana.gov/wildlife/mammals-louisiana

Rice, Dale W. (1998). *Marine Mammals of the World: Systematics and Distribution*. Society of Marine Mammalogy Special Publication Number 4: 231pp.

MARSUPIALS
   ___Virginia Opossum *Didelphis virginiana*

EDENTATES
   ___Nine-banded Armadillo *Dasypus novemcinctus*

INSECTIVORES
   ___Southern Short-tailed Shrew *Blarina carolinensis*
   ___Elliot's Short-tailed Shrew *Blarina hylophaga*
   ___Least Shrew *Cryptotis parva*
   ___Southeastern Shrew *Cryptotis parva*
   ___Eastern Mole *Scalopus aquaticus*

BATS
   ___Brazilian Free-tailed Bat *Tadarida brasiliensis*
   ___Big Brown Bat *Eptesicus fuscus*
   ___Silver-haired Bat *Lasionycteris noctivagans*
   ___Eastern Red Bat *Lasiurus borealis*
   ___Hoary Bat *Lasiurus cinereus*
   ___Seminole Bat *Lasiurus seminolis*
   ___Northern Yellow Bat *Lasiurus intermedius*
   ___Southeastern Myotis *Myotis austroriparius*
   ___Northern Long-eared Myotis *Myotis septentrionalis*
   ___Evening Bat *Nycticeius humeralis*
   ___Tri-colored Bat *Perimyotis subflavus*
   ___Rafinesque's Big-eared Bat *Corynorhinus rafinesquii*

RODENTS
   ___American Beaver *Castor canadensis*
   ___Plains Pocket Gopher *Geomys bursarius*

___Hispid Pocket Mouse *Chaetodipus hispidus*
___Woodland Vole *Microtus pinetorum*
___Marsh Rice Rat *Oryzomys palustris*
___Golden Mouse *Ochrotomys nuttalli*
___Common Muskrat *Ondatra zibethicus*
___White-footed Mouse *Peromyscus leucopus*
___Cotton Mouse *Peromyscus gossypinus*
___Fulvous Harvest Mouse *Reithrodontomys fulvescens*
___Eastern Harvest Mouse *Reithrodontomys humulis*
___Hispid Cotton Rat *Sigmodon hispidus*
___Eastern Woodrat *Neotoma floridana*
___Southern Flying Squirrel *Glaucomys volans*
___Eastern Chipmunk *Tamiaus striatus*
___Eastern Gray Squirrel *Sciurus carolinensis*
___Eastern Fox Squirrel *Sciurus niger*

LAGOMORPHS
___Swamp Rabbit *Sylivagus aquaticus*
___Eastern Cottontail *Sylivagus floridana*

CARNIVORES
___Coyote *Canis latrans*
___Red Fox *Vulpes vulpes*
___Gray Fox *Urocyon cinereoargenteus*
___Bobcat *Lynx rufus*
___Florida Panther *Puma concolor*
___Striped Skunk *Mephitis mephitis*
___Spotted Skunk *Spilogale putorius*
___Northern River Otter *Lutra canadensis*
___Mink *Mustela vison*
___Long-tailed Weasel *Mustela frenata*
___Common Raccoon *Procycon lotor*
___Ringtail *Bassariscus astutus*
___American Black Bear *Ursus americanus*

CETACEANS
___Blue Whale *Balaenoptera musculus*
___Bryde's Whale *Balaenoptera brydei*
___Common Minke Whale *Balaenoptera acutorostrata*
___Fin Whale *Balaenoptera physalus*

___Sei Whale *Balaenoptera borealis*
___Humpback Whale *Megaptera novaeangliae*
___Rough-toothed Dolphin *Steno bredanensis*
___Common Bottlenose Dolphin *Tursiops truncatus*
___Indo-Pacific Bottlenose Dolphin *Tursiops aduncus*
___Clymene Dolphin *Stenella clymene*
___Pantropical Spotted Dolphin *Stenella attenuata*
___Spinner Dolphin *Stenella longirostris*
___Striped Dolphin *Stenella coeruleoalba*
___Fraser's Dolphin *Lagenodelphis hosei*
___Risso's Dolphin *Grampus griseus*
___Melon-headed Whale *Peponocephala electra*
___Pygmy Killer Whale *Feresa attenuata*
___False Killer Whale *Pseudorca crassidens*
___Killer Whale *Orcinus orca*
___Short-filled Pilot Whale *Globicephala macrorhynchus*
___Sperm Whale *Physeter macrocephalus*
___Dwarf Sperm Whale *Kogia sima*
___Pygmy Sperm Whale *Kogia breviceps*
___Cuvier's Beaked Whale *Ziphius cavirostris*
___Blainville's Beaked Whale *Mesoplodon densirostris*
___Gervais' Beaked Whale *Mesoplodon europaeus*

ARTIODACTYLS
___Wild Boar [introduced]
___White-tailed Deer *Cervus virginianus*

REPTILES AND AMPHIBIANS OF LOUISIANA

SALAMANDERS
___Western Lesser Siren *Siren intermedia nettingi*
___Gulf Coast Waterdog *Necturus beyeri*
___Red River Waterdog *Necturus louisianensis*
___Two-toed Amphiuma *Amphiuma means*
___Three-toed Amphiuma *Amphiuma tridactylum*
___Eastern Spotted Newt *Notophthalmus viridescens*
___Spotted Salamander *Ambystoma maculatum*
___Marbled Salamander *Ambystoma opacum*
___Mole Salamander *Ambystoma talpoideum*
___Small-mouthed Salamander *Ambystoma texanum*
___Eastern Tiger Salamander *Ambystoma tigrinum*
___Southern Dusky Salamander *Desmognathus auriculatus*
___Spotted Dusky Salamander *Desmognathus conanti*
___Southern Two-lined Salamander *Eurycea cirrigera*
___Three-lined Salamander *Eurycea guttolineata*
___Dwarf Salamander *Eurycea quadridigitata*
___Four-toed Salamander *Hemidactylium scutatum*
___Louisiana Slimy Salamander *Plethodon kisatchie*
___Mississippi Slimy Salamander *Plethodon mississippi*
___Southern Red-backed Salamander *Plethodon serratus*
___Webster's Salamander *Plethodon websteri*
___Gulf Coast Mud Salamander *Pseudotriton montanus flavissimus*
___Southern Red Salamander *Pseudotriton ruber vioscai*

TOADS AND FROGS
___Eastern Spadefoot *Scaphiopus holbrookii*
___Hurter's Spadefoot *Scaphiopus hurterii*

___Dwarf American Toad *Bufo americanus charlesmithi*
___Fowler's Toad *Bufo fowleri*
___Gulf Coast Toad *Bufo nebulifer*
___Oak Toad *Bufo quercicus*
___Southern Toad *Bufo terrestris*
___East Texas Toad *Bufo velatus*
___Eastern Cricket Frog *Acris crepitans crepitans*
___Coastal Plain Cricket Frog *Acris gryllus gryllus*
___Western Bird-voiced Tree Frog *Hyla avivoca avivoca*
___Cope's Gray Tree Frog *Hyla chrysoscelis*
___Green Tree Frog *Hyla cinerea*
___Pine Woods Tree Frog *Hyla femoralis*
___Barking Tree Frog *Hyla gratiosa*
___Squirrel Tree Frog *Hyla squirella*
___Greater Gray Tree Frog *Hyla versicolor*
___Spring Peeper *Pseudacris crucifer*
___Upland Chorus Frog *Pseudacris feriarum*
___Ornate Chorus Frog *Pseudacris ornata* [extirpated]
___Strecker's Chorus Frog *Pseudacris streckeri*
___Southern Crawfish Frog *Rana areolata areolata*
___American Bullfrog *Rana catesbeiana*
___Bronze Frog *Rana clamitans clamitans*
___Pig Frog *Rana grylio*
___Pickerel Frog *Rana palustris*
___Dusky Gopher Frog *Rana sevosa* [extirpated]
___Southern Leopard Frog *Rana sphenocephala utricularia*
___Eastern Narrow-mouthed Toad *Gastrophryne carolinensis*
___Rio Grande Chirping Frog *Syrrhophus cystignathoides campi* [introduced]
___Greenhouse Frog *Eleutherodactylus planirostris* [introduced]

CROCODILIANS
___American Alligator *Alligator mississippiensis*

TURTLES
___Eastern Snapping Turtle *Chelydra serpentina serpentina*
___Alligator Snapping Turtle *Macrochelys temminckii*
___Mississippi Mud Turtle *Kinosternon subrubrum hippocrepis*
___Razor-backed Musk Turtle *Sternotherus carinatus*
___Stripe-necked Musk Turtle *Sternotherus minor peltifer*
___Common Musk Turtle *Sternotherus odoratus*

___Southern Painted Turtle *Chrysemys dorsalis*
___Eastern Chicken Turtle *Deirochelys reticularia reticularia*
___Western Chicken Turtle *Deirochelys reticularia miaria*
___Pascagoula Map Turtle *Graptemys gibbonsi*
___Ringed Map Turtle *Graptemys oculifera*
___Ouachita Map Turtle *Graptemys ouachitensis ouachitensis*
___Sabine Map Turtle *Graptemys ouachitensis sabinensis*
___Mississippi Map Turtle *Graptemys pseudogeographica kohnii*
___Mississippi Diamondback Terrapin *Malaclemys terrapin pileata*
___River Cooter *Pseudemys concinna*
___Gulf Coast Box Turtle *Terrapene carolina major*
___Three-toed Box Turtle *Terrapene carolina triunguis*
___Ornate Box Turtle *Terrapene ornata ornata*
___Red-eared Slider *Trachemys scripta elegans*
___Florida Gopher Tortoise *Gopherus polyphemus*
___Midland Smooth Softshell *Apalone mutica mutica*
___Gulf Coast Smooth Softshell *Apalone mutica calvata*
___Gulf Coast Spiny Softshell *Apalone spinifera aspera*
___Pallid Spiny Softshell *Apalone spinifera pallida*
___Loggerhead Sea Turtle *Caretta caretta*
___Green Sea Turtle *Chelonia mydas*
___Atlantic Hawksbill *Eretmochelys imbricata imbricata*
___Kemp's Ridley *Lepidochelys kempi*
___Leatherback *Dermochelys coriacea*

LIZARDS
___Mediterranean Gecko *Hemidactylus turcicus turcicus* [introduced]
___Northern Green Anole *Anolis carolinensis carolinensis*
___Brown Anole *Anolis sagrei* [introduced]
___Texas Horned Lizard *Phrynosoma cornutum*
___Prairie Lizard *Sceloporus consobrinus*
___Southern Coal Skink *Plestiodon anthracinus pluvialis*
___Common Five-lined Skink *Plestiodon fasciatus*
___Southeastern Five-lined Skink *Plestiodon inexpectatus*
___Broad-headed Skink *Plestiodon laticeps*
___Southern Prairie Skink *Plestiodon obtusirostris obtusirostris*
___Little Brown Skink *Scincella lateralis*
___Eastern Six-lined Racerunner *Aspidoscelis sexlineatus sexlineatus*
___Western Slender Glass Lizard *Ophisaurus attenuatus attenuatus*

REPTILES AND AMPHIBIANS OF LOUISIANA 249

___Eastern Slender Glass Lizard *Ophisaurus attenuatus longicaudatus*
___Eastern Glass Lizard *Ophisaurus ventralis*
SNAKES
___Brahminy Blind Snake *Ramphotyphlops braminus* [introduced]
___Midland Worm Snake *Carphophis amoenus helenae*
___Western Worm Snake *Carphophis vermis*
___Southeastern Scarlet Snake *Cemophora coccinea copei*
___Buttermilk Racer *Coluber constrictor anthicus*
___Tan Racer *Coluber constrictor etheridgei*
___Eastern Yellow-bellied Racer *Coluber constrictor flaviventris*
___Black-masked Racer *Coluber constrictor latrunculus*
___Southern Black Racer *Coluber constrictor priapus*
___Eastern Coachwhip *Coluber flagellum flagellum*
___Mississippi Ring-necked Snake *Diadophis punctatus stictogenys*
___Western Mud Snake *Farancia abacura reinwardtii*
___Northern Rainbow Snake *Farancia erytrogramma erytrogramma*
___Eastern Hog-nosed Snake *Heterodon platirhinos*
___Prairie King Snake *Lampropeltis calligaster calligaster*
___Mole King Snake *Lampropeltis calligaster rhombomaculata*
___Scarlet King Snake *Lampropeltis elapsoides*
___Speckled King Snake *Lampropeltis getula holbrooki*
___Louisiana Milk Snake *Lampropeltis triangulum amaura*
___Gulf Salt Marsh Snake *Nerodia clarkii clarkii*
___Mississippi Green Water Snake *Nerodia cyclopion*
___Yellow-bellied Water Snake *Nerodia erythrogaster flavigaster*
___Broad-banded Water Snake *Nerodia fasciata confluens*
___Northern Diamond-backed Water Snake *Nerodia rhombifer rhombifer*
___Midland Water Snake *Nerodia sipedon pleuralis*
___Northern Rough Green Snake *Opheodrys aestivus aestivus*
___Red Corn Snake *Pantherophis guttata*
___Western Rat Snake *Pantherophis obsoleta*
___Kisatchie Corn Snake *Pantherophis slowinskii*
___Gray Rat Snake *Pantherophis spiloides*
___Black Pine Snake *Pituophis melanoleucus lodingi* [extirpated]
___Louisiana Pine Snake *Pituophis ruthveni*
___Graham's Crayfish Snake *Regina grahamii*
___Delta Glossy Crayfish Snake *Regina rigida deltae*
___Gulf Glossy Crayfish Snake *Regina rigida sinicola*

___Pine Woods Snake *Rhadinaea flavilata*
___Marsh Brown Snake *Storeria dekayi limnetes*
___Texas Brown Snake *Storeria dekayi texana*
___Midland Brown Snake *Storeria dekayi wrightorum*
___Southern Red-bellied Snake *Storeria occipitomaculata obscura*
___Southeastern Crowned Snake *Tantilla coronata*
___Flat-headed Snake *Tantilla gracilis*
___Orange-striped Ribbon Snake *Thamnophis proximus proximus*
___Gulf Coast Ribbon Snake *Thamnophis proximus orarius*
___Eastern Ribbon Snake *Thamnophis sauritus sauritus*
___Eastern Garter Snake *Thamnophis sirtalis sirtalis*
___Rough Earth Snake *Virginia striatula*
___Western Smooth Earth Snake *Virginia valeriae elegans*
___Harlequin Coral Snake *Micrurus fulvius*
___Texas Coral Snake *Micrurus tener tener*
___Southern Copperhead *Agkistrodon contortrix contortrix*
___Western Cottonmouth *Agkistrodon piscivorus leucostoma*
___Eastern Diamondback Rattlesnake *Crotalus adamanteus*
___Timber Rattlesnake *Crotalus horridus*
___Western Pygmy Rattlesnake *Sistrurus miliarius streckeri*

BUTTERFLIES OF LOUISIANA

SWALLOWTAILS (Family Papilionidae)
___Pipevine Swallowtail *Battus philenor*
___Polydamas Swallowtail *Battus polydamas*
___Zebra Swallowtail *Eurytides marcellus*
___Black Swallowtail *Papilio polyxenes*
___Giant Swallowtail *Papilio cresphontes*
___Eastern Tiger Swallowtail *Papilio glaucus*
___Spicebush Swallowtail *Papilio troilus*
___Palamedes Swallowtail *Papilio palamedes*

WHITES and SULPHURS (Family Pieridae)
Whites (Subfamily Pierinae)
___Checkered White *Pontia protodice*
___Cabbage White *Pieris rapae*
___Great Southern White *Ascia monuste*
___Florida White *Appias drusilla*
___Falcate Orangetip *Anthocharis midea*

Sulphurs (Subfamily Coliadinae)
___Clouded Sulphur *Colias philodice*
___Orange Sulphur *Colias eurytheme*
___Mustard White *Pieris rapae*
___Southern Dogface *Zerene cesonia*
___Cloudless Sulphur *Phoebis sennae*
___Orange-barred Sulphur *Phoebis philea*
___Large Orange Sulphur *Phoebis agarithe*
___Barred Yellow *Eurema daira*
___Mexican Yellow *Eurema mexicana*
___Little Yellow *Eurema lisa*
___Sleepy Orange *Eurema nicippe*
___Dainty Sulphur *Nathalis iole*
___Lyside Sulfur *Kricogonia lyside*

GOSSAMER-WING BUTTERFLIES (Family Lycaenidae)
  Harvesters (Subfamily Miletinae)
    ___Harvester *Feniseca tarquinius*
  Hairstreaks (Subfamily Theclinae)
    ___Great Purple Hairstreak *Atlides halesus*
    ___Banded Hairstreak *Satyrium calanus*
    ___King's Hairstreak *Satyrium kingi*
    ___Striped Hairstreak *Satyrium liparops*
    ___Southern *(Oak)* Hairstreak *Fixsenia (Satyrium) favonius*
    ___Frosted Elfin *Callophrys irus*
    ___Henry's Elfin *Callophrys henrici*
    ___Eastern Pine Elfin *Callophrys niphon*
    ___Juniper Hairstreak *Callophrys gryneus*
    ___White M Hairstreak *Parrhasius m-album*
    ___Gray Hairstreak *Strymon melinus*
    ___Red-banded Hairstreak *Calycopis cecrops*
  Blues (Subfamily Polyommatinae)
    ___Western Pygmy-Blue *Brephidium exile*
    ___Eastern Pygmy-Blue *Brephidium isophthalma*
    ___Marine Blue *Leptotes marina*
    ___Cassius Blue *Leptotes cassius*
    ___Ceraunus Blue *Hemiargus ceraunus*
    ___Reakirt's Blue *Hemiargus isola*
    ___Eastern Tailed-Blue *Everes comyntas*
    ___Spring Azure *Celastrina "ladon"*
    ___Summer Azure *Celastrina neglecta*

METALMARKS (Family Riodinidae)
    ___Little Metalmark *Calephelis virginiensis*

BRUSH-FOOTED BUTTERFLIES (Family Nymphalidae)
  Snouts (Subfamily Libytheinae)
    ___American Snout *Libytheana carinenta*
  Heliconians and Fritillaries (Subfamily Heliconiinae)
    ___Gulf Fritillary *Agraulis vanillae*
    ___Julia Heliconian *Dryas julia*
    ___Zebra Heliconian *Heliconius charithonius*
    ___Variegated Fritillary *Euptoieta claudia*
    ___Diana *Speyeria diana*
    ___Great Spangled Fritillary *Speyeria cybele*

True Brush-foots (Subfamily Nymphalinae)
___Gorgone Checkerspot *Chlosyne gorgone*
___Silvery Checkerspot *Chlosyne nycteis*
___Texan Crescent *Phyciodes (Anthanassa) texana*
___Phaon Crescent *Phyciodes phaon*
___Pearl Crescent *Phyciodes tharos*
___Question Mark *Polygonia interrogationis*
___Eastern Comma *Polygonia comma*
___Mourning Cloak *Nymphalis antiopa*
___American Lady *Vanessa virginiensis*
___Painted Lady *Vanessa cardui*
___Red Admiral *Vanessa atalanta*
___Common Buckeye *Junonia coenia*
___White Peacock *Anartia jatrophae*

Admirals and Relatives (Subfamily Limenitidinae)
___Red-spotted Purple *Limenitis arthemis*
___Astyanax' Red-spotted Purple *Limenitis arthemis astyanax*
___Viceroy *Limenitis archippus*
___Common Mestra *Mestra amymone*

Leafwings (Subfamily Charaxinae)
___Goatweed Leafwing *Anaea andria*

Emperors (Subfamily Apaturinae)
___Hackberry Emperor *Asterocampa celtis*
___Tawny Emperor *Asterocampa clyton*

Satyrs (Subfamily Satyrinae)
___Southern Pearly Eye *Enodia portlandia*
___Northern Pearly Eye *Enodia anthedon*
___Creole Pearly Eye *Enodia creola*
___Gemmed Satyr *Cyllopsis gemma*
___Carolina Satyr *Hermeuptychia sosybius*
___Georgia Satyr *Neonympha areolata*
___Little Wood Satyr *Megisto cymela*
___Common Wood Nymph *Cercyonis pegala*

Monarchs (Subfamily Danainae)
___Monarch *Danaus plexippus*
___Queen *Danaus gilippus*

SKIPPERS (Family Hesperiidae)
  Spread-wing Skippers (Subfamily Pyrginae)
    ___Silver-spotted Skipper *Epargyreus clarus*
    ___Long-tailed Skipper *Urbanus proteus*
    ___Dorantes Longtail *Urbanus dorantes*
    ___White-striped Longtail *Chiodes catillus*
    ___Hoary Edge *Achalarus lyciades*
    ___Southern Cloudywing *Thorybes bathyllus*
    ___Northern Cloudywing *Thorybes pylades*
    ___Confused Cloudywing *Thorybes confusis*
    ___Hayhurst's Scallopwing *Staphylus hayhurstii*
    ___Sleepy Duskywing *Erynnis brizo*
    ___Juvenal's Duskywing *Erynnis juvenalis*
    ___Horace's Duskywing *Erynnis horatius*
    ___Mottled Duskywing *Erynnis martialis*
    ___Zarucco Duskywing *Erynnis zarucco*
    ___Funereal Duskywing *Erynnis funeralis*
    ___Wild Indigo Duskywing *Erynnis baptisiae*
    ___Persius Duskywing *Erynnis persius*
    ___Common Checkered-Skipper *Pyrgus communis*
    ___Tropical Checkered-Skipper *Pyrgus oileus*
    ___Common Streaky-Skipper *Celotes nessus*
    ___Common Sootywing *Pholisora catullus*
  Grass Skippers (Subfamily Hesperiinae)
    ___Swarthy Skipper *Nastra lherminier*
    ___Neamathla Skipper *Nastra neamathla*
    ___Clouded Skipper *Lerema accius*
    ___Least Skipper *Ancyloxypha numitor*
    ___Southern Skipperling *Copaeodes minima*
    ___Fiery Skipper *Hylephila phyleus*
    ___Leonard's Skipper *Hesperia leonardus*
    ___Cobweb Skipper *Hesperia metea*
    ___Dotted Skipper *Hesperia attalus*
    ___Meske's Skipper *Hesperia meskei*
    ___Tawny-edged Skipper *Polites themistocles*
    ___Crossline Skipper *Polites origenes*
    ___Whirlabout *Polites vibex*
    ___Southern Broken-Dash *Wallengrenia otho*

___Northern Broken-Dash *Wallengrenia egeremet*
___Little Glassywing *Pompeius verna*
___Sachem *Atalopedes campestris*
___Arogos Skipper *Atrytone arogos*
___Delaware Skipper *Anatrytone logan*
___Zabulon Skipper *Poanes zabulon*
___Aaron's Skipper *Poanes aaroni*
___Yehl Skipper *Poanes yehl*
___Broad-winged Skipper *Poanes viator*
___Palatka Skipper *Euphyes pilatka*
___Dion Skipper *Euphyes dion*
___Dukes' Skipper *Euphyes dukesi*
___Dun Skipper *Euphyes vestris*
___Dusted Skipper *Atrytonopsis hianna*
___Pepper and Salt Skipper *Amblyscirtes hegon*
___Lace-winged Roadside-Skipper *Amblyscirtes aesculapius*
___Common Roadside-Skipper *Amblyscirtes vialis*
___Celia's Roadside-Skipper *Amblyscirtes celia*
___Dusky Roadside-Skipper *Amblyscirtes alternata*
___Eufala Skipper *Lerodea eufala*
___Twin-spot Skipper *Oligoria maculata*
___Brazilian Skipper *Calpodes ethlius*
___Salt Marsh Skipper *Panoquina panoquin*
___Obscure Skipper *Panoquina panoquinoides*
___Ocola Skipper *Panoquina ocola*
Giant-Skippers (Subfamily Megathyminae)
___Yucca Giant-Skipper *Megathymus yuccae*
___Strecker's Giant-Skipper *Megathymus streckeri*

LOUISIANA BIRDING ROUTES

*With landscapes ranging from coastal wetlands
to rolling hills and prairies.*

http://www.louisianatravel.com/louisiana-birding-trails

America's Wetland Birding Trail

America's Wetland Birding Trail consists of 115 birdwatching sites in 22 Louisiana parishes The trail guides you to come of the state's most productive natural places along the Gulf Coast.

* Atchafalaya Loop: *http://bit.ly/14iviSU*
* Orleans Loop: *http://bit.ly/1aFOyPi*
* Barataria Loop: *http://bit.ly/11Xy8uU*
* Sabine Loop: *http://bit.ly/19tlXKt*
* Creole Loop: *http://bit.ly/11ULIOl*
* St. Mary Loop: *http://bit.ly/1341Zs0*
* East Florida Parishes Loop: *http://bit.ly/189aRO0*
* Terrebonne Loop: *http://bit.ly/12XMdO2*
* Grand Isle Loop: *http://bit.ly/10e62hy*
* Vermilion Loop: *http://bit.ly/19tJ7Bt*
* Lacassine Loop: *http://bit.ly/10e65K8*
* West Florida Parishes Loop: *http://bit.ly/11yFad7*

Mississippi River Birding Trail

Sparsely populated and heavily cultivated in cotton, corn, and soybeans, the Northeast Louisiana Delta has served as one of the last homes for the Ivory-billed Woodpecker and Louisiana Black Bear. Agriculture and hardwood timbering fragmented this once-contiguous mosaic of bottomland hardwood and cypress/tupelo swamp habitats, exterminating the woodpecker and almost the bear. The Ivory-billed Woodpecker may be lost forever, but the bear is making an impressive comeback, thanks to an intensive wildlife conservation program initiated by both federal and state wildlife agencies. To date, hundreds of thousands of acres of abandoned farmland in this region have been purchased and restored to their former forested glory.

The Mississippi River Birding Trail consists of 30 birdwatching sites in 13 Louisiana parishes.

* Mississippi River Guide 1: *http://bit.ly/12IRXuJ*
* Mississippi River Guide 2: *http://bit.ly/11WRvTU*
* Mississippi River Guide 3: *http://bit.ly/12eP7Mq*
* Mississippi River Guide 4: *http://bit.ly/16vzyjP*
* Mississippi River Guide 5: *http://bit.ly/14tD7Wu*
* Mississippi River Guide 6: *http://bit.ly/11Jnpo7*
* Complete Mississippi River Guide (This file is a compilation of the files above and is quite large, 20 MB. It may take several minutes to download.): *http://bit.ly/11WRNdr*

Red River Birding Trail

Long storied throughout American history for its role in U.S. "Wild West" culture, the Red River changes character considerably as it enters Louisiana. Red clay bluffs, vast pine forests, and Pileated Woodpeckers replace the rocks, Bison, and rattlesnakes of the river's upper reaches in the Southern Great Plains. Geologically, the Red River neatly bisects a large shield of exposed, high-elevation tertiary outcroppings, which form the entire northwestern quadrant of the state. This tertiary shield supports many of Louisiana's rarest plants. To this day, the Louisiana segment of the Red River Valley is best known for its timber resources, and interest in its mixed-pine forests culminated in the formation of the 600,000-acre Kisatchie National Forest system. Most of the forest's districts lay along the Red River Trail.

The Red River Birding Trail consists of 82 birdwatching sites in 18 Louisiana parishes.

* Red River Guide 1: *http://bit.ly/19wCDlp*
* Red River Guide 2: *http://bit.ly/1aINWsp*
* Red River Guide 3: *http://bit.ly/16vzPmL*
* Red River Guide 4: *http://bit.ly/10h3fEi*
* Red River Guide 5: *http://bit.ly/11CulH3*
* Red River Guide 6: *http://bit.ly/19muDa0*

* Complete Red River Guide (This file is a compilation of the files above and is quite large, 22 MB. It may take several minutes to download.): http://bit.ly/14mwWTN

Zachary Taylor Parkway Birding Trail

Stretching nearly 150 miles eastward through the "boot" of southeastern Louisiana, the Zachary Taylor Parkway leg of the America's Wetland Birding Trail encompasses almost every major habitat type native to the state. At its western end, within the Tunica-Biloxi Loop, the trail slogs through the low bottomland hardwoods and cypress/tupelo swamps of the lower Mississippi River floodplain. Farther east, the Audubon Loop climbs into the prominent upland hardwood blufflands of the Mississippi River's east bank. This is the only region of the state where the Eastern Chipmunk and American Ginseng live and grow and represents the southernmost extensions of these two species' North American ranges. Finally, the trail meanders higher up into the dry, 300+-foot pineland ridges near its boundary with southern Mississippi.

The Zachary Taylor Parkway Birding Trail consists of 27 birdwatching sites in 10 Louisiana parishes.

* Zachary Taylor Parkway Guide 1:   http://bit.ly/12ISJI6
* Zachary Taylor Parkway Guide 2:   http://bit.ly/14tDD6P
* Zachary Taylor Parkway Guide 3:   http://bit.ly/14TTZYi
* Zachary Taylor Parkway Guide 4:   http://bit.ly/18c3yFs
* Zachary Taylor Parkway Guide 5:   http://bit.ly/17yH9CB
* Complete Zachary Taylor Parkway Guide (This file is a compilation of the files above and is quite large, 14 MB. It may take several minutes to download.): http://bit.ly/14tDHn1

Creole Nature Trail

Creole Nature Trail is home to more than 400 bird species making it one of the Top 10 Birding Destinations in the country. Year round you will be treated to a seemingly endless array of raptors, waterfowl, wading birds and shorebirds residing in this lush environment. http://www.louisianatravel.com/creole-nature-trail-all-american-road

* Sabine National Wildlife Refuge, the largest waterfowl sanctuary on the Gulf Coast
* Rockefeller State Wildlife Refuge, near Grand Chenier
* Cameron Prairie National Wildlife Refuge on LA 27 south of Holmwood
* Peveto Woods Bird & Butterfly Sanctuary eight miles west of Holly Beach

SELECTED READING

Dickson, Paul, Laurence M. Hardy, Hubert Hervey, James L. Ingold, A. Bradley McPherson, Nancy M. Menasco, Larry R. Raymond, Jeff F. Trahan, and Bill Wood. 2004. *Birding Hot Spots of Northwestern Louisiana*, Second Edition. Bird Study Group of the Shreveport Society for Nature Study, Inc., Shreveport.

Fermata Incorporated. 2009. *America's Wetland Birding Trails* (downloaded from Louisiana Tourism website *http://www.louisianatravel.com/birding*, 16 August 2009).

Lowery, George H., Jr. 1955. *Louisiana Birds*. Louisiana State University Press, Baton Rouge.

Oberholser, Harry C. 1938. *The Bird Life of Louisiana*. Louisiana Department of Conservation Bulletin 28, New Orleans.

Purrington, Robert D., Al Smalley, Gwen Smalley, Ronald J. Stein, and James Whelan. 1987. *A Birdfinder's Guide to Southeastern Louisiana*. Orleans Audubon Society, New Orleans.

Wiedenfeld, David A., and M. Mark Swan. 2000. *Louisiana Breeding Bird Atlas*. Louisiana Sea Grant College Program, Louisiana State University, Baton Rouge.

AMERICAN BIRDING ASSOCIATION
PRINCIPLES OF BIRDING ETHICS

Everyone who enjoys birds and birding must always respect wildlife, its environment, and the rights of others. In any conflict of interest between birds and birders, the welfare of the birds and their environment comes first.

CODE OF BIRDING ETHICS

1. Promote the welfare of birds and their environment.

1(a) Support the protection of important bird habitat.

1(b) To avoid stressing birds or exposing them to danger, exercise restraint and caution during observation, photography, sound recording, or filming.

Limit the use of recordings and other methods of attracting birds, and never use such methods in heavily birded areas or for attracting any species that is Threatened, Endangered, or of Special Concern, or is rare in your local area.

Keep well back from nests and nesting colonies, roosts, display areas, and important feeding sites. In such sensitive areas, if there is a need for extended observation, photography, filming, or recording, try to use a blind or hide, and take advantage of natural cover.

Use artificial light sparingly for filming or photography, especially for close-ups.

1(c) Before advertising the presence of a rare bird, evaluate the potential for disturbance to the bird, its surroundings, and other people in the area, and proceed only if access can be controlled, disturbance can be minimized, and permission has been obtained from private land-owners. The sites of rare nesting birds should be divulged only to the proper conservation authorities.

1(d) Stay on roads, trails, and paths where they exist; otherwise keep habitat disturbance to a minimum.

2. Respect the law and the rights of others.

2(a) Do not enter private property without the owner's explicit permission.

2(b) Follow all laws, rules, and regulations governing use of roads and public areas, both at home and abroad.

2(c) Practice common courtesy in contacts with other people. Your exemplary behavior will generate goodwill with birders and non-birders alike.

3. Ensure that feeders, nest structures, and other artificial bird environments are safe.

3(a) Keep dispensers, water, and food clean and free of decay or disease. It is important to feed birds continually during harsh weather.

3(b) Maintain and clean nest structures regularly.

3(c) If you are attracting birds to an area, ensure the birds are not exposed to predation from cats and other domestic animals, or dangers posed by artificial hazards.

4. Group birding, whether organized or impromptu, requires special care.

Each individual in the group, in addition to the obligations spelled out in Items #1 and #2, has responsibilities as a Group Member.

4(a) Respect the interests, rights, and skills of fellow birders, as well as those of people participating in other legitimate outdoor activities. Freely share your knowledge and experience, except where code 1(c) applies. Be especially helpful to beginning birders.

4(b) If you witness unethical birding behavior, assess the situation and intervene if you think it prudent. When interceding, inform the person(s) of the inappropriate action and attempt, within reason, to have it stopped. If the behavior continues, document it and notify appropriate individuals or organizations.

Group Leader Responsibilities [amateur and professional trips and tours].

4(c) Be an exemplary ethical role model for the group. Teach through word and example.

4(d) Keep groups to a size that limits impact on the environment and does not interfere with others using the same area.

4(e) Ensure everyone in the group knows of and practices this code.

4(f) Learn and inform the group of any special circumstances applicable to the areas being visited (e.g., no tape recorders allowed).

4(g) Acknowledge that professional tour companies bear a special responsibility to place the welfare of birds and the benefits of public knowledge ahead of the company's commercial interests. Ideally, leaders should keep track of tour sightings, document unusual occurrences, and submit records to appropriate organizations.

PLEASE FOLLOW THIS CODE— DISTRIBUTE IT AND TEACH IT TO OTHERS.

American Birding Association
1618 West Colorado Avenue, Colorado Springs, CO 80904
(800) 850-2473 or (719) 578-9703
e-mail: member@aba.org; website: www.aba.org

This ABA Code of Birding Ethics may be reprinted, reproduced, and distributed without restriction.

Please acknowledge the role of ABA in developing and promoting this code.

rev: 7/1/96

Join Today!

Name _____

Address _____

_____

City _____ State _____ Zip _____

Country _____ Phone _____

Email _____

Each level entitles members to certain benefits.
Visit <https://www2.aba.org/join> or call 800-850-2473 to find out more.

o Individual . . . . US $45

o Joint . . . . US $52

o Student . . . . US $25

o International / Canada Individual . US $55

o International / Canada Joint . . . US $63

o International / Canada Student . . US $35

Send this form to:
ABA Membership
1618 W. Colorado Ave.
Colorado Springs, CO
80904

You may also join by phone or web:
Phone 800-850-2473
www.aba.org/join

Membership: $ _____
Additional Contribution: $ _____ for: o Unrestricted o Conservation o Education
Total: $ _____

US dollars; check or money order payable to American Birding Association, or charge to:

o VISA   o Mastercard   o Discover

Card # _____ Exp Date _____

INDEX

A

Abbeville 58
Albatross, Yellow-nosed vii, 228
Alexander State Forest 155
Alexandria 129, 151
All About Birds 11
American Birding Association 15, 260-262
Anhinga 48, 62, 69, 75, 77, 81, 92, 97, 109-110, 112, 127, 131, 149, 153, 155, 159, 181, 186, 193, 202, 221, 229
Ani
  Groove-billed 43, 119, 125, 209, 233
  Smooth-billed 233
Arboretum, Louisiana State 158-159
Arsenal Park (Baton Rouge) 80
Atchafalaya Basin vi, 51, 69, 94
Atchafalaya National Heritage Area v, 71
Atchafalaya National Wildlife Refuge 69
Atchafalaya River 71
Audubon Park (New Orleans) 110, 223
Audubon Society
  Baton Rouge 9, 34
  Orleans 10, 109
Audubon State Historic Site 87-88
Avery Island 67
Avocet, American 24, 31, 38, 155, 205, 231

B

Bastrop 186, 188
Baton Rouge 73
Baton Rouge Audubon Society 9, 34
Bayou Bodcau Wildlife Management Area 166
Bayou D'Arbonne Lake Spillway 197
Bayou Manchac 93

Bayou Pierre Wildlife Management Area 177
Bayou Sauvage National Wildlife Refuge 113-114
Bayou Teche 71
Bayou Teche National Wildlife Refuge 119
Belle Chasse 123
Bentley 141
Big Branch Marsh National Wildlife Refuge 118
Big Days 23
Bird Louisiana 12
Birding seasons 5-6
Bishop Point Recreation Area 181
Bittern
  American 41, 47, 118, 174, 202, 229
  Least 30, 41, 46, 118, 127, 202, 229
Black Bayou Lake (Hosston) 162
Black Bayou Lake National Wildlife Refuge (Monroe) 185
Blackbird
  Brewer's 129, 133, 164, 219, 241
  Red-winged vi, 97, 102, 219, 241
  Rusty 121, 129, 133, 151, 153, 159, 163-164, 167, 219, 241
  Yellow-headed 32, 37, 102, 129, 133, 219, 241
Blackwater Conservation Area (Baton Rouge) 81
Bluebird
  Eastern 88, 131, 141, 163, 166, 189, 214, 238
  Mountain 6, 53, 238
Bluebonnet Swamp Nature Center (Baton Rouge) 85
Bobolink 25, 32, 121, 132, 219, 241
Bobwhite, Northern 145, 148, 201, 227

Bonnet Carré Spillway 121
Booby
  Brown 229
  Masked 7, 202, 229
  Red-footed vii, 229
Bossier City 173
Boyce Recreation Area 152
Brant 6, 226
Breeding Bird Surveys 12
Broussard 64
Broussard Beach 43
Bufflehead 23, 114, 117, 132, 152, 167, 201, 227
Bunting
  Blue vii, 241
  Indigo vii, 27, 37-38, 48, 55, 65, 71, 81, 115, 131-133, 139, 148, 156, 171, 177, 185, 219, 241
  Lark 240
  Lazuli 34, 241
  Painted 25-26, 37-38, 48, 55, 71, 81, 93, 115, 131-133, 139, 156, 164, 177, 181, 185, 219, 225, 241
  Varied vii, 241
Buras Boat Harbor 124

C

C. Bickham Dickson Park (Shreveport) 171
Calcasieu River ferry 37
Cameron 37-38
Cameron Parish 5, 23, 37
Cameron Prairie National Wildlife Refuge 41
Camp Claiborne 148
Canvasback vi, 23, 30, 80, 132, 135, 139, 155, 167, 201, 227
Capitol Lake (Baton Rouge) 80
Caracara, Crested 25, 28-29, 40, 47, 210, 224, 235
Cardinal, Northern 59, 75, 88, 218, 241
Caroline Dormon Trail (Longleaf Trail Scenic Byway) 145
Castor Plunge Road 147
Catahoula National Wildlife Refuge 135
Catbird, Gray vi, 27, 135, 139, 149, 178, 214, 238

Causeway, Lake Pontchartrain 5, 19, 117
Chat, Yellow-breasted 24, 34, 81, 115, 133, 155, 178, 191, 217, 240
Cheneyville 129-133
Chickadee, Carolina 27, 59, 61, 75, 88, 91, 131, 213, 237
Chicot State Park 157-159
Christmas Bird Counts 12
Chuck-will's-widow 118, 142, 155, 209, 234
City Park Lake (Baton Rouge) 76
Coastal hiatus 73, 109, 170
Collared-Dove, Eurasian 208, 233
Conservation Area
  Blackwater 81
  Frenchtown Road (Baton Rouge) 83
  White Lake Wetlands 57
Coot, American 66, 75, 113, 205, 230
Cormorant
  Double-crested 66, 76, 97, 167, 197, 202, 229
  Neotropic 30, 42, 47, 55, 59, 62, 76, 159, 202, 221, 229
Cotile Recreation Area 152
Couturie Forest (New Orleans City Park) 109
Cowbird
  Bronzed 37, 42, 219, 225, 241
  Brown-headed 102, 219, 241
  Shiny 42, 97, 127, 225, 241
Crane
  Sandhill 5-6, 23, 40, 131, 133, 205, 230
  Whooping 3, 57, 230
Crawfish Research Center 64
Creeper, Brown 27, 88, 129, 147, 159, 163, 180, 189, 213, 237
Creole 42
Crescent Bird Club 9
Cross Lake (Shreveport) 167-168
Crossbill, Red 242
Crow
  American 212, 236
  Fish 87, 212, 237
Crowley 53
Cuckoo
  Black-billed 34, 209, 233
  Mangrove 233

Yellow-billed 34, 77, 88, 114, 131-132, 185, 209, 233
Curlew
  Eskimo 231
  Long-billed 24, 38, 107, 206, 223, 231
Cypremort State Park 119
Cypress Island Preserve 62

D

Delhi 190, 192
Dewey W. Wills Wildlife Management Area 135
Dickcissel 25, 29, 37, 48, 55, 65, 93, 115, 121, 131-132, 177, 189, 219, 241
Dove
  Inca 37, 107, 209, 233
  Mourning 208, 233
  White-winged 37, 107, 208, 223, 233
Dowitcher
  Long-billed 24, 49, 55, 132, 207, 232
  Short-billed 24, 102, 207, 232
Duck
  American Black 132, 183, 227
  Long-tailed 23, 32, 43, 102, 152, 227
  Masked vii, 227
  Mottled 23, 30, 55, 59, 66, 97, 131, 200, 221, 227
  Ring-necked vi, 80, 109, 132, 139, 162, 201, 227
  Ruddy 23, 32, 66, 102, 132, 152, 167, 197, 201, 227
  Wood 75-77, 81, 109-110, 112, 131, 149, 151, 155, 159, 185-186, 189, 191, 200, 227
Dunlin 55, 132, 207, 232
Duson 53
D'Arbonne National Wildlife Refuge 195, 197

E

EBird 11
Eagle
  Bald 66, 93-94, 97, 112, 132, 135, 149, 153, 155-156, 162, 167, 181, 187, 197, 204, 230
  Golden 6, 49, 55, 132, 183, 230
Egret
  Cattle 67-68, 153, 203, 229
  Great 65, 67-68, 75, 153, 186, 202, 229
  Reddish 31, 43, 102, 203, 222, 229
  Snowy 41, 48, 65, 67-68, 75, 153, 186, 203, 229
Eider, King 227
Elbow Slough Wildlife Management Area 133
Elmer's Island Wildlife Refuge 103
Empire 123-124
Estherwood 53
Evariste Nunez Woods Bird Sanctuary 45

F

Falcon
  Peregrine 31, 47, 66, 80, 93, 99, 102, 132, 135, 177, 181, 211, 235
  Prairie vii, 235
False River (New Roads) 93
Farmerville 197
Finch
  House 75, 220, 242
  Purple 77, 121, 129, 147, 156, 169, 220, 242
Flamingo, American vii, 228
Flicker, Northern 131, 210, 235
Flycatcher
  Acadian 27, 59, 61, 71, 85-86, 114, 119, 131, 137, 145, 149, 159, 197, 211, 235
  Alder 211, 235
  Ash-throated 49, 53, 124, 211, 224, 236
  Brown-crested vii, 124-125, 236
  Cordilleran vii, 235
  Crowned Slaty vii, 236
  Dusky-capped 236
  Empidonax 5, 34, 42, 65
  Fork-tailed vii, 53, 236
  Gray vii, 235
  Great Crested 27, 34, 48, 61, 71, 75, 77, 86, 88, 114, 119, 137, 141, 147, 149, 155, 159, 185, 189, 197, 211, 236
  Hammond's vii, 235
  Least 152, 211, 235
  Myiarchus 6, 125
  Olive-sided 211, 235
  Pacific-slope vii, 235
  Scissor-tailed 25, 40, 55, 123-124, 146, 148-149, 152, 164, 177, 195, 211, 236

Sulphur-bellied vii, 107, 236
Vermilion 6, 47, 53, 132, 211, 236
Willow 211, 235
Yellow-bellied 152, 211, 235
Fontainebleau State Park (Mandeville) 117
Ford Park (Shreveport) 167
Fort Jackson 124
Fort Polk 143
Fort Randolph-Buhlow State Historic Site 138
Frenchtown Road Conservation Area 83
Frigatebird, Magnificent 77, 107, 117, 127, 153, 202, 221, 228
Fruge Road 40

G

Gadwall 23, 30, 45, 80, 113, 132, 152, 200, 227
Gallinule
  Common 30, 124, 131, 181, 205, 230
  Purple 30, 41, 47, 118, 127, 132, 153, 205, 223, 230
Gannet, Northern 39, 43, 102-103, 202, 229
Geography 3
Gnatcatcher, Blue-gray 5, 66, 71, 75, 147, 169, 177, 191, 213, 237
Godwit
  Black-tailed vii, 53, 231
  Hudsonian 24, 49, 55, 206, 231
  Marbled 24, 102, 206, 231
Golden-Plover, American 25, 49, 54, 107, 125, 153, 177, 205, 231
Goldeneye, Common 23, 30, 109, 114, 117, 162, 167, 197, 201, 227
Goldfinch
  American 5, 75, 88, 129, 147, 156, 166, 183, 220, 242
  Lesser 242
Goose
  Cackling 23, 200, 226
  Canada 226
  Greater White-fronted 23, 200, 226
  Ross's 23, 55, 132, 200, 226
  Snow vi, 23, 132, 200, 226
Goshawk, Northern 230

Grackle
  Boat-tailed vi, 219, 241
  Common 88, 163, 219, 241
  Great-tailed vi, 219, 241
Grand Cote National Wildlife Refuge 171
Grand Isle 5, 97, 99-100, 104-107
Grand Isle State Park 107
Grassy Lake 171
Grebe
  Eared 117, 202, 228
  Horned 39, 114, 117, 153, 156, 202, 228
  Least vii, 228
  Pied-billed 66, 75, 113, 149, 162, 186, 202, 228
  Red-necked 167, 228
  Western 149, 167, 228
Grosbeak
  Black-headed 6, 34, 218, 241
  Blue vii, 29, 37-38, 48, 65, 93, 115, 131-132, 139, 149, 156, 164, 178, 180, 219, 241
  Evening 242
  Rose-breasted 27, 34, 65, 107, 218, 241
Ground-Dove, Common 209, 223, 233
Gueydan 53
Gulf Coast Bird Club 9
Gull
  Black-headed 232
  Bonaparte's 31, 38, 76, 102, 155, 181, 197, 207, 232
  California 39, 102, 232
  Franklin's 38, 149, 207, 232
  Glaucous 39, 43, 208, 232
  Great Black-backed 39, 102, 232
  Herring 31, 38, 102, 127, 207, 232
  Iceland 127, 232
  Kelp vii, 232
  Laughing 26, 31, 38, 102, 127, 207, 232
  Lesser Black-backed 24, 39, 102, 127, 207, 232
  Little 232
  Ring-billed 31, 38, 102, 127, 156, 162, 197, 207, 232
  Sabine's 167, 232
  Thayer's 43, 127, 232
  Western vii, 232

H

Habitat types 3
Hackberry 30
Handy Brake National Wildlife Refuge 186-187
Harrier, Northern 32, 131-132, 177, 204, 230
Harrisonburg 137
Hawk
  Broad-winged vi, 5, 61, 124, 132, 139, 145, 159, 204, 230
  Cooper's 66, 204, 230
  Ferruginous 6, 49, 55, 204, 230
  Harris's vii, 230
  Red-shouldered 59, 66, 71, 81, 87, 97, 112, 169, 204, 230
  Red-tailed 32, 129, 204, 230
  Red-tailed (Fuertes') 177
  Red-tailed (Harlan's) 129, 177
  Red-tailed (Krider's) 129, 177
  Rough-legged 49, 132, 230
  Sharp-shinned 88, 204, 230
  Swainson's 25, 48, 123-124, 204, 222, 230
  White-tailed vii, 230
  Zone-tailed vii, 230
Henderson Lake 71
Heron
  Great Blue 186, 202, 229
  Green 30, 41, 46, 48, 55, 75, 81, 131, 149, 155, 177, 181, 185-186, 203, 229
  Little Blue 41, 48, 65, 153, 155, 186, 203, 229
  Tricolored 41, 48, 59, 63, 65, 68, 127, 131, 155, 186, 203, 229
Holleyman-Sheely Migratory Bird Sanctuary 34
Hollister Chenier Preserve 45
Holly Beach 31-32, 34
Holmwood 23, 40-41
Honey Island Swamp 114-115
Hosston 162-163
Houma 97, 99
Hummingbird
  Allen's 6, 234
  Anna's 6, 234
  Black-chinned 6, 210, 234
  Blue-throated vii, 7, 234
  Broad-billed 6, 234
  Broad-tailed 6, 234
  Buff-bellied 6, 210, 234
  Calliope 6, 234
  Magnificent vii, 7, 234
  Ruby-throated vii, 5-6, 27, 59, 210, 234
  Rufous 6, 210, 234
Hurricanes 2, 8, 34, 112

I

Ibis
  Glossy 59, 99, 203, 229
  White 41, 59, 65, 68, 80, 131, 155, 203, 229
  White-faced vi, 41, 48, 59, 64-65, 99, 132, 155, 203, 229
Indian Bayou 71
Indian Creek Recreation Area 155

J

Jabiru 228
Jaeger
  Long-tailed 233
  Parasitic 102, 167, 208, 233
  Pomarine 102, 167, 208, 233
Jay, Blue 75, 88, 212, 236
Jean Lafitte National Historic Park 119
Jefferson Island 68
Joe W. Brown Memorial Park (New Orleans) 112
Junco, Dark-eyed 75, 97, 166, 218, 241
Jungle Gardens (Avery Island) 67

K

Kaplan 53
Kestrel, American 32, 131-132, 145, 177, 189, 210, 235
Killdeer 205, 231
Kincaid Lake Recreation Area 149
Kincaid Reservoir 146-147, 149
Kingbird
  Cassin's vii, 236
  Couch's vii, 236
  Eastern vi, 40, 55, 77, 86, 131-132, 137, 141, 148, 177, 181, 189, 211, 236

Gray 97, 105, 211, 224, 236
Tropical vii, 236
Western 41, 123-124, 164, 171, 181, 211, 236
Kingfisher
  Belted 27, 30, 75, 81, 97, 112, 153, 156, 159, 162, 166, 210, 234
  Ringed vii, 6, 167, 234
Kinglet
  Golden-crowned 27, 63, 65, 75, 88, 135, 147, 159, 163, 166, 169, 180, 189, 197, 214, 238
  Ruby-crowned vi, 24, 59, 63, 65, 75, 88, 112, 129, 147, 159, 163, 166, 189, 197, 214, 238
Kisatchie Bayou Recreation Area 145
Kisatchie National Forest 139, 145
Kiskadee, Great vii, 42, 45, 236
Kite
  Mississippi vi, 59, 71, 75, 87, 112, 115, 131-132, 152, 157, 159, 191, 204, 222, 230
  Swallow-tailed vi, 1, 59, 69, 115, 157, 203, 222, 230
  White-tailed 27-29, 123, 204, 230
Kittiwake, Black-legged 39, 167, 232
Knot, Red 102-103, 206, 231
Krotz Springs 69

L

LABIRD 11
LSU Museum of Natural Science 49, 78
Lacassine National Wildlife Refuge 46-47
Lafayette 53, 61, 64
Lake
  Black Bayou (Hosston) 162
  Cross (Shreveport) 167-168
  Henderson 71
  Pontchartrain 5, 117
Lake Buhlow (Alexandria) 138
Lake Charles 25, 27-28, 30, 40
Lake Dautrieve 71
Lake District of Alexandria 151
Lake Fausse Pointe State Park 71
Lake Martin (Lafayette) 62
Lake Martin Bird Sanctuary 62
Lake Ophelia 171

Lake Pontchartrain 5, 117
Lake Pontchartrain Causeway 5, 19, 117
Lake Verret 119
Lark, Horned 55, 129, 153, 164, 177, 180, 191, 212, 237
Leeville 100
Little Chenier Road (Cameron Parish) 41
Little Cypress Pond Recreation Area 142
Lock and Dam #5 (Red River) 179
Longleaf Scenic Area 143
Longleaf Trail Scenic Byway 145
Longspur
  Chestnut-collared 43, 238
  Lapland 55, 129, 153, 165, 177, 180, 215, 238
  McCown's vii, 238
  Smith's 238
Longwood 169
Loon
  Common 117, 149, 153, 156, 197, 201, 228
  Pacific 228
  Red-throated 167, 228
Louisiana Bayou Bluebird Society 10
Louisiana Bird Records Committee 8, 226
Louisiana Bird Resource Office iv, 8
Louisiana Birders Anonymous 9
Louisiana Breeding Bird Atlas 12
Louisiana Department of Wildlife and Fisheries 10
Louisiana Office of Culture, Recreation and Tourism 152
Louisiana Ornithological Society 7-8, 23-24, 226
Louisiana State Arboretum 158-159
Louisiana State Parks 11
Louisiana State University (Main Campus) 74-75

M

Mallard 23, 30, 113, 132, 162, 200, 227
Mandalay National Wildlife Refuge 119
Mandeville 117
Mango, Green-breasted vii, 7, 234
Martin
  Brown-chested vii, 237

Purple 5, 19, 212, 237
Mary Ann Brown Preserve 88
Meadowlark
  Eastern 141, 219, 241
  Western 132, 164-165, 219, 241
Merganser
  Common 167, 227
  Hooded 80, 103, 132, 152, 164, 181, 201, 227
  Red-breasted 23, 32, 43, 102-103, 201, 227
Merlin 32, 47, 102, 132, 164, 177, 210, 235
Milford Wampold Memorial Park (Baton Rouge) 77
Mockingbird, Northern 75, 214, 238
Monroe 194-195, 197
Morganza Spillway 91-93
Morse 54
Murrelet, Ancient vii, 233

N

National Forest, Kisatchie 139, 145
National Historic Park, Jean Lafitte 119
National Wildlife Refuge
  Atchafalaya 69
  Bayou Sauvage 113-114
  Bayou Teche 119
  Big Branch Marsh 118
  Black Bayou Lake (Monroe) 185
  Cameron Prairie 41
  Catahoula 135
  D'Arbonne 195, 197
  Grand Cote 171
  Handy Brake 186-187
  Lacassine 46-47
  Mandalay 119
  Red River 173
  Sabine 30, 37
  Tensas River 191-192
  Upper Ouachita 187
Nature Center
  Bluebonnet Swamp 85
New Orleans 108-111
New Orleans Zoo 110
New Orleans' City Park 109

Night-Heron
  Black-crowned 30, 55, 75, 109, 127, 131, 155, 186, 203, 229
  Yellow-crowned 55, 75, 80, 109, 127, 131, 186, 191, 203, 229
Nighthawk
  Antillean vii, 234
  Common 209, 234
  Lesser 34, 209, 234
Noah Tyson Park (Vivian) 163
Noddy, Brown 232
Northshore Bird Club 9
Nutcracker, Clark's vii, 236
Nuthatch
  Brown-headed 27, 88, 112, 117-118, 145, 147, 163, 167, 185, 213, 224, 237
  Red-breasted 167, 169, 213, 237
  White-breasted 153, 166-167, 169, 185, 191, 213, 237

O

Oak Grove Sanctuary 42
Oriole
  Baltimore 27, 34, 65, 107, 152, 171, 185, 220, 242
  Bullock's 242
  Hooded vii, 242
  Orchard 37-38, 41, 48, 71, 75, 81, 86, 88, 93, 115, 148-149, 164, 178, 180, 189, 220, 242
  Scott's vii, 242
Orleans Audubon Society 10, 109
Ornithology in Louisiana 1
Osprey 30, 93, 97, 103, 124, 127, 132, 135, 149, 155-156, 162, 181, 197, 203, 230
Ovenbird 34, 106, 192, 215, 239
Overton Lock and Dam 132-133
Owl
  Barn 177, 209, 233
  Barred 27, 48, 58, 61, 85, 97, 112, 114, 169, 189, 209, 234
  Burrowing 43, 234
  Eastern Screech- 27, 48, 209, 234
  Flammulated vii, 234
  Great Horned 48, 209, 234
  Long-eared 234
  Northern Saw-whet 234

Short-eared 28, 30, 43, 48, 55, 132, 177, 209, 234
Snowy 234
Oystercatcher, American 24, 35, 38, 107, 205, 231

P

Palmetto Island State Park 58-59
Parakeet, Carolina 235
Park
  Arsenal (Baton Rouge) 80
  Audubon (New Orleans) 110
  C. Bickham Dickson (Shreveport) 171
  Cameron Parish Police Jury (Cameron) 38
  Fontainebleau State (Mandeville) 117
  Ford (Shreveport) 167
  Grand Isle State 107
  Joe W. Brown Memorial (New Orleans) 112
  Milford Wampold Memorial (Baton Rouge) 77
  New Orleans' City 109
  Noah Tyson (Vivian) 163
  Richard Fleming (Longwood) 169
  Robert A. Nance (Hosston) 162
  Sam Houston Jones State 27
  Walter B. Jacobs Memorial Nature (Longwood) 169
Parula
  Northern 5, 24, 27, 34, 59, 61, 63, 71, 81, 85-86, 100, 106, 112, 114, 119, 131, 137, 147, 155, 166, 169, 174, 185, 189, 216, 239
  Tropical vii, 167, 239
Pearl River Wildlife Management Area 112, 114-115
Pelagic birding 7, 127
Pelican
  American White 38, 77, 93, 135, 149, 181, 202, 229
  Brown 38, 153, 202, 229
Peveto Woods Migratory Bird Sanctuary 5, 32-34
Phalarope
  Red 232
  Red-necked 232
  Wilson's 41, 55, 102, 207, 232

Phoebe
  Eastern vi, 27, 87-88, 129, 163, 211, 235
  Say's 49, 53, 132, 236
Pigeon
  Band-tailed 233
  Passenger 233
  Rock 208, 233
Pintail, Northern 23, 30, 132, 152, 200, 227
Pipit
  American 77, 129, 132, 153, 177, 189, 214, 238
  Sprague's 55, 129, 132, 164-165, 181, 214, 224, 238
Pitkin 142
Plaquemines Parish 123
Plover
  Black-bellied 31, 39, 102, 125, 205, 230
  Mountain vii, 231
  Piping 24, 31-32, 39, 43, 102-103, 205, 223, 231
  Semipalmated 24, 31, 43, 49, 55, 102, 205, 231
  Snowy 24, 31, 39, 43, 102-103, 205, 223, 231
  Wilson's 24, 31, 39, 43, 205, 223, 231
Pointe a la Hache 123
Pomme de Terre Wildlife Management Area 171
Port Fourchon 100-101
Port Hudson State Historic Site 86
Poverty Point State Historic Site 189-190
Powers Junction 114
Powhatan 223
Prairie-Chicken, Greater 3, 227
Preserve
  Hollister Chenier 45
  Mary Ann Brown 88

R

Raccourci Old River 93
Raceland 99
Rail
  Black 30, 204, 230
  Clapper 38, 54, 100, 124, 204, 230
  King 26, 49, 55, 113, 204, 230
  Virginia 30, 41, 49, 55, 181, 204, 230
  Yellow vii, 30, 49, 55, 174, 204, 222, 230

Rainey Lake Hiking Trail (Tensas River NWR) 192
Raven, Chihuahuan vii, 237
Rayne 53
Razorbill 233
Recreation Area
  Bishop Point 181
  Boyce 152
  Cotile 152
  Indian Creek 155
  Kincaid Lake 149
  Kisatchie Bayou 145
  Little Cypress Pond 142
  Stoner Avenue (Shreveport) 172
  Stuart Lake 141
  Tom Merrill 166
  Valentine Lake 149
Red River National Wildlife Refuge 173
Redhead 23, 30, 80, 109, 132, 139, 152, 155, 167, 201, 227
Redstart
  American 24, 34, 61, 65, 71, 85, 106, 114, 137, 169, 191, 216, 239
  Painted vii, 34, 240
Refuge
  Elmer's Island Wildlife 103
Refuge, Rockefeller Wildlife 45
Reporting Unusual Sightings 13
Richard Fleming Park (Longwood) 169
Rip Van Winkle Gardens 68
Roadrunner, Greater 148, 195, 209, 233
Robert A. Nance Park (Hosston) 162
Robin, American vi, 75, 131, 214, 238
Rock Falls Nature Trail (Sicily Island Hills WMA) 137
Rockefeller Wildlife Refuge 45
Ruff 53, 232
Russell Sage Wildlife Management Area 192, 194
Rutherford Beach 43

S

Sabine Bridge 35
Sabine National Wildlife Refuge 30, 37
Sam Houston Jones State Park 27

Sanctuary
  Evariste Nunez Woods Bird 45
  Grilletta Tract (Grand Isle) 106
  Laffite Woods (Grand Isle) 106
  Lake Martin Bird 62
  Oak Grove 42
  Peveto Woods Migratory Bird 5, 33
Sand-Plover, Lesser vii, 231
Sanderling 24, 39, 102, 206, 231
Sandpiper
  Baird's 24, 49, 55, 102, 207, 231
  Buff-breasted 25-26, 28, 49, 54-55, 107, 121, 132, 139, 141, 177, 207, 223, 232
  Curlew 53, 232
  Least 24, 49, 55, 102, 132, 206, 231
  Pectoral 121, 125, 207, 231
  Purple 105, 232
  Semipalmated 24, 49, 55, 132, 206, 231
  Solitary 49, 206, 231
  Spotted 125, 205, 231
  Stilt 24, 55, 102, 207, 232
  Upland 25, 28, 49, 107, 121, 139, 141, 177, 206, 231
  Western 24, 49, 55, 102, 132, 206, 231
  White-rumped 24, 49, 55, 132, 206, 231
Sapsucker
  Red-naped vii, 235
  Williamson's vii, 235
  Yellow-bellied vi, 27, 81, 87-88, 97, 129, 210, 235
Scaup
  Greater 23, 30, 43, 132, 155, 197, 201, 227
  Lesser 23, 32, 43, 66, 80, 102, 117, 132, 197, 201, 227
Scenic Area, Longleaf 143
Scenic Byway, Longleaf Trail 145
Scoter
  Black 23, 32, 43, 167, 201, 227
  Surf 23, 32, 167, 201, 227
  White-winged 23, 32, 43, 149, 167, 201, 227
Shearwater
  Audubon's 7, 228
  Cory's 7, 228
  Great 228
  Manx 228

Sherburne Wildlife Management Area 69-71
Sherburne Wildlife Management Area (South Farm) 94-95
Shoveler, Northern 23, 30, 65, 113, 132, 139, 200, 227
Shreveport 170-172
Shreveport Society for Nature Study 10
Shreveport's Bird Study Group 172
Shrike, Loggerhead 131, 212, 236
Sicily Island Hills Wildlife Management Area 136-137
Siskin, Pine 129, 169, 220, 242
Skimmer, Black 31, 38, 153, 208, 233
Slidell 113-114
Snipe, Wilson's 55, 164, 207, 232
Sod farm 25
Solitaire, Townsend's vii, 30, 238
Sora 30, 41, 49, 55, 181, 205, 230
South Farm (Sherburne Wildlife Management Area) 94-95
Spanish Lake (Lafayette) 66
Sparrow
  American Tree 240
  Bachman's 1, 5, 117, 129, 142, 147, 185, 217, 225, 240
  Baird's vii, 240
  Brewer's vii, 240
  Cassin's vii, 240
  Chipping 88, 121, 129, 148, 166, 177, 185, 217, 240
  Clay-colored 217, 240
  Field 81, 88, 121, 133, 147-148, 178, 217, 240
  Fox 121, 132, 148, 169, 178, 218, 240
  Golden-crowned 241
  Grasshopper 28-29, 55, 132, 164-165, 177, 217, 240
  Harris's 28-29, 55, 177, 180, 218, 241
  Henslow's 117, 129, 142, 147, 166, 217, 225, 240
  House 220, 242
  Lark 178, 217, 240
  Le Conte's 55, 121, 132-133, 166, 175, 177, 217, 240
  Lincoln's 29, 55, 132, 218, 240
  Nelson's 38, 100, 124, 218, 240

Savannah vi, 81, 88, 121, 132-133, 217, 240
Seaside 35, 38, 42-43, 100, 103, 124, 218, 240
Song 81, 88, 97, 121, 132-133, 148, 177-178, 218, 240
Swamp vi, 81, 97, 121, 132-133, 163, 177, 218, 240
Vesper 121, 132-133, 135, 148, 164, 217, 240
White-crowned 121, 132-133, 177, 218, 241
White-throated vi, 27, 59, 77, 81, 88, 121, 132-133, 163, 177, 218, 241
Spillway
  Bayou D'Arbonne Lake 197
  Bonnet Carré 121
  Chicot State Park 159
  Morganza 91-93
Spoonbill, Roseate vi, 23, 30, 38, 41, 55, 62, 65, 68, 92, 129, 131, 155, 159, 203, 222, 229
Spring Bayou Wildlife Management Area 171
St. Francisville 90
Starling, European 214, 238
State Forest, Alexander 155
State Historic Site
  Audubon 87-88
  Fort Randolph-Buhlow 138
  Port Hudson 86
  Poverty Point 189-190
State Park
  Chicot 157-159
  Cypremort 119
  Fontainebleau 117
  Grand Isle 107
  Lake Fausse Pointe 71
  Palmetto Island 58-59
  Sam Houston Jones (Lake Charles) 27
Stilt, Black-necked 30, 48, 54-55, 65, 131, 155, 157, 205, 231
Stoner Avenue Recreation Area (Shreveport) 172
Stork, Wood vi, 5, 55, 59, 71, 91, 93, 97, 132, 155, 202, 221, 228
Storm-Petrel
  Band-rumped 7, 228

Leach's 7, 228
Wilson's 7, 228
Stuart Lake Recreation Area 141-142
Sulphur 28-29
Swallow
 Bank 132, 212, 237
 Barn 132, 213, 237
 Cave 35, 213, 237
 Cliff 35, 132, 152, 213, 237
 Northern Rough-winged vi, 132, 139, 177, 212, 237
 Tree vi, 16, 97, 132, 192, 212, 237
Swamp, Honey Island 114
Swan
 Trumpeter 227
 Tundra 227
Swift
 Chimney 27, 75, 209, 234
 Vaux's vii, 77, 80, 234

T

Tanager
 Hepatic vii, 241
 Scarlet 27, 34, 65, 107, 183, 218, 241
 Summer 5, 27, 65, 71, 86, 88, 107, 115, 141, 145, 147, 155, 159, 169, 171, 185, 189, 218, 241
 Western 218, 241
Teal
 Blue-winged 23, 30, 97, 113, 200, 227
 Cinnamon 23, 30, 132, 200, 227
 Green-winged 23, 30, 45, 99, 113, 152, 181, 200, 227
Tensas River National Wildlife Refuge 191-192
Tern
 Arctic 233
 Black 38, 149, 153, 155, 208, 233
 Bridled 7, 232
 Caspian 24, 31, 38, 181, 208, 233
 Common 38, 208, 233
 Forster's 38, 75, 77, 81, 127, 162, 208, 233
 Gull-billed 24, 30, 41-42, 110, 208, 223, 232
 Least 24, 103, 172, 208, 232
 Royal 24, 31, 38, 208, 233
 Sandwich 24, 31, 38, 103, 127, 208, 233
 Sooty 7, 110, 232

Terrebonne Bird Club 9
The Nature Conservancy 45, 62, 88, 106, 112
Thistlewaite Wildlife Management Area 71
Thornwell 48-49
Thrasher
 Brown 61, 88, 97, 131, 148, 189, 214, 238
 Curve-billed vii, 238
 Sage vii, 238
Thrush
 Gray-cheeked 34, 106, 192, 214, 238
 Hermit vi, 24, 65, 77, 88, 147, 159, 163, 166, 197, 214, 238
 Swainson's 34, 61, 106, 214, 238
 Varied 107, 238
 Wood 27, 34, 61, 63, 83, 106, 114, 147, 189, 214, 238
Tidewater 127
Titmouse, Tufted 27, 61, 88, 91, 131, 213, 237
Tom Merrill Recreation Area 166
Towhee
 Eastern 27, 81, 91, 121, 135, 145, 147-148, 166, 178, 191, 217, 240
 Green-tailed 124, 240
 Spotted 240
Trail
 Cardinal Nature (Audubon SHS) 88
 Caroline Dormon (Longleaf Trail Scenic Byway) 145
 Chicot State Park 159
 John Haygood Nature Trail (Bayou Bodcau WMA) 166
 Rainey Lake Hiking (Tensas River NWR) 192
 Rock Falls Nature (Sicily Island Hills WMA) 137
 Wild Azalea (Kisatchie National Forest) 146, 148
Tropicbird, Red-billed 228
Tunica Hills Wildlife Management Area 90-91
Turf Grass Road (Welsh) 25
Turkey, Wild 69, 145, 147, 191, 201, 228
Turnstone, Ruddy 31, 55, 102, 206, 231

U

U.S. Fish and Wildlife Service 10
U.S. Forest Service 10
ULL Experimental Farm 64
University Lake (Baton Rouge) 76
Upper Ouachita National Wildlife Refuge 187

V

Vacherie 16, 20
Valentine Lake Recreation Area 149
Veery 34, 106, 192, 214, 238
Venice 127
Vermilion Bay 119
Violetear, Green vii, 7, 234
Vireo
  Bell's 164, 212, 236
  Black-whiskered 97, 107, 236
  Blue-headed 27, 65, 87-88, 135, 147, 159, 169, 180, 212, 236
  Cassin's vii, 236
  Philadelphia 34, 42, 106, 152, 169, 212, 236
  Plumbeous vii, 236
  Red-eyed 27, 61, 71, 86, 91, 106, 114, 131, 147, 149, 155, 163, 166, 191, 212, 236
  Warbling 34, 42, 106, 152, 159, 169, 171, 212, 236
  White-eyed vi, 27, 48, 59, 61, 65, 88, 91, 97, 106, 114, 133, 139, 147, 169, 177, 212, 236
  Yellow-green vii, 236
  Yellow-throated 5, 27, 34, 61, 85, 88, 91, 106, 112, 114, 131, 147, 149, 155, 163, 166, 191, 212, 236
Vivian 163
Vulture
  Black 203, 229
  Turkey 203, 229

W

Wagtail, White vii, 238
Walter B. Jacobs Memorial Nature Park (Longwood) 169
Warbler
  Bachman's 191, 239
  Bay-breasted 34, 61, 106, 192, 216, 239
  Black-and-white 24, 34, 61, 71, 85, 91, 106, 112, 137, 166, 191, 197, 215, 239
  Black-throated Blue 34, 42, 107, 216, 239
  Black-throated Gray 6, 24, 42, 125, 240
  Black-throated Green 24, 34, 61, 107, 169, 217, 240
  Blackburnian 34, 65, 106, 192, 216, 239
  Blackpoll 34, 107, 192, 216, 239
  Blue-winged 34, 106, 169, 192, 215, 239
  Canada 5, 34, 107, 192, 217, 240
  Cape May 34, 42, 107, 167, 216, 239
  Cerulean 34, 171, 183, 192, 216, 239
  Chestnut-sided 34, 61, 106, 192, 216, 239
  Connecticut 34, 239
  Golden-winged 34, 107, 171, 192, 215, 239
  Hermit vii, 34, 240
  Hooded 5, 27, 34, 59, 61, 63, 65, 71, 83, 86, 88, 91, 106, 114, 137, 141, 147, 149, 155, 166, 189, 191, 197, 216, 225, 239
  Kentucky 27, 34, 61, 65, 68, 71, 83, 88, 91, 106, 114, 137, 141, 147, 149, 155, 166, 191, 197, 215, 239
  Lucy's vii, 239
  MacGillivray's vii, 6, 239
  Magnolia 34, 65, 106, 169, 216, 239
  Mourning 5, 34, 169, 215, 239
  Nashville 34, 171, 215, 239
  Orange-crowned vi, 5, 27, 63, 65-66, 75, 81, 88, 97, 112, 129, 135, 147, 163, 169, 178, 189, 197, 215, 239
  Palm 43, 87, 216, 239
  Pine 27, 75, 81, 87-88, 91, 97, 112, 117, 142, 145, 147, 166, 197, 216, 239
  Prairie 107, 118, 145, 148, 155, 217, 240
  Prothonotary vi, 34, 59, 61, 63, 69, 71, 81, 83, 85, 100, 106, 112, 114, 119, 131, 147, 149, 159, 163, 166, 169, 171, 174, 180, 185, 215, 225, 239
  Red-faced vii, 240
  Swainson's vi, 1, 34, 59, 71, 83, 91, 115, 156, 159, 169, 171, 215, 225, 239
  Tennessee 34, 106, 215, 239
  Townsend's 34, 125, 240
  Virginia's vii, 34, 239
  Wilson's 66, 217, 240

Worm-eating 34, 106, 137, 142, 159, 171, 197, 215, 239
Yellow vi, 5, 34, 106, 113, 169, 216, 239
Yellow-rumped vi, 5, 27, 65-66, 75, 81, 87-88, 97, 112, 159, 163, 169, 178, 197, 216, 240
Yellow-throated 5, 34, 61, 63, 65, 71, 85, 91, 100, 106, 112, 114, 119, 124, 131, 141-142, 155, 159, 166, 169, 185, 191, 216
Waterthrush
  Louisiana 5, 34, 88, 106, 137, 145, 147, 149, 159, 169, 215, 239
  Northern 34, 106, 215, 239
Waxwing, Cedar 27, 88, 129, 214, 238
Wheatear, Northern vii, 6, 53, 238
Whimbrel 35, 38, 55, 206, 231
Whip-poor-will, Eastern 209, 234
Whistling-Duck
  Black-bellied 46, 59, 110, 113, 124, 131, 159, 200, 221, 226
  Fulvous 46, 51, 55, 59, 110, 131, 200, 221, 226
White Kitchen Area (Slidell) 112
White Lake Wetlands Conservation Area 57
Wigeon
  American 23, 30, 113, 132, 155, 181, 200, 227
  Eurasian 227
Wild Azalea Trail (Kisatchie National Forest) 146, 148
Wild Louisiana 14
Wildlife Management Area
  Bayou Bodcau 166
  Bayou Pierre 177
  Dewey W. Wills 135
  Elbow Slough 133
  Pearl River 112, 114-115
  Pomme de Terre 171
  Russell Sage 192, 194
  Sherburne 69-71
  Sherburne (South Farm) 94
  Sicily Island Hills 136-137
  Spring Bayou 171
  Thistlewaite 71
  Tunica Hills 90-91
Willet 24, 31, 102, 107, 206, 231

Wood Stork and Wading Bird Event (South Farm) 94
Wood-Pewee
  Eastern 34, 137, 141, 147, 155, 169, 171, 189, 197, 211, 235
  Western 235
Woodcock, American 135, 148, 207, 232
Woodpecker
  Downy 61, 65, 71, 75, 87, 91, 131, 163, 210, 235
  Hairy 27, 71, 87, 91, 97, 129, 147, 210, 235
  Ivory-billed 3, 183, 191-192, 235
  Ladder-backed vii, 235
  Pileated 27, 58-59, 71, 88, 91, 97, 159, 163, 191, 210, 235
  Red-bellied 61, 85, 87-88, 91, 131, 163, 210, 235
  Red-cockaded 5, 27, 117-118, 129, 139, 141, 143, 145, 147-148, 155, 185, 195, 210, 224, 235
  Red-headed 88, 93, 135, 149, 181, 189, 210, 235
Woodworth 148, 155
Wren
  Bewick's 164, 177, 180, 213, 237
  Carolina 59, 88, 213, 237
  House 27, 63, 65, 87-88, 97, 129, 147, 178, 197, 213, 237
  Marsh 41, 97, 100, 118, 180, 197, 213, 237
  Rock vii, 237
  Sedge 35, 97, 100, 166, 171, 197, 213, 237
  Winter 27, 49, 63, 87-88, 97, 147, 159, 167, 169, 189, 197, 213, 237

Y

Yearwood Road 177-178
Yellow Rails and Rice Festival 49, 222
Yellowlegs
  Greater 54-55, 125, 206, 231
  Lesser 54-55, 125, 206, 231
Yellowthroat
  Common 81, 97, 106, 131, 133, 148, 163, 181, 215, 239

Z

Zoo, New Orleans 110

ABA Birdfinding Guide Series

A Birder's Guide to Alaska
George C. West

A Birder's Guide to Arkansas
Mel White

A Birder's Guide to the Bahamas
Anthony R. White

A Birder's Guide to Belize
Bert Frenz

A Birder's Guide to Colorado
Harold R. Holt

A Birder's Guide to Eastern Massachusetts
Bird Observer

A Birder's Guide to Florida
Bill Pranty

A Birder's Guide to Metropolitan Areas of North America
Paul Lehman

A Birder's Guide to Michigan
Allen T. Chartier and Jerry Ziarno

A Birder's Guide to New Hampshire
Alan Delorey

A Birder's Guide to Planning North American Trips
Jerry A. Cooper

A Birder's Guide to the Rio Grande Valley
Mark W. Lockwood, William B. McKinney, James N. Paton, Barry R. Zimmer

A Birder's Guide to Southeastern Arizona
Richard Cachor Taylor

A Birder's Guide to Southern California
Brad Schram

A Birder's Guide to the Texas Coast
Mel Cooksey and Ron Weeks

A Birder's Guide to Virginia
David Johnston

A Birder's Guide to Washington
Hal Opperman

A Birder's Guide to Wyoming
Oliver K. Scott

ABA SALES
www.aba.org/abasales

www.ingramcontent.com/pod-product-compliance
Lightning Source LLC
Chambersburg PA
CBHW052104230426
43671CB00011B/1925